CHRIST
IN HIS
SAINTS

by Patrick Henry Reardon

Conciliar Press
Ben Lomond, California

CHRIST IN HIS SAINTS
© Copyright 2004 by Patrick Henry Reardon

All Rights Reserved

Published by   Conciliar Press
                    P.O. Box 76
                    Ben Lomond, California 95005-0076

Printed in the United States of America

ISBN 1-888212-68-3

Manufactured under the direction of Double Eagle Industries.
For more manufacturing details, call 888-824-4344
or e-mail to info@publishingquest.com

for my archbishop and father in God

METROPOLITAN PHILIP

to whose wisdom

paternal care

and missionary fervor

so many of us

are so deeply in debt

CONTENTS

FOREWORD

⁂

I have always appreciated Father Patrick Reardon as a philosopher and an accomplished Orthodox theologian, but I was not aware of his other, important gift: he is a fine exegete and an inspiring teacher of Christian spirituality. His book *Christ in His Saints* is the proof of this.

Father Patrick offers to all those who are interested in knowing Christ and His Church through His saints an exciting, spiritually uplifting and refreshing presentation of the lives of close to 150 saints who manifest Christ's presence. He makes the saints come alive, as they are alive in Christ; in writing about their lives, the teachings of Christ and the Church, the Body of Christ, also come alive. It is the kind of literature that, when you begin reading it, you can't put it down.

Father Patrick utilizes his broad knowledge of scriptural exegesis, knowledge of the Church's Fathers, and personal penetrating insights to portray Christ in His Saints. Let me lift a few examples from his book to illustrate this.

Saint Peter's story is a very striking one: he is the enthusiastic disciple, always ready to speak first and represent the others; however, he is not always aware of the distinction between "the pumping of adrenaline" and the "infusion of grace." He promises faithfulness to Christ, and moments later he denies Christ three times! Thank God, he repents, and seeks Christ's forgiveness. After the Resurrection, Christ restores him to apostleship, by inviting him three times to love Him. Finally, Saint Peter trusts Christ's feelings, and gives his life for Him, being martyred at the Vatican Hill in Rome.

Saint Paul's life is another example of a repenting Christian. As with every one else, he is not given "to choose the framework and shape" of his repentance; he was commanded to comply with the practices and wishes of the Church, the very "organized religion" which he persecuted.

The case of the Canaanite prostitute, Rahab, who instructed the Israelite spies, as a matter of faithfulness to God, is an edifying story of

9

yet another repenting sinner. She is also considered to be an image of the repenting Church.

Saint Andrew's case is a very interesting one: being self-effacing, he is the opposite of his brother Peter; he is the person who, because of his cordial, unassuming ways, was able to know that there was in the crowd a young man who had five loaves of barley and two salted fish, needed for the miracle of the feeding of the multitudes in the wilderness.

Mary Magdalene was not one of the "official" witnesses, but rather a "mediational" witness of Christ's Resurrection, representing the women apostles. Her witness is an "in-house" witness, and "it can only be understood in the community of salvation, for it describes a wisdom otherwise not available to this world."

Finally, the example of Nehemiah of the Persian court is that of a person of the world who is also a man of God. He did his work in the Persian court; yet, at the same time, he was a man of prayer and faithfulness to God. He became a role model for Christians who find themselves in situations like his.

Overall, Father Patrick's very exciting book honors the Church's teaching that the saints have no independent existence. They live in Christ, as Christ lives in them, and lead to salvation in Christ, "the Son of God, who is wondrous amongst His Saints."

Metropolitan MAXIMOS of Pittsburgh
October 15, 2003

INTRODUCTION:
THE CLOUD OF WITNESSES
ॐ

The Epistle to the Hebrews, which repeatedly speaks of Christian worship in terms of "approach" (4:16; 7:25; 10:1, 22; 11:6), "entrance" (10:19), and "drawing near" (7:19) to God, describes this worship as a complex liturgical gathering: "But you have come [literally 'approached'] to Mount Zion and to the city of the living God, the heavenly Jerusalem, to an innumerable company of angels, to the general assembly and church of the firstborn *who are* registered in heaven, to God the Judge of all, to the spirits of just men made perfect, to Jesus the Mediator of the new covenant, and to the blood of sprinkling that speaks better things than *that of* Abel" (12:22–24). That is to say, when the Christian comes to God, he doesn't come "one on one," so to speak; he approaches also the company of angels and saints.

This text is particularly striking because of its explicit reference to Christ our Lord as the Mediator of the covenant that gives us access to God. The unique mediation of Christ, an important theme in Hebrews (cf. also 8:6; 9:15), has rather often been cited in recent centuries to negate the role of the saints in heaven with respect to the Christian worship on earth. Yet, here in this description of Christian worship, along with the mediation of Christ and His redemptive blood, the author of Hebrews speaks also of "the spirits of just men made perfect." The author obviously saw nothing incompatible between the unique mediation of Christ and the communion of the glorified saints in the Church's worship.

Although the bodies of the departed saints are elsewhere described as "sleeping" (1 Thessalonians 4:13; 1 Corinthians 15:6–20), their spirits are very much alive and alert; indeed, they are already "made perfect," even though they still await the glorification of their bodies. The departed saints are certainly not "dead," because those who believe in Christ will never die (John 11:26). The departed saints did not simply live a long time ago and now they are gone. Oh no, they are still very much alive, standing in worship with the angels before God's throne, and that is why, in the mediation of Christ and through His blood, we may join them in worship.

These "spirits of just men made perfect" are, of course, identical to the "great cloud of witnesses" spoken of only a few verses earlier (12:1). Indeed, the previous chapter had just narrated their biblical stories: Abel, Enoch, Noah, Abraham, Sarah, Moses, and the others, most of whom the author did not name because "time would fail" him to do so (11:32).

By these heavenly "witnesses" we saints on earth are said to be "surrounded," as though to suggest that they themselves form a larger group than we. To describe their company, the author uses the image of a cloud, a classical metaphor designating a thickly packed crowd of people (cf. *Iliad* 4.274; *Aeneid* 7.797). In the density of their representation these "spirits of just men made perfect" are comparable to the "innumerable company of angels."

These texts from the Epistle to the Hebrews, then, indicate that all of these glorified saints, "the spirits of just men made perfect," are part of the awareness and experience of Christians at worship. The reason that the Church adorns her houses of worship with the icons of the glorified saints is that Christian worship raises believers up in mind and spirit to pray with those saints at the throne of God. We believers have access to their company in God's presence because of the saving blood of Jesus our Mediator. Symbolized in the twenty-four elders, these saints offer our prayers to God with their own and with the praises of the angels (Revelation 5:8; 8:3). Christian worship is inseparable from the communion of the saints.

Besides this, the departed saints (and so many more have been added since the Epistle to the Hebrews was written) are also held out as models for our emulation. This was the whole point of the list of the champions of faith in Hebrews 11. This list invites us to study the biblical saints especially, "who through faith subdued kingdoms, worked righteousness, obtained promises" (11:33). On page after page, Holy Scripture tells the stories of these men and women, members of that ancient family into which, by baptism, we have been incorporated. Let us now examine their examples, "considering the outcome of *their* conduct" (13:7).

I.
REPENTANT SAINTS

In the biblical narrative of the creation, it is noteworthy that the original day of creation is not designated "the first" day. It is called, rather, "one day" (*yom 'ehad*). Although this difference of expression in Genesis 1:5 has proved too subtle for virtually all biblical translations into modern languages, its significance caused it to be maintained in the ancient versions, such as the Septuagint (*hemera mia*) and the Vulgate (*dies unus*). In addition, that difference of expression ("one day" instead of "first day") was the object of explicit discussion in nearly all ancient commentaries on Genesis 1:5, whether Jewish (e.g., Philo and Rashi) or Christian (e.g., Basil and Augustine).

In those classical comments on the text, moreover, we find the common assertion that the words "one day" served to elevate that day to something more than part of a sequence. There is a profound reason why the original day of creation is appropriately called "one," whereas the second day is not appropriately called "two," nor the third day "three," and so forth. The original day is "one" in a manner analogous to the number itself. "One" is not simply the numeral that precedes two; it is, rather, the number out of which that second number comes. There is a formal disparity between one and the other numbers. One (*to hen*) is the font determining the identity of two and the subsequent numbers. "One" is not just "first" as part of a sequence; it is what we call a principle, an *arche*. The principle of something possesses its qualitative form.

For example, there is a parallel and corresponding proposition to be argued with respect to repentance, *metanoia*. Repentance is the *arche*, the foundational principle, of the life in Christ; it functions in the life of grace as the number "one" functions in arithmetic. It is not simply the "first" step of the Christian life. Repentance, rather, provides the abiding and formative structure of the whole life in Christ. Repentance is not a first step that we take with a view to getting past it. We are called to remain forever repentant. Although there is certainly progress to be made in the life of grace, all genuine progress is indicated by a renewal of repentance. A Christian does not "grow" in Christ by diminishing in repentance. True growth and authentic progress in Christ always imply growth and progress in repentance.

There are several very important inferences to be drawn from this premise of repentance as a principle of the life in Christ:

First, as the initial effect of grace, repentance is not of an order different from holiness. This needs emphatically to be said, because for some few centuries now there has roamed abroad the fallacious theory that God's act by which we are justified remains external to us. This rather recent theory effectively separates repentance from holiness, as though God would declare a man righteous without actually making him righteous, pronounce him to be just without causing him to be a "saint," and convert him but without giving him a new heart. Against this theory, the Bible indicates that the conversion of repentance is not just an act of God; it is also an act of man's free will under the accepted influence of God's grace. Man's heart, his interior, is altered by repentance.

Second, because repentance is the free decision of man as well as the free gift of God, the grace of repentance, if not properly safeguarded, can also be lost. Again, this truth has been obscured in recent centuries by an erroneous theory asserting that repentance, if genuine, cannot perish. However, a more complete reading of the Bible obliges us to say that the blessed assurance given us in Christ (cf. Romans 8:31–39) is no substitute for humility and vigilance. At no point in our Christian lives can we afford to forget that we must work out our salvation with fear and trembling (Philippians 2:12), with discipline lest we fall away (1 Corinthians 9:27). "Therefore let him who thinks he stands take heed lest he fall" (10:12).

Third, if repentance is a sustained constant in the life of grace, it is also repetitive. This repetition is both possible and required, not only for the daily shortcomings that befall us all, but also for those more serious infidelities that may even constitute apostasy. Once again, a fairly recent pernicious theory, interpreting the adjective "impossible" in Hebrews 6:4 in an excessively literal sense, has imagined that there is no return for a believer who has deliberately fallen from grace. This mischievous theory, however, is dashed to pieces by the biblical examples of such men as David and Peter. The command "Repent!" is addressed, not only to non-Christians (Acts 2:38; 3:19; 8:22), but to Christians as well (Revelation 2:5, 16; 3:3, 19).

Repentance is the non-negotiable, foundational constant of the life in Christ. However much God's saints differ from one another in style, tone, and emphasis, repentance is a grace and discipline—a principle—shared by them all.

⚜

1. PETER AT THE CHARCOAL FIRE

The Greek word *anthrakia* (cf. the English derivative "anthracite," a type of coal), meaning a charcoal fire, is found only twice in the New Testament, both times in the Gospel according to St. John. The first instance is in 18:18 and designates the courtyard fire where the officers and servants of the high priest stood warming themselves through the chilly night of Jesus' trial before the Sanhedrin. Simon Peter likewise came to that place and stood near a cousin of Malchus, a servant of the high priest. It was there by the charcoal fire that Simon thrice denied even knowing our Lord, going so far as to confirm the denials with an oath.

It is most significant, surely, that that event, so embarrassing to the chief of the Twelve Apostles, is narrated in detail in each of the four canonical Gospels, for it is thus made to stand fixed forever in the memory of Holy Church. From this story, all believers down through the ages are to learn two lessons that they must never forget.

First, anyone may fall, at any time. If Simon Peter could deny Jesus, any one of us could do so. Simon, after all, had not believed himself capable of such a thing. "Even if *all* are made to stumble," he boasted, "yet I will not be" (Mark 14:29). He was so utterly resolved on the matter that, when the soldiers came to arrest Jesus in the garden, Simon had attacked them with violence. Alas, he was neither the first man nor the last to confuse human excitement with divine strength, nor to mistake the pumping of adrenaline for the infusion of grace. Within a very short time after he swung his sword at the unsuspecting Malchus (cf. John 18:10), we find Peter backing down embarrassed before the pointing finger of a servant girl. The Holy Spirit took particular care that Christians throughout the ages would never forget that falling away remains a real possibility for any of them. In the words of yet another converted sinner, "Therefore let him who thinks he stands take heed lest he fall" (1 Corinthians 10:12).

Second, Christians were also to learn from this story that, as long as they are alive, repentance and a return to forgiveness are always live options. In this respect, the repentance of Simon Peter is to be contrasted with the despair of Judas. Thus, the Gospel stories tell us, until our very last breath, it is never too late to return to God in answer to the summons of His grace. It is probably Luke's Gospel that gives the most poignant description of this conversion: "And the Lord turned and looked at Peter. . . . So Peter went out and wept bitterly" (22:61–62). This event is turned into a prayer in an ancient Latin hymn composed to be sung at cockcrow, the very hour of the denial: *Jesu, labantes respice / et nos videndo corrige / Si respicis labes cadunt / et fletu culpa solvitur—* "Jesus, gaze upon those who are falling, and set us right by the gaze. Our sins fall away at Your glance, and guilt is dissolved in weeping."

The second charcoal fire in John's Gospel is the one in its final scene, the fire kindled by the Lord Himself, over which He prepared breakfast for His dispirited Apostles (21:9). After breakfast it was at this fire that Jesus would put to that same Simon Peter his threefold question: "Do you love Me?" The Apostle understood, of course, why the question was asked of him three times, for it was the very number of his own denials. At this point the chastened Peter, no longer trusting himself, relies completely on the Lord's knowledge of his heart (21:17).

But there is more to the story. Simon Peter's threefold profession is followed by a reference to his eventual martyrdom, which had already happened by the time this text was written down later in the first century. Indeed, the author of John 21 clearly presupposes his readers' familiarity with Peter's martyrdom. The story of the Apostle's crucifixion on Vatican Hill in Rome in the mid-60s was so widely reported among the churches that John could simply refer to the stretching out of Peter's hands as "signifying by what death he would glorify God" (21:18–19). The point required no further explanation. The early Christians were so familiar with the circumstances of Peter's martyrdom in Rome that around the turn of the century Clement of Rome (*Ad Corinthios* 5.4), writing *from* Rome, and Ignatius of Antioch (*Romans* 4), writing *to* Rome, felt no need to elaborate on the details and circumstances. That this Johannine passage ("you will stretch out your hands . . . signifying by what death he would glorify God") did in fact refer to Peter's crucifixion in

Rome was perfectly obvious to Tertullian, writing in Africa slightly after the year 200. Citing that Johannine verse, he wrote: "Then was Peter 'bound by another,' when he was fastened to the cross" (*Scorpiace* 15.3).

⁊

2. JUDAH AND HIS BROTHERS

The personality of the patriarch Judah is chiefly elaborated in the story of Joseph, where Judah is part of a rather complex narrative.

Thus, in the encounter between Joseph and Potiphar's wife (Genesis 39), the example of Joseph's chastity is heightened by a contrast with two of his older brothers, the incestuous Reuben in Chapter 35 (cf. 49:4) and the lustful Judah in Chapter 38. This contrast, moreover, is quietly introduced by the specific attention directed to both of these brothers (37:21f, 26f, 29) in the context of Joseph's being sold to Potiphar (37:36). Later on, of course, both Reuben and Judah will be important to the developing tension of the Joseph story (42:22–24, 37; 43:3, 8).

The tale of Judah and his daughter-in-law in Genesis 38 is particularly relevant here, for it deliberately interrupts the account of Joseph's trials near their very beginning. Nor is this break in the story a distraction from the theme. Inserted between Joseph's arrival at Potiphar's house and the incident of Potiphar's wife, this tale of Judah manifestly serves three purposes.

First, it provides a literary "meanwhile," hinting at the passage of time in Joseph's life. This "Judah interlude" allows the reader to put Joseph out of his mind for a while, so that he can "get settled," as it were, down in Egypt. Only then will attention be drawn back to Joseph.

Second, as already noted, the incident of Judah's lust offers an immediate contextual contrast to Joseph's chastity.

Third, this position of Judah near the beginning of the drama of Joseph prepares the reader for Judah's essential role in its resolution (44:18–34). Thus, when Jacob's sons finally arrive at Joseph's home for the story's memorable denouement, it is significant that they are called "Judah and his brothers" (44:14). Even as the story of Joseph comes to an end, we learn that "Judah is a lion's whelp" and that "the scepter shall not depart from Judah" (49:9–10). Indeed, in this final section of Genesis, properly known as the Joseph Cycle, one easily detects another motif that can be called "the conversion of Judah."

Born fourth among the twelve brothers, Judah will rise to prominence after the moral failings of the older three (49:3–7). It is in the Joseph story that he is brought specifically to the reader's notice, when he proposes that the younger brother be sold instead of killed. There is a moral emphasis here. Whatever his other moral failings, Judah is at least sensitive to the sin of fratricide: "Let not our hand be upon him, for he is our brother and our flesh" (37:27).

There immediately follows the extended interlude that recounts the mutual deception of Judah and Tamar. Bereaved of a wife and two sons within six verses (38:7–12), the wily Judah deceives his daughter-in-law by withholding his youngest son from his levirate responsibilities (38:11). He is in turn deceived by Tamar's impersonation of a harlot (38:12–23).

Once again there is a moral note in the story. Judah, at first indignant about Tamar's alleged adultery (38:24–25), is smitten in conscience when the truth is revealed (38:25–26). Tamar has turned the tables on her father-in-law; he can only acknowledge his paternity of the children whom she carries in her womb. This narrative, in addition to its importance in the genealogy of the chosen people, is a chief component in the moral development of Judah.

Judah's finest hour arrives with his lengthy pleading for the delivery of Benjamin (44:16–34), which leads directly to Joseph's revelation to his brothers (45:1–15). It is essential for Joseph to know that his brothers have really changed over the years. Will these men simply go back to their father with heartbreaking news about Benjamin, as they did in his own case so many years before? Or will they come clean about their offense? Are they yet the coldhearted men of yesteryear? Joseph has to know.

It is at this point that "Judah came near to him and said" (44:18), and, in answering these moral questions, he assumes his destined leadership among the sons of Jacob. To the yet unrecognized Joseph he pleads with tears that their aged father be spared any further distress, and the supple, forgiving soul of Joseph needs to hear no more. Judah has repented with all his heart.

⁂

3. THE FALL AND RISE OF DAVID

In its story of David's double sin, the Bible describes certain theological aspects of all sin, by portraying David's offense through a series of striking parallels with the earlier account of Adam's Fall in the Garden.

First, regarding the circumstances and immediate consequences of David's infidelity, there are several points of correspondence with the offense of Adam. Thus, both Adam and David were tempted by women, Eve (Genesis 3:6) and Bathsheba (2 Samuel 11:2–4). Likewise, in both cases the two men were abruptly confronted with the gravity of their sin: "Have you eaten from the tree . . . ?" (Genesis 3:11) and "You are the man!" (2 Samuel 12:7). Next, judgment was pronounced on the house of each offender in the shape of death (Genesis 3:19; 2 Samuel 12:14). Indeed, Adam and David would each be preceded to the grave by a son born of that same woman (Genesis 4:8; 2 Samuel 12:18). That is to say, in both instances sin led immediately to death (cf. Romans 5:12). On the other hand, in each example, a new son was born as a sign of promise and renewed hope (Genesis 4:25; 2 Samuel 12:24). Thus, in the circumstances of Adam's and David's sins, we see a narrative sequence of fall, judgment, curse, and mercy.

Second, with respect to the more extended effects of their transgressions, both Adam and David became the fathers of fratricides, Cain (Genesis 4:8) and Absalom (2 Samuel 13:29). Their fall, that is to say, led to hatred and murder. Indeed, there is a remarkable similarity between the description of Cain's murder of Abel and the parabolic portrayal of Absalom's killing of Amnon. In each instance the murderer rises up and slays his brother in a field (compare Genesis 4:8 and 2 Samuel 14:6). We observe, moreover, that in each case, the murderer himself is initially spared (Genesis 4:15; 2 Samuel 14:11), though a restricting curse still hangs over him (Genesis 4:16; 2 Samuel 14:24). Thus, even though in neither instance is the murder punished by death, guilt remains as an active element in the story, a source of continuing narrative tension.

Third, the biblical text goes to some length to demonstrate the long-term consequences of the sins of Adam and David, which intensify through the fratricides committed by Cain and Absalom. Both of the latter act in hatred, which in turn provokes the fear of vengeance (Genesis 4:14; 2 Samuel 14:7). The consequences of these offenses will eventually include full-scale rebellions. In the account of Adam this rebellion is indicated both before and after the Flood (Genesis 6:5; 11:3, 4), while in the case of David the resulting rebellion takes shape in Absalom's civil war (2 Samuel 15—18).

Thus, by this remarkable series of parallels with the fallen founder of the human race, the biblical tale portrays the offending David as the symbol of all human offenders since Adam. David's sin becomes, like Adam's, a kind of archetype of man's rebellion against God's command.

This was not a theory. The tenth-century BC narrator of this story had seen it happen, and his sixth-century editor had witnessed its later fruits toward the end of the Davidic monarchy, culminating in the fall of Jerusalem in 586 BC.

Within the full canonical context of the biblical account, nonetheless, David's swift repentance serves as the proper pattern of conversion and pardon. The contrition of this fallen king is the story of all who fall and rise.

It is instructive, then, that the Bible's great psalm of contrition, the *Miserere* (Psalm 50 in Greek, 51 in Hebrew), is traditionally ascribed to David. It is significant, too, that the Church prescribes this prayer of a repentant adulterer and murderer to be recited daily in the Canonical Hours and again by her priests during the incensing before the Great Entrance at every celebration of the Divine Liturgy. The Church thus places the repentance of David very close to the center of her own relationship to Christ our Lord.

Indeed, at the "tenth prayer" of Orthodox Matins, which quotes several verses of that penitential psalm, the Church opens each day by thinking of David. It begins: ". . . O Lord our God, who hast granted unto men pardon through repentance, and hast set us, as an example of the acknowledgment of sin and of the confession which is unto forgiveness, the repentance of the Prophet David, do Thou, the same Lord, have mercy on us according to Thy great mercy . . . Blot out our transgressions."

⁂

4. THE PARALYTIC FROM THE ROOF

In all three Synoptic Gospels, the healing of the paralytic (Matthew 9:1–8; Mark 2:1–12; Luke 5:17–26) is followed immediately by the calling of the tax collector and the Lord's eating with sinners (Matthew 9:9–13; Mark 2:13–17; Luke 5:27–32). This common sequence of the two narratives probably reflects an early preaching pattern, explained by the fact that both stories deal with the same theme: Jesus' relationship to sin and sinners. The paralytic was healed, after all, "that you may know that the Son of Man has power [authority] on earth to forgive sins," and the point of the second story is that "I did not come to call the righteous, but sinners."

Thus, the most significant thing about the paralytic is not his paralysis, but his "sins," so this is what Jesus addresses first. Indeed, even when He heals the paralysis, Jesus does so in order to demonstrate His authority over the man's sins. In what He does in this scene, then, Jesus inserts Himself between God and the man, speaking to the man with God's authority. It is not without significance that all three versions of the story also include the detail that Jesus could, like God, read His accusers' inner thoughts.

In each of the three Synoptic Gospels, moreover, the Lord's claim to authority over sin here becomes the first occasion on which His enemies accuse Him of blasphemy. This is significant too, because at His judicial process before the Sanhedrin, blasphemy will be the crime of which He is accused. In a sense, then, Jesus' trial begins with His healing of the paralytic, because this scene is recognized by even His enemies as the occasion on which He forcefully claims divine authority.

This more dramatic aspect of the account is perhaps clearest in the versions of Mark and Luke, where it is the first of five conflict stories that cast an ominous cloud over Jesus' activity through the rest of those Gospels (Mark 2:1—3:5; Luke 5:17—6:11). In Mark's rendering, furthermore, the resolve to "destroy" Jesus is explicitly taken at the end of this sequence (3:5).

In all three Synoptic Gospels, the paralytic becomes the "type" of the sinner. He is helpless, carried by others because he cannot carry himself. He is utterly in need of mercy above all things. Indeed, even his forgiveness and his cure are not credited to his own faith. All three accounts mention that the Lord sees the faith, not of the paralytic, but of the men who support him. This point of "corporate faith" in the forgiveness of sins is accentuated in Matthew's version, where the authority of Jesus to forgive sins is shared with "men" (9:8). The plural here is significant and touches on an important theme in Matthew, the Church's authority to bind and loose in God's name (16:19; 18:18). This theme is related to the Great Commission at the end of that Gospel, where the entire mission of the Church is rooted in the total "authority" of Christ (28:18).

Even functioning as a literary and theological type, however, this paralytic is certainly not reduced to an abstraction. Indeed, because of the detail of the removal of the roof (in Mark and Luke) in order to lower the paralytic down into Jesus' presence, still dangling between earth and heaven, this is one of the more colorful and unforgettable scenes in the Gospels.

Matthew's slightly shorter and less colorful version, which comes quite a bit later in his narrative sequence, has certain notable features proper to that Gospel. It is the sixth in his series of ten specific miracles that fill chapters 8 and 9, demonstrating Jesus' "authority" (*exsousia*) in deed. The Lord's authority in works of wonder corresponds to His authority in teaching, demonstrated in the Sermon on the Mount, which immediately precedes this section of Matthew. The latter had noted that Jesus "taught them as one having authority [*exsousia*]" (7:29). The Lord's authority to forgive sins, in Matthew, thus stands in sequence with His authority over sickness (8:9), fever (8:15), demonic possession (8:16, 32), blindness (9:29), muteness (9:32), hemorrhage (9:22), and even death (9:25).

Matthew is alone in placing this story immediately after the stilling of the storm and the driving out of the Gergesene demons. When the healing of the paralytic is effected to demonstrate that Jesus is possessed of the "authority to forgive sins," it is done with that same ready dispatch with which He stilled the storm and drove the devils into the swine.

❧

5. THE TAX COLLECTOR AND HIS FRIENDS

Since the call of Levi falls in exactly the same sequence in the Gospels of Mark and Luke as Matthew's call in the Gospel of Matthew, we are surely correct in regarding these two men as identical, notwithstanding the contrary opinions mentioned by Heracleon, Clement of Alexandria, and Origen. Mark and Luke place this tax collector's calling fairly early, soon after the calling of the fishermen, where we might naturally expect it. Matthew puts it somewhat later in the narrative, after the Sermon on the Mount.

It is much more significant, however, that all three Synoptic Gospels treat the call of the tax collector (Levi/Matthew) as a centerpiece bracketed between two stories about sinners: the paralytic being forgiven his sins and Jesus having dinner with notorious sinners. Thus set between these two events, the call of the tax collector represents above all the evangelical summons to repentance and the forgiveness of sins.

The dialogue connected with the meal at his house illustrates this meaning of the tax collector's call. Jesus, criticized for his association with sinners on this occasion, explains that "those who are well have no need of a physician, but those who are sick" (Mark 2:17). In thus addressing sin through the metaphor of sickness, the Lord strikes again the note recently sounded by His healing the paralytic as proof of His authority to forgive the man's sins (2:5–12).

Furthermore, summoning sinners to repentance and salvation is not just one of the things Jesus happens to do. There is a sense in which this is the defining thing that Jesus does, the very reason He came into this world. This truth is affirmed at the meal at the tax collector's house, where He proclaims, "I did not come to call the righteous, but sinners, to repentance" (Luke 5:32; cf. Matthew 9:13; Mark 2:17). Again, it is in the context of the call of yet another tax collector, Zacchaeus, that Jesus says, "the Son of Man has come to seek and to save that which was lost" (Luke 19:10).

One of those "lost" was the Apostle Paul, who remembered himself to have been "a blasphemer, a persecutor, and an insolent man." But then he recalled that the same Lord who received the friends of the tax collector also received him: "This is a faithful saying and worthy of all acceptance, that Christ Jesus came into the world to save sinners, of whom I am chief" (1 Timothy 1:13–15).

Christ can call sinners, only because He can really do something about their sins. And He can forgive their sins precisely because He has paid the price of those sins. Therefore, Jesus' forgiveness of sins is theologically inseparable from His dying for sinners. Correct repentance, then, brings the sinner to the foot of the Cross.

In truth, this soteriological dimension of the call to repentance is implied in the Gospel stories under consideration. Both at the forgiveness of the paralytic and at the tax collector's dinner, all three Synoptics speak of the hostile presence of Jesus' enemies, the very men who will contrive to kill Him. They accuse Him of blasphemy on the first occasion ("This man blasphemes"—the very charge for which He will be condemned to death) and find fault with Him on the second ("Why does your Teacher eat with tax collectors and sinners?"). In both cases Jesus confronts them on this matter of His relationship to sin and to sinners.

Every time an Orthodox Christian approaches the Cup of Salvation, the Church exacts of him a twofold confession, explicitly and out loud. First, "I confess that Thou art the Christ, the Son of the Living God." And second, "who didst come into the world to save sinners, of whom I am chief." This double formula, combining the confessions of St. Peter and St. Paul, means "You-Lord, me-sinner," which pretty much puts us tax collectors in our place at Communion time. Truly this is the meal at the tax collector's house, and only sinners have been summoned.

But calling myself "chief of sinners" is not a quantitative statement. It is not a thesis that I prove by demonstrating that I have committed a larger number of sins than other people. To think of myself as the chief of sinners is not an inference based on a comparison of myself with others. Indeed, the notion of "other sinners" here is nearly a metaphor; there are no other sinners right now, at this moment of Holy Communion. Only one sinner, and only one Savior.

❦

6. THE DEMONIAC AND THE PIGS

Except for the Passion narratives, it is not often that several consecutive Gospel stories are told in the identical order in all or even several of the Gospels. Indeed, apart from events that obviously belong near either the beginning or the end of Jesus' earthly life, factual chronology seems not to have been of great concern to the four evangelists, and the differing positions and juxtapositions of individual stories within their Gospels seem determined less by a care for historical precision than by the literary and theological considerations that guided their minds. (Early in the second century, Papias of Hierapolis already remarked on this feature in the Gospel according to St. Mark.)

Consequently, when we find four consecutive stories told in exactly the same order in three of the Gospels, the fact is noteworthy. Indeed, in such a case we are justified in suspecting that the sequence of the narrative was determined by very early tradition, perhaps even the historical memory established by an apostolic eyewitness.

We have such an instance in the order of the following four stories: the stilling of the storm, the driving of the demons into the pigs, the healing of the woman with the blood-flow, and the raising of Jairus's daughter. These accounts appear in each of the three Synoptic Gospels in exactly the same sequence.

The likelihood of strict chronological precision is even stronger in the sequence of the storm scene and the episode involving the demons and the pigs. Since the latter event was remembered to have taken place in Gentile territory (Jews not being permitted to tend pigs) on the east side of the Sea of Galilee, we naturally find it preceded by a boat trip to arrive at the place. Beyond simple historical sequence, however, the two narratives are appropriately juxtaposed for two other reasons.

First, both stories are concerned with the mysterious identity of Jesus in a context symbolic of baptism. First, the marveling Apostles raise the question of Jesus' identity in reaction to His manifest authority over the storm (Matthew 8:27; Mark 4:41; Luke 8:25), and then the demons address Him as "Son of God" (Matthew 8:29; Mark 5:7; Luke 8:28): "Who is this? The Son of God." This combination of query and response, found in all three Synoptics, suggests that the demons themselves are answering the question that the Apostles have just asked: "Who?" The joining of this specific doctrinal question and this specific dogmatic answer, given at the waterside, follows the ancient interrogation of the Sacrament of Baptism (cf. Acts 8:36–37, for example), which in the Church has always been prefaced by an exorcism. To this very day, when someone is presented for baptism, that person is first exorcised of demons, who are explicitly rejected, and is then asked to confess Jesus as Son of God, Savior, and Lord.

Second, the juxtaposition of these two stories suggests an imaginative analogy between the outer, physical storm on the lake and the inner, spiritual storm afflicting a tortured soul. (This suggestion is not at all affected by Matthew's having two demoniacs here, apparently moving the second one to this scene from Mark 1:23–26. Such doublings are typical of Matthew.)

Both of these storms, the outer and the inner, have a "before and after." Thus, of the first one we read, "a great windstorm arose, and the waves beat into the boat," and then, "the wind ceased and there was a great calm" (Mark 4:37, 39). Of the second storm we are told, "he was in the mountains and in the tombs, crying out and cutting himself with stones," and then, they "saw the one who had been demon-possessed and had the legion, sitting and clothed and in his right mind" (Mark 5:5, 15). In both cases, it is the encounter with Jesus that produces the calm. In each instance, Jesus' command is inexorable: "Even the wind and the sea obey Him" and "Send us to the swine" (4:41; 5:12).

Prior to meeting Jesus, this poor demoniac is the very type of the lost soul, his heart and mind fractured and fragmented into thousands of warring parts. (There were six thousand foot soldiers in a Roman legion, besides cavalry. Now, if six thousand demons entered into two thousand pigs, that would mean . . . well, you can do the math.) This meeting with Christ is baptismal; the demons perish in those same deluge waters from which the Church has just been delivered.

More specifically, that raging demoniac, living in Gentile territory, represented the hopeless plight of the uncovenanted Gentiles described by St. Paul: "without Christ, being aliens from the commonwealth of Israel and strangers from the covenants of promise, having no hope and without God in the world" (Ephesians 2:12). Prior to meeting Christ in the mystery of baptism, he was day and night dwelling in tomb caves, the realm of the dead, breaking iron chains with his bare hands, crying out in despair and gashing himself in anguish; it was truly the case that "he saw Jesus from *afar*" (*makrothen*—Mark 5:6). Indeed, from very far, and without hope. But even to those in such a state was St. Paul able to write, "But now in Christ Jesus you who once were *far off* [*makran*] have been brought near by the blood of Christ" (Ephesians 2:13).

⁊

7. THE WOMAN AT THE WELL

Among the loveliest lines ever penned for Christian prayer, I think, are those in the tenth strophe of Thomas of Celano's *Dies Irae: "Quaerens me sedisti lassus / Redemisti crucem passus / Tantus labor non sit cassus!"* or "Seeking me, You sat down weary, / Redeeming me, You bore the cross, / Let not such labor be in vain!"

No Calvinist was Thomas of Celano. He believed, from the Scriptures, that the Lamb of God suffered and died for everyone, atoning for the sins of the whole world, not just the sins of the elect. *"Copiosa apud Eum redemptio!"* says Psalm 129 in the *Vetus Latina*, "With Him is copious redemption." Broadly flooding in libation, Jesus' blood was shed even for the sake of those sinners who, by their own choice (not God's!), would be damned. And that Lamb's dear blood would be, in the latter case, without avail, *cassus*. Thus Celano prayed that the wide labor of Christ's redemption be not wasted in his own regard.

But these second and third lines of Celano's *terza rima* are so rich that one might easily miss the delicate allusion of its first line: "Seeking me You sat down weary." Once the line is noticed, nonetheless, its allusion is perfectly clear. These words refer to the scene in John 4:6— "Jesus therefore, being wearied from His journey, sat thus by the well." Just why did Jesus sit down weary by Jacob's well? Celano answers that He was waiting for someone special whom He had in mind to meet that day. He was seeking *me*. The Samaritan woman at the well is each of us.

The Evangelist John surely knew that woman's name, just as he knew the names of the paralytic at the pool and the man born blind, because he narrates all of these one-on-one encounters with details that he could only have obtained from the individuals themselves. So John most certainly knew their names. His omission of those names in the stories, then, has literary significance, and Celano is probably right to suppose that we are dealing here with anonymity for the sake of reader identification. That is to say, each of us, as we ponder the text prayerfully, becomes that paralytic, that blind man, and that woman at the well, encountering the Lord in the power of His Scriptures.

As an "every Christian" account, the story of the Samaritan woman at Jacob's well serves to illustrate certain distinct stages in the path of conversion.

We observe, for instance, what might be called a growth in Christology as the story progresses; there is a pronounced evolution in the terms by which the Lord is regarded. Thus, when the woman first meets Jesus, He is called simply "a Jew" (4:9). This is important to the story as a whole, of course, because the Lord Himself will presently declare that "salvation is of the Jews" (4:22). On the woman's lips, nonetheless, the designation "Jew" indicates two things: First, it says that Jesus is at first assessed only within a certain class of people. He is not yet a distinguishable person, important on His own account. And second, the word "Jew" indicates the woman's sense of separation from Jesus, because "Jews have no dealings with Samaritans."

Next, Jesus is addressed as "Sir" (4:11; presumably the Aramaic *Mar*). This term of respect is a great step for the woman to make, indicating her change of attitude toward Jesus. But then, within four verses "Sir" becomes "prophet" (4:19), when the Lord directs the woman's attention to her own sins. Then Jesus takes the initiative in His own identification, calling Himself the Messiah, the Christ (4:25–26), and the woman immediately departs.

Nonetheless, she leaves the well with a question in her mind, a question about the identity of Jesus. It is the fundamental question that would in due time be addressed by the Ecumenical Councils: "Who do you say that I am?" Just exactly who is Jesus? "Come," she invites her friends, "see a *Man* who told me all things that I ever did. Could this be the Christ?" (4:29). Everyone in John's Gospel seems to be asking such questions: "'This is the Prophet.' Others said, 'This is the Christ'" (7:40, 41).

At the end of the woman's story, the designation "Christ" is embraced by her Samaritan friends, who promptly complete it with another important Christological title: "We know that this is indeed the Christ, the Savior of the world" (4:42).

The lady from Samaria has now come all the way. Starting out that day, hardly suspecting what lay ahead, she laboriously carried her sins to the well, where she met a Jew, who asked her for a drink of water. The Jew presently became a Sir, and then a prophet who reminded her that she was a sinner. No matter, though, because this prophet was also the Christ, who, because He was the Savior of the world, knew exactly what to do with her sins. Seeking her He sat down weary, and to redeem her He would, in due course, endure the cross.

⅗

8. THE PARALYTIC AT THE POOL

Although our Lord evidently cured a number of people from various kinds of paralysis (cf. Mark 4:24; 8:6), the Gospels narrate only two such instances in much detail: the paralytic lowered through the roof (Mark 2:1–12; Matthew 9:1–8; Luke 5:17–26), and the man lying at the pool of Bethesda (John 5:1–15). It also happens that these are the only two occasions of physical healing in which Jesus refers to the sins of the person whom He heals. Thus, He says to the man lowered through the roof, "Your sins are forgiven you" (Mark 2:5), and after restoring the man at the pool of Bethesda the Lord exhorts him, "Sin no more" (John 5:14).

Now it is worthy of remark that we find no references to personal sins in Gospel stories about Jesus cleansing lepers, or restoring sight to the blind, or curing other sorts of ailments. He does not say to Peter's feverish mother-in-law, for example, "Your sins are forgiven you," nor does He exhort the man born blind, "Go, and sin no more." Indeed, in this latter instance the Lord specifically denies that the blind man was blind because of his personal sins (9:3). In short, only in those two instances of paralysis does Jesus refer to the sins of the people He cures, even addressing one of them with the exact words that He spoke to the woman caught in adultery: "Sin no more" (8:11).

One is disposed to wonder if there is some special reason why the restorations of the paralytics are alone distinguished in this way. Though the Gospels do not specifically address the question, one is prompted to inquire if there is not, in this kind of disability, some feature particularly symbolic of sin. Is there perhaps some aspect of paralysis itself that serves as an allegory of sin, something about the affliction that narrates the properties of sin?

This question of allegory is especially urged in the case of the paralytic at the pool, because of the recorded dialogue between this man and Jesus. The Lord's question, when He asks the paralytic, "Do you want to be made well?" is apparently elicited by the fact that the fellow has been lying in that place for thirty-eight years. It is because Jesus knows that "he already had been in that condition a long time" that He makes the inquiry, "Do you *want* to be made well?" In other words, there is room for doubt about the man's genuine desire for healing. Maybe his heart and soul have become as helpless and lethargic as his body.

Moreover, his response to our Lord's question is hardly reassuring. Instead of answering, like the blind men, "Yes, Lord" (Matthew 9:28), the paralytic immediately begins to make excuses: "Sir, I have no man to put me into the pool when the water is stirred up; but while I am coming, another steps down before me" (John 5:7). There is his answer. It is always somebody else's fault, somebody else's advantage over him, that he has not been cured. He is not to blame, poor victim; he has been lying there at the pool of Bethesda for nearly four decades, using the same excuse to explain why, in a place where healings took place frequently, he has never been healed. Year after year he just lies there. It gets easier all the time. It becomes a way of life.

This seems to be the point, then, of the question that Jesus puts to the man: "Do you *want* to be healed?" Perhaps, in his deeper heart, he does not want to be healed, not really, and perhaps that is the sin to which Jesus is referring when He tells him, "See, you have been made well. Sin no more, lest a worse thing come upon you" (5:14).

In removing his paralysis, the Lord also gives the man a straight, unambiguous order: "Rise, take up your bed and walk" (5:8). If this paralytic wants to walk in the way of the Lord, he must begin now. No more excuses. He must not lie around one minute longer, theorizing about the mysterious relationship between divine grace and human effort. This lethargic soul must not worry whether he may be slipping into semi-Pelagianism or whatever. He must get up on his feet, put his bed away, and get busy walking.

Conversion is grace, but it is also command. Surely wisdom too is God's gift, but what is the first step we take to attain wisdom? Obedience to an emphatic command: "Get wisdom! Get understanding!" (Proverbs 4:5). No more lying around, making excuses (usually involving other people who are to blame), no more theorizing abut the nature of wisdom. Just get up and get it!

⁂

9. THE PRODIGAL SON

"I have acquired Thy testimonies by inheritance," prayed the Psalmist, clearly appreciative of his legacy. Alas, such opulent legacies are not always cherished. Few sins, indeed, are so common, and fewer still, perhaps, so distressing, as the squandering of birthrights.

The Bible is very concerned about this sin. For example, the various warnings that fill the Book of Proverbs, especially those concerned with discipline among young men, are based on the fear that a son's goodly inheritance may be lost because of a failure to recognize its worth. In truth, Holy Scripture records examples of such loss. One thinks of the sons of Eli (1 Samuel 2:12–17, 22–25), the sons of Samuel (8:1–5), the son of Hezekiah (2 Kings 21), and so on. These were all foolish young men who, failing to recognize the worth of their birthright, thoughtlessly tossed it away. The Bible gives more ample treatment to two such young men, whose cases, I suggest, warrant comparison: Esau in Genesis 25 and the younger son in the Lord's parable in Luke 15:11–32.

First, we note that both of these young men enjoyed the fortune of good and godly fathers. Esau, the elder son of Isaac, ostensibly stood in the direct line of the divine promises made to Abraham, while in the household of the other man's father, even the hired servants had "bread enough and to spare" (15:17).

Second, both of these young men were utter fools, the very sort about whom the Book of Proverbs has so much to say, none of it very good, and, being fools, both young men treated their heritage with disrespect. We know that Esau was a "profane person . . . who for one morsel of food sold his birthright" (Hebrews 12:16), while the other "gathered all together, journeyed to a far country, and there wasted his possessions with prodigal living" (Luke 15:13).

Third, in due course both young fools came to regret their mistakes. It is in respect to those regrets, however, that our comparison between the two of them must be modified into a significant contrast. Whereas one of those men simply regretted his loss, the other genuinely repented of his sin.

We may start with Isaac's elder son, of whom Holy Scripture tells us, "Thus Esau despised his birthright" (Genesis 25:34). He certainly regretted the loss of that birthright. There was no sign, however, that he ever assumed responsibility for its loss. It was always Jacob's fault, not his. "He took away my birthright" (27:36), Esau complains of his younger brother. Never do we perceive in Esau an awareness of himself as a sinner. Thus, laying elsewhere the blame for his misfortune, Esau never found his way to repentance.

If Esau espoused any recognizable theology, it was the theology of "cheap grace," which claims godly favor without godly repentance. Having bargained off his birthright for a bowl of lentil soup, Esau imagined that he could later turn around and procure the blessing of the firstborn with a plate of venison. Having treated so lightly his paternal heritage, he traipsed in carelessly for what he fancied to be an easy paternal blessing. Esau never reflected that he had sinned against his father on that day when, merely to appease a moment's hunger, he had contemned his father's legacy. Esau spoke not a syllable of regret for any loss except his own. And now it was too late. The birthright was gone; the blessing of the firstborn was gone, and Esau "was rejected, for he found no place for repentance, though he sought it diligently with tears" (Hebrews 12:17).

Not like Esau was that younger son in the parable, for his was genuine repentance. When his folly drove him to the dire straits of destitution (as the Book of Proverbs, page after page, had warned that it would), the young man did not take to blaming others for his plight. He did not start expressing jealousy and bitterness toward his brother, for example, nor complaining of his father's discipline, or some possible shortcoming in his own education or opportunities. On the contrary, we are told that "he came to himself" (Luke 15:17), and, coming to himself, he realized that he was the one who had sinned, and the responsibility was entirely his own. His had been, moreover, a twofold sin, an offense against both God and that man whom God had given him to be his father: "Father, I have sinned against heaven and in your sight, and am no longer worthy to be called your son" (Luke 15:21). Such is the voice of genuine repentance, that "fear of the LORD" which is, according to Psalm 111:10, "the beginning of wisdom."

⁂

10. THE CONVERSION OF SAINT PAUL

We are not free to choose the framework and shape of our repentance— surely this is one of the clearest teachings of the Bible. Jesus "poured water into a basin," says the Sacred Text, "and began to wash the disciples' feet" (John 13:5). The Lord determined the basin, the instrument that gave specific contour and dimensions to the shape of His cleansing water. He then came to each of the disciples, one by one, and they understood that they had to put their feet into that basin, so that He could wash them.

In other words, the Lord Himself chooses the manner and pattern of our washing; how we are cleansed by Christ is not a decision for our personal choice. "Here is the bowl," the Lord's action affirms; "put your feet right in here, this specific basin, and I will wash you clean, for if I do not wash you, you have no part with Me."

This truth was among the most important that Saul of Tarsus had to learn, and God took special care that he learned it well. As he was ruefully to reflect so many times during his later life, Saul had been a persecutor of the Holy Church (1 Corinthians 15:9; Galatians 1:13, 23; Philippians 3:6; 1 Timothy 1:13). "As for Saul," we are told, "he made havoc of the church, entering every house, and dragging off men and women, committing them to prison" (Acts 8:3). So when the Lord converted Saul on the road to Damascus, He made an explicit point of obliging that persecutor to submit to the Church that he had afflicted.

Some modern Christians imagine that they can come to God by "Christ alone and not by an organized religion," but the Lord would suffer Saul to entertain no such illusion. On the contrary, in Saul's conversion Jesus most explicitly identified Himself with the Church: "Saul,

Saul, why are you persecuting *Me*? . . . I am Jesus, whom you are persecuting" (9:4, 5). It was in this moment that Saul learned that Jesus and His Church are inseparable.

Thus, Saul would never be able to say that he came to God by "Christ alone and not by an organized religion." Indeed, after Jesus identified Himself to Saul, He gave him not one word of further direct instruction. When Saul asked Him, "Lord, what do You want me to do?" Jesus simply directed him to make that same inquiry of the Church: "Arise and go into the city, and *you will be told* what you must do" (9:6).

That is to say, not even the Apostle Paul, in the very hour of his conversion, was permitted to deal with Jesus "one on one." The contour and shape of his repentance had to be determined by a specified "organized religion." Paul would have no "personal relationship to Jesus as Lord and Savior" except through obedience to the doctrine, discipline, sacramental worship, and corporate life of the Church; he could not have a "personal relationship to Christ" on his own terms. Apart from the Church, the saving knowledge of God in Christ was not available even to St. Paul. He was constrained, rather, humbly to submit his heart and conscience to the divinely commissioned authority of that same body of Christians that he had hitherto been persecuting.

Paul's sins were not taken away simply by his "asking Jesus to enter his heart." There is nothing in the biblical text to suggest that he did any such thing on the road to Damascus. On the contrary, Paul's sins were taken away by his deliberate submission to the Church's sacramental discipline: "Arise and be baptized, and wash away your sins, calling on the name of the Lord" (Acts 22:16), because he "who believes and is baptized will be saved" (Mark 16:16). Paul was obliged to adhere to the same procedure as every other believer, a prescription enunciated in the Church's very first sermon on Pentecost: "Repent, and let every one of you be baptized in the name of Jesus Christ for the remission of sins" (Acts 2:38). Paul was forgiven his sins in exactly the same way required of everyone else, by joining the sole organization in this world that has the authority to forgive sins (cf. John 20:23).

Surely, then, it was in the experience of his conversion that the Apostle Paul received the seed of all his later teaching about the Church, which he identified as "the pillar and ground of the truth" (1 Timothy 3:15). Paul knew nothing of any noninstitutional Christianity. He was familiar with no Christ except the Christ of the Church, that constituted, organized communion of believers so intimately identified with Christ as to be called His "body" (Ephesians 1:22; 4:15–16; 5:23; Colossians 1:18, 24).

II.
SAINTS IN NEED OF IMPROVEMENT
ॐ

It never fails to jar my soul when Christians want to *feel* that they are "making progress in the spiritual life." Personal impressions of progress are undiluted nonsense; our feelings have nothing to do with it. Indeed, among all possible barometers of our spiritual state, hardly any are more likely to be deceptive than our feelings about ourselves. Yet, in spite of the uniform testimony of the saints, who warn us to distrust subjective perceptions of our spiritual state, there must be some perverse component in contemporary culture that drives people to consult (and trust) their own self-analysis in order to determine their standing in the sight of God. Thus, if they "feel good about themselves," they rather presume that God feels the same way about them too. If, on the contrary, they are distressed with themselves, they imagine that God also is displeased with them. It is all perfectly absurd.

Convinced that real saints are always in need of real improvement, I suggest the following list of three useful maxims for the life in Christ.

The top of the list should probably read: "I am still a sinner and will be a sinner until the day I die, and the subtler impulses of my heart are quietly conspiring to conceal that truth from my mind." In the life of grace, absolutely nothing is less reliable than my own assessment of my spiritual progress. Indeed, any thought or sentiment suggesting to me that I have made even the slightest spiritual progress should be regarded as a temptation coming straight from the Evil One. I dally with such a thought only at my peril. Temptations to fornication, homicide, and blasphemy are more safely entertained than this one. I should flee such an impulse as I would a fire, giving it not the faintest indulgence.

A second useful maxim of the life of grace may be: "It is in no way required that I feel good about myself." God does not require it; the Bible does not require it, and the entire ascetical tradition of the Church sternly warns against it. Self-approval is expected only within certain very dubious canons of contemporary behavioral sciences. A "positive self-image" is the most overrated of modern commodities and a very bad bargain at any price. Most often, in fact, the price is a concomitant compulsive disposition to pass judgment on other struggling servants of God.

A third useful maxim of the life of grace may be this: "I am just as likely to offend God because of my virtues as I am because of my vices, and if ever I am completely undone, my fall will more probably involve my strengths than my weaknesses. Consequently, in the spiritual life it is highly deceptive and even perilous to 'play to my strengths.'"

Each of us, when we place our lives under the guidance of the Holy Spirit, brings along an assortment of personal traits, to be regarded as either strengths or weaknesses depending on their compatibility with that guidance. For example, some individuals are already possessed of a certain natural patience and a spontaneous sense of humble deference. Perhaps they were raised that way in their youth. These qualities are strengths, of course, inasmuch as the Holy Spirit leads us to patience and personal humility. Such a person is less likely to sin by impatience and arrogance.

But suppose that same person, playing to his strengths, concentrates his mind's attention mainly on patience and deference, which he may do simply because these virtues come more easily to him. Watch for such a one to offend God by failing to be properly impatient and appropriately intolerant in circumstances where impatience and intolerance are the only godly options. This seems to be the fault of which the Apostle Paul accuses Barnabas in Galatians 2:13.

Thus too, a person naturally given to righteous zeal, when playing to this strength, may sin by making too abrupt a decision (David in 1 Samuel 25). Someone else, with a temperament disposed to gravity of soul, if he overly indulges this strength, may wax morbid in his heart and become despondent (Elijah in 1 Kings 19). Again, someone tolerant by native instinct may fail to impose discipline when it is morally necessary (Eli in 1 Samuel 2). Another, falling prey to a mix-up between divine grace and excessive adrenaline (a confusion common among those possessed of the latter), commits himself beyond his strength (Simon Peter in Matthew 26:33). In King Saul, it would seem, we find a man ultimately done in by that very quality that had initially made him so effective a servant of God. His executive impatience, the charismatic can-do that was his clear strength against the Ammonites in 1 Samuel 11, grew to monstrous proportions throughout the ensuing chapters, until King Saul, unto his own ruin, was completely dominated by it. Far from being improved by playing to his strength, Saul made it an instrument of his destruction.

$\mathcal{R}$

1. THE BEGUILING OF EVE

The humanity of Adam is the origin of all humanity. Every human being, that is to say, including Eve, comes forth from Adam. Consequently, from a theological perspective the whole of humanity fell in Adam's fall, because he was font and father of our race (cf. Romans 5:14; 1 Corinthians 15:22, 45).

From the perspective of chronology, nonetheless, Adam was not the first human sinner, for Genesis 3 testifies that that distinction belonged to Eve. Hence the rather corny story of postlapsarian Adam, pointing out the Garden of Eden to young Cain and Abel, "Boys, that garden there yonder is where your Ma ate us out of house and home." More reliable is the plain testimony of St. Paul: "Adam was not deceived, but the woman being deceived, fell into transgression" (1 Timothy 2:14).

Eve, moreover, was not only the first person to commit sin, but also the first to give scandal—to cause someone else to sin. "She also gave to her husband with her," says the Sacred Text, "and he ate" (Genesis 3:6). Hers was the offense of Jeroboam, so to speak, sinning and teaching Israel to sin.

Probably because she was the world's first offender, Holy Scripture goes into some detail to describe the temptation to which Eve succumbed. Her temptation serving as a kind of paradigm of all temptation, Eve stands as the Bible's first negative model of the moral life; her lapse provides the initial description of how the demons deal with the human soul.

Perhaps, indeed, St. Paul was indicating as much when he wrote to the church at Corinth, "I fear, lest somehow, as the serpent deceived Eve by his craftiness, so your minds may be corrupted from the simplicity that is in Christ" (2 Corinthians 11:3). Thus, if we want to understand how temptation functions in human psychology, we can hardly do better than to examine the temptation of Eve.

Prior to succumbing, Eve is tempted in three stages: (1) "So when the woman saw that the tree was good for food," (2) "that it was pleasant to the eyes," (3) "and a tree desirable to make one wise"—"she took of its fruit and ate" (Genesis 3:6). We may reasonably say that these three steps in the temptation correspond to "all that is in the world"—namely, "the lust of the flesh ['good for food'], the lust of the eyes ['pleasant to the eyes'], and the pride of life ['desirable to make one wise']" (1 John 2:16). At each stage in the temptation, Eve indulges a specious reasoning begotten of her passions. Objective moral strictures are not consulted. Eve's fall results from a distorted pattern of reasoning, for her thoughts are dictated by her desires.

And how did Eve stumble into this tripartite temptation? By giving ear to the deceptive arguments of the serpent. The latter begins with a factual question: "Has God indeed said, 'You shall not eat of every tree of the garden'?" (Genesis 3:1). The idea is preposterous, and Eve hastens to correct the questioner. She feels justified in this, of course, because in answering the serpent she can even feel herself to be God's defender. Alas, however, a conversation with the deceiver has therewith begun, and fickle Eve is a poor match for him. Her first mistake, then, was tactical. She should never have answered him at all.

Eve's mind now engaged, the deceiver prompts her to question the very reason that God had given for the command, "for in the day that you eat of it you shall surely die" (2:17). In fact, Eve had never heard God say these words, for they were spoken before she was formed from Adam's rib. Eve knew of the prohibition only through Adam. That is to say, God's mandate, as far as Eve knew, was simply a moral tradition, perhaps subject to improvement. Why need she submit her moral judgment to the apodictic command that Adam had shared with her? She, after all, had a mind of her own. She was just as intelligent as Adam, who after all had not really been in this world much longer than she. She could figure things out for herself. Thus did our ancient mother commence the process of her own personal moral theory.

St. Paul describes Eve's beguilement as a corruption from "simplicity" (2 Corinthians 11:3). In place of God's emphatic command, known solely through the moral tradition available to her, Eve declared the autonomy of her own thought, not pausing to consider that her thinking was hardly more than the perverse assertion of her passions.

৵৶

2. THE NEIGHBORHOOD LOT

Abraham's nephew Lot was no good judge of neighborhoods.

First, there was Sodom. With the whole Promised Land from which to choose, "Lot dwelt in the cities of the plain and pitched his tent even as far as Sodom" (Genesis 13:12). It was a perfectly awful choice. Hardly had Lot and his family moved in when a group of Bedouin kings came and raided the place, taking the whole bunch of them captive (14:1–12). Were it not for the prompt intervention of Uncle Abraham, that probably would have been the last we heard of Lot (14:13–17).

In addition, Sodom was hardly a salubrious place to live, because "the men of Sodom were exceedingly wicked and sinful against the LORD" (13:13). We know that Lot did not enjoy living there. The Scriptures speak of "righteous Lot, who was oppressed by the filthy conduct of the wicked (for that righteous man, dwelling among them, tormented his righteous soul from day to day by seeing and hearing their lawless deeds)" (2 Peter 2:7, 8).

Why, then, did Lot continue to live in such a vile place? He seems to have been one of those many people who, once they have settled down somewhere, are reluctant to move away, long after the situation has proven itself hopeless. Such souls are excessively fond of the familiar, the sort of folk who imagine all manner of evil that may befall them if they should change neighborhoods. "I cannot escape to the mountains," insisted Lot, "lest some evil overtake me and I die" (19:19). If anyone in Holy Scripture, however, should ever have heeded the warning, "Come out of her, my people, lest you share in her sins, and lest you receive of her plagues" (Revelation 18:4), surely that man was Lot.

Still, Lot stayed put in Sodom, until it was almost too late. That time of crisis that Jesus called "the days of Lot" (Luke 17:28) had well nigh run its course. Loudly sounded, even now, the hour of its overthrow. The brimstone was ready, with the pitch pots boiling to the brim, and the rescuing angels were urging Lot to hurry: "Arise, take your wife and your two daughters who are here, lest you be consumed in the punishment of the city. . . . Escape for your life! . . . Escape to the mountains, lest you be destroyed" (Genesis 19:15, 17).

Second, there was Zoar. Even as he fled from Sodom, Lot already began to miss the old neighborhood and was reluctant to move too far away! When the angels pressed him to flee to the mountains, he begged them for a compromise. How about Zoar, little Zoar, not far from Sodom? "See now," Lot pleaded pathetically, "this city is near enough to flee to, and it is a little one; please let me escape there (is it not a little one?) and my soul shall live" (19:20).

So Lot moved to Zoar, and his soul did live, but not his wife's, alas. Zoar was simply too proximate to Sodom, and it was not safe for Lot's family to remain so immediate to the scene of the overthrow. His wife succumbed to the temptation to look back, in spite of the angelic ad-monition not to do so (19:17, 26). Her backward glance to Sodom became, for all time, the symbol of those unwilling to put sufficient distance between themselves and sin. Her punishment stands forever as a portent to God's people: "Remember Lot's wife!" (Luke 17:32).

In spite of the unflattering picture of him in these biblical stories, Lot is remembered in the Bible as a righteous man. As we have seen, the Apostle Peter uses the word "righteous" three times in the two verses he devotes to Lot. In this respect Peter followed the example of the Wis-dom of Solomon, which spoke thus of Lot: "When the ungodly per-ished, [Wisdom] delivered the righteous man, who fled from the fire which fell upon the five cities. Of such wickedness, even to this day, the smoking wasteland is a testimony, and plants bearing salt that never come to ripeness; and a standing pillar of salt is a monument of an unbelieving soul" (10:6–7).

One observes that when the Bible calls Lot righteous, the term is somewhat relative; that is, he is called righteous by way of contrast with those around him, whether his wife or the citizens of Sodom. It is largely in this contrast that Lot is held forth as a model. In the words of St. John of Mount Sinai, "So we had better imitate Lot, and certainly not his wife" (*Ladder of Divine Ascent* 3).

৯৫

3. THE RESTLESS CAREER OF JACOB

The Greeks were not agreed what to make of Odysseus. A "very versa-tile man" (*aner polytropos*), as Homer called him, expert in ruse and master of disguise, this son and heir of Laertes was certainly among the most interesting and entertaining characters in classical memory. Both sagacious in counsel and brave in combat, moreover, his role in the routing of Troy placed Odysseus with the heroes honored in the annals of valor.

Some Greeks, nonetheless, did not feel entirely comfortable with this cunning warrior, "ever resourceful" (*polymetis*), never at a loss for the ingenious plan or the artful word. Even while admiring his various stratagems—his clever escape from the Cyclops's cave, for instance—they wondered if all that talented guile was entirely a good thing. Was there not something rather sneaky, duplicitous, and a tad too fast about it all? Indeed, might there not be some deeper, even darker significance in the fact (proved in the footrace at the funeral games of Patroclus) that Odysseus was simply much faster than everyone else?

Even conceding that Odysseus would never have arrived safely back home in Ithaca except for that wild, wily aspect of his character, was a man of so much deception to be held up for the emulation of the young? Were the ways of guile to be regarded as models in education? Would the imitation of shrewd Odysseus lead to a more virtuous citizenry and the enhancement of public trust? Doubting it, Pindar and Sophocles expressed their reservations about Odysseus. Plato, in fact, raised those same questions in the shorter dialogue between Socrates and Hippias, which contrasted the cunning of Odysseus with the candor of honest Achilles. In short, the example of Odysseus was a bit of a problem.

Now, with no possible rival, I think, the Odysseus of the Bible is Jacob. Truth to tell, the several parallels between the two are striking, if not always edifying. For starts, both were utter con men, unscrupulous deceivers, fluent, even eloquent, in falsehood. The one tricked blinded Polyphemus by hiding under a sheep, while the other deceived his blind father by hiding under a goatskin. Both, moreover, were blessed by blind men, the one by Teiresias, the other by Isaac. Each man struck a deal to win his wife, the one with Tyndareus, the other with Laban. The one took from the herds of Helios, the other from the flocks of his father-in-law Laban.

Both Odysseus and Jacob, furthermore, were accomplished, wide-ranging travelers. Whereas Odysseus returned home in disguise, Jacob left home because of a disguise. In the course of those journeys, the reader is struck by the attention given to events that happened while the two travelers slept, whether near Aeolia and at the Bay of Porcys, or at Bethel and the ford at Peniel. Both travelers, likewise, left their aging fathers, but even after many years each returned to find his father still alive. Indeed, the paternal home was the goal of each man's journey.

Jacob's flamboyant career began even in his mother's womb, where he and his twin brother wrestled to see who would be born first. Esau won the match, but Jacob emerged still clinging to his sibling's heel, determined never to lose again. He seldom did. Many years later he would walk with a limp from an injury sustained in another wrestling match, that time with an angel. Jacob won that contest too.

The great Baptist preacher, Charles Haddon Spurgeon, was once approached by a woman distressed by her recent reading of Romans 9:13: "Jacob I have loved, but Esau I have hated." "I cannot understand," she said, "why God should say that He hated Esau." "That is not my problem, madam," Spurgeon replied. "My difficulty is to understand how God could love Jacob!"

But God sees all things, including the future, and He knew how Jacob would turn out in the end. God foresaw the finishing days of an old man finally purified by much pain. God foreknew the aging heart chastened by grief for a lost son and disappointment in the other sons. God saw, already, the latter exile of Jacob in the land of Egypt, much humbled now, long bereft of the woman he really loved, and waiting to die on alien soil. God could hear already the much wiser ancient who told Pharaoh, "The days of the years of my pilgrimage are one hundred and thirty years; few and evil have been the days of the years of my life, and they have not attained to the days of the years of the life of my fathers in the days of their pilgrimage" (Genesis 47:9).

※

4. THE IMPATIENCE OF ELIHU

By the end of chapter 31 of the book named for him, Job has answered all of the objections and arguments made to him by his three friends, thus reducing them to silence. One might even think that this would be a good place for the book to end.

But then, as though out of nowhere, a completely new person appears on the scene, "Elihu, the son of Barachel the Buzite, of the family of Ram," who wants to add his own remarks. Hitherto keeping silence, he tells us, in order to show deference to the four older men (Job 32:4), young Elihu has been listening to the give-and-take of their lengthy discussion, a debate that has lasted through twenty-nine chapters of the book.

Outwardly patient while enduring their discussions, Elihu has nonetheless been inwardly seething with indignation at both Job and his three alleged comforters (32:2, 3). Hardly can he contain himself any longer, disagreeing with nearly everything said so far. Now, therefore, with a considerable show of indignation he begins his discourse (which will run on for the next seven chapters, easily the longest single speech in the book). Elihu informs the four older men just how patient he has remained during their pointless meanderings. But even as he boasts about his heroic longsuffering, we note the irony that Elihu mentions his own anger four times in five consecutive verses!

The failure of the three friends to answer Job's arguments adequately has confirmed Elihu's suspicion that wisdom is not an inevitable quality of old age. "Great men are not always wise, / Nor do the aged always understand justice" (32:9), he affirms. Indeed, Elihu addresses the company with some sarcasm on the point: "Age should speak, / And multitude of years should teach wisdom. . . . Indeed I waited for your words, / I listened to your reasonings, while you searched out what to say" (32:7, 11).

Job's three comforters, having exhausted their arguments, seem content now to leave the suffering Job to God, they themselves having nothing more to say. Not so Elihu. He will release in a torrent the pressure that has been building up within him: "For I am full of words; / The spirit within me compels me. / Indeed my belly is like wine that has no vent; / It is ready to burst like new wineskins. / I will speak, that I may find relief; / I must open my lips and answer" (32:18–20).

Even as he answers his elders, however, Elihu demonstrates the self-consciousness of youth and inexperience. He must justify himself by explaining that he is a plain-spoken man, a fellow both candid and proud of it: "Let me not, I pray, show partiality to anyone; / Nor let me flatter any man. / For I do not know how to flatter" (32:21, 22). Well, the reader of the Book of Job will concede this point to him, surely, for what Elihu has to say will be singularly innocent of flattery.

Somewhat pompous and verbose as he is in the beginning, we nonetheless observe that the young man does have some important things to say, and his truly is a fresh voice in the discussion. More than Job's three older friends, Elihu appreciates the basic soundness of Job's case. Although unwilling to admit that Job is completely undeserving of his afflictions, Elihu appears not to be bound by any theory that would render Job simply a sinner being punished for his sins. In the first part of his speech (Job 33), Elihu contends that, in dealing with Job's sufferings, inadequate attention has been given to the mysterious ways of God. Job's sufferings, he argues, do not show God to be Job's enemy. This observation represents a genuine advance over the various theses argued by Job's three other friends.

Even as he rebukes Job, Elihu spends most of chapter 34 talking about the just and merciful attributes of God, who is all-powerful and all-wise. No one can really demand an explanation from God, he goes on to argue in chapter 35. God is not someone against whom a man may lay just claims. Knowing this, Elihu contends in chapter 36, man must consider that God may see in human suffering something a great deal more than a means of punishing evil. Elihu closes his discourse in chapter 37 by exhorting Job to dwell more on what he knows of God and to assess his own suffering in the light of that knowledge. In this way Elihu's long discourse prepares the way for God's revelation to Job in the book's closing chapters.

⌘

5. JONAH AND THE NINEVITES

The Book of Jonah is a story full of paradox and irony, characteristics that mark both the person of the prophet and his career. Commanded by the Lord to go and preach repentance to the Ninevites, he proceeds in the very opposite direction, boarding a ship at the port of Joppa, headed to Tarshish (Cadiz, beyond the Straits of Gibraltar) at the other end of the Mediterranean Sea.

While other biblical prophets, such as Moses and Jeremiah, showed themselves reluctant to comply with their prophetic call, Jonah seems to be the only one whose reluctance was inspired by the fear of being successful! It is an important feature of this story that Jonah did not *want* the Ninevites to be converted; he wanted them justly punished, not spared. The original account of Jonah's call does not tell us this fact; we learn it only at the end of the book: "Ah, LORD, was not this what I said when I was still in my country? Therefore I fled previously to Tarshish; for I know that You are a gracious and merciful God, slow to anger and abundant in lovingkindness, One who relents from doing harm" (4:2).

Then, in his very flight Jonah discovers another paradox of the Lord's mercy, its uncanny capacity for bringing good out of evil. Thus, the prophet's very infidelity to God's call is turned into the means by which the pagan sailors come to know and worship the true God (1:16). Thus, Jonah's prophetic ministry, precisely because of his attempted disobedience to it, is enhanced by the conversion of *two* sets of people.

Next, because of Jonah's disobedience, God shifts to what may be called "Plan W" in His project to save the Ninevites. A great whale or sea monster swallows the prophet, but then, in the belly of this beast, Jonah proceeds to sing a hymn of praise for God's salvation (2:9). This too is paradoxical, because the salvation celebrated in this book is manifold. It is God's twofold liberation of Jonah, both the deliverance from his own infidelity by the sending of the whale and his coming rescue from the whale itself; it is the Lord's care for the pagan sailors; and, finally, it is the mercy shown to the Ninevites.

The three days spent by Jonah in the whale's belly comprise half of his active ministry; his next three days are spent walking through Nineveh (3:3). After those six days, of course, it is time for the Sabbath rest, and Jonah plans to spend his Sabbath reclining under the shade of a vine. Like murderous Cain going to the land of Nod (cf. Genesis 4:16), he proceeds to the east of the city (Jonah 4:5).

Jonah reflects on what has happened. Complying with the barest literal sense of the Lord's command, he had simply announced the city's destruction, with not a single word about repentance nor the faintest ray of hope. Indeed, his entire prophetic message took only half a verse of the story's text (3:4).

Alas, Jonah saw, his half verse of apparently unfulfilled prophecy bore more immediate fruit than any other preaching recorded in the Bible! It was enough to make the vindictive prophet wish for death (4:3, 8). This detail, reminiscent of the identical wish of Elijah (1 Kings 19:4), is ironic by reason of the sharp contrast between the two men. The final chapter portrays our poor vindictive prophet lamenting the loss of his sheltering vine, feeling the sun and hot wind beating on his head, and arguing with the God who endeavors to bring him to repentance. Will Jonah too repent, as did the Ninevites, and be converted? It is most significant that the Book of Jonah ends with this question put to the prophet himself.

Moreover, the very presence of Jonah within the biblical canon is itself a point of paradox. As we have seen, the burden of the story is that God spared sinful Nineveh because its citizens repented at Jonah's preaching. Yet the rabbinical authorities who placed this book into the canon were well aware that Nineveh, spared for its repentance in Jonah's century, was finally punished for its sins during the century of Jeremiah and Nahum. They had to realize that Jonah's desire for Nineveh's destruction, while it certainly casts no credit on the prophet in the book that bears his name, was somehow vindicated by subsequent history. Indeed, in the Book of Nahum we seem to find raised to canonical dignity those identical sentiments for which Jonah, in his book, was divinely reprimanded. It is a sort of canonical irony that Jonah and Nahum stand only a few pages from one another in the Sacred Text.

Finally, there is the sharper irony in Our Lord's appeal to reluctant, vindictive Jonah as a type even of Himself: "For as Jonah became a sign to the Ninevites, so also the Son of Man will be to this generation. . . . The men of Nineveh will rise up in the judgment with this generation and condemn it, for they repented at the preaching of Jonah; and indeed a greater than Jonah is here" (Luke 11:30, 32).

⊰ঔ৵

6. THE ROUGH LIFE OF BARUCH

Though Baruch's name means "blessed," his was a pretty rough life, because he served one of the most turbulent men in an extraordinarily turbulent period of Israel's history. Long before anyone thought of an annual "Secretaries' Appreciation Day," Baruch was the secretary for the Prophet Jeremiah.

Baruch, "son of Neriah" (Jeremiah 32:12), had he lived in normal times, would surely have fared better. Perhaps as talented as his brother Seraiah, the quartermaster to King Zedekiah (51:59), he might have gone into royal service. How he came into the service of Jeremiah the Bible does not tell us, but one is probably right in thinking that a perceived divine call was the determining factor. Indeed, hardly anything else would explain it.

Jeremiah had fallen silent in 622 BC, when King Josiah's workmen, in the course of some repairs on the temple, had discovered the Book of Deuteronomy lying on a shelf somewhere under several layers of dust. This discovery led, in turn, to a very serious religious reform of the kingdom under royal auspices (2 Kings 23; 2 Chronicles 34), so Jeremiah, a somewhat reluctant prophet anyway (Jeremiah 1:6), felt that he could retire from public life. Even when the Assyrian capital of Nineveh fell to the Babylonians in 612, much to the literary inspiration of the Prophet Nahum, Jeremiah held his peace.

But then disaster struck. King Josiah, who had thrown in his lot with the rising Babylonian power, was killed by the Egyptian army under Pharaoh Neco at the Battle of Megiddo in 609. It was the beginning of very hard times in Jerusalem. The new king, Jehoahaz (Shallum), reigned less than a hundred days (2 Kings 23:31), and from this point on, kings would reign in Jerusalem only at the pleasure of either Egypt or Babylon. Judah's religious and political life began rapidly to unravel, ending with Jerusalem's destruction in 587.

The crisis inaugurated by the death of Josiah in 609, addressed with such pathos by Habakkuk, also brought Jeremiah out of retirement. At the divine command he went to the temple to preach the sermon that began the second phase of his long prophetic ministry (Jeremiah 7:1–15; 26:1–24). It was during this phase that Baruch entered his service as the prophetic secretary.

What made Baruch's task particularly difficult was that many folks, Judah's kings in particular, were not especially fond of what Jeremiah had to say. They thought his tone a bit too stark and stern, in contrast to the gentler, more nuanced approach favored by themselves. So when Jeremiah delivered his oracles, and Baruch dutifully wrote them down, there was normally not much applause.

We find a typical reaction in Jeremiah 36, where one of those oracles conveyed some hint of divine displeasure (at least, "great is the anger and the fury that the LORD has pronounced against this people," verse 7, could be taken in that sense). The king, who preferred a broader, more flexible view of things, took exception to the point. Although it was a fairly lengthy message, which had cost poor Baruch several hours of careful transcription, how did the king receive it? Well, as the scroll was read before him, we are told, he "cut it with the scribe's knife and cast it into the fire that was on the hearth, until all the scroll was consumed in the fire that was on the hearth" (36:23). And how did Jeremiah respond to this? He instructed Baruch to take a new scroll and write the whole thing down again!

Naturally, sometimes Baruch would get discouraged. There is an example of this in the shortest chapter of the Book of Jeremiah, chapter 45, a message from the prophet to his secretary in the year 605. He quotes Baruch as saying, "Woe is me now! For the LORD has added grief to my sorrow. I fainted in my sighing, and I find no rest." By way of response to this lament, Jeremiah reminds his secretary that he is not alone in his suffering. Indeed, insists the prophet, God is suffering more than anyone. God is tearing down what He built; God is plucking up what He planted. So who was Baruch to be complaining and feeling sorry for himself? Jeremiah leaves the message there, confident that the loyal Baruch will hear it wisely and brace his mind for the greater catastrophes yet to fall. After the destruction of Jerusalem in 587, the faithful secretary shares the prophet's exile in Egypt (43:2–7).

ॐ

7. THE SILENCE OF ZACHARIAS

The Angel Gabriel, at the beginning of the Gospel according to St. Luke, is sent to make two announcements—the first to the priest Zacharias in Jerusalem, and the other to the virgin Mary in Nazareth, both of whom are told that they will soon become the parents of children miraculously conceived. Now among the several points of resemblance between these two stories is the detail that both Zacharias and Mary, upon receiving this message, requested some sort of explanation from Gabriel.

It is at this point that the two accounts go in quite different directions. To Mary's request Gabriel gives an adequate and very reassuring response, whereas Zacharias's request is not only denied, but he is punished for even making it!

The difference between the two cases is not hard to discern. Mary's question—"How can this be, since I do not know a man?" (1:24)—is actually a request for further instruction. Since she is a virgin, and Gabriel is telling her she is about to become a mother, Mary really does need more information. Her question to Gabriel means something like "Tell me what I am supposed to do." There is no arrogance here, nor doubt. On the contrary, Mary's attitude is summed up in her final words to Gabriel: "Behold the maidservant of the Lord! Let it be to me according to your word" (1:38).

Such is clearly not the case with Zacharias. His question is a request not for further instruction but for an explanation: "How shall I know this? For I am an old man, and my wife is well advanced in years" (1:18). To ask "How shall I know?" does not convey a spirit of faith and obedience, but a spirit of skepticism. Indeed, "How shall I know?" is entirely an epistemological question. Even as he offers incense in God's house, Zacharias is a cultivated doubter.

The gravity of Zacharias's doubt is rendered more obvious if we consider it in contrast to Abraham's response to an identical promise. Both married to women beyond childbearing years, Abraham and Zacharias were each told that his wife would bear him a son. These sons would be "children of promise," conceived by God's special intervention. Zacharias very well knew the story of Abraham, but still he insisted, "How shall I know this?"

In punishment for such arrogance, Zacharias is struck speechless for the next nine months and eight days, thus given an opportunity to ponder the serious nature of his offense. He must repent. If he is to become a fit father for John the Baptist, than whom there is no one greater among those born of women (7:28), Zacharias has much to learn about the ways of God.

Until he repents, the doubting Zacharias strikes one as the "thoroughly modern man," far less concerned with what he knows than with how he can know it. Burdened with an excessive, even morbid preoccupation with the psychology of knowledge, modern man no longer seems sure of knowing anything at all. In this respect Zacharias bears some resemblance to Descartes, the philosopher chiefly responsible for introducing the intentional, systematic cultivation of doubt as the basis of the philosophical pursuit. Doubting everything possible to doubt, Descartes concluded that he knew for certain only that he was thinking, and from his thinking he went on to demonstrate (but only to himself!) his existence. He arrived, that is, at the Self, the first single reality not subject to doubt.

In the nearly four centuries since Descartes began this reductionist path, we have been living in what is called the modern world, where the question "How shall I know?" receives answers progressively smaller, age after age. Once modern man accepted sustained, systematic doubt as the proper philosophical procedure, there could be no end to the business, because *everything* can be doubted. The very Self, which Descartes had thought to prove by his thinking, was soon put in doubt by the thinking of Hume, and eventually Nietzsche would suggest that the Self might be only a product of thought. And so it goes to this day. A snake that began by swallowing its tail is currently munching on its brain.

In this respect the silence imposed on Zacharias may serve as a parabolic warning to modern man, because the relentlessly doubting mind must finish by asserting nothing at all. Zacharias may start as a Cartesian, but Gabriel reduces him to a Deconstructionist. Indeed so, for the doubt that begins by destroying faith must end by destroying reason.

⟡

8. MARK, GROWING UP

Only in the Gospel according to Mark do we find the brief but colorful account of the young man who was apparently "spying" on the Lord's arrest in Gethsemane: "Now a certain young man followed Him, having a linen cloth thrown around his naked body. And the young men laid hold of him, and he left the linen cloth and fled from them naked" (14:51–52). There seems more than ordinary merit in the attractive view that that young man was the author of this Gospel, John Mark himself. Who else?

Not much older than a boy, John Mark was the son of a woman named Mary, in whose home the earliest Christians in Jerusalem met for their common worship (Acts 12:12). Also a relative of the Apostle Barnabas (Colossians 4:10), Mark was included in the missionary team of his kinsman and St. Paul (Acts 12:25; 13:5).

After their mission to Cyprus, where Barnabas and Mark may have been among relatives (cf. Acts 4:36), the young man evidently became discouraged and probably homesick, so he left the party and returned to his mother (13:13). His departure, understandably, did not sit well with St. Paul, to whom Mark must have seemed something of a wimp and a mommy's boy, hardly suitable for the rough work of the ministry. Later, when Barnabas wanted to take his youthful kinsman along on the next missionary journey, Paul objected. Indeed, the altercation between Paul and Barnabas became so heated that they decided to split up the mission into two teams, leaving Barnabas free to take John Mark with him back to Cyprus (15:37–41).

St. Paul's disapproval of Mark did not last long, though it is possible that the latter's reputation became damaged in the Pauline churches.

This would explain why Paul, even several years later, thought it necessary to tell the Colossians to welcome Mark (Colossians 4:10), who was apparently with him at the time (Philemon 24). It is instructive that St. Paul very favorably mentioned Mark within the very last lines that we have from his pen: "Get Mark and bring him with you, for he is useful to me for ministry" (2 Timothy 4:11).

This verse would also explain how Mark got to Rome, for he most certainly got to Rome. We find him there with St. Peter shortly afterwards (1 Peter 5:13). John Mark stayed on at Rome several years more as an assistant to St. Peter, following whose death he went to Alexandria in Egypt, becoming the first bishop of that city.

When he arrived at Alexandria, Mark was carrying a copy of a small work that he had written while he was still back in Rome. It was the Gospel that bears his name (Eusebius, *Ecclesiastical History* 2.16.1).

Early historical testimony to Mark's writing is remarkably uniform. Eusebius cites our first witness, Papias of Hierapolis, about AD 140, who quoted an anonymous elder: "Mark, having become an interpreter of Peter, recorded accurately whatever he could remember, though not in order, of the things said and done by the Lord. For he had neither heard the Lord nor followed him, but later, as I said, he followed Peter, who crafted the teachings according to needs, but not as though making a correct sequence of the Lord's sayings. Thus Mark did not err in writing the single components as he remembered them" (3.39.15).

The expression "interpreter of Peter" as a description of Mark appears also within a generation in the Roman *Anti-Marcionite Prologue*, which further testifies that "after the death of Peter himself, [Mark] recorded this present gospel in the regions of Italy." Irenaeus of Lyons uses the identical expression to describe Mark (*Adversus Haereses* 3.1.2), and both the *Prologue* and Irenaeus agree in dating Mark's composition just after Peter's death. Clement of Alexandria likewise states that Mark's Gospel contains the preaching of Peter at Rome (quoted by Eusebius, 2.15.1–2).

By the year 200, then, we are dealing with an impressive, uniform, and widespread agreement, evidenced in material from Hierapolis, Rome, Lyons (and therefore Asia Minor), and Alexandria, and against which there is not the slightest shred of dissent or contradiction during the entire period. This unquestioned historical consensus asserts that Mark's Gospel was written at Rome, and reflects the preaching of St. Peter.

That was pretty good for a young man who had flunked his first test as a missionary!

⚹

9. THE HEALING OF AENEAS

In the ancient stories of the Trojan War, Aeneas the Dardanian was a relatively minor character. From Homer, Hesiod, and Hyginus, we know something of his origins (fathered by the mortal Anchises and born of the goddess Aphrodite) and a bit of his part in the nine-year conflict that culminated in the fall of Troy. After that, however, the Greeks had no clear focus on the career of Aeneas. The older accounts varied with respect to his end, some saying he died at Pellene in Thrace, others at Orchomenus in Arcadia. In any case, the post-Troy days of Aeneas, unlike those of Achilles, Agamemnon, Odysseus, Ajax, and other characters in that famous adventure, inspired no abiding theme for Greek theater or poetry. He had fought, after all, on the losing side.

This Greek uncertainty about the latter days of Aeneas invited the later speculation of the Latins, whose most famous account thereof comes to us in Vergil's *Aeneid*. According to this story, Aeneas and his companions escaped during the burning of Troy and, after a lengthy, circuitous voyage around various corners of the Mediterranean, finally landed on the western coast of the Italian peninsula, founding the city of Lavinium. They were the forebears, that is to say, of Rome.

When Vergil died at Brindisi in Calabria on September 22, 19 BC, his *Aeneid* was not yet ready for publication, and he had left instructions with his literary executors to burn the manuscript in the event of his death. At the intervention of the Emperor Augustus, however, this did not happen. Convinced that Vergil's great epic version of the Trojan origin of the Roman people would inspire them to an heroic sense of their destiny, Augustus ordered the work to be published. There is every reason to believe that the *Aeneid*, which became a standard text in the teaching of Latin grammar and literature, served the intention of Augustus very well, prompting the Romans to assume the burden of political greatness that history had placed into their hands.

Because of the literary and political importance of this work within the century following its publication, no carefully educated, internationally cultured man in the Roman Empire would have been unfamiliar with the Roman story of Aeneas. Even those unable to read Latin would know Vergil's account secondhand, as part of the officially endorsed mythology of the Empire. Vergil's story was certainly familiar, therefore, to the physician Luke, a truly cosmopolitan man of letters, whose style of historiography has often been compared to that of Herodotus and Thucydides.

In any case, the parallels between the *Aeneid* and Luke's Acts of the Apostles are many and difficult to miss. For instance, both epics begin in a doomed city (Troy/Jerusalem) and finish in Rome. Indeed, Luke, who accompanied Paul to Rome (Acts 28:13–16; 2 Timothy 4:11), seems to have a Roman fixation from the beginning. After noting the presence of Romans at Jerusalem on Pentecost (Acts 2:10), Luke follows the movement of the Gospel relentlessly westward.

Moreover, one of the major steps in that progression is made at Troas, the site of the ancient Troy, where Paul receives the message that brings him to Europe (16:8–12). He will again visit Troas (20:5–6) on the journey that would at last take him to Rome (cf. Romans 1:15; 15:22–25). Going to Rome will be Paul's own carefully considered decision (Acts 25:16–21; 26:32), and, like Aeneas in Vergil's account, his Rome-ward voyage will include long delays (24:27 and the context *passim*), as well as a shipwreck (27:13–44). (At Rome, Paul will again think of Troas; cf. 2 Timothy 4:13.)

Before ever narrating the journeys of Paul, however, Luke sounds the Roman theme already in the ministry of Peter, whose baptism of the centurion Cornelius, the first official representative of Rome to become a Christian (Acts 10), is a crucial event in the whole mission of the Church and its movement to Rome. Just prior to that event, furthermore, Luke suggests its immense significance by describing Peter's healing of . . . Aeneas! Of the many persons healed through the ministry of Peter (3:7; 5:15–16), it is noteworthy that only Aeneas and Dorcas are named (9:32–41). In the case of Aeneas, the name suggests some connection to the Rome-ward motif of the book itself.

Thus, Vergil's older account of the Trojan survivor is now completed by the Gospel. The message of salvation goes to Rome, where Peter too (as Luke and his readers well knew) will finish his course (1 Peter 5:13). We are surely right in reading Peter's declaration to Aeneas as Luke's proclamation to the whole Roman world: "Aeneas, Jesus the Christ heals you" (9:34).

III.
LOYAL SAINTS

⁂

The loyalty of the saints is an inner, even hidden trait. If the true identity of Christ our Lord, His inner Person begotten of the Father, remains a mystery concealed from the world (John 14:22), something similar is also said rightly of those who put their hope in Christ, because they too are defined by their communion with the Father in Christ. They are *known* by God (John 10:14; 1 Corinthians 8:3; 13:12). To be sure, the world is able to look at Christians and label them for social and demographic purposes (Acts 11:26), but it does not really *know* them.

"You died," wrote Paul to the Colossians, "and your life is hidden with Christ in God" (3:3). These Christians, whom the world can outwardly distinguish by remarking on peculiar cultural and social patterns, carry about in their lives, amid circumstances however humble, the only force available to mankind for the redemption and transformation of its history. On this earth, the treasure of God is veiled and borne about in earthen vessels (2 Corinthians 4:7). Like the clay pitchers of Gideon, the disciples of Christ convey the secret flame that must, in the end, force flight upon the Midianite.

Consequently, the coming of Christ at the end of time will reveal to the world, not only His own glory, but the glory of those who have hoped in Him: "When Christ who is our life appears, then you also will appear with Him in glory" (Colossians 3:4). Until that day when the inner meaning of history is manifest, it stays concealed except to the eyes of faith. "Beloved," wrote the Apostle John, "now we are children of God; and it has not yet been revealed what we shall be, but we know that when He is revealed, we shall be like Him, for we shall see Him as He is" (1 John 3:2).

For Christians themselves, this truth implies practical applications of piety and a disciplined life. Both in John's First Epistle and in Paul's Letter to the Colossians, the Christian hope of the final revelation of

the believer leads promptly to the theme of holiness and personal purification. The Apostle John, immediately after the verse just cited, went
on to say, "And everyone who has this hope in Him purifies Himself,
just as He is pure" (3:3). Likewise the Apostle Paul, right after telling
the Colossians that their hidden life in Christ will be revealed at His
coming, exhorted those Christians to radical and strenuous moral and
ascetical effort: "Therefore put to death your members which are on the
earth: fornication, uncleanness, passion, evil desire, and covetousness,
which is idolatry" (3:5). While they await the final revelation of glory,
Christians quietly labor in the inner pursuit of that "holiness, without
which no one will see the Lord" (Hebrews 12:14).

This characteristic of "concealment" that marks the loyal lives of
Christians explains why the Church for many centuries has celebrated
an annual Feast of All Saints. Quite simply, there are more saints than
even the Church can identify, because the inner holiness of most Christians is concealed even from the scrutiny of the Church. For example,
we know that there were "many other women" (*heterai pollai*) who served
and provided for Jesus "from their substance," but only three of those
women are named. And even of those three, we know nearly nothing
(Luke 8:2–3). Likewise, there were about one hundred twenty Christians waiting for the coming of the Holy Spirit on the morning of Pentecost (Acts 1:15), but the Church herself preserved hardly more than a
tithe of their names (1:13–14). Who were those unnamed believers on
whom the Holy Spirit fell in the home of Cornelius (10:24, 44)? And
who were those widows that wept around the body of Dorcas (9:39)?
The Church remembered Antipas as the first Christian martyr at
Pergamos (Revelation 2:13), but who were those other early Christians
at Smyrna and Philadelphia who suffered the same fate (2:10; *The Martyrdom of Polycarp* 19.1)?

Thus has it always been. The great majority of the saints have lived
very hidden lives. Their inner communion with God, their fidelity to
His will, was so quiet and concealed that only He knew it. Even those
saints recognized by the Church in their own generation were often
enough recognized for some trait distinct from personal holiness, such
as preaching, pastoral ministry, or theological writings. Although all the
saints lived in great loyalty to God, the overwhelming majority of them
are beyond our ability to name. No matter. The Good Shepherd knows
them by name and by name calls them.

ॐ

1. RAHAB AND THE SPIES

Near the end of his list of the "spirits of just men made perfect" (Hebrews 12:23), those Old Testament saints who form his "great cloud of witnesses" (12:1), the author of the Epistle to the Hebrews speaks of the first pagan that the chosen people encountered inside the Promised Land: "By faith the harlot Rahab did not perish with those who did not believe, when she had received the spies with peace" (11:31). Thus a Canaanite prostitute becomes a model of faith for believing Christians.

In this text the faith of Rahab is contrasted with the unbelief of those who perished. Just who were the latter? The immediate context suggests that they are the other citizens of Jericho, who for seven days beheld the Ark of the Covenant circling their city and listened to the blast of the warning trumpets. They thus had ample opportunity to repent before it was too late, remarked St. John Chrysostom, more than twice as long as the citizens of Nineveh! (*On Repentance* 7.4.14)

Nonetheless, in the wider context of the Epistle to the Hebrews, it may be the case that the saving faith of Rahab is being contrasted with the unbelief of the Israelites themselves, those who failed to reach the Promised Land. Of those inexcusable unbelievers the author asks, "Now with whom was He angry forty years? Was it not with those who sinned, whose corpses fell in the wilderness? And to whom did He swear that they would not enter His rest, but to those who did not obey? So we see that they could not enter in because of unbelief" (3:17–19). Following this line of interpretation, Chrysostom writes: "She accepted the spies and the One whom Israel denied in the desert; Rahab preached this One in the brothel." And again: "What Israel heard—he who was surrounded by so many miracles and who was tutored by so many laws—he completely denied, whereas Rahab, who lived in a brothel, gives them instruction. For she says to the spies, 'We learned all that your God did to the Egyptians'" (*op. cit.* 7.5.16).

The faith of Rahab was not an idle or lazy faith, says the Epistle of St. James: "Likewise, was not Rahab the harlot also justified by works when she received the messengers and sent them out another way? For as the body without the spirit is dead, so faith without works is dead also" (2:25–26). Both of these perspectives were preserved by St. Clement of Rome, who said that "Rahab the harlot was saved because of her faith and hospitality" (Clement 12.1).

Perhaps because she was the first "Gentile convert" incorporated into God's people, Rahab has always had a special place in Christian affection and esteem. Chrysostom imagines God saying of Rahab: "Yes, I had inside their city to teach them repentance that wonderful Rahab, whom I saved through repentance. She was taken from the same dough, but she was not of the same mind, for she neither shared in their sin nor resembled them in their unbelief" (*op. cit.* 7.4.14).

Joshua's spies were sent out as a pair, like the Apostles of the Lord, and Rahab received them as the Lord's own emissaries. They came and remained at her home, as though following the Lord's instruction, "In whatever place you enter a house, stay there till you depart from that place" (Mark 6:10). Once again, we may consult the insights of Chrysostom: "Rahab is a prefiguration of the Church, which was at one time mixed up in the prostitution of the demons and which now accepts the spies of Christ, not those sent by Joshua the son of Nun, but the apostles who were sent by Jesus the true Savior. . . . The Jews received these things but did not guard them; the Church heard these things and preserved them. So Rahab, the prefiguration of the Church, is worthy of all praise" (*op. cit.* 7.5.16).

The Church Fathers thus saw significance in nearly every detail of the biblical story of Rahab. For instance, the scarlet cord, hung from her window for her family's deliverance, was interpreted by Clement of Rome (12.7), Justin Martyr (*Dialogue With Trypho* 111), and others as a foreshadowing of the redemptive blood of Christ.

And because she was the first to be delivered when Israel entered the Promised Land, there is surely a great propriety in Dante's speculation that the soul of "tranquil Rahab" was the first to be assumed from Hades by Christ our Lord when He descended there in the hour of His victorious death (*pria ch'altr'alma del triunfo di Cristo fu assunta*—*Paradiso* 9.115–120).

⁓

2. FAITHFUL RUTH

Very important to the Gospel of Matthew is the theme of the calling of the nations into the Church. "Make disciples of all the nations [*ethne*, *goyim*]," Jesus commands the eleven Apostles at the end of that Gospel

(28:19), and Matthew, alone among the four evangelists, quotes the prophecy of Isaiah to the effect that Jesus "will declare justice to the Gentiles" and "in His name Gentiles will trust" (12:18, 21). Early in his story Matthew gives us, moreover, the firstfruits of that call of the nations in the story of the distant Magi who came to worship the Christ Child (2:1–2).

Even earlier, however, Matthew faintly intimates this universal call in the genealogy with which he begins his Gospel. Students of the Bible have long remarked that three of the four women named in that genealogy are Gentiles: the Canaanites Tamar and Rahab, and the Moabite Ruth. All three of these women are the subjects of very interesting stories in the Old Testament.

Among these three, nonetheless, the Old Testament takes a singular care to tie Ruth most closely to the genealogy of David (Ruth 4:13–22), and it is on Jesus' relationship to David that Matthew commences his entire account: "The book of the genealogy of Jesus Christ, the Son of David" (Matthew 1:1). Let us speak, then, of Ruth, the great-grandmother of David and distant ancestor to the Son of God.

We may begin by reflecting on the sheer improbability of the thing. Generally speaking, after all, the Moabites seem not to have been among the Bible's favorite folks. When Zephaniah predicted that "Moab shall be like Sodom" (Zephaniah 2:9), the news hardly came as a shock to anybody. Pronouncements such as "I will send a fire upon Moab" and "Moab shall die with tumult" (Amos 2:2) pretty much sum up the prevailing biblical sentiment on Ruth's fellow countrymen. Moses had, in fact, made that sentiment a national policy: "An Ammonite or Moabite shall not enter the assembly of the LORD; even to the tenth generation none of his descendants shall enter the assembly of the LORD forever" (Deuteronomy 23:3). Such was the un-nuanced "official line" of the Old Testament on the subject of the Moabites.

Such was the context in which the young Moabite widow Ruth said to her widowed Israelite mother-in-law Naomi, "Wherever you go, I will go; / And wherever you lodge, I will lodge; / Your people shall be my people, / And your God, my God. / Where you die, I will die, / And there will I be buried" (Ruth 1:16–17). Ruth was biting off a great deal by accompanying Naomi back to Bethlehem. Indeed, her faith is properly likened to that of Abraham, who also left his family and his father's house in order to follow God's summons to a strange land.

And with due respect to the immortal John Keats (who needed a word to rhyme with "forlorn"), there is scant evidence that Ruth, after she arrived in Bethlehem, "stood in tears amid the alien corn." There was no time for that sort of thing. Ruth was far too busy, bent over all day long in the fields of Boaz, gleaning one by one the fallen grains of barley and wheat.

The townspeople at Bethlehem, much impressed that Ruth remained so deeply devoted to her mother-in-law, adopted a lenient view of the injunction about avoiding Moabites. "It is the young Moabite woman," they said to one another, "who came back with Naomi from the country of Moab" (Ruth 2:6). Though she regarded herself as a foreigner at first (2:10), the rumor of her loyalty had gotten around: "It has been fully reported to me, all that you have done for your mother-in-law since the death of your husband, and how you have left your father and your mother and the land of your birth, and have come to a people whom you did not know before. The LORD repay your work, and a full reward be given you by the LORD God of Israel, under whose wings you have come for refuge" (2:11–12).

It is one of the great ironies of this highly ironical book that the man who spoke those lines became the instrument by which God rewarded Ruth for what she had done. Boaz answered his own prayer, as it were, and Ruth in due course became his wife. Centuries later, Matthew felt it appropriate to mention this young woman who caused Moabite blood to be included in the great price poured out on the Cross.

3. THE TRANSFORMATION OF NAOMI

When she came back, at last, from Moab to Bethlehem, Naomi was a broken soul. Nor is it hard to see why. In just the first five verses of the Book of Ruth, she had swallowed a series of bitter cups in abrupt succession: famine, exile, and then the deaths of her husband and two sons. Indeed, the names conferred on those two boys at their birth suggest that the infants were weak, ailing, and not destined to enjoy the proverbial length of days; Mahlon means "sickly" and Chilion "wasting away," so it likely surprised no one when each young man died shortly after his marriage. Naomi, then, bereaved and beaten, returned to Bethlehem lamenting, "Do not call me Naomi ["my joy"]; call me Mara ["bitter"], for the Almighty has dealt very bitterly with me. I went out full, and the

LORD has brought me home again empty" (Ruth 1:20–21). On this sad note ends the first chapter of Ruth.

This tone of sadness will change rather quickly, nonetheless, and the rest of that book may be described as Naomi's transformation. As the second chapter begins, it is Ruth, not Naomi, who takes the initiative to go out and make them a living (2:2). Taking advantage of an ancient rule permitting the poor to glean in fields already harvested (Leviticus 19:9–10), Ruth comes into contact with Boaz, described as "a relative of Naomi's husband, a man of great wealth" (2:1). Treating her kindly (2:8, 12, 14), Boaz encourages Ruth to remain in his own fields and instructs his laborers to leave extra grain for her to find (2:15–16).

Thus, when Ruth returns home that evening, she brings her mother-in-law a great deal more grain than a gleaner normally would (2:17). Suspicious, the inquiring Naomi learns where her daughter-in-law was gleaning that day and that the hand of Boaz has been at work in the matter.

At this point we discern the first trace of Naomi's coming transformation. When she instructs Ruth not to leave the fields of Boaz, the admonition need not, on its surface, indicate anything more than an appreciation of the better gleaning available in Boaz's fields. Naomi has something more in mind, however, and her first remark—"This man is a relation of ours, one of our close relatives" (2:20)—betrays her deeper intention. She immediately realizes that Ruth, following the customs of the time, has a particular social claim on her dead husband's next of kin. Namely, a levirate marriage, by which Boaz would raise up children to Ruth's deceased husband. This is the message quietly contained in Naomi's remark that the Lord "has not forsaken His kindness to the living *and the dead*" (2:20). The "dead" here refers to Ruth's husband. This is no more than hinted at, and perhaps Ruth herself does not yet grasp the significance of the words, but Naomi understands the situation very well, and her instruction to Ruth is a first step in her emerging plan. The deeply depressed woman of the story's beginning is now recovering an energetic initiative and sense of life.

Following the older woman's counsel, Ruth remains "close by the young women of Boaz, to glean until the end of barley harvest and wheat harvest" (2:23), but nothing happens to advance Naomi's plan. Deciding that more drastic measures are indicated, she then gives Ruth detailed instructions how to press the point with Boaz by more explicitly stirring up his interest (3:1–4). When Ruth follows these instructions (3:6–9), we discover that Boaz's own thoughts about Ruth have already been running along romantic lines (3:10–11). Indeed, he has even researched the situation, for he knows that he is not actually the next of kin (3:12) and that the matter will require further adjudication (3:13).

Boaz is well aware that Naomi's is the guiding hand behind this whole business. When he sends Ruth home, therefore, he gives her as much barley as she could glean in six days, telling her: "Do not go empty-handed to your mother-in-law" (3:17). It is a line of great irony. Naomi, for her part, is confident that Boaz will see the thing through. She assures Ruth that "the man will not rest until he has concluded the matter this day" (3:18).

And Boaz does, of course. Thus, the story that began with famine, exile, death, and bereavement closes with a harvest, a marriage, and the birth of a child. Naomi's transformation is complete. The book's final scene presents what is arguably the finest picture known to man, a grandmother dandling a new grandchild in her lap.

❧

4. THE STRENGTH OF BOAZ

In *Far from the Madding Crowd,* Thomas Hardy portrays a steady, dependable, hard-working man, on whom he confers the name Gabriel Oak. He is a strong, independent character, deeply rooted in the land and its labor, and his wonderfully virile name, suggesting the feel of sinewed firmness, conveys a great deal of who he is. Indeed, one can hardly imagine a name more manly than Gabriel. Derived from the Semitic root *gbr*, signifying "man" or "strength," and *El*, the biblical word for "God," Gabriel means either "man of God" or "strength of God." As for "Oak," of course, the very sound evokes that mightiest, most stable of ancient trees, *Quercus robur*, the "hard wood" of Cicero and Vergil. Surely, any man alive might envy Gabriel Oak his sturdy name.

When I think of Gabriel Oak, a deeper memory invariably summons to my mind another steady man of strength, who went by the name of Boaz. Like Hardy's character, Boaz too lived far from the madding crowd, hard-working on his land, and his name was likewise significant. Also Semitic, Boaz (*bo 'oz*) means "in him is strength."

A further similarity between the two men is that both of them married young widows. Aside from that curious particular, it must be said, there is scant similarity between Boaz's Ruth and Gabriel's Bathsheba Everdeen, and I confess that former gentleman seems to me by far the more fortunate in his choice. How Boaz came to make that choice involves the plot of some of the most charming pages in the Bible.

Boaz lived in Bethlehem, "the house of bread," and made his very substantial living by growing barley and wheat. (Indeed, the story's emphasis on Boaz's abundant grain harvests stands in stark contrast to the famine or "hunger," *ra'av*, with which the Book of Ruth begins.) Maintaining a residence in the town, Boaz went out daily to oversee the workers in his fields. He also labored with them and was known sometimes to sleep out on the threshing floors during the winnowing days.

The Bible describes Boaz as a kind and godly man, and both traits were picked up by his field laborers. "The LORD be with you," he greeted them each morning, to which they responded, "The LORD bless you!" (2:4). Blessing, indeed, rose easily to the lips of Boaz (2:12; 3:10). He likewise took good care of his workers, making certain that they had water to drink under the hot sun (2:9) and seasoned food when they broke for the midday meal (2:14).

Himself a kind and godly man, it is not surprising that Boaz appreciated kindness and godliness in others, and such were exactly the traits that he admired in Ruth, the woman who had accompanied the unfortunate Naomi back from her recent, sad sojourn in Moab. Arriving at work one morning, Boaz found the young Moabite woman gleaning the fallen heads of grain dropped by his reapers, a privilege that the Mosaic Law reserved for the poor. Boaz treated Ruth with his accustomed kindness, further enhanced by knowing of her own kindness to Naomi. He encouraged Ruth to remain in his own fields, instead of wandering elsewhere (2:21–22), and instructed his reapers to leave extra grain lying in her path to be gleaned (2:16). In short, he "took notice" of her (2:19).

We do not know at what point Boaz's admiration for Ruth assumed an amorous tone, but it did so before the summer was over. Aware of being a kinsman to her deceased husband, Boaz was alert to the possibility of marrying Ruth by levirate law. Indeed, he must have researched the question, because he learned that there was another male relative, whose claims in the matter were stronger than his own. Because Boaz was older than Ruth (3:10), perhaps he felt embarrassed to present himself as a possible husband.

Then, one night as he slept on the grain at the threshing floor, the suddenly chilled Boaz was awakened to find the perfumed presence of a woman lying at his feet. It was Ruth, asking him to marry her (3:9). He needed no further coaxing. As the two of them lay there the rest of that night, Boaz devised a plan to advance his claim over his possible rival.

After discreetly sending Ruth home in the final hour before daylight, Boaz arranged a meeting at which he employed a clever stratagem that outwitted his rival (4:1–10). Thus, Boaz became the husband of Ruth, at the end of one of the very few truly romantic stories in the Bible.

⚬

5. JONATHAN, LOYAL AND BRAVE

When Jonathan, the son of Saul, perished at the Battle of Mount Gilboah in 1000 BC, he was cherished in memory as a peerless warrior, a faithful son, and a loyal friend.

Jonathan the warrior, unlike most godly men of the Old Testament, died young. Indeed, combat being a pursuit commonly ungenerous in respect to longevity, his prospects for maturing to ripe years were never promising. As we shall see presently, however, Jonathan fought with a derring-do that lowered those chances further yet. He did that fighting, moreover, during a period marked by unusually frequent battles, even for the Middle East.

As for the enemies of Jonathan, their odds for old age were even worse, for he was truly fearsome in the arts of war. The times called for it. When his father Saul became king about 1020, Israel was sore oppressed by several marauding adversaries. These included the invading Ammonites from the east, the Amalekites from the south, and from the west the garrisoned Philistines, who raided the land and ravaged the countryside at will. In fact, it was a military crisis that brought Saul to the throne (1 Samuel 11:1–11).

But Jonathan not only fought back; he habitually provoked the battles. General to a third of Saul's army, he took it upon himself to initiate a war with the Philistines (1 Samuel 13:2–4). Then, at a point when Israel's diminishing forces, hemmed in at Gibeah, were threatened with annihilation, Jonathan and his armor-bearer conspired to leave the camp and deliberately incite the enemy. In a rapid series of single-handed encounters, the two of them slaughtered "about twenty men within about half an acre of land," thus rallying Israel's forces to an unexpected victory (14:1–23).

Though he was manifestly adept as a swordsman, it was chiefly as an archer that men remembered Jonathan. They often watched him begin his day in the discipline of that skill (20:20–22, 35–38). The funeral dirge of Saul and Jonathan, memorized by the Israelites and in due course recorded in the Book of Jasher, was known, in fact, as the "Song of the Bow" (2 Samuel 1:18), named for that line that reads, "the bow of Jonathan did not turn back" (1:22).

Jonathan's pursuit of warfare was contoured by, and inseparable from, a warm commitment to his father's throne. He was a faithful son. Faithful, furthermore, to a father who did not make the matter easy. In fact, that battle at Gibeah was the first occasion when Jonathan's fidelity to Saul was sorely tried. Putting himself in danger of execution by inadvertently violating his father's rash oath, Jonathan was delivered at last only by the resolute intervention of the soldiers, who refused to see him die (1 Samuel 14:24–46).

The loyalty of Jonathan as a friend is chiefly seen in his association with David. Was it not from their first meeting that "the soul of Jonathan was knit to the soul of David, and Jonathan loved him as his own soul" (18:1)? That occasion itself reveals the attraction that drew these two together. It was the day that David stepped forward to take up the challenge of the giant Goliath, who "defied the armies of the living God" (17:36). David's abrupt intervention on the battlefield, at the hour when "Saul and all Israel . . . were dismayed and greatly afraid" (17:11), seized the attention of Jonathan. His eyes fixed on this newcomer walking calmly back into the camp, his one hand gripping the giant's sword and his other the giant's head. It was then that Jonathan, in a dramatic gesture of undying loyalty, "took off the robe that was on him and gave it to David, with his armor, even to his sword and his bow and his belt" (18:4).

Events would soon test both Jonathan's loyalty as a friend and his fidelity as a son. The very chapter that tells us "Jonathan and David made a covenant" (18:3) also describes the mounting jealousy of Saul toward David (18:6–13), even to the point of plotting to kill him

(20:9–18). As it became obvious to both father and son that David, not Jonathan, would be the next king (20:15; 24:20), the situation grew tense and progressively complex. Saul, increasingly deranged and acting in rage, not only disputed the fidelity of Jonathan (20:30, 31), but even made an impetuous attempt on his life (20:33). Remaining ever loyal to David, however, Jonathan stayed steadfast at the side of his doomed father, finally dying with him on the desperate slopes of Gilboah, brave and faithful to the end.

᪣

6. ELISHA THE WONDER-WORKER

In the Books of Kings it is not difficult to perceive the ways in which the prophets Elijah and Elisha resemble the great Moses. Indeed, emphasizing that resemblance pertained very much to the author's purpose, for he had in mind to portray them both as Moses' latter-day successors, each providing some measure of fulfillment to Moses' own prophecy that he would be succeeded by a prophet like himself (Deuteronomy 18:15–18). This perspective is likewise part of the Bible's more general care to regard the prophetic corpus as the proper sequence to the Law. In fact, the expression "the Law and the Prophets" is sometimes employed to mean simply the whole Hebrew Bible.

Elijah resembles Moses, then, in several particulars of his story: a miraculous provision of meat and bread in the wilderness (1 Kings 17:4–7), a fast of forty days while journeying through the desert on the strength of miraculously provided bread and water (19:4–8), and an encounter with the Lord on Mount Horeb, complete with all the sounds and sights associated with Moses' own experience in that place. Elijah receives his prophecies on the very mountain where Moses received the Law. Like Moses too, Elijah covers his face in response to his mountaintop experience (19:9–13). Then, when the time comes for Elijah to leave this life, he repeats Moses' act of parting the waters and then disappears east of the Jordan, where Moses disappeared (2 Kings 2:8–18).

Though perhaps more subtle, Elisha's resemblance to Moses is nonetheless unmistakable, and it has to do with his ministry as a worker of miracles. Indeed, Moses and Elisha are clearly the Old Testament's two great thaumaturges. This is not to say that Elisha is portrayed as a miracle-worker in order to make him look like another Moses. Indeed, the very opposite presumption is made here. That is to say, it is presumed here that the Bible portrays Elisha as resembling Moses the miracle-worker because he did, in fact, work miracles as Moses had done. Nonetheless, that point understood, it is reasonable to suggest that the author of Kings does tell his story in such a way as to accentuate the similarities between the two men in this matter of miracles. In this respect it is worth examining the context and sequence of 2 Kings 2—6 rather closely.

First, the prophetic ministry of Elisha begins where that of Elijah left off; namely, with the miraculous parting of the waters (2:14), this repetition of the miracle putting one in mind, of course, of both Moses and Joshua. Next, in grudging response to the persistent requests made by "the sons of the prophets," Elisha authorizes a search for Elijah's body. Knowing what had happened to Elijah, Elisha is hardly surprised at their failure to find it (2:15–17), and the attentive reader will remember that, among the last recorded facts about Moses, it was said that "no one knows his grave to this day" (Deuteronomy 34:6).

Such is the context in which Elisha begins his ministry as a worker of miracles. These latter immediately come in a fairly rapid sequence reminiscent of the ten plagues of Moses. And, like those Mosaic plagues, these recorded miracles of Elisha are also ten in number: the purification of the spring at Jericho (2:19–21), the efficacious cursing of his foes (2:23–25), the wondrous flow of water (3:16–20), the miraculous production of oil (4:1–7), the raising of the dead boy (4:18–37), the purging of the pot of stew (4:38–41), the multiplication of food (4:42–44), the cleansing of Naaman's leprosy and its transferal to Gehazi (5:1–27), the floating ax head (6:1–7), and the blinding and enlightenment of the Syrian soldiers (6:8–23).

As both prophet and miracle-worker, Elisha stands in Holy Scripture as a very special foreshadowing of Christ. In truth, except for Moses, no other Old Testament figure so completely combines both of those characteristics of our Lord as does this ninth-century prophet, who was also a healer of leprosy, provider of food and water, and raiser of the dead. It is particularly proper, then, that Elisha appears as an illustration in Jesus' first recorded public words, the sermon in the synagogue at Nazareth. In that sermon, the Lord recalls that "many lepers were in Israel in the time of Elisha the prophet, and none of them was cleansed except Naaman the Syrian" (Luke 4:27).

༄

7. JOANNA, THE WIFE OF CHUSA

Alone among the four evangelists, Luke tells the story of Jesus' judicial appearance before Herod Antipas on the day of the Crucifixion (23:6–12). This is the same Herod whom Luke mentions closer to the beginning of his Gospel, at the inauguration of the ministry of John the Baptist (3:1). Thus, in Luke's literary construction, these two references to Herod Antipas serve to frame Jesus' public ministry, which, as that evangelist was careful to note, extended "all the time that the Lord Jesus went in and out among us, beginning from the baptism of John to that day when He was taken up from us" (Acts 1:21–22).

Luke also tells how the animosity of Herod Antipas toward Jesus (cf. Luke 13:31) was later directed against Jesus' disciples (cf. Acts 12:1, 11). Indeed, Luke regarded the collusion of Antipas and Pontius Pilate, which was sealed at Jesus' trial (Luke 23:12), as the fulfillment of David's prophecy (Psalm 2:1–2) of the gathering of the world's leaders "against the LORD and against His Christ" (Acts 4:25–27).

It is significant that Luke, when he tells us of Jesus' appearance before Antipas on Good Friday, does more than state the bare event. He goes into some detail about how "Herod, with his men of war, treated Him with contempt and mocked Him, arrayed Him in a gorgeous robe, and sent Him back to Pilate" (Luke 23:11). This description implies that Luke had access to an eyewitness account of the event, an event at which, as far as we know, no Christian disciple was present. The historian rightly inquires how Luke knew all this.

Moreover, in addition to these external items of the narrative, Luke even addresses the motive and internal dispositions of Antipas, saying that "he was exceedingly glad; for he had desired for a long time to see Him, because he had heard many things about Him, and he hoped to see some miracle done by Him" (23:8). Once again the historian properly wonders how Luke was privy to these sentiments. What was his source for this material, a source apparently not available to the other evangelists?

Luke himself provides a hint toward answering this historical question when he mentions a certain Chuza, described as a "steward" of Herod Antipas. The underlying Greek noun here is *epitropos*, the same word that refers to the vineyard foreman in Matthew 20:8, but in the

Lukan context it more likely points to a high political office, such as a chief of staff.

It does not tax belief to imagine that such a person would be present at Jesus' arraignment before Herod Antipas. Indeed, this would be exactly the sort of person we would expect to be present on that occasion, when Herod was in Jerusalem to observe the Passover. Furthermore, Chuza is also the sort of person we would expect to be familiar with Herod's own thoughts, sentiments, and motives with respect to Jesus.

And how did Chuza's information come to Luke? Most certainly through Chuza's wife, Joanna, whom Luke includes among the Galilean women who traveled with Jesus and the Apostles, providing for Him "from their substance" (Luke 8:3). Joanna, whom Luke is the only evangelist to mention by name, was surely his special channel of information that only he, among the evangelists, seems to have had. Married to a well-placed political figure in the Galilean court, Joanna was apparently a lady of some means, who used her resources to provide for the traveling ministry of Jesus and the Apostles. Acting in this capacity, she must have been very well known among the earliest Christians. Only Luke, however, speaks of her by name, a fact that seems to indicate that he had interviewed her in the composition of his Gospel.

We can guess that Joanna's adherence to Jesus was not without its difficulties for her domestic life. Here she was, the wife of a high political official, providing support for someone who would die as a political criminal.

Her loyalty was supremely rewarded, however, because the risen Lord saw fit to number Joanna among the Holy Myrrhbearers, those surprised women who "came to the tomb bringing the spices which they had prepared," found the stone rolled away from the tomb, then prostrated before the two herald angels of the Pascha, and subsequently "told these things to the apostles" (Luke 24:1, 5–7, 10). One suspects that Joanna also had a thing or two to tell her husband Chuza later that day.

୬୬

8. BARNABAS, THE SON OF CONSOLATION

Although the history of icons may give us an idea of what some early saints looked like (the very primitive sketch of Peter and Paul in the excavation under the Vatican, for example), it is generally hard to gain knowledge of this sort from the New Testament. It is true that, unless the expression "of short stature" in Luke 19:3 refers to Jesus (which is grammatically possible), we know that Zacchaeus the tax collector was not tall, and we are probably justified in suspecting that Mary of Bethany was blest with ample tresses (cf. John 11:2; 12:3). On the whole, however, the New Testament is not a copious source for such information.

It differs, in this respect, from the Old Testament, which more often remarks on the physical characteristics of this or that individual. We are told, for example, of David's handsome complexion (1 Samuel 16:12; 17:42), Saul's unusual height (9:2; 10:23), and the density of Absalom's hair (14:26; 18:9). We learn too, with no little distress, that Esau's skin felt like a goat's (Genesis 27:16–23), and of Elisha we are informed, not only that he was bald, but that he was more than slightly sensitive on the subject (2 Kings 2:23–24). Regarding the women of the Old Testament, the reader may lose track of how many are described as beautiful.

If the New Testament is less satisfactory in providing these engaging details, there is a major exception in the case of Barnabas. We really do have a good idea of what Barnabas looked like, because some ancient devotees of Zeus mistook him for the object of their devotion.

It happened in the city of Lystra, where Paul had just healed a lifelong cripple. In immediate response to this marvel, the citizens of the city "raised their voices, saying in the Lycaonian language, 'The gods have come down to us in the likeness of men!'" After that, matters got very much out of hand. In the enthusiasm of the moment, "the priest of Zeus, whose temple was in front of their city, brought oxen and garlands to the gates, intending to sacrifice with the multitudes." Because of the language barrier, which apparently required them to speak through an interpreter, it took several minutes for the two apostles to put a stop to the business, but they eventually did so, proceeding then to preach one of the shortest sermons in history (three verses). Even then, says the text, "with these sayings they could scarcely restrain the multitudes from sacrificing to them" (Acts 14:8–18).

Now the curious point here is that the crowd, persuaded that the gods had just arrived in town, took Barnabas for Zeus. It was somewhat natural, given their premise, that they thought Paul to be Hermes, the messenger god, "because he was the chief speaker." Indeed, it was Paul who had healed the lame man with a simple command. But why Barnabas as Zeus? It must have had something to do with his appearance. These folks would never have taken an average-looking guy to be Zeus.

Now it happens that we know exactly what sort of fellow those people thought Zeus, should he ever come to visit his temple, would look like, because Zeus is portrayed in dozens of extant old art works and described in scores of ancient texts. This "father of gods and men" was massive in height and powerfully muscular in bulk. His great brow extended broad and serene over clear, far-seeing eyes, and a full majestic beard lay upon his barrel chest. Brother to Poseidon, god of the sea, Zeus, when he condescended to speak, spoke with the deep rumblings of oceanic authority. Now this . . . this is what the citizens of Lystra saw in Barnabas! No wonder they were impressed.

In fact, they never quite lost their awe in the presence of Barnabas. A few days later, when some Jews from Iconium arrived and stirred up the crowd against the two apostles, it was Paul that they stoned, nearly to death. Nobody dared throw a stone at Barnabas! (14:19–20)

The impressive appearance of Barnabas was matched by his generosity and nobility of soul. He made one of the first large financial donations to the Christian Church, and it was the trusted Barnabas who could introduce the recently converted Saul of Tarsus to the frightened Jerusalem church, oversee the new ministry at Antioch, lead the first mission to Cyprus and Pisidia, and later restore young John Mark to the mission field (4:36–37; 11:22–25; 13:2–14; 15:36–39). Reassured even to be in the presence of this huge, competent, and gentle human being, all Christians knew Barnabas as the "Son of Consolation."

☙

9. THE ZEAL OF TIMOTHY

When the Apostle Paul appointed St. Timothy to be the bishop at Ephesus in the mid-50s, he sent the young pastor a series of wise pastoral directions. He told him, for example, to "give attention to reading, to exhortation, to doctrine" (1 Timothy 4:13). He urged Timothy to "fight the good fight of faith" (6:12) and to "reject profane and old wives' fables" (4:7). He warned him to "observe these things without prejudice, doing nothing with partiality" (5:21). He exhorted him to "be an example to the believers in word, in conduct, in love" (4:12), and so on. Paul instructed Timothy, in short, with many pieces of wise counsel.

Of all Paul's exhortations to Timothy, however, my own favorite is, "No longer drink only water, but use a little wine for your stomach's sake and your frequent infirmities" (5:23). Yes, as I think over the matter yet again, this is my favorite.

What sort of man was Timothy? Well, we know what Paul thought of him. He told the Macedonians, "I have no one like-minded, who will sincerely care for your state" (Philippians 2:20), and went on to speak of his "proven character" (2:22). Indeed, Paul refers to Timothy as "our brother" (2 Corinthians 1:1; Colossians 1:1; 1 Thessalonians 3:2; Philemon 1), "as a son with his father" (Philippians 2:22), and "my beloved and faithful son in the Lord" (1 Corinthians 4:17). Paul addresses him, moreover, as "son Timothy" (1 Timothy 1:18), "Timothy, a true son in the faith" (1:2), and "Timothy, a beloved son" (2 Timothy 1:2).

Paul knew that Timothy had been raised in a devout, believing family (2 Timothy 1:5), where he was trained in the Holy Scriptures (3:15). Still young, Timothy had joined Paul's company during the second missionary journey (Acts 16:1–3) and remained with him through the ensuing years, carefully following his "doctrine, manner of life, purpose, faith, longsuffering, love, perseverance, persecutions, afflictions, which happened to me at Antioch, at Iconium, at Lystra" (2 Timothy 3:10–11).

Along the way, Paul found that he could entrust Timothy with important responsibilities in the ministry. The young man had not been a missionary even a year before Paul sent him from Athens to Thessaloniki for a needed pastoral visit (1 Thessalonians 3:1–5). Later, from Ephesus, Paul sent Timothy to visit the Macedonians (Acts 19:22; Philippians 2:19–23) and the quarrelsome, spiteful congregation at Corinth (1 Corinthians 4:17; 16:10). It was to Timothy, finally, that Paul wrote the last letter of his life, asking him to "be diligent to come to me quickly" (2 Timothy 4:9).

It is arguable, however, that the whole New Testament contains not a single verse that tells us more about Timothy than 1 Timothy 5:23: "No longer drink only water, but use a little wine for your stomach's sake and your frequent infirmities." Here we gain a genuine insight into the young man's character. This verse informs us, first, that Timothy, throughout his many labors, also suffered from poor health. It also indicates that Timothy was an ascetic man, whose self-denial and mortification were sufficiently austere to raise the concern of even so disciplined an ascetic as Paul. Timothy, in short, lived a life of mortified habits and self-control, even to the point of endangering his health.

It seems ironic that Paul was obliged to exhort Timothy to "ease up" on the asceticism, because we suspect that Timothy was deliberately modeling himself on what he beheld in Paul. Was this not the same Paul who wrote, "I discipline [literally 'give a black eye to,' *hypopiazo*] my body and bring it into subjection" (1 Corinthians 9:27) and spoke of himself as "in hunger and thirst, in fastings often, in cold and nakedness" (2 Corinthians 11:27)?

These apostolic examples of self-discipline illustrate the importance of ascetic striving in the Christian life. Emulating Christ our Lord, whose forty-day fast in the wilderness provided the model for the Christian Lent, believers recall that He placed fasting along with prayer and almsgiving in the Sermon on the Mount. In the life in Christ, fasting and mortification of the flesh are not optional. Jesus never said, "If you fast . . ." but rather "*when* you fast" (Matthew 6:16–17). In the case of Timothy, we learn of these things by what Paul believed to be his excessive zeal in the matter.

IV.
THE SAINTS IN WORSHIP
֍

Perhaps among the least appreciated, and most seldom thought on, descriptions of Jesus our Lord is the one given by John the Baptist: "His winnowing fan is in His hand, and He will thoroughly clean out His threshing floor, and gather His wheat into the barn; but He will burn up the chaff with unquenchable fire" (Matthew 3:12).

Threshing is a violent activity, which consists in pounding the harvested grain repeatedly on a stone floor with a shovel or a flail, in order to separate it from the husks that enclose it. The discarded husks are called chaff. When this beating of the grain has been done, the thresher uses his shovel to throw it into the air, so that the wind will carry away the light and useless chaff, leaving the heavier kernels to fall once more to the threshing floor. This latter action is called winnowing.

Yes, threshing and winnowing are violent activities; they are likewise, if one may say so, very judgmental activities. Threshing and winnowing are emphatic, even ferocious ways of asserting "this, and not that." The thresher addresses the grain and the chaff, making an aggressive distinction, as it were: "You stay put, but you get out of here." The separation of the two things is truly final. The grain and the chaff grew up together, but they will never be together again.

This definitive separation of wheat and chaff, which means the final acceptance and rejection of human decisions, is essential to the Gospel itself, because it affirms the everlasting significance of those decisions. Consequently, this biblical threshing stands directly at variance with those religious philosophies constructed on "the myth of the eternal return," in which all human decisions rendered in the course of history are "subject to further review," so to speak, and final correction in an afterlife, in order to achieve a universal reconciliation. This latter heresy was appropriately condemned at the Fifth Ecumenical Council in 553.

The biblical teaching about God's judgmental threshing, then, is asserted as though to answer the question contained in the provocative title of a book by a well-known theologian of the twentieth century, *Dare We Hope "That All Men Be Saved"?* (*Allversöhnung?*). No, we do not dare to hope for such a thing. It is a delirious fantasy, neither a proper object of Christian hope, nor a proper subject of Christian speculation. In fact, St. John of Mount Sinai warns us of the grave spiritual danger of even entertaining such a thought (*The Ladder of Divine Ascent*, Step 5, "On Repentance"). If wheat and chaff are ultimately the same thing, then human choice is a mirage, human history only a theatrical production, and the death and Resurrection of Christ ultimately meaningless. For this reason, Jesus as Savior must not be disconnected from Jesus as Thresher.

Just where in the Gospels, however, do we detect Jesus acting as Thresher? In answering that question, most readers of the Bible would probably refer to our Lord's driving the money changers from the temple, and they would surely be correct in that reference. When Jesus drove the money changers from the temple, an event recorded in all four canonical Gospels, it was the most eschatological of actions. Jesus thereby affirmed that the temple really is a precinct separated from an "outside," where are found "dogs and sorcerers and sexually immoral and murderers and idolaters, and whoever loves and practices a lie" (Revelation 22:15). Thus, the Bible's final book does not portray an afterlife of universal reconciliation, but an everlasting separation of wheat and chaff.

Even that earthly temple purged by Jesus was constructed on a threshing floor (2 Chronicles 3:1), Arauna's ancient rock where David's soul, for his final sin, was flailed by the angel of judgment (2 Samuel 24:15–25). Indeed, the place of worship, where man meets God and places himself under the divine gaze, is ever the hard surface of his purging. Prayer itself is a pounding of the soul, that the wheat may be beaten free of the chaff. Hence, in this world the true temple is necessarily constructed on a threshing floor. There, before the face of God, the heart is afflicted in repentance, the contrite and broken heart that God will not despise; indeed, this very breaking of the heart is the sacrifice that God requires (Psalm 51[50]:17). Such is the authentic worship of God in the soul's true temple, the prayer of repentant sinners who never cease to beat their breasts and plead for the divine mercy (Luke 18:13; 23:48).

৯৭

1. MELCHIZEDEK, KING AND PRIEST

The Old Testament provides a genealogy, at least in brief, for most of its "persons of the drama." The clear exception is Melchizedek, who suddenly enters the biblical story in Genesis 14 and just as abruptly leaves it. Nothing whatever is said of his ancestry, the rest of his life, or his death. Melchizedek simply appears "without father, without mother, without genealogy, having neither beginning of days nor end of life" (Hebrews 7:3). In fact, Genesis 14 tells us only five things about him.

First, Melchizedek was a king. "Salem," the city of his kingship, was an old name for Jerusalem (Psalm 76[75]:2). Indeed, the Jewish historian, Flavius Josephus, took Melchizedek to be the founder (*ho protos ktisas*) of the holy city (*The Jewish War* 6.438). Regarding Melchizedek as the king who founded the city of Jerusalem, we may discern a noteworthy correspondence he shares with two other figures in whom Plutarch (*Parallel Lives* 1.2) perceived a match: Romulus, who "founded Rome" (*ektise ten Romen*), and Theseus, "who built up Athens" (*synoikise tas Athenas*). Pliny's description of those two urban organizers as "of unknown and obscure origins" (*anegguo kai skotio genomenoi*) corresponds to the portrayal of Melchizedek, the founder of Jerusalem, who was "without father, without mother, without genealogy."

Speculating on the etymology of Melchizedek's name (*melek-hassedeq*), Josephus calls him a "righteous king" (*basileus dikaios*) (*Antiquities* 1.10.2). Exploiting the resemblance of the name "Salem" to the Hebrew word for "peace," *shalom*, the author of the Epistle to the Hebrews calls Melchizedek "king of peace." Like Josephus, he sees etymological symbolism in Melchizedek's own name, calling him "king of righteousness" (*basileus dikaiosynes*) (7:2).

Second, Melchizedek was "the priest of God Most High." In fact, he is the first man to whom Holy Scripture gives the title "priest" (*kohen*), and it is Melchizedek's priesthood that receives the greater attention in the Bible. For example, while the Book of Psalms speaks of the Messiah's kingship as derived from David (Psalm 78[77]:70; 89[88]:3–4, 20, 39, 45; 110[109]:1–3), the Messiah's priesthood is said to be "according to the order of Melchizedek" (110[109]:4).

Melchizedek was "the first to serve as priest to God" (*ierasato to Theo protos*), Josephus wrote, and long before Solomon built a temple at Jerusalem, Melchizedek had already done so (*to hieron protos deimamenos*). Indeed, Josephus traces the very name of Jerusalem (in Greek *Hierosolyma*) to the "priest of Salem" (*hierus Salem*) (*The Jewish War* 6.438).

Following the lead of Psalm 110(109), the author of Hebrews sees in the priesthood of Melchizedek the "order" (*taxsis*) of the definitive priesthood of Christ the Lord (5:6, 10; 6:20; 7:17). The Bible's very silence with respect to the death of that ancient priest of Salem is taken as a prefiguration of the "unchangeable priesthood" (7:24) of God's Son, to whom Melchizedek was "made like" (7:3). The latter was a living prophecy of the definitive Priest who "has become a surety of a better covenant" (7:22).

Third, Abraham gave a tithe to Melchizedek, just as Abraham's children gave tithes to the Levitical priests (7:8–10). That detail argues for the superiority of the "order of Melchizedek" over the "order of Aaron" (7:11).

Fourth, Melchizedek blessed Abraham, saying: "Blessed be Abram of God Most High, Possessor of heaven and earth; and blessed be God Most High, who has delivered your enemies into your hand" (Genesis 14:19–20). This priestly blessing too indicates the superiority of the "order of Melchizedek," inasmuch as "the lesser is blessed by the better" (Hebrews 7:7).

Fifth, Melchizedek "brought out bread and wine" (Genesis 14:18). His offering of bread and wine, moreover, was recognized as a priestly act; that is to say, Melchizedek did this precisely "because he was" a priest (as is clear in the Septuagint's *en de* and the Vulgate's *erat enim*).

Melchizedek's offering of bread and wine, of course, was a type and prefiguration of what transpired that night when God's priestly Son took the loaf of bread and the cup of wine into His holy and venerable hands and identified them as His Body and Blood. This is how the Christian Church has always interpreted the act of that first priest, Melchizedek, "who gave the wine and bread, the sanctified food, as a type of the Eucharist [*eis typon Eucharistias*]" (Clement of Alexandria, *Stromateis* 4.25). Melchizedek was the "type of Christ, and he offered the same gifts that prefigured the Mystery" (John Chrysostom, *Homilies on Genesis* 36.3). "Who had the bread and wine?" asked Ambrose of Milan. "Not Abraham," he answered, "but Melchizedek. Therefore he is the author of the Sacraments" (*De Sacramentis* 4.10). The living memory of Melchizedek thus abides deeply in the worship of the Christian Church.

꙳

2. THE PRAYERS OF HANNAH

Among the characters from Holy Scripture used as models of prayer in traditional Christian literature, few appear as often as Hannah, the mother of Samuel. Starting with Clement of Alexandria and Hippolytus of Rome near the dawn of the third century, those who wished to be instructed in the ways of prayer have had recourse to Hannah's example, as contained in the first two chapters of First Samuel.

It is worth observing that Hannah's prayer serves a significant purpose in the literary structure of that book. Bearing in mind that the Books of Samuel were originally a single book, not two, we readily discern that both the opening and closing scenes of that book have to do with worship. Thus, chapter 1 of First Samuel describes the regular pilgrimages that Elkanah's family made to the ancient shrine at Shiloh, while the last chapter of Second Samuel finishes with David's purchase of the site of the future temple at Jerusalem. At the beginning of the book, the Ark of the Covenant is in Shiloh, but the Ark has been moved to the new site as the book ends. Sacrifices are offered in each place, whether by the priest Eli or by David. In both places, likewise, there is a description of prayer. First Samuel starts with two prayers of Hannah, and Second Samuel closes with two prayers of David (24:10, 25).

Moreover, these prayers themselves are similar. Hannah's petition, inspired by her great distress, takes the form of a vow; if the Lord should give her a son, she promises, she will dedicate him to the Lord. And at the end of the book, David's prayer, made in response to the plague that afflicts the people through his own sin, takes the form of resolve to dedicate a new temple to the Lord. David's resolve, implicit in 2 Samuel 24, is elaborated in 1 Chronicles 21 and Psalm 131(132). Thus, the Book of Samuel begins and ends with similar prayers, in the context of sacrifice.

There are further parallels between the canticle of Hannah in 1 Samuel 2 and the canticle of David in 2 Samuel 22. Indeed, these canticles form an "inclusion" to the book. Thus, in David's canticle God is praised for having kept the promises contained in Hannah's canticle. For example, while Hannah says of the Lord that "He will guard the feet of His saints, but the wicked shall be silent in darkness"

(1 Samuel 2:9), David will say of Him, "He makes my feet like the feet of deer" (2 Samuel 22:34) and "You enlarged my path under me; so my feet did not slip. I have pursued my enemies and destroyed them" (22:37–38). Once again, too, there is the shared image of the shrine or temple. Whereas Hannah's canticle is chanted at the house of the Lord in Shiloh, David's canticle says of the Lord, "He heard my voice from His temple" (22:7). This parallel is all the more striking inasmuch as the new temple has not yet been constructed.

Because the Davidic rise and reign form the substance of the Book of Samuel, these various parallels between the prayers of Hannah and David are hardly surprising. Indeed, Hannah ends her canticle with a promise and prophecy about David, saying of the Lord, "He will give strength to His king, and exalt the horn of His anointed" (1 Samuel 2:10). This theme is later taken up in David's own canticle, which declares that God is "my shield and the horn of my salvation, my stronghold and my refuge" (2 Samuel 22:3).

We may observe, in this respect, that Hannah's canticle near the beginning of Samuel serves much the same purpose as Mary's Magnificat near the beginning of St. Luke's Gospel, both of them introducing themes about the putting down of the mighty and the raising up of the lowly. In fact, one wonders if there has ever been written a commentary on the Magnificat that did not mention its many lines and sentiments shared with the canticle of Hannah.

Furthermore, several Christian writers, including Saints Basil, John Chrysostom, and Bede the Venerable, have drawn attention to the similarities between Hannah and the publican in Luke 18. Both of them pray quietly in the temple and with great humility, neither of them responding to the contempt with which they are treated by their two antagonists, Peninnah and the Pharisee. Both of them thus model the proper sentiments and attitudes of Christian prayer.

In summary, then, when Origen in the mid-third century described Hannah as "praying in the Holy Spirit," he certainly spoke for the whole Tradition.

৵৽

3. THE DUET OF TOBIT AND SARAH

Whatever the objections raised against the canonicity of the Book of Tobit, it is readily acknowledged that its moral and spiritual teaching is

of a piece with the covenantal ethics of the Bible generally. This observation seems especially true of its teaching on prayer.

After the first two chapters of the Book of Tobit have set the stage
on which the book's drama is to be enacted, chapter 3 is of special importance for its description of the simultaneous prayers of Tobit and
Sarah. The sentiments of these two believers in a common hour of darkness and despondency are strongly reminiscent of the prayers of Moses
(Numbers 11:15), Elijah (1 Kings 19:4), Job (7:15), Jonah (4:3, 8), and
Baruch (1:15–22; 2:4; 3:8), but the scene in the Book of Tobit is even
darker. This is the only place in all of biblical literature in which *two*
people, simultaneously, pray to die.

To begin with, there is a clear emphasis on the simultaneity of the
two prayers. Though separated from one another by a great geographical distance, Tobit and Sarah both make that common prayer at exactly
the same hour. They prayed "on the same day" (3:7) and even "at the
very time" (3:17). The prayers, each exactly five verses, are of pretty
much equal length, a feature that also serves to emphasize their simultaneity. By way of speculation, it is not difficult to reconstruct an arrangement of those prayers in either Hebrew or Aramaic, so that both would
have exactly the same number of words. Indeed, if the Book of Tobit
were performed as an opera, the two prayers would constitute a duet.

The structure and general contents of these two prayers are similar,
as well, not only with reference to the afflictions and the common desire to die, but also in their shared emphasis on the acclamation and
praise of God's works. Albeit unwittingly, then, the hearts of Tobit and
Sarah were united in prayer on earth.

But prayer likewise unites earth to heaven, and in the Book of Tobit
this joining of heaven and earth especially has to do with the ministry
of the angels. Prayed simultaneously down below, the suffrages of Tobit
and Sarah are also heard up above at exactly the same time. Indeed, the
very same angel, Raphael ("the healing of God"), receives their petitions
together as a common offering in the presence of the Holy Glory (3:16;
12:12). When believers pray "under the gaze of God," Tertullian was to
write a few centuries later, there is standing with them "the angel of
prayer" (*De Oratione* 16.6). In prayer, then, Tobit and Sarah are united
not only to one another but also to the powers on high.

Near the end of the book, Raphael identifies himself as "one of the
seven holy angels who present the prayers of the saints and enter into

the presence of the glory of the Holy One" (12:15). The very last book of the Bible will take up this image, speaking of these "seven Spirits who are before His Throne" (Revelation 1:4; 4:5).

A further comparison between Tobit and the Book of Revelation is instructive here. In the latter, seven trumpets are given to the seven angels that they may announce the righteous judgments of God. These trumpets are integral parts of the heavenly liturgy; when the prayers of the saints are offered as incense before God, there are immediate repercussions on the earth (Revelation 8:3–5). The blowing of the seven trumpets by the seven angels then announces God's intervention in history on behalf of his righteous ones. Chapter 3 of Tobit serves a very similar function in the structure of that book. All of the events narrated in the remainder of the story are a response to the twin prayers offered at the book's beginning.

The Book of Tobit abounds in further references to prayer, including numerous short prayers—especially fleeting expressions of blessing—from almost every character in the story. Chapter 8 contains the fervent benedictions (*berakoth*) of Tobias and Raguel in response to the heavenly intervention that saved the former and his new wife on their wedding night, and in chapter 11 there are several benedictions associated with Tobias' return and the recovery of Tobit's sight. The entire chapter 13 is a lengthy *berakah* celebrating God's merciful interventions well beyond the dimensions of the narrative itself. The whole story of Tobit is permeated with prayer.

ॐ

4. JESHUA, THE HIGH PRIEST

When the Persian conqueror, Cyrus, after overthrowing Babylon in 539 BC, permitted the deported Jews to return to the Holy Land from their Babylonian Captivity, relatively few of them did so. Indeed, from an investigation of Ezra 2 and Nehemiah 7, it appears that only 49,897 individuals returned to the land of Palestine over the next century. The reason for this is not hard to discern. Most Jews, settled down now and living good, profitable lives in Babylon, were reluctant to come back and assume the drudgeries of life in what could hardly be called, any longer, "a land flowing with milk and honey."

The priests, nonetheless, did not share that reluctance to come home, and this circumstance, too, was understandable. Since the Deuteronomic reform of 622 had limited the sacrificial worship of the Jewish religion exclusively to Jerusalem, there was certainly no reason for priests to remain in Babylon. Consequently, the number of priests who returned—4,289—seems disproportionately large (Ezra 2:36–39).

Chief among them was the high priest Jeshua, or Joshua, whose father Jehozadak had been carried away to Babylon back in 586 (1 Chronicles 6:15). Jeshua's name invariably appears second among the returning exiles (Ezra 2:2; Nehemiah 7:7; 12:1, 10, 26), right after Zerubbabel, the governor appointed by the Emperor Cyrus to oversee Jerusalem's restoration. In the Bible, Zerubbabel and Jeshua were often paired as the political and spiritual leaders of the people. Thus, the Prophet Zechariah described them as "the two anointed ones, who stand beside the Lord of the whole earth" (Zechariah 4:14).

When Jeshua first took up his duties in Jerusalem, there was no temple, of course, for the Babylonians had destroyed it in 586. Accordingly, the first sacrifices were offered on an outdoor altar (Ezra 3:2–3). The first major feast day they observed that year was Tabernacles, celebrated in September (3:1, 4). That was a feast very appropriate to the actual living conditions of the returned exiles, who were still obliged to live in tents, lean-tos, and other makeshift dwellings. The next spring they laid the new temple's foundations (3:7–13), but roughly two decades would elapse before Zerubbabel and Jeshua were able to supervise the temple's completion, largely under the prophetic urging of Haggai and Zechariah (Ezra 5:1–2; 6:15–18; Haggai 1:1–2; Zechariah 1:1).

The high priest Jeshua also appeared several times in the prophetic visions of Zechariah. In one of those the prophet beheld him standing before God with an angel and with Satan. He saw Satan doing for Jeshua what he did for Job, namely, "opposing" him, saying bad things to God about him (Zechariah 3:1; cf. Job 1:9–11; 2:4–5). In both these cases Satan was the "accuser of our brethren, who accused them before our God day and night" (Revelation 12:10). In the case of Jeshua, Satan's accusation had to do with the "filthy garments" of the high priest (Zechariah 3:3). Could such a one, so improperly vested, properly offer sacrifices to the Almighty?

At this point the angel of the Lord rebuked Satan for his accusation against the priest: "The LORD rebuke you, Satan! The LORD who has chosen Jerusalem rebuke you!" (Zechariah 3:2). (In case anyone inquires,

"The LORD rebuke you!" is the execration regularly preferred by angels who are obliged to deal with Satan; cf. Jude 9.)

Jeshua may be taken to represent any and all of God's servants aware of their total unworthiness as they come to worship. Their hearts are full of such sentiments as, "Depart from me, for I am a sinful man, O Lord" (Luke 5:8), "I am not worthy that You should enter under my roof" (7:6), and "God, be merciful to me a sinner!" (18:13). Satan, of course, is ever at hand on such occasions, ready even further to discourage these saints who feel guilty in their filthy garments, suggesting to their minds that they may as well give the whole thing up as useless.

But what do the angels say? "Take away the filthy garments from him. . . . Let them put a clean turban on his head." We do not come before God with any righteousness of our own. "See," the Lord says, "I have removed your iniquity from you, and I will clothe you with rich robes" (Zechariah 3:4–5). We approach the worship of God only in the pure grace of our redemption. "Is this not," asks our good angel, "a brand plucked from the fire?" (3:2).

৵

5. SIMON, THE HIGH PRIEST

The Jewish high priest Simon II did not leave a big mark on history. In fact, his death in 198 BC was the sole occasion of Simon's career that the historian of the race, Flavius Josephus, bothered to mention, and this only in passing (*Antiquities* 12.4.10). Simon was less prominent than his father, Onias II (12.4.1), and a great deal less significant than either of his two sons, Onias III (2 Maccabees 3—4; *Antiquities* 12.4.11) and Jason (2 Maccabees 4—5). In short, as the world normally appraises historical importance, Simon was not an important man.

This fact renders very remarkable the high esteem in which Simon was held by Joshua Ben Sirach, the author of the Book of Ecclesiasticus, who eulogized the high priest shortly after his death. The book's final long section, which contains a detailed panegyric of Israel's heroes, begins with the words, "Let us now praise famous men and our fathers that begot us" (Ecclesiasticus 44:1). Then, beginning with Enoch and Noah, it goes on to extol the deeds of Israel's prophets, warriors, kings, and sages throughout history: Abraham, Moses, Joshua, Samuel, David, Solomon, and the others. But the final and climactic figure in Sirach's long account is this otherwise obscure high priest, Simon II, to whose description he devotes almost a whole chapter (50).

And what was it about Simon that Ben Sirach found so impressive? His solicitude for the divine worship, his refurbishing of the temple, his care for its appointments, the personal dignity with which he enhanced the solemnity of its rituals. The reverent grandeur of Israel's liturgical worship was of great moment to Ben Sirach. Earlier in his historical panegyric he had paid detailed attention to the vestments and accoutrements of the Aaronic priesthood and its rites of sacrifice (45:6–17), in which he savored the mystic compound of holiness, beauty, and devotion. It was in the temple ministry of Simon, however, that Ben Sirach supremely discerned what it meant to "worship the Lord in the beauty of holiness."

Ben Sirach, one fears, would have scant sympathy with current trends to simplify and popularize the forms of worship in order to make them more "accessible," more "relevant," and less "foreign" to the man on the street. Ben Sirach would have scoffed at "seeker friendly" services that reflect everyday culture and "make people feel at home." Notions of this sort, had he known about them (which he didn't, of course, for they are very recent), Ben Sirach would have considered monstrous. He knew very well—and in his description of Simon he would teach us—that worship involves dignifying man by elevating him up to God, not by celebrating what man already is on his own.

To "worship the Lord in the beauty of holiness" requires, first of all, holiness, and in this respect Simon the high priest was a model. Indeed, according to Ben Sirach, "when he went up to the holy altar, he made the garment of holiness honorable" (50:11).

This holiness of worship is clothed in beauty, and beauty is simply truth as lovable, truth discerned in its loveliness. The perception of truth is the discernment of form, nor is there any beauty apart from form. This is why worship is formal, structured, patterned on a determined model. With respect to the form of worship, Moses on the mountain was told to make all things according to the heavenly pattern that he beheld. This sane prescription would safeguard Israel from the worship of Canaanite gods and from silly Philistine heresies like that which thinks "beauty is in the eye of the beholder." Because every form of truth is heavenly and eternal, true liturgy is not simply old; it is necessarily timeless.

Ben Sirach, in his account of Simon, has left us the Bible's finest description of Israel's worship. He gloried in the high praise of God according to the forms that God Himself prescribed. His eyes beheld the fire, the precious stones and beaten gold, the beauty of stately shapes and extravagant colors in vestments and sacred vessels. The air he breathed was laden with the richness of incense and aromatic oils, and his ears were filled with the silver trumpets and the chanting of the worshippers. He contemplated in the rituals of the temple the culminating adornment of creation itself. In Sirach's estimation, then, Simon's task was not to make his mark on history, but to serve in the dignified and solemn worship that transcends the mere events of men.

꙾

6. SPIRIT-FILLED ELIZABETH

In the Gospel according to St. Luke and its companion work, The Acts of the Apostles, there are clear indications of the author's sustained and explicit preoccupation with the Holy Spirit. This characteristic of Luke becomes obvious if one simply counts the number of his references to the theme. While Matthew mentions the Holy Spirit twelve times and Mark only six, there are no fewer than seventeen such references in Luke's Gospel and fifty-seven in Acts.

Some of the evidence for Luke's preoccupation is subtle and likely to be detected only by close inspection, comparing him to the other evangelists. For example, whereas Matthew's version of a certain teaching of the Lord on prayer reads, "If you then, being evil, know how to give good gifts to your children, how much more will your Father who is in heaven give good things to those who ask Him" (7:11), in Luke's rendering of that verse the Lord's closing comment says: "How much more will your heavenly Father give the Holy Spirit to those who ask Him" (11:13). Similarly, if we examine a prayer of our Lord as recorded in both Matthew 11:25–27 and Luke 10:21–24 ("I thank You, Father, Lord of heaven and earth . . ."), we observe that only Luke begins by saying that "Jesus rejoiced in the Holy Spirit" ("Holy" being the better textual reading here, included in the two earliest codices of the New Testament).

Not all the evidence is so subtle, however, nor will most readers fail to observe that both of Luke's books begin and end with the Holy Spirit (Luke 1:15, 35; 24:49; Acts 1:4, 5, 8; 2:4ff; 28:25). Likewise, Luke especially speaks of individuals designated, or acting, or speaking under the influence of the Holy Spirit. These include Simeon (Luke 2:25–27), Philip (Acts 8:29, 39), Peter (10:19; 11:12), Paul (20:22–23; 21:4), Agabus (11:29; 21:11), the presbyters at Ephesus (20:28), the Apostles generally (Acts 5:32; 13:2, 4; 15:28; 16:6–7), and especially Jesus Himself (Luke 4:1, 14, 18; Acts 10:38).

"Filled with the Holy Spirit," moreover, is a favorite expression of Luke, which he uses to describe Zacharias (Luke 1:67), Peter (Acts 4:8), Paul (9:17; 13:9, 52), Barnabas (11:24), and even the entire congregation at Jerusalem (Acts 4:31). This expression is especially prominent with respect to Stephen, who is several times described this way (Acts 6:3, 5, 10; 7:55).

Luke's earliest and arguably most significant use of this expression refers to John the Baptist, of whom Gabriel tells Zacharias: "He will be filled with the Holy Spirit, even from his mother's womb" (Luke 1:15). This striking prophecy is fulfilled only twenty-six verses later, when the unborn infant's response to this filling with the Holy Spirit is to jump for joy inside his mother's body. Indeed, the mother herself is filled with the Holy Spirit: "And it happened, when Elizabeth heard the greeting of Mary, that the babe leaped in her womb; and Elizabeth was filled with the Holy Spirit" (Luke 1:41). Furthermore, Elizabeth will credit this outpouring of the Holy Spirit to the sound of Mary's voice: "For indeed, as soon as the voice of your greeting sounded in my ears, the babe leaped in my womb for joy" (1:44).

And what does the Holy Spirit prompt Elizabeth to say to Mary? "Blessed are you among women, and blessed is the fruit of your womb" (1:42). This is the way that one addresses the Mother of God, if one is filled with the Holy Spirit. This point is emphatic.

The word "blessed" in Elizabeth's greeting to Mary is not the *makarios*, or "happy," of the Beatitudes (though this *is* used in the same context in Luke 1:45, 48). It is, rather, *eulogemene*, the participle of the verb "to bless." This particular "blessed" is of the same root as the "blessed" (*eulogetos*) in Zacharias's "Blessed is the Lord God of Israel," a detail surely significant inasmuch as Zacharias himself is also described in that passage as "filled with the Holy Spirit" when he said it (1:67–68).

Elizabeth's greeting to Mary was bound to become part of the faith and piety of God's Church, inasmuch as it is explicitly said to have been given by the Holy Spirit. Like "Abba, Father" (Galatians 4:6; Romans

8:15) and "Jesus is Lord" (1 Corinthians 12:3), "Blessed are you among women" is a pronouncement prompted by the Holy Spirit. "Blessed are you among women" pertains to the Spirit-given substance of the Christian faith. Like Elizabeth who "cried out with a loud voice," Christians render this identical greeting to the one whom they know as "the mother of my Lord" (1:42–43).

⳨

7. NATHANAEL UNDER A FIG TREE

Nathanael's meeting with our Lord, as described by John, is one of the most striking such encounters in Holy Scripture. Just as Nathanael approaches Him, Jesus exclaims: "Behold, an Israelite indeed, in whom is no deceit!" As such a judgment implies an ability to discern someone's heart, Nathanael's response does not surprise us: "How do You know me?" The mystery is only deepened by the Lord's answer to this query: "Before Philip called you, when you were under the fig tree, I saw you" (John 1:47–48).

What does this all mean? The dialogue between Jesus and Nathanael clearly refers to some recent experience of the latter as he was sitting under a fig tree. Apparently it was a spiritual perception, an awareness that his soul was being scrutinized by the Omniscient Reader of men's hearts. As a result of this experience, Nathanael felt God's gaze into his soul. He knew himself to be "seen." In this respect his experience was like that of the Psalmist: "O LORD, You have searched me and known me. / You know my sitting down and my rising up; / You understand my thought afar off. / You comprehend my path and my lying down, / And are acquainted with all my ways. / For there is not a word on my tongue, / But behold, O Lord, You know it altogether" (Psalm 139:1–4).

Sitting there under the fig tree, Nathanael doubtless is profoundly affected by this experience, when suddenly his friend Philip comes with a summons: "We have found Him of whom Moses in the law, and also the prophets, wrote" (John 1:45). And when he then meets Jesus, Jesus reveals Himself to Nathanael as the very One who had been reading his heart as he sat there under the fig tree. Now beholding, in front of him, the face of that mysterious Presence that he had perceived in his own soul, Nathanael exclaims with the voice of faith: "Rabbi, You are the

Son of God!" (1:49). He identifies Christ as the One who sees into his heart. Nathanael's knowledge of Christ comes from his experience of being known by Christ.

Our knowledge of God is born of our encounter with His knowledge of us, and we are able to love Him only by reason of His salvific recognition of us: "But if anyone loves God, this one is known by Him" (1 Corinthians 8:3). Thus, in speaking of the conversion of the Galatians, St. Paul says to them: "But now after you have known God, or rather are known by God . . . ." (Galatians 4:9).

In gracing us with the knowledge of the true God, the Christian revelation also entrusts to us the knowledge of our true selves. Moreover, only in knowing God do we even *become* our true selves. "For you did not receive the spirit of bondage again to fear," St. Paul tells us, "but you received the Spirit of adoption by whom we cry out, 'Abba, Father.' The Spirit Himself bears witness with our spirit that we are children of God" (Romans 8:15–16). That is to say, the Holy Spirit testifies in our hearts, not only to who God is, but also to who we are—not only to God as Father, but to us as His children. More precisely, we know the true God as our Father only by reason of that sustained outpouring through which He makes us His children. Our own self-understanding is poured into our hearts by God's Holy Spirit.

This revelation, this "riches of the full assurance of understanding, to the knowledge of the mystery of God" (Colossians 2:2), is grace in the strict sense. We are not able, of ourselves, to establish or claim this identity as God's children, for it springs entirely of the Father's own initiative. We know Him only because He has first known us.

This, our new identity, is conferred upon us as a costly trust, our inheritance purchased with the blood of Christ. Though in this earthly life we see God "in a mirror, dimly," such vision is still our most precious holding, for God's knowledge of us leads at last to our knowing Him "face to face." "Now I know in part," says St. Paul, "but then I shall know just as I also am known" (1 Corinthians 13:12).

Our new identity precludes anonymity, too, for the Good Shepherd truly knows His own, and each of them He calls by name. And should those sheep endeavor, foolishly, to remain nameless, He will not suffer them very long to stay concealed. Like that desperately ill woman hiding in the folds of the crowd while extending her finger toward the fringe of Christ's garment, they will be summoned forth. "Somebody," the Lord will say, "touched Me" (Luke 8:46). Oh, "somebody" indeed, for there are no nobodies in Christ.

ॐ

8. THE PRAYER OF THE PUBLICAN

Virtually from the beginning, it would seem, Christians sensed that the Lord's account of the "two men who went up to the temple to pray" (Luke 18:9–14) contained some of the most important lessons they were obliged to learn. The parable's teaching about humility and contrition of heart embodied the major characteristic of a true disciple of Christ.

The Parable of the Pharisee and the Publican bears striking affinities to other passages in Luke. For example, its closing statement, about the humbling of the self-exalting and the exalting of the humble, is identical with the final verse of the Lord's exhortation about seeking the lower place at table (14:11). It is a theme that Luke establishes early, with the song of Mary in 1:52. Again, the differing features and fates of the two men in the temple readily put the reader in mind of the opposition between the Rich Man and Lazarus in 16:19–31; each story has to do with the divergence of the divine judgment from the human.

Even clearer, perhaps, is this parable's resemblance to the story of the Prodigal Son in 15:11–32. Both stories elaborate differences between a self-righteous keeper of the law and a miserable offender pleading for forgiveness and grace. Similarly, the humble contrition of the Publican resembles that of the repentant woman in 7:36–50, while his gentle confidence in the divine mercy is like that of the chronically bleeding woman in 8:43–44. Most of all, however, the petition of the Publican in the temple closely resembles the prayer of the Thief on the Cross in 23:42; since neither man could bring to God anything but a plea for divine mercy, their cases are precisely parallel.

Within Luke's Gospel, chapters 11 and 18 are concerned with prayer in a more concentrated way. The former begins with Jesus at prayer, a scene that prompts the disciples to request that He teach them also the proper way to pray. Thus is introduced Luke's version of the Lord's Prayer, which is promptly followed by two further dominical teachings on the subject. The first (11:5–8), specific to Luke, is the parable of the importunate seeker who repeatedly bothers his friend for help. This emphasis on repetition introduces the next dominical teaching on prayer, the famous "ask, seek, knock" sequence (11:9–13).

The teaching on prayer in Luke 18 also emphasizes indefatigability and persistence. Beginning with the exhortation that Christians are to "pray always" (18:1), an ideal also found in St. Paul (Romans 12:12; Ephesians 6:18; Colossians 4:2; 1 Thessalonians 5:17), Luke 18 gives three models of persevering prayer: the two parables of the Widow and the Judge (vv. 2–8) and the Pharisee and the Publican (vv. 9–14), and also the story of the blind man of Jericho (vv. 38–39). Each is a case of sustained, relentless, and repeated petition. The characters in each of these accounts pray without ceasing by making the same request over and over again. In the teaching of Luke, then, constant, uninterrupted prayer means ceaselessly repeated prayer. In Luke, the Publican's petition became a major feature in the Christian quest for steady, persistent, and constant prayer.

Following an historical development not fully documented in the sources, the prayer of the Publican was gradually joined to the blind man's prayer in Luke 18:38—"Jesus, son of David, have mercy on me"— and augmented with more ample Christological affirmations. It thus became "the Jesus Prayer": "Lord, Jesus Christ, Son of the living God, have mercy on me, a sinner."

Above all else, this ancient prayer, rooted in the biblical text, is an affirmation of the Lordship of Jesus as the defining revelation of God in human history: "Lord, Jesus Christ, Son of the living God." It is a proclamation of faith in the form of a direct address, an interpersonal prayer in which the believer invokes the Savior of the world. Since only in the Holy Spirit can we proclaim that Jesus is Lord, this is a prayer permeated with the divinizing grace of the Holy Spirit.

Furthermore, the Jesus Prayer is a confession of one's sinfulness, designed to place a broken and contrite heart continuously in the Presence of the living Christ and under the bounteous mercy of His blood: "Have mercy on me, a sinner." One may think of this prayer as the biblical doctrine of "justification by faith" shaped into a petition, enshrined in the form of a confession of Jesus' lordship.

⁂

9. CLEOPAS AND HIS COMPANIONS

The story of the two disciples walking to Emmaus on the afternoon of the day of the Lord's Resurrection (Luke 24:13–35) is of great importance to biblical exegesis and the structure of Christian worship.

First, with respect to biblical exegesis, it may be said that the conversation of the risen Christ, as He walked with Cleopas and his unnamed companion and interpreted the Holy Scriptures for them, was the Church's first formal course in the proper Christian interpretation of the Sacred Scriptures. From time to time, as we know, Jesus had interpreted individual passages of Moses, Isaiah, David, and other Old Testament writers, normally in reference to Himself. In that discourse on the road to Emmaus, however, Jesus devoted the entire effort and time to this theme, laying the foundation for the proper Christian understanding of the Bible. It may be said that all orthodox Christian exegesis goes back to that conversation, and we are surely correct in going to the writers of the New Testament as illustrating the interpretive patterns put forward in that conversation.

The "allegory" (Galatians 4:21–31) or "spiritual sense" (1 Corinthians 2:6–16; 2 Corinthians 3:18) of God's holy Word is that Word's underlying Christological reference, its relationship to the Incarnate Lord who brings it to historical and theological fulfillment. Clothed in the literary forms of history, parable, and poetry, the Bible's deeper doctrinal message is ever its reference to the Mystery of Christ, who is at once God's only path to us and our only path to God. Thus, every line of the Bible, every symbol and every story, every prophecy, proverb, and prayer bears its deeper significance in Christ, its meaning conveyed in the catechesis of the Church and sacramental sharing in the Christian Sacraments. It is this more profound Christological "sense" of Holy Scripture that separates the Christian from the Jew.

We may also say, in this respect, that all of Christian doctrine is rooted in our Lord's paschal discourse to the two disciples on the way to Emmaus. The timing of that discourse is likewise significant, for it took place on the very day of His rising from the dead; on that day "the Lion of the tribe of Judah, the root of David," demonstrated that He "was worthy to take the scroll and to open its seals." He was worthy to do this because He was slain and had redeemed us to God by His blood (Revelation 5:5, 9). Jesus interprets Holy Scripture—indeed, He is the very interpretation of Holy Scripture—because He "fulfills" Holy Scripture by the historical and theological events of His death and Resurrection. His blood-redemption of the world is the formal principle of biblical interpretation.

Second, in the paschal experience of those two disciples we have the initial paradigm of proper Sunday worship as the Apostles handed it down to us. The experience of those men, hearing and understanding God's Word while their hearts burned within them, led to their recognition of Him in the breaking of the Bread. Holy Church has always understood this intricate combination of Word and Sacrament to indicate the structure of correct Sunday worship. This is the format we find in the New Testament (Acts 20:7–11) and in the earliest explicit description of Christian Sunday worship left us from the second century (St. Justin Martyr, *First Apology* 67).

In the Orthodox East this binary principle of Word and Sacrament is expressed in the two Entrances. The Little Entrance, which takes place after the litanies and psalmody at the beginning of the Divine Liturgy, gives prominence of place to the Gospel book, which the deacon carries high in the procession. This procession may be regarded as the walk to Emmaus, for it introduces the public reading of God's Word. Or, in the words of Justin, "the memoirs of the Apostles or the writings of the prophets are read, as long as time permits; then, when the reader has ceased, the Presider verbally instructs and exhorts to the imitation of these good things."

With the Great Entrance, in which the bread and wine are borne solemnly into the sanctuary, we arrive in the inn at Emmaus, taking our place at "the Lord's table" (1 Corinthians 10:21), that we may know Him in the Breaking of the Bread. The Scriptures are interpreted by the sacramental context of their proclamation, while the knowledge of the risen Christ thus proclaimed reaches its proper fulfillment in the Holy Communion, the mystic reception of the risen, glorified Body and Blood of the Lion of Judah. "Lord, abide with us," we say, "for it is toward evening, and the day is far spent."

V.
ZEALOUS SAINTS
⨏

Many of the biblical zealots, though certainly not all of them, are found in the Books of Joshua and Judges, the two books that continue Israel's history from the death of Moses to the beginnings of the monarchy. These two books, which begin with the conquest of the Holy Land by the chosen people, are dominated by the imagery of warfare. It is not surprising that many modern readers are shocked and concerned about the great emphasis on combat in these books, the bloodshed, the conquest, the seizure of the property of others, and so forth. If taken literally, these two books might be used to justify all sorts of dreadful behavior, and some Christians deliberately avoid them for that very reason. These arguments against the Books of Joshua and Judges run parallel, then, to those alleged against the "cursing psalms."

In both cases, the question is legitimately posed: Are we not dealing here with a very primitive and immature level of religion that we should not pursue? Should not Christians, who have been enlightened with the greater grace of the Gospel, simply ignore such an early and more barbarous expression of religion?

It is arguably in connection with these problematic texts that we perceive most clearly the Pauline distinction between the letter that kills and the Spirit that gives life (cf. 2 Corinthians 3:6). We Christians today are hardly the first biblical readers to sense a problem with too literal an application of these more aggressive parts of Holy Scripture. From the earliest periods of the Christian Church, in fact, great care has been taken to interpret the Bible's battles, bloodshed, cursing, and hostility in a more spiritual sense, applying them to the great struggle that Christians must exert to do battle with Satan, who goes about the world as a roaring lion, seeking whom he may devour (1 Peter 5:8). A good number of sermons and Christian commentaries on these texts have come down to us from the early centuries of the Church, and all of them are marked by this concern. The vigorous fighting recorded in Joshua and Judges, as well as the robust cursing of enemies that one finds in the Book of Psalms, were habitually understood by those ancient preachers and commentators as symbolic of the considerable struggles involved in the daily Christian life.

To appreciate the validity of this approach, I offer two reflections here.

First, the application of these historical events to the more spiritual dimensions of our life in Christ is not farfetched. Ancient Israel's struggles with the Canaanites and her other enemies were not simply political and military. Those were idolatrous cultures, devoted to the worship of demonic powers. The religion of these peoples was hateful to God. As offensive as this sounds to modern ears, Israel was involved in a godly task in undertaking their destruction. Even though Christians today are forbidden to employ such violent means to eradicate idolatry and perversion from our modern culture, we are no less obliged to dedicate ourselves to that struggle and that eradication. Indeed, the idolatry and perversions of ancient Canaanite culture sometimes seem rather tame in comparison with the demonic conditions that surround us Christians in the world today. At this very moment, we Americans know far more about the evils of the Amorites, the atrocities of the Jebusites, and the cruelties of Moloch-worship than did the Israelites in those distant times.

Second, for far too long, and at much too deep a level, Christians have failed to take seriously their obligation to struggle against the forces of evil in their own souls. Too often this strenuous, biblically enjoined obligation to "work out our salvation in fear and trembling" has been dismissed as simply a species of works-righteousness. There is no question here, of course, of "earning" our salvation. There is, however, the elementary concern that in all things God be glorified, and often enough God is not glorified by how little concern we show for rooting out of our souls the various faults, habits, and dispositions that stand inimical to His grace. It was to Christians, after all, and not to pagans, that the Apostle Paul sent the warning not to grieve the Holy Spirit (Ephesians 4:30). It is a mammoth perversion of the teaching of Holy Scripture to use the doctrine of salvation by faith as an excuse for remaining spiritually lazy and self-indulgent.

જ્જ

1. PHINEHAS THE PRIEST

After wandering in the Sinai and Negev deserts for most of a generation, the people of Israel had now arrived at a place called Shittim, just east of the Jordan River and only about ten miles from Jericho. Then came a new crisis.

It was a moral crisis, involving some Israelite men of slack discipline with certain Moabite women of relaxed virtue. Fornication was the problem, that term understood both literally and in the figurative sense of their falling prey to the idolatrous worship of the Moabite god, Baal of Peor (Numbers 25:1–3).

The seduction of these Israelites, moreover, was not a mere boy-meets-girl happenstance. It resulted, rather, from a deliberate machination on the part of the Moabites, plotting to weaken the military resolve and moral will of the Israelites. Indeed, there is reason to believe that the scheme had been concocted in the mind of the religious philosopher Balaam, who was at that time in the service of the Moabite king (cf. Revelation 2:14).

Seeing it happen, the young priest Phinehas discerned the peril of the hour, for an earlier experience had taught him the hazards of moral compromise. If he was sure of anything at all, Phinehas was certain that God's punishment of sin was invariably decisive and might very well be swift.

Phinehas had been hardly more than a child when he saw the divine retribution visited on two of his priestly uncles, Nadab and Abihu, for a single offense in the service of God. Nor had those been insignificant men who were thus punished. On the contrary, Nadab and Abihu, sons of Aaron and his heirs in the priesthood, were men of stature and respect among the people. They had accompanied Moses, their very uncle, as he began his climb of Mount Sinai (Exodus 24:1), and had partly shared in his vision of the divine glory (24:9–10). Nonetheless, Nadab and Abihu had been instantly struck dead, devoured by a fire from the divine presence for just one moral lapse (Leviticus 10:1–3). The memory of that swift retribution had seared itself into the memory of young Phinehas. He knew by experience that Israel's Lord was a morally serious God, not some feather of a deity to be brushed away at one's convenience.

At the time of the Moabite crisis, then, Phinehas's reaction was utterly decisive and equally swift. Responding to the Lord's decree to punish the offenders (Numbers 25:4–6), he resolutely took the matter in hand and thus put an end to the divine wrath already plaguing the people (25:7–15). For his part in averting the evil, Phinehas came to enjoy great respect in Israel. Not long afterwards, for instance, he was the priest chosen to accompany the army advancing against the Midianites (Numbers 31:6). After the conquest, Phinehas inherited land among the Ephraimites (cf. Joshua 24:33) and continued to be consulted by Israel, especially in times of crisis (cf. Judges 20:28). He would be remembered throughout the rest of biblical history, furthermore, as the very model of zeal in God's service (cf. Psalm 105[106]:30; 1 Chronicles 9:20; Sirach 45:23).

If we knew only of Phinehas's decisive action at the time of the Moabite trouble, it might be easy to think of him solely as an energetic, resolute, executive sort of man, but this would be an incomplete perspective. Phinehas was also a thoughtful person, able to consider a delicate question in its fully nuanced complexities.

This latter trait of his character was revealed in the crisis later created by the construction of an altar to the east of the Jordan River by the Israelites who lived in that region (Joshua 22:10). Regarded as a rival altar outside of the strict confines of the Holy Land, this construction proved so provocative to the rest of Israel that there arose the real danger of civil war (22:12). Fortunately, cooler heads prevailed, and the decision was made to establish an eleven-member committee of inquiry to investigate the matter. Phinehas was the head of that committee (22:13–14).

Probing into the construction of that altar, Phinehas's committee concluded that it was not intended to be used as such, but would serve merely as a monument to remind all the Israelites of their solidarity in the worship of their one God. Civil war was thus averted, and Phinehas, once so swift unto bloodshed, was thus in large measure responsible for preventing it (22:21–34).

⚜

2. THE PRAYER OF JOSHUA

When, after the death of Moses, the leadership of Israel passed to Joshua, everyone in the camp must have experienced a sudden new energy and sense of resolve. The long trek through the desert was over. In his first statement on assuming command, Joshua announced that the Jordan would be crossed "within three days" (Joshua 1:11).

For a long time Joshua had been awaiting that hour. Many years before, when he and Caleb had been part of a twelve-man surveillance party sent to scout the land of Canaan (Numbers 13:1–27), they had been frustrated at Israel's refusal to invade that country. Joshua and Caleb were outvoted ten-to-two (14:1–9). Their "minority report" was so badly received, in fact, that they were nearly stoned to death (14:10).

For many years Joshua had suffered from the frustration of that earlier period. He knew that the death of Moses must precede the people's passage into the Promised Land, and he had maintained his patience all those years. Now, however, a new day of resolve had dawned. No matter that Joshua was no longer a young man; the rest of his life would be taken up by the utmost zeal in God's purposes.

Even God's most zealous servants in Holy Scripture, however, are still frail human beings, as manifested in their times of discouragement. Joshua was no exception to that pattern.

The text illustrating this point in the case of Joshua is his prayer in response to the defeat of the Israelites in the siege of Ai: "Alas, Lord GOD, why have You brought this people over the Jordan at all—to deliver us into the hand of the Amorites, to destroy us? Oh, that we had been content, and dwelt on the other side of the Jordan! O Lord, what shall I say when Israel turns its back before its enemies? For the Canaanites and all the inhabitants of the land will hear it, and surround us, and cut off our name from the earth" (Joshua 7:7–9).

Though this desperate prayer of Joshua was doubtless sincere, its inflections strike us as exaggerated and unreasonable, perhaps even melodramatic, not to say hysterical. One has the impression that Joshua was perhaps not thinking very clearly that day. It was hardly his finest hour. Indeed, the Lord's response to the prayer seems to display even a certain measure of impatience with Joshua: "Get up! Why do you lie thus on your face?" (7:10).

The exaggerated tone and unreasonable quality of Joshua's prayer are indicated by two considerations:

First, the general context. Within the previous few days, after all, Joshua had beheld the Jordan River dried up in order for the chosen people to walk over on its bed. Now, nonetheless, we find him wishing that they had remained on the other side! Likewise, just prior to the debacle at Ai, Joshua had witnessed the dramatic conquest of Jericho, its walls reduced to rubble at the blast of Israel's trumpets. But the dust of that victory has hardly settled before Joshua is rendered fearful that Israel will be wiped out by the Canaanites. This single setback at Ai seems to erase, in his mind, all remembrance of recent and more auspicious events.

Second, the immediate context. Simply put, the defeat at Ai hardly signaled the darkest hour of Israel's history. True, it was an unexpected setback, but scarcely more. Joshua had sent out about three thousand troops; though these were overcome in battle, they sustained only thirty-six casualties. To hear Joshua tell it, however, one would think that Israel had just suffered the worst slaughter in military history.

Is this the same Joshua, we wonder, who had boldly announced to the Israelites that "within three days you will cross over this Jordan" (1:11)? Is this the level of discouragement we would have expected from the same man who could announce: "But as for me and my house, we will serve the LORD" (24:15)? The least to be said is that Joshua's anxiety and distress over the vanquishing at Ai seem out of character with what we know of him in the rest of Scripture.

But is it out of character with a man of flesh and blood? May it not be that even Joshua's distress serves as a source of comfort for the rest of us during our own times of anxiety? If our reactions to adversity are, on occasion, somewhat exaggerated and unreasonable, it may be useful to remember that this was true likewise of a figure so zealous and brave as the conqueror of Jericho.

☙

3. CALEB AND THE GIANTS

Caleb wanted to be, more than anything, a slayer of giants, and the giants he especially had in mind to slay were the Anakim. Who could blame him?

Caleb was not alone in his sentiments about the Anakim. This Semitic tribe of giants, living in the southern portion of the land of Canaan, was very familiar to its disgruntled neighbors. The Egyptians, for example, who knew all about the Anakim, certainly did not like them; they left us our earliest reference to these giants on an execration text from the dawn of the second millennium BC. Such texts are inscriptions on shard pieces containing the names of Egypt's adversaries; those shards are fragments of pottery, originally inscribed with appropriate curses against enemies. Thus adorned, the pottery was ritually broken, to exorcise and annul, as it were, the military might of the foe. Well, sure enough, on one of those Egyptian shards there is a curse against "the ruler of Iy-'anaq" and his confederates.

These Anakim were the descendants of Arba, the father of Anak (Joshua 15:13). Arba is described as "the greatest man among the Anakim" (14:15). For this reason, their major city was named "the city of Arba," Kirjath-Arba (21:11). Although that same place was known to the Israelites as Hebron, to this day the Arabic name for it, Deir el-Arba'in, recalls the earlier Canaanite tradition.

Caleb knew the Anakim firsthand and up close. Representing the tribe of Judah, he was one of twelve spies whom Moses commissioned to investigate the Promised Land: "Go up this way into the South, and go up to the mountains, and see what the land is like" (Numbers 13:17–18). Since it was the time for the grape harvest, Moses exhorted the spies especially to bring back some of the land's vintage (13:20).

The latter, in fact, proved to be extraordinary: "Then they came to the Valley of Eshcol, and there cut down a branch with one cluster of grapes; they carried it between two of them on a pole" (13:23). With such evidence of the land's largesse, one would have thought that the Israelites could hardly wait to invade the place. Indeed, the report of the spies, who had investigated the land for forty days, was rather enthusiastic with respect to its fertility: "It truly flows with milk and honey, and this is its fruit" (13:27).

Had this information been the only element in the report of the spies, Israel's invasion of the land might have begun at once. Unfortunately, however, ten of the twelve spies were simply overawed by the size of the Anakim that the invaders would be obliged to fight: "Nevertheless the people who dwell in the land are strong; the cities are fortified and very large; moreover we saw the descendants of Anak there. . . . We are not able to go up against the people, for they are stronger than we. . . . And we were like grasshoppers in our own sight, and so we were in their sight" (13:28, 31, 33).

This report of the majority of the spies so discouraged the Israelites that "all the congregation lifted up their voices and cried, and the people wept that night" (14:1). There ensued the litany of Israelite complaints, like "If only we had died in the land of Egypt!" and "Why has the LORD brought us to this land to fall by the sword?" (14:2–3). Indeed, there even arose a movement to go back to the condition of slavery: "Let us select a leader and return to Egypt" (14:4). It became clear, in any event, that the case for invading Canaan enjoyed no popular support.

This report of the espionage delegation, and more especially the people's reaction to it, brought great distress to the delegation's only two members who dissented, Joshua and Caleb. In vain did these two exhort the Israelites to begin the invasion (13:30; 14:6–9). They were nearly stoned to death for their efforts (14:10).

Israel's infidelity in this matter would rankle Joshua and Caleb for decades to come, until at last, after the death of Moses, Joshua assumed command of a new generation of Israelites and accomplished what the Lord had commanded in the first place. Caleb was given the task of attacking and conquering the three sons of Anak: Ahinam, Sheshai, and Talmai (Joshua 15:14; Judges 1:10), the very tribes that had earlier struck such fear into the hearts of his companions (Numbers 13:22). To his family was given the city of Kirjath-Arba, renamed Hebron. One suspects that Caleb insisted on this arrangement. He had a score to settle with those giants.

৵৽

4. LEFT-HANDED EHUD

In the sixth century *The Holy Rule* of St. Benedict determined that monks must not read from certain books of the Bible just before going to bed. The *Rule* does not say why, but it was apparently felt that some biblical stories might stimulate the monks' imaginations too much at bedtime, either keeping them awake or giving rise to troublesome dreams. The books mentioned by St. Benedict in this respect were "the Heptateuch and Kings," the "Heptateuch" being the Bible's first seven books, and "Kings" including those four books that today we call Samuel and Kings. We recognize, of course, that St. Benedict was right. Some of the accounts in those eleven books are among the most graphic and exciting in the Bible.

Included among the stories that might keep the monk awake at night, or haunt his dreams if he did manage to fall asleep after reading them, was the adventure of Ehud, one of the most violent, dramatic, and memorable narratives in all of Holy Scripture. Ehud, we recall, was the Benjaminite leader charged to carry Israel's tribute to Moab's big, fat king, Eglon, under whom Israel was oppressed for eighteen years. Raised up by God, Ehud resolved to set the Israelites free, and Judges 3 tells how he did it.

His first step was to procure what the King James Bible calls a "dagger." This blade, however, specifically identified as double-edged, was longer than most daggers; its length was a cubit, the distance between a man's elbow and the tip of his little finger. Ehud concealed this cumbersome weapon under his clothing, attached along his right thigh, for he was, you see, a left-handed man. (This latter detail is ironic, because Ehud belonged to the tribe of Benjamin, a name meaning "son of my right hand.") Why, then, a weapon so large and therefore easier to detect? Well, Ehud had a plan.

After dismissing his delegation, which had delivered the annual tribute to the Moabites, Ehud asked to speak to Eglon in private, mentioning that he had a message from God for the king. Eglon suspected nothing amiss; after all, the tribute had just been paid, and Ehud's retinue had been sent away, nor did the man appear to be armed. The unsuspecting Eglon, therefore, took his visitor to the privacy of a cool apartment on his roof. When they were alone, Ehud's left hand quickly reached under the garment covering his right leg and drew forth the long twin-edged blade. Suddenly, as hard as he could, he rammed it into the immense stomach of Eglon. He drove the point so forcefully that the entire length of the blade became buried in Eglon's copious flesh. Indeed, the king's flab oozed out around the haft and covered it, so that the weapon could not be extracted. Then, taking the king's key and locking the door to the apartment, Ehud went out to rally the troops that he had placed on the road to Moab. Eglon's astonished courtiers had barely discovered his corpse when Ehud returned with an army and took the Moabites by surprise at the fords of the Jordan. There he "killed about ten thousand men of Moab, all stout men of valor; not a man escaped" (Judges 3:29). Thus did Ehud deliver Israel from the oppressor.

Now if a monk should read this story before going to bed, St. Benedict believed, its vividness and violence might keep him awake or give him nightmares. The monk might forget that the account of Ehud possessed a deeper, mystic level of meaning. His imagination thus stimulated by a racy story, he might not reflect on the story's more important theological significance. He might fail to observe that the account of Ehud's deliverance is a type or allegory (two terms entirely interchangeable in ancient Christian literature) of our own salvation from Moabites far worse than fat Eglon. The overly agitated monk might miss the spiritual significance of the two-edged sword used to slay God's glutted enemy. He might also fail to recognize the "power of the keys" symbolized in Ehud's locking of Eglon's door. Distracted by the very dynamism of the adventure, the insomniac monk might not notice the reference to Holy Baptism, mystically signified in the fords of the Jordan, that sacramental river where God's enemies are crushed and put to flight. Who, after all, is this Ehud? He is Christ our Savior, from whose mouth issues the sharp, two-edged sword of His holy Word (Revelation 19:15), in whose hand are the keys that lock so that no man may open (20:1; 3:7), whose forces are rallied at the fords of the Jordan, and whose Israelites are delivered from their oppressor.

$$\mathcal{R}$$

5. SHAMGAR THE FARMER

The career of Ehud, Israel's defender against Moab, comes to an end in Judges 3:30, with the note that "the land had rest for eighty years." The fourth chapter begins with the note, "When Ehud was dead." The two verses would seem to provide an untarnished and seamless narrative transition.

They don't, however, because between them falls another verse, introducing yet another character, as though out of nowhere: "After [Ehud] was Shamgar the son of Anath, who killed six hundred men of the Philistines with an ox goad; and he also delivered Israel." Just who was this Shamgar, of whom we are told so very little?

Well, the Bible places Shamgar, like Deborah and Barak, after Ehud, which would make him roughly a contemporary of those two. This impression is later confirmed by the mention of him in Deborah's canticle in Judges 5:6. In addition, we can fix Shamgar geographically, because the Sacred Text tells us that he fought against the Philistines, a fact which places him in the west of the Holy Land. Thus, while Deborah and Barak were occupied with Israel's enemies to the east, Shamgar was dealing with those in the west.

But there is more. Shamgar is called the "son of Anath," a designation that appears not to be a patronymic, because Anath is not a masculine name. It is more likely a reference to Shamgar's birthplace, the Canaanite city of Beth-Anath ("house of Anath"), which served under tribute to Israel since the time of Joshua (Judges 1:33). Consequently, Shamgar was likely not an Israelite by blood. He certainly belonged to the chosen people by allegiance, however, and Israel's enemies were his own.

Some biblical historians, realizing that "son of Anath" (*ben-Anath*) is a geographical and not a patronymic reference, propose emending the Hebrew text to "of Beth-Anath" (*beth-Anath*), which would require changing only a single letter. Even this is unnecessary, however, because we know of another "son of Anath" a century or so earlier, during the reign of Pharaoh Ramses II; he was a Syrian sea captain allied to Egypt. Thus, the name itself was not unique, and no emendation of the Hebrew text is required to make Beth-Anath Shamgar's city of origin.

This Canaanite city Anath and the Greek city Athens were both named after the same patronal goddess, a lady well known in all the lands bordering the eastern Mediterranean, including Africa. The Ugaritic texts from Ras Shamra indicate that she was a goddess of war for the peoples of the Middle East, and Shamgar showed himself worthy of that martial tradition.

However, this does not mean that Shamgar was a warrior. Indeed, he seems to have preferred farming, as indicated by the reference to his ox goad. It is entirely reasonable to picture Shamgar, when there were no pesky Philistines around to distract him, patiently pacing hour by hour behind the plow, steadily looking straight ahead and not looking back (Luke 9:62). Resting on the plowshare, meanwhile, lay the pointed end of a sturdy piece of lumber, roughly eight feet long and about two inches in diameter at the other end, which Shamgar, while he plowed, kept tucked under his arm. Should the draught animals slow down more than he thought proper, the plowman let the thicker end of the long pole drop down into his hand and gave them a modest thrust with its point. Over time the oxen learned that it was hard to kick against the pricks (Acts 9:5; 26:14).

Shamgar was a steady, patient fellow who loved to till the soil, a man so quiet that the Bible tells us not a single word he ever spoke. He was also a pacific man, who did not even own a weapon. For all that, Shamgar was not someone safely messed with. He was particularly ill-disposed toward the Philistines, those recent invaders from Crete, uncouth and troublesome fools who, neglecting their own fields, bothered and wearied honest plowmen during working hours. Shamgar expressed his annoyance, over the years, by employing his trusty ox goad to dispatch some six hundred of the rascals to the nether regions. Six hundred was a respectable figure, evidence of a conscientious citizen doing his part to preserve decency and advance the public order. It earned Shamgar his brief place in the Bible, where he appears as a kind of Semitic Cincinnatus, occasionally obliged to interrupt the simple joys of agriculture in order to deal with knaves and ne'er-do-wells.

☙

6. DEBORAH MEETS THE CHALLENGE

Early in the history of the chosen people's occupation of the Promised Land appears the matriarchal and prophetic Deborah, the only woman listed among the "judges" that guided Israel's various tribes during the two centuries or so between the conquest and the rise of Saul. Most of what we know of Deborah comes from Judges 4—5, an historical account followed by a canticle showing signs of great antiquity. This material, prior to its incorporation into the literary sources of the Book of Judges, was probably preserved for a long time in Ephraim's narrative traditions at the shrine of Bethel, not far from which stood the palm tree under which Deborah was known to sit and deliver oracular guidance to the people. Although we are not explicitly told so, the reference to forty years of peace in Judges 5:31 has suggested to some readers that this was the length of Deborah's ministry.

The story of Deborah is chiefly preoccupied with two themes, soteriology and the moral life.

First, soteriology. The Deborah story is mainly an account of God's deliverance of Israel from her oppressing enemies ("And the LORD routed Sisera"—Judges 4:15), and it stands within a lengthy series of such stories united mainly by this common theme. Indeed, if the several traditions within Judges, drawn from quite diverse local settings and tribal traditions, are joined by any element beyond mere chronology, the motif of God's deliverance is certainly that element. The Book of Judges is essentially a detailed account of God's repeated deliverance of His people through the agency of charismatic figures prior to the rise of the monarchy. The key to understanding Deborah, surely, is through that general consideration.

With regard to the theme of the moral life, on the other hand, one readily admits that this consideration is of far less importance to the purposes of the Book of Judges. Truly, if the inculcating of moral example ranked very high among those purposes, it would be difficult to explain how some of the juicier stories in Judges ever managed to find their place at all! In the Deborah account, nonetheless, such a moral interest is certainly present, at least in a minor key, and it is to be discovered chiefly in the accented contrast between Deborah and the timid Barak.

Thus, St. Jerome observed that, if Barak had been a brave and decisive man to begin with, Deborah's intervention in the battle with Sisera would not have been necessary. He went on to compare her to Mary Magdalene, whom the Gospels likewise show to have been a courageous woman at the time of the Lord's death and burial, in conspicuous contrast to the intimidated, bewildered, and discouraged Apostles.

It is not surprising, then, that Christian readers have always seen the Deborah story as evidence of God's equal regard for men and women. Their comments in this respect are rooted, of course, in the particulars of the story itself. Indeed, the contrast between the forthright Deborah and the timid, reluctant Barak is one of the most obvious and entertaining examples of this literary technique in all of Holy Scripture. The robust directives of Deborah in Judges 4:6f ("Go . . . deploy . . . take") are met by the poltroonish foot-dragging of Barak in verse 8. His pathetic response is composed of two hypothetical pronouncements that leave all the initiative to Deborah: "If you will go with me, then I will go; but if you will not go with me, I will not go!" The very sounds of the Hebrew text mimic both the bee-like, rapid-fire delivery of Deborah (*lek wumashakta . . . welaqahta*) and the lifeless, melancholic mumbling of Barak (*'im telki 'immi wahalakti, we'im lo' telki 'immi lo'elek*).

This highly amusing contrast is further heightened by the fact that Barak's very name means "lightning bolt." The energetic Deborah is manifestly frustrated, having a difficult time persuading this lightning to strike! A few verses later, Deborah must sting the sluggard again: *Qum*—"Up!" (4:14). This sharp command, *qum*, is repeated in the canticle in Judges 5:12.

It is not surprising, perhaps, that Christian readers have traditionally seen the Deborah story as evidence of God's equal regard for men and women. On the other hand (if one may safely venture the remark), the woman in this contrast seems to be quite a bit more reliable than the man.

⋙

7. GIDEON AND THE MIDIANITES

It is a point of historical irony that the military success of Deborah and Barak, narrated in Judges 4—5, is what produced the crisis faced by Gideon in the chapters that follow. By his overthrow of the powerful Canaanite kings, Barak had removed a formidable military presence which prevented various tribes of Bedouin nomads, notably the Midianites and their confederates, from ravaging the cultivated fields, orchards, vineyards, and granaries of the Promised Land. Now, with the elimination of that impediment, those marauders could ride in on their camels and pillage the countryside at will.

Fearsome and unscrupulous predators, the Midianites were also cunning, for they habitually scheduled their invasions at harvest times, causing economic disaster, even famine, among the Israelites (cf. Ruth 1:1). Judges 6 describes how the Lord raised up Gideon as a champion to meet this crisis.

Gideon's task, however, would be more than merely political and military, because the crisis itself was more than political and military. In the Bible's analysis, the theological root of the problem was Israel's infidelity to the Covenant of Mount Sinai. Beyond the political aspects of their plight, it was clear to Gideon that God was punishing the Israelites for their involvement in the worship of Canaanite gods, whose chief was Baal. Indeed, Gideon's own father was a worshipper of Baal. The success of Gideon's mission would depend, therefore, on his first addressing that theological root of the difficulty.

He did so at once, taking ten men to assist him in the overthrow of the Baal shrine maintained by his father. From that point on, events began to unroll pretty rapidly, for a large invasion force of Midianites and others suddenly arrived from the east, crossed the Jordan River, and camped in the fertile valley of Jezreel. Probably impressed by the sheer boldness of Gideon, manifest in his attack on the worship of Baal, his countrymen spontaneously accepted his leadership to meet the impending attack.

It was clear to everyone, anyway, that Gideon was in charge of the situation, for the Spirit of the Lord took decisive hold of him (Judges 6:34). The Hebrew verb used to describe this transformation is especially striking, for it literally says that the Spirit "clothed itself" (*labshah*) with Gideon. This expression, sometimes used for the putting on of armor, indicates that Gideon would serve as the instrument of God's Spirit in the events to come.

The transformation of Gideon was evident to all. Whereas fear had prompted him to use the cover of night in destroying Baal's shrine (6:27), Gideon now began to act with open, executive boldness, sending out messengers to the other Israelites for their assistance in the impending battle.

Three scenes in particular have rendered most memorable the story of Gideon. First, there was a consultation of the Lord by means of "putting out a fleece" (6:36–40). The purpose of this experiment was to determine whether Gideon's resolve was truly of God, and not simply a human impulse for glory and vengeance. Just as Israel's crisis was radically spiritual, its resolution would have to be radically spiritual, so Gideon wanted to be quite certain that the new strength he felt was truly of the Holy Spirit, and not just a burst of what we today call adrenaline. It is most important not to confuse the flesh and the Spirit, especially during a crisis.

Second, there was the curious exercise by which, at the Lord's bidding, Gideon reduced the size of his gathered army. Indeed, the reduction was of ridiculous proportions—from thirty-two thousand to three hundred (7:1–8)! If this victory was to be truly of God, it was important that no human being could take credit for it, because the Sprit of God is not to be identified with any human force or fleshly impulse.

Third, there was Gideon's defeat of the Midianites by the singularly improbable means of the breaking of jars and the blowing of trumpets (7:15–23). This latter action is, of course, reminiscent of Joshua's overthrow of the walls of Jericho and conveys the identical message. Namely, that God, alone victorious over His enemies, alone deserves the praise, a truth to which Gideon himself bore witness by his subsequent refusal to become king (8:22–23). This was a lesson God's humbled people needed to learn, and their defeat of the Midianites would be in vain if they did not learn it.

ༀ

8. THE ENTERPRISING JUDITH

Ancient Christian interpretation of the Book of Judith was nearly always inspired by certain moral and ascetic themes. Almost invariably it was a matter of holding up some edifying aspect of the character of Judith, the book's heroine, for Christian emulation.

Among the virtuous aspects of the character of Judith especially emphasized as ethical and ascetic standards were her courage and self-sacrifice, her prayer and fasting, her sobriety and level-headedness, and the chastity of her consecrated widowhood, all of which features made her a ready instrument in the workings of God's salvific providence. For all the *risqué* elements of her story, Judith was especially regarded as a model of the Christian life.

Our earliest Christian reference to Judith's courage is early indeed. Addressing the church at Corinth about the year 96, Clement of Rome wrote: "Blessed Judith, during the siege of her city, begged of the elders that she might be permitted to go out into the camp of the enemies. So, exposing herself to peril, she went forth out of love for her fatherland and her people in the siege, and the Lord delivered Holofernes into a woman's hand." He then went on to compare Judith to Esther, who likewise risked her life for her people. God used both women to deliver the nation from destruction by specific threatening individuals, Haman in the instance of Esther, Holofernes in the case of Judith.

Clement's ideas on Judith were to become common themes in the traditional understanding of the book. First, there was the example of Judith's courage, which inspired her to place her life at risk for the sake of others. Ambrose of Milan and Isidore of Seville picked up this theme: "She did not fear death"; a model of fortitude, she showed herself to be "stronger, by ignoring danger and despising death." In all of this, Judith was motivated by "a fetching contempt for her own safety."

Second, there was Judith's striking similarity to Esther. Since the heroines in both stories were used by God to overcome cruel enemies in circumstances of great danger, it is not surprising that the two books were almost always named sequentially in the traditional lists of biblical literature. Both women, after all, defeated and destroyed specific enemies of God's people. As Ambrose observed, a more specific resemblance between Judith and Esther was the fact that both women also took to fasting as an integral component of their fight with evil.

Judith's fasting, moreover, was combined with prayer. Origen observed that she provided a model for both these features of the ascetic life. Said an anonymous medieval preacher: "Most holy Judith, whose prayers opened heaven, formed victorious weapons by the art of prayer."

In addition, Judith's prayer was the secret to her chastity, the continence that she carefully preserved inviolate. Her chastity was integral to the consecration of her widowhood, a celibacy dedicated to the glory of God, inseparable from her holiness.

Judith became, in short, the very ideal of the Christian widow, giving herself over to asceticism, fasting, and a life of consecrated celibacy, praying day and night for the Church. As such she was to be compared to the prophetess Anna, who was part of the welcoming committee that received the infant Jesus on his first visit to the temple. Some Christians commented that the biblical descriptions of both women are, in fact, very similar.

The story of Judith, finally, is an account of great irony, a feature of the narrative, the dialogues, and the characters. Much of the irony is found in the lady herself, this respectable widow turned seductress, this matronly and meticulous keeper of Israel's dietary laws plying her victim with alcohol, this almost monastic devotee of prayer and fasting who comes walking home one morning with a man's head tucked in her purse, returning once more to her simple, sanctified life of prayer and fasting, as though nothing out of the ordinary had ever happened!

Judith is a living example of the truth that God's ways are past finding out. Ultimately, the victory is God's, Judith being His mere instrument. At the end it is God's accomplishment that Judith praises: "I will sing unto the Lord a new song: O Lord, Thou art great and glorious, wonderful in strength, and invincible" (Judith 16:13).

※

9. ZOPHAR THE NAAMATHITE

Because he was the last to speak among Job's (alleged!) comforters, we should presume that Zophar was the youngest of those three. Whereas the Masoretic text speaks of him as a "Naamathite," likely in reference to a site in northwestern Arabia called Jebel-el-Na'ameh, the much older Septuagint version identifies him as "the king of the Mineans," a tribe in southern Arabia. Zophar was, in either case, an Arab.

Rather Arabian, too, was his attitude toward Job's problem, because Zophar's was a God experienced in the starkness of the desert. Arabs and other ancient nomads, unlike the tillers of the soil who were their contemporaries, were not people accustomed to thinking of God in terms of agricultural cycles and seasons. Gods of fertility, to say nothing of goddesses, were not much worshipped in the desert. While the nomad certainly invoked a Sky Father, that invocation normally had nothing to do with an Earth Mother, for only seldom did the desert dweller witness the rain that prompted the farmer to think of the Sky Father as a god of fertility.

Little preoccupied with earth, the religion of the Arabian nomad was not burdened with the complex and intricate rites and narratives associated with the agricultural divinities. It was, rather, a simpler religion concentrated on heaven, that vast vault overarching the trackless sands. For if the desert provided the Arabian with no constant and discernible path, heaven certainly did, because across its face moved the myriad celestial bodies in their appointed rotations and everlasting courses. The dweller in the desert would very quickly become lost unless he took his guidance from the stars above, so the religion of the desert was at once less complex and more predictable, its lines marked by a steadiness and predetermination unfamiliar to the rather undependable and often uncertain future of the farmer. And while the vastness and height of the sky proclaimed its independence from every human hope and need, the order—even the punctuality—of its regular gyrations conveyed the stable transcendence of solidly simple truths, entirely dependable because utterly unalterable. It was from the relentless desert that the mind of mankind learned the eternal and apodictic moral law.

Zophar, whose arguments are found in chapters 11 and 20 of the Book of Job, was the spokesman for that stern, demanding, moral religion learned across the sands beneath the vaulted heavens. He argued that if Job was suffering, then Job most certainly deserved to suffer: "The heavens will reveal his iniquity, / And the earth will rise up against him" (20:27). Eternally just is the moral structure of the universe. Indeed, he tells Job, "God exacts from you / Less than your iniquity deserves" (11:6).

Zophar, a man familiar with "the poison of cobras" and "the viper's tongue" (20:16), regarded Job's protestations of innocence as mere exercises in pretense:

Do you not know this of old,
Since man was placed on earth,

That the triumphing of the wicked is short,
And the joy of the hypocrite is but for a moment?
Though his haughtiness mounts up to the heavens,
And his head reaches to the clouds,
Yet he will perish forever like his own refuse;
Those who have seen him will say, "Where is he?"
He will fly away like a dream, and not be found. (20:4–8)

Even Zophar's abrupt rhetorical style resembles some turbaned rider from the desert, swooping down swiftly from the dunes, camel at the gallop, robes flowing in the wind, scimitar whirling aloft and menacing. Speaking of "my anxious thoughts" and "the turmoil within me" (20:2), Zophar's is the fierce, impetuous voice of the sandstorm. Whereas Bildad and Eliphaz speculated about Job's afflictions as a philosophical problem, Zophar will have none of this, but is even insulting to the sufferer. Job accuses Zophar of mockery (cf. 21:3, where the verb is in the singular) and the insensitivity of someone unfamiliar with personal affliction (12:4–5).

Zophar, in short, is not much given to calm, detached dialogue. Unlike Eliphaz the Temanite, he makes no appeal to his personal experience, nor, like Bildad the Shuhite, does he argue from the studies of the ancients. Zophar believes that things are what they are. The laws overarching the world are unalterable, and if Job cannot accept that fact, then he is "a man full of talk" (11:2), "an empty-headed man" (11:12), to be numbered among the "deceitful" (11:11) and "the wicked" (11:20). In the book's structure, Zophar's fierce impatience with Job functions as a major foil to Job's patience.

VI.

THE FELLOWSHIP OF CHRIST'S SUFFERINGS
_&^_

After the first half of the Gospel of Mark climaxes with Simon Peter's confession of Jesus as the Messiah (8:29), there immediately commences the dominating theme of the Gospel's second half, the way of the Cross. This latter half of Mark manifestly breaks into two parts. First, a narrative section (8:30—10:52) structured around the Lord's three prophecies of His coming Passion (8:31; 9:31; 10:32–34). Second, a detailed account of the last week of Jesus' earthly life (chapters 11—16).

The first part of Mark's second half is structured geographically, inasmuch as each of the three aforesaid prophecies is made in a location ever nearer to Jerusalem, where the final part of Mark takes place. These three prophecies are given in Caesarea Philippi (8:27), Capernaum in Galilee (9:30, 33), and the neighborhood of Jericho (10:46), each a step closer to Jerusalem. The importance of this journey to Jerusalem is emphasized by Mark's sustained use of the word "way" or "road" (_hodos_ in Greek, the root of our English word "odometer") all through this section (cf. 8:27; 9:33–34; 10:17, 32, 46, 52). Each of these Markan passages may be contrasted, in this respect, to their parallels in Matthew and Luke. Except for Matthew 20:30 and Luke 18:36 (corresponding to Mark 10:46), the word _hodos_ is not found in any other instance of Synoptic parallels to Mark. This fact indicates clearly that we are dealing with a special Markan accent on the "way" of the Cross. It is a Markan word.

In Mark's narrative, moreover, each of Jesus' three predictions of His Passion is met by some completely inappropriate response on the part of His disciples. In the first case, Simon Peter answers the Lord by declaring the whole idea of the Cross to be unacceptable: "And Peter took Him aside and began to rebuke Him" (8:32). In the second instance, Mark comments that the disciples "did not understand this

115

saying, and were afraid to ask Him" (9:32). Instead, they begin immediately to dispute "among themselves who would be the greatest" (9:34)! By way of response to the Lord's third prophecy of His Passion, "James and John, the sons of Zebedee, came to Him, saying, 'Teacher, we want You to do for us whatever we ask'" (10:35). Each time Jesus speaks of the Cross, the disciples fail Him miserably.

In all three examples, that is to say, the Lord's preaching to His disciples about the necessity of the Cross falls on various sorts of infertile soil. The first seed falls "by the *wayside* [*para ten hodon*]. . . . Satan comes immediately and takes away the word that was sown in their hearts" (4:15). Such is the case of Simon Peter, who refuses to hear the word of the Cross. Satan takes it from his heart. Testifying to this, Jesus addresses Peter, "Get behind Me, Satan! For you are not mindful of the things of God, but the things of men" (8:33).

In the second case, the seed "fell on stony ground, where it did not have much earth" (4:5). This is the instance exemplified by the shallow disciples who, when they hear the word of the Cross, promptly begin to argue among themselves for preeminence (9:33–34), illustrating how "when tribulation or persecution arises for the word's sake, immediately they stumble" (4:17).

In the third case, the "seed fell among thorns; and the thorns grew up and choked it" (4:7). This response is illustrated by James and John, who answer the word of the Cross by asking Jesus if they may sit on either side of Him in His glory (10:37). Their spirit of ambition and self-aggrandizement corresponds to "the cares of this world, the deceitfulness of riches, and the desires for other things" (4:19).

In short, the disciples of Jesus are still men of the world, mindful of the things of men and not the things of God; they are still self-centered and ambitious. To counter this "apostolic resistance" to His message of suffering and death, then, Jesus three times preaches a more elaborate sermon on "the word of the Cross," on the necessity of taking up the Cross and its shame (8:34–38), on the imitation of the Suffering Servant by becoming the servant of all (9:35; 10:42–45), and the commitment to live by the standard of the Cross implicit in the ordinances of Baptism and Holy Communion (10:38–40).

At the end of this section of Mark, and just prior to the Lord's entrance into Jerusalem to suffer and die (11:1), we meet blind Bartimaeus, who sits "by the road [or "way," *para ten hodon*]" and is given sight by Jesus. This new sight enables Bartimaeus to do what the other disciples have all along resisted doing: "And immediately he received his sight and followed Jesus on the road [or "way," *en te hodo*]" (10:46–52). Bartimaeus thus represents the true disciple who follows Jesus on the way of the Cross. At last the seed falls on good ground and bears fruit (4:8, 20).

శ్ర

1. ZECHARIAH THE PROPHET

Two passages from the sixth-century Prophet Zechariah are understood in the Gospel of Matthew as especially pertaining to the Passion and death of our Lord.

The first of these texts is Zechariah 9:9—"Tell the daughter of Zion, / 'Behold, your King is coming to you, / Lowly and sitting on a donkey, / A colt, the foal of a donkey'" (Matthew 21:5). The background of this passage is the story in 2 Samuel 15—17, where King David is portrayed fleeing from the rebellion of Absalom. Crossing the Kidron Valley eastwards and ascending the Mount of Olives, David is the king rejected by his people, while a usurper is in full revolt. The King leaves in disgrace, riding on a donkey, the poor animal of the humble peasant. David is the very image of meekness in the face of defeat. In his heart is no bitterness; he bears all with patience and plans no revenge.

As he goes, David suffers further humiliation and deception from those who take advantage of his plight. One of his most trusted counselors, Ahithophel, betrays him to his enemies; another citizen curses and scorns him in his flight.

Moreover, in the description of David fleeing from Jerusalem on the back of a donkey, there is a striking contrast with the victorious Absalom, the usurper, who is driving "chariots and horses, and fifty men to run before him" (2 Samuel 15:1). Absalom represents worldly power and worldly wisdom, contrasted with the humility and meekness of the king.

Incorporating this image of David as a mystic prefiguration of the Messiah yet to come, Zechariah prophesied the messianic entry of Jesus into Zion. The Savior arrives by the very path that David used to flee from the Holy City. Riding the donkey, our Lord comes down westward from the Mount of Olives, crosses the Kidron Valley, and finally enters Jerusalem. He thus begins the week of His meekly borne sufferings, including betrayal by a friend and rejection by His people.

The second such passage invoked by Matthew is Zechariah 11:13— "And they took the thirty pieces of silver, the value of Him who was priced, whom they of the children of Israel priced, and gave them for the potter's field, as the LORD directed me" (Matthew 27:9–10). Matthew cited this text as a prophecy fulfilled by Judas Iscariot in his betrayal of the Lord for thirty pieces of silver, the prescribed price of a slave (Exodus 21:32).

There is a curious confusion of words in this text of Zechariah, however, apparently seen by Matthew as pointing to a deeper layer of meaning. In the traditional Hebrew reading, the Lord tells the prophet: "Cast it to the potter [el-hayoser]." Zechariah goes on to say, "So I cast it, in the house of the Lord, to the potter," a reading reflected in several modern translations. With the change of only one letter, however, the Hebrew text would read: "Cast it into the treasury [el-hahoser]," and "So I cast it, in the house of the Lord, into the treasury." This latter reading is followed by other translations.

Rather than choose between these two possible readings, however, the Gospel of Matthew conflates them, maintaining both the temple treasury *and* the potter. Thus, Judas Iscariot, realizing the gravity of his betrayal but despairing of God's mercy, returns to the temple and throws in the thirty shekels. The clinking of those silver coins, bouncing and rolling across the stone floor of the temple, has been resounding in the ears of the Church for the past two thousand years, summoning every sinful soul back from the perils of final despair.

The temple officials collect the coins. Their first thought is to put them into the temple treasury (*hahoser*), but they are afflicted by a hypocritical scruple about such a use of blood-money. Instead, they take the coins and purchase the "field of the potter [*hayoser*]." The double disposition of these coins of Judas, the inspired evangelist saw clearly, was a fulfillment of a prophetic word spoken centuries earlier in that mystic text of Zechariah.

This "field of the potter," perhaps so named because of broken shards lying about in it, came to be known as the "field of blood," says Matthew, because it was purchased with blood-money. As such, this field is a very rich symbol of redemption. This obscure piece of real estate, bought with the price of the blood of Christ, became a sort of down payment on that ultimate redemption by which "the Lord's is the earth and the fullness thereof." By the price of His blood, Christ became the "Landlord," the Lord of the Earth. All this Matthew saw in the prophecy of Zechariah.

᪣

2. THE MOTHER OF THE SONS OF ZEBEDEE

The Gospels of Matthew (20:20–23) and Mark (10:35–40) record the occasion on which the two sons of Zebedee, James and John, request of the Lord the privilege of sitting to His immediate right and left when He enters into His kingdom. Still worldly and without understanding, the two brothers are portrayed as resistant to the message of the Cross.

In both Gospel accounts, the Lord's response to their request is to put back to the brothers a further query about their ability to "drink the cup that I am about to drink," and Mark's version contains yet another question about their being "baptized with the baptism that I am baptized with."

Both images used by our Lord in this context, baptism and the cup, are found elsewhere in the New Testament as symbolic of the Lord's Passion. Relative to baptism, one thinks immediately of Luke 12:50— "But I have a baptism to be baptized with, and how distressed I am till it is accomplished!" Interpreters since the second century have appealed to this Lukan passage to interpret the story of James and John. Relative to the cup, of course, the Synoptic descriptions of the Lord's agony in the Garden and His arrest show it to refer to His sufferings.

Obviously, in the context of the New Testament churches, the baptism and the cup referred symbolically to two of the sacraments, and it was understood, moreover, that these two sacraments place their communicants into a special relationship with the Lord's Passion. With respect to the Sacrament of Baptism, one thinks of Romans 6:3–4 ("Or do you not know that as many of us as were baptized into Christ Jesus were baptized into His death? Therefore we were buried with Him through baptism into death") and Colossians 2:12 ("buried with Him in baptism"). The sacramental relationship to the Lord's Passion is no less clear with respect to the Eucharist: "For as often as you eat this bread and drink this cup, you proclaim the Lord's death till He comes" (1 Corinthians 11:26). The questions about baptism and the cup, then, were most instructive for the Christians attending divine worship where these Gospel texts were read and interpreted.

Matthew's version, moreover, presents Zebedee's wife, the mother of the two brothers, approaching the Lord to make the request on their behalf. Nothing would be easier, of course, than to regard the wife of Zebedee as simply the unscrupulous promoter of her sons' selfish aspirations. Scenes of ambitious mothers endeavoring to promote the political fortunes of their sons are absolutely commonplace in ancient history, with examples from Assyria (Sammurammat, mother of Adad-Nerari III), Macedonia (Olympias, mother of Alexander), Rome (Agrippina the Younger, mother of Nero), and so forth. The Bible's memorable instance is the mother of Solomon, Bathsheba, in 1 Kings 1:11–12.

For all that, traditional Christian comments on the incident tend to "go easy" on Zebedee's wife, excusing her request as a weakness born of excessive maternal affection, pardonable anxiety, and so forth. Indeed, does not Mark's very omission of the detail indicate that the fault lay rather with the sons than with their mother? Surely the whole idea was theirs, not their mother's, it was argued. Her two sons had prevailed upon her, thinking thereby more easily to prevail upon the Lord.

Whatever the merits of these suggestions, it seems that they do less than full justice to a certain subtlety in Matthew's account, for he is surely implicating the mother in her sons' failure to understand the message of the Cross. This woman, elsewhere known as Salome, Matthew calls simply "the mother of Zebedee's sons." The detail is certainly significant, inasmuch as this designation, "mother of Zebedee's sons," appears only twice in the entire New Testament, both times in Matthew: here in 20:20 and later, in 27:56, at the foot of the Cross. In the first of these instances, Zebedee's wife is portrayed as an enterprising and somewhat ambitious worldling who fails to grasp the message of the Cross, while in the later scene we find her standing vigil as her Lord dies, now a model of the converted and enlightened Christian who follows Jesus to the very end. This marvelous correspondence between the two scenes—a before and after—is proper to Matthew and points to a delicate nuance of his thought.

⁂

3. MALCHUS

It is unlikely that Simon Peter and Malchus knew each other, the one being a Galilean fisherman and the other a servant of Caiaphas the high priest, living in Jerusalem. Nor is it probable, in the normal course of affairs, that the paths of these two men would ever have crossed.

Affairs were not following a normal course, however, on that fateful night just prior to Passover, when the destinies of Malchus and Simon came to an abrupt and dramatic confrontation in an olive orchard on the side of a hill just east of the Kidron Valley.

Malchus was part of an armed band sent by the high priest to arrest Jesus of Nazareth secretly, away from the eyes and impulses of the Passover crowds. This band was guided by Judas Iscariot, a defector from the small group of Jesus' close companions, for he was the one who could identify Jesus from within their number. The giveaway sign was an easy one; Judas would simply walk up to Jesus and kiss His hand, the customary greeting that a disciple gave to his rabbi.

Moreover, there is no reason to believe that Malchus himself regarded the coming event as especially significant. It had nothing to do with him, after all; he was simply the faithful servant of the high priest, expected to perform this task loyally, leaving to his betters the determination of such matters.

It was somewhat after midnight when that armed band left the house of Caiaphas, well to the south of the temple, proceeded northward along the Kidron Creek, and approached the little bridge by which they could cross over to the Mount of Olives on the opposite side. Those in the front carried lanterns and flambeaus to light the way, for the night was dark, in spite of the full moon of Passover. Some of the band were armed with swords, while others carried only clubs (Matthew 26:47). We are not sure just what Malchus had in hand.

Meanwhile, Simon Peter was once again awakened by the voice of Jesus, having fallen asleep three times in as many hours, even as he listened to the prayer of Jesus. Weak in flesh, Simon had utterly failed in the Master's command to watch and pray with Him (Matthew 26:41).

What a night. At the Passover Seder, just a few hours before, Jesus had disclosed the presence of a traitor among them and foretold that the rest of the little group would fail Him in His coming hour of trial (26:21–24, 31). Simon himself had been singled out for a special warning, as the Lord predicted his triple denial before that very night should run its course (26:33–35). It was all entirely too much for a man to bear, so Simon had slept there on the ground, under the olive trees.

But now he was awakened by the Lord's voice: "Rise, let us be going. See, My betrayer is at hand" (26:46). And here they were, a band of armed men already on the scene. Simon leapt up, holding a sword that he had brought to make good his promise of loyalty in the face of danger. He recognized Judas Iscariot, who came forward to Jesus and, in the customary fashion, kissed the hand of his rabbi. Just what was this all about?

The response of Jesus explained it all: "Judas, are you betraying the Son of Man with a kiss?" (Luke 22:48). Simon waited no further.

Malchus saw the sword coming from the right, aimed at his throat, and he ducked quickly to his left to avoid decapitation. Even so, his right ear was partly severed by the tip of the blade (Luke 22:50). Then Jesus stepped up, grabbed his dangling ear, and replaced it entirely to his head, as though nothing had ever happened. The rest of that night was a blur, and the whole next day, as he walked around in a daze, going to Pilate's and elsewhere, but ever reaching up from time to time to feel his ear and trying to make sense of it all.

Some decades later, Malchus, a Christian now for many years and long repentant of his actions on that dreadful night, sat down and described his part in the event to a physician named Luke, who happened to be writing a new account of the life and teaching of Jesus. Malchus told how the Lord reached out His hand through the enveloping darkness and reattached his dangling ear. "He made it as good as new, really. But, please, leave out my name," Malchus requested of Luke. He was not aware that another writer would put it in anyway (John 18:10). This other writer, John, had been present when it happened, and he may have learned the name of Malchus from a cousin, who encountered Simon in the courtyard of the high priest somewhat later that night (18:26).

৵৹

4. SIMON OF CYRENE

Although we know on the authority of Plutarch that every criminal condemned to crucifixion by a Roman court was obliged to carry his own cross to the place of execution, those soldiers charged with crucifying Jesus evidently believed that His weakened state would not permit Him to do so. Consequently, they obliged a "certain man . . . passing by" (says Mark) to carry Jesus' cross to the place of crucifixion. That man was returning to the city "from the country" (say Mark and Luke), perhaps for his midday repast. His name was Simon of Cyrene (Matthew 27:31–32; Mark 15:20–21; Luke 23:26).

A descendant of certain Jews who had settled on the north coast of Africa (in modern Libya) about 300 BC, Simon doubtless belonged to that synagogue in Jerusalem particularly frequented by Cyrenian Jews who had moved back to the Holy Land (Acts 6:9). These were among the Jews responsible for the stoning of Stephen.

Bearing the cross of Jesus was not Simon's idea. He was "compelled" (says Matthew, using the same verb as in 5:41). We are surely right, however, in thinking that the event proved to be a moment of providential grace for Simon, because he certainly became a Christian. Indeed, about forty years after the event, the Evangelist Mark mentioned him as the father of two Christians well known to the Roman church for whom he was writing: "Then they compelled a certain man, Simon a Cyrenian, *the father of Alexander and Rufus*, as he was coming out of the country and passing by, to bear His cross."

Simon's family was cherished by the Apostle Paul, who evidently had known them a generation earlier at Jerusalem. Some of them were living in Rome when Mark and Paul wrote. Very early in 58, about seven years before Mark's Gospel was written, Paul sent Rufus and his mother greetings in Rome: "Greet Rufus, chosen in the Lord, and his mother and mine" (Romans 16:13).

With respect to Simon's other son, Alexander, we are less certain. In late 1941, however, archeologists excavating the southwestern side of the Kidron Valley in Jerusalem made a stunning discovery. They uncovered a burial cave owned by a family of Cyrenian Jews, the graves in which were all earlier than the destruction of the Holy City in the summer of 70. Here the archeologists found an ossuary (bone box) with the Greek inscription, "Alexander the son of Simon." Same Simon and same Alexander? One would like to believe so, but the matter is far from certain.

However that may be, Simon of Cyrene himself lives on in the New Testament, intimately associated with the cross of Jesus. Luke's description of the event is especially instructive: "Now as they led Him away, they laid hold of a certain man, Simon a Cyrenian, who was coming from the country, and on him they laid the cross that he might bear it *after Jesus*" (*opisthen tou Iesou*). Luke is the only evangelist to express the matter in this way.

In order to see the significance this expression held for Luke, it is useful to compare the text with other Lukan passages. For example, Luke 9:23: "If anyone desires to come after Me [*opiso mou*], let him deny himself, and take up his cross daily, and follow Me." And 14:27: "And whoever does not bear his cross and come after Me [*opiso mou*] cannot be My disciple." Luke's latter text (particularly if we contrast it with the parallel in Matthew 10:38) shows that the bearing of the cross "after Jesus" is the true mark of *discipleship*. That is to say, Simon of Cyrene, bearing the cross and following after Jesus on the way to Golgotha, becomes the symbolizing embodiment of Christian discipleship.

Holy Scripture gives us no reason to think that Simon of Cyrene had been a believer in Christ before that day when Roman soldiers compelled him to assume the weight of the Holy Cross. That was the very beginning of his discipleship. He became, however, the model of those who follow Jesus to the place of His crucifixion, outside the walls of Jerusalem ("as they came out," says Matthew 27:32; "led Him out," says Mark 15:20). Carrying Jesus' cross, he shared in Jesus' shame. Simon paid heed to that exhortation of the Epistle to the Hebrews which is addressed equally to us all: "Therefore Jesus also, that He might sanctify the people with His own blood, suffered outside the gate. Therefore let us go forth to Him, outside the camp, bearing His reproach" (13:12–13).

※

5. THE DYING THIEF

Referring to the two thieves who died on either side of Jesus, St. Mark records that "those who were crucified with Him reviled Him" (15:32). At least they did so for some time. During the course of the afternoon, however, one of them came to think better of the matter, as he watched our Lord hang there in patience, praying for His enemies. St. Luke describes the scene:

> Then one of the criminals who were hanged blasphemed Him, saying, "If You are the Christ, save Yourself and us." But the other, answering, rebuked him, saying, "Do you not even fear God, seeing you are under the same condemnation? And we indeed justly, for we receive the due reward of our deeds; but this Man has done nothing wrong." Then he said to Jesus, "Lord, remember me when You come into Your kingdom." And Jesus

said to him, "Assuredly [lit., *Amen*] I say to you, today you will be with Me in Paradise" (23:39–43).

This profoundly moving scene is best considered, I believe, within both its immediate and its wider context in the Gospel of Luke. Three considerations suggest themselves with respect to Luke's immediate context. First, this scene with the thieves is the second of three times that Jesus is pronounced innocent. The first pronouncement was made by Pilate and Herod (23:14–15), and the third will issue from the lips of the centurion under the Cross (23:47). This verdict of the second thief, then, is added to the chorus of those who profess Jesus to be executed unjustly (23:41).

Second, the blasphemy by the unrepentant thief is the third and culminating instance in which the crucified Jesus is reviled in identical terms. First, there were the Jewish rulers who challenged Jesus to *save* Himself if He was the Messiah (23:35). Then the Gentile soldiers defied Him to *save* Himself, if He was a king (23:37). Finally, the unrepentant thief challenges Jesus to *save* Himself, adding "and us" (23:39). We observe that the same verb, "save" or *sozein*, is used in all three instances. The thief's reviling of the Lord thus forms a climax to the theme.

This sequence prepares for its foil, the scene's culminating irony, in which only one man, the "good thief," perceives the true path to salvation. He boldly grasps the salvific meaning of Jesus' death. He is the "good thief," indeed. In his final and defining act of theft, as it were, he extends his soul and clutches hold of eternal life.

Third, the encounter with the two thieves immediately precedes the death of Jesus, so that Jesus' words to the second thief, promising to meet him that day in Paradise, are His last recorded words to another human being during His earthly life. The good thief represents the repentant Church gathered at the Cross, and the words that he hears are the last thing that Jesus has to say to His people on earth.

With regard to the wider context of Luke's Gospel, there are two points particularly worthy of note in this story of the thieves. First, in drawing a contrast between the two men, Luke follows a pattern of antithesis that he has employed throughout his entire narrative. For instance, it is Luke who immediately opposes the Beatitudes with the Woes (6:20–26). It is Luke who elaborates in detail the differences between the Pharisee and the woman who came into his house (7:44–47). It is Luke, likewise, who contrasts two men who went up to the temple to pray (18:9–14), the two sons of the same father (15:27–32), the rich man and the pauper (16:19–22), the faithful and unfaithful servants (12:35–39), the leper and his nine companions (17:17), the rich donors and the poor widow (21:1–2). Luke's opposition between the two thieves, then, is the climax in a lengthy series of contrasts.

Second, Luke's good thief is the final example of individuals who confess their guilt in the hope of obtaining divine mercy. Earlier instances include the Publican in the Temple (18:13), the Prodigal Son (15:21), and the repentant woman (7:36–50). In all of these examples, Luke's narrative resonates with the Pauline emphasis on justification by faith. While in each of these examples the characters come to God with no justifying works of their own, this note is especially obvious in the thief on the cross, who turns to Jesus for mercy with literally no time left to do anything except repent and die.

Finally, this thief seems to ask for so very little. Sensing that our Lord is about to go to some destiny different from his own, he modestly pleads, "Remember me." Ah, but "the grace shown is more abundant than the request made," commented St. Ambrose. That very day the dying thief will be with Jesus. Here the Sacred Text employs the very expression, *with*, habitually used by St. Paul to describe eternal life. Everlasting glory consists in being *with the Lord* (Romans 6:8; 2 Corinthians 5:8; Philippians 1:22–23; 1 Thessalonians 4:17; 5:10). It has been justly remarked that the good thief was canonized even before his death. In the words of St. John Chrysostom, "The thief, after doing so many evil things, entered into Paradise before everyone else, because he did not become discouraged" (*Homilies of Repentance* 1.15). It is hardly a wonder, therefore, that Holy Church, when chanting the evangelical Beatitudes during the Divine Liturgy, habitually uses as an antiphon the prayer of the dying thief, "Lord, remember me when You come into Your kingdom."

⸰꙳

6. JOSEPH OF ARIMATHEA

Because Jesus could not rise from the grave unless He had been buried, an explicit insistence on His burial may be noted in the Church's earliest proclamation. Paul himself, who knew its importance from the earlier tradition (1 Corinthians 15:4), included it in his own preaching (Acts 13:29) and writing (Romans 6:4). All the canonical Gospels, moreover, agree that Jesus was buried by Joseph of Arimathea, a prominent member of the Sanhedrin.

Joseph himself is variously portrayed by the four inspired writers. Mark (15:43) and Luke (23:51) describe him as someone who "was waiting for the kingdom of God," an expression which, taken without context, might indicate no more than that Joseph was a devout Jew. (I will argue presently that it does mean more.) Luke adds that Joseph, though a member of the Sanhedrin, had not consented to its plot against Jesus. Matthew (27:57) and John (19:38) are more explicit about Joseph's faith, both of them calling him a "disciple"—that is, a Christian—though John observes that he was so "secretly, for fear of the Jews."

In their slightly differing descriptions, the evangelists may have been portraying Joseph of Arimathea at somewhat different stages of his "spiritual pilgrimage," to use the customary expression. If this is the case, then it appears that the death of Jesus, the very hour of His apparent failure and defeat, was the occasion Joseph chose for getting really serious in his commitment, going public about his Christian discipleship. He approached Pontius Pilate—"boldly," says Mark—and asked for the body of Jesus.

This Joseph, precisely because he "waited for the kingdom of God," had intended to be buried, not in Ramathaim, his native village, but in Jerusalem itself. The grand prophecies of messianic restoration, after all, especially those of Ezekiel and Zechariah, were centered in Jerusalem. Accordingly, in the holy city, Joseph had purchased for himself a special burial vault that was situated, says John (18:41–42), in a garden not far from where Jesus had died. According to Matthew and Mark, this tomb was carved out of solid rock. Luke and John both mention that it was brand new.

This elaborate burial arrangement suggests that Joseph of Arimathea was a man of some means. Indeed, Matthew (27:57) explicitly records that he was rich. This detail is, furthermore, of theological significance, because God's Suffering Servant, according to prophecy, was to be buried "with the rich" (Isaiah 53:9).

Luke features certain parallels between the account of Joseph of Arimathea and the infancy narrative, near either end of his Gospel. First, of course, a Joseph is prominent in each story. Second, in each account the naked, helpless body of Jesus is decently wrapped (2:7, 12; 23:53). Third, Luke's portrayal of Joseph of Arimathea is strikingly similar to his description of Simeon, who welcomed the newborn Jesus on His first visit to the temple (2:25). Thus, both stories begin with "and behold" (*kai idou*). Both men are called "just" (*dikaios*), and both are said to be "waiting." Simeon is "waiting for the Consolation of Israel," and Joseph is "waiting for the Kingdom of God." This complex set of parallels establishes a literary inclusion in the Lukan structure.

In all of the Gospels, Joseph's actions are contrasted with those of the other members of the Sanhedrin. Whereas they blindfolded, mocked, and abused Jesus, Joseph treats even his dead body with dignity and respect. Although executed criminals were often buried in a common grave, or even left as carrion for wild beasts, Joseph carefully places the body of Jesus in a special tomb, a place befitting the dignity of the coming Resurrection.

An image of Jesus lying in Joseph's grave is inscribed on the antimens on every altar of the Orthodox Church. Facing that image each Sunday during Matins, the priest proclaims one of the Resurrection accounts from the Gospels. The altar is thus preeminently the liturgical *situs* of the Resurrection. Michelangelo, in his final and less famous *Pieta*, the one at Florence, portrayed Joseph of Arimathea in his own likeness. I have long thought, similarly, that that just man who buried Jesus in his own sepulcher serves as a model for all believers. That tomb, originally planned for Joseph, has been unoccupied these many centuries, a symbol of the hope we have for our own graves.

⁓

7. NICODEMUS, THE VISITOR BY NIGHT

The Pharisee Nicodemus, "a ruler of the Jews" and "a teacher of Israel," appears only three times in the New Testament. Each time Nicodemus appears in St. John's Gospel, it is always in the context of the Lord's redemptive death.

First, it was to Nicodemus that Jesus made His earliest explicit reference to His coming crucifixion: "And as Moses lifted up the serpent in the wilderness, even so must the Son of Man be lifted up, that whoever believes in Him should not perish but have eternal life. For God so loved the world that He gave His only begotten Son, that whoever believes in Him should not perish but have everlasting life" (3:14–16).

John next speaks of Nicodemus as the sole member of the Sanhedrin to raise his voice against the plot to take Jesus' life (7:45–52).

We do not hear of Nicodemus again until immediately after the death of Jesus, who was, at last, "lifted up" on Golgotha. In this third instance, Nicodemus appears as the companion of Joseph of Arimathea, assisting him in the Lord's burial: "And Nicodemus, who at first came to Jesus by night, also came, bringing a mixture of myrrh and aloes, about a hundred pounds. Then they took the body of Jesus, and bound it in strips of linen with the spices, as the custom of the Jews is to bury" (19:39–40).

The expression "be lifted up," used by our Lord in His discourse with Nicodemus, is repeated halfway through John's Gospel, again with reference to the crucifixion: "'And I, if I am *lifted up* from the earth, will draw all peoples to Myself.' This He said, signifying by what death He would die" (12:32–33). In addition to being a reference to the crucifixion, the expression "lifted up" also alludes to a prophecy of God's Suffering Servant: "Behold, My Servant will prosper; He shall *be lifted up* and glorified exceedingly" (Isaiah 52:13, LXX). As this text makes clear, the Lord's *lifting up* refers not only to His crucifixion but also to His exaltation in glory.

In this respect it is useful to compare the Lord's words to Nicodemus, as recorded in John, to the predictions He makes about His coming sufferings, as recorded in the Synoptic Gospels. It is noteworthy that what Jesus proclaims to His closest disciples in the Synoptics, He proclaims to the Pharisee Nicodemus in John. We may take Mark 8:31 as an example. In the Markan text, as in John, the defining verb is "must" (*dei*), which refers to God's determined plan of redemption. In each text also, Jesus calls Himself "the Son of Man." Thus, in Mark 8:31, "the *Son of Man must* suffer many things . . . and be killed, and after three days rise again," while in John 3:14, "so *must* the *Son of Man* be lifted up." If these verses are to be regarded as theological equivalents (which seems reasonable), Mark's inclusion of the Resurrection among the things that *must* happen suggests that John's "lifted up" includes the Lord's glorification as well as His crucifixion.

In John's theological vision, the Lord's glorification is manifest even in His mounting of the Cross. His very death is an assertion of His authority: "I lay down My life that I may take it again. No one takes it from Me, but I lay it down of Myself. I have power to lay it down, and I have power to take it again" (10:17–18).

It is in discoursing with Nicodemus, then, that Jesus first calls Himself "the Son of Man" and refers to the necessity of His sacrificial death. We do not know the immediate response of Nicodemus, but the Lord's words finally smite this Pharisee's heart when he sees them being fulfilled on Golgotha.

John's account of the Lord's sufferings stresses that Jesus died as a king (18:36–37; 19:2, 15, 19, 21), and Nicodemus certainly witnessed the death of a king. Whereas all the Gospels credit Joseph of Arimathea with the burial of Jesus, John tells us that it was Nicodemus who determined that Jesus would be buried as a king. First, Jesus would be laid to rest in a garden (19:41), like His royal ancestors, the ancient kings of Judah (2 Kings 21:18, 26). Then, to the ministry of properly burying this King of the Jews, the now-converted Nicodemus would bring a kingly measure of myrrh and precious spices, about a hundred pounds. This burial garden was, after all, the King's garden of which Holy Church says, "My beloved has gone to his garden, / To the beds of spices" (Song of Solomon 6:2). It is on this "mountain of myrrh" that He will lie in rest "until the day breaks and the shadows flee away" (4:6).

⁂

8. THE INEFFICIENT MYRRHBEARERS

Among the figures with whom Christians gather round the empty Tomb in paschal season, there is a special prominence pertaining to the Myrrhbearers, those women disciples who shouldered their newly purchased spices and came to anoint the body of Jesus. They formed the first "women's guild" of the Church, one might say, and they had just done duty a couple of days earlier at the foot of the Cross. Excluded from the public "official list" of the Resurrection eyewitnesses (preserved in 1 Corinthians 15:5–8), these women are nonetheless featured with distinction in the narratives of Pascha morning in all four canonical Gospels. Only a few of them we know by name: Mary Magdalene, "the other Mary" (manifestly a kinswoman of the Mother of Jesus, because she is "the mother of James and Joses"—Matthew 27:56; 28:1; Mark 16:1; Luke 24:10), Salome (Zebedee's wife), Joanna.

Now there is a certain kind of "practical" person, an efficiency expert, who does not much appreciate what the Myrrhbearers were up to. Had he encountered them on the road that morning, he might well have asked them, "Just what good do you think you are going to accomplish?" You see, anointing a dead body does not make good business sense. It achieves nothing very practical. It is the sort of activity that fails to contribute to the Gross National Product. Except for its very small influence on the myrrh market, spice trading, and nard futures, it barely shows up on the Dow Industrials. It has no measurable results. The corpses thus anointed cannot be interviewed to ascertain if they are satisfied with the product, or which brand they prefer, or whether they would recommend it to their neighbors. Anointing dead bodies resists a quantitative analysis. So an economist like Ludwig von Mises, were he to discuss it in his very long and unbelievably boring book, *Human Action* (which I read all the way through for a Lenten penance one year), would call this activity of the Myrrhbearers "autistic." That is to say, it is the kind of activity that produces only a subjective and emotional benefit to the one who does it. It involves no "transaction," which Von Mises and his sort think to be the truly valuable sort of human activity.

Another economist and efficiency expert, this one from an earlier period, also adopted an emphatically negative perspective on a certain lady's pouring out of ointment. "To what purpose is this waste?" he objected. "This ointment might have been sold for more than three hundred pence and given to the poor." (The final part of his analysis is interesting for its suggestion of altruism in his calculation. The evangelist, however, did not fall for the ruse—see John 12:5–6.) Judas Iscariot, you see, was heavily engaged in quantitative thinking. He wanted measurable results. Judas was a practical man. He knew a good price when he saw one. Shrewdly he could size up any situation and calculate what it was worth on the basis of cost and output. Like Francis Bacon, Jeremy Bentham, Ludwig von Mises, Rudolph Carnap, and Ayn Rand, Judas Iscariot believed that objective, verifiable truth is invariably logical and quantitative. Only then does it have "significance." If you can measure it, these folks tell us, then you can know it. Everything else is just opinion, purely subjective and unverifiable.

Over against this modern point of view is the completely unproductive, uneconomical, inefficient assessment of the ointment-pouring scene at Bethany: "She has done what she could" (Mark 14:8). In that assessment of the thing, we arrive very near the heart of the Gospel.

Quite simply: We do what we can. We do not attempt to measure what we do, certainly not by its perceived results. We act solely out of love, letting God alone determine whether we have "loved much" (Luke 7:47). The final quality of our lives will not be assessed by what we have accomplished, but by our love (1 Corinthians 13:24). Only the God who reads the heart can put a value on that love.

Prominent in the midst of the Church, then, are those Myrrhbearers who came that morning loaded down with their spices and without the foggiest idea how they were going to enter a sealed tomb guarded by a massive stone. What an exercise in inefficiency, lack of cost analysis, and failure in planning. As it turned out, they could not even find a body to anoint. All that myrrh, just going to waste.

⁘

9. DOUBTING THOMAS

St. Thomas was a philosopher. Lest, however, this statement sound too obvious, let me promptly say that I don't mean Thomas Aquinas but Thomas the Apostle.

The philosophy embraced by Thomas the Apostle was not of an academic brand. It was, rather, the peasant variety, a common type, the truly useful school of thought that aids an ordinary man to brace up in adversity, face disaster bravely, and cope with valor on the bitter day. A philosopher of this sort is less interested in exploring the essence of things, and more concerned about how to get through life without falling to pieces. Thus, he emphasizes sobriety of soul and is deeply suspicious of anything even faintly resembling fun. His aspirations are modest, the better to soften the inevitable disappointments that life will bring. Ever resigned to the next unforeseen but inexorable tragedy, fairly certain that all will come to a bad end, this philosopher tightens the reins on enthusiasm and dissuades his heart from inordinate hope. The last thing he would trust is a bit of good news.

If such a school of thought can be summarized in two sentences, those sentences might be an hypothesis and an imperative: "If anything can go wrong, it probably will. Get used to it." One could never be too cautious, after all, or he risked getting too rosy a picture of things. Therefore, be careful. Near every silver lining lurks a cloud. Some, I suppose, would call this philosophy pessimism, but those who espouse it usually think of themselves as realists.

Such a philosopher was Thomas the Apostle, significantly known to history as "Doubting Thomas." One suspects, however, that the doubting of Thomas had less to do with his epistemological system than with his nervous system. Ever brave to drain the draught of sadness and misfortune, he dared to imbibe joy, if ever, only in small sips.

Thomas, therefore, was very cautious about all those miracles and healings that he witnessed. Things were going far too well. There had to be a downside to the whole business. All these blind people were receiving their sight, to be sure, but who could say what they would see before the thing was all over?

It came as no great surprise to Thomas, then, when he learned that disaster lay just down the road. Indeed, Thomas was the first among the Apostles to embrace the imperative of the Cross. Unlike Peter ("Get behind Me, Satan!"), he put up no resistance to the news. When Jesus declared His intention of going to Jerusalem to "wake up" Lazarus, the other Apostles expressed their fear at the prospect. "Rabbi," they answered, "lately the Jews sought to stone You, and are You going there again?" It was Thomas who found within himself the generous strength to say, "Let us also go, that we may die with Him" (John 11:8, 16). In this scene, Thomas is no skeptic. He is, rather, very much the realist, the man who discerns the stark realities awaiting His Lord at Jerusalem, and he is resolute with respect to his own course in the matter. When it comes to the prospects for tragedy, Thomas is not deceived by any inappropriate optimism. Nor, let it be said, by cowardice. If there is one thing he knows how to take with a stiff upper lip, it is bad news. It is, so to speak, his specialty.

Thomas may also have been something of a loner, which would explain why, when the risen Lord paid His first visit to the assembled Apostles, Thomas "was not with them when Jesus came" (20:24). He apparently had gone off to get a better grip on himself. It had been a very tough week. Just as Thomas had foreseen, Jesus' life had ended in tragedy. This, the Apostle was sure, was the biggest tragedy he had ever seen. Yet he was coping with it somehow. Years of an inner docility to inevitable fate had schooled him in the discipline of endurance. Yes, he would get through this too. He was a man who could deal with misfortune and sorrow.

Thomas returned to the other Apostles in the "upper room" that evening, having wrestled his soul into a quiet acquiescence. It was the first day of a new week. He had faced down the disaster, and his control over life was starting to return. What he had not anticipated, however, was that the other Apostles, in his absence, would completely lose their minds. "Well, Thomas," one of them announced, "fine time to be gone. We have seen the Lord, and you just missed Him!"

Thomas knew how to deal with sorrow. His real problem had always been how to deal with happiness. And that problem was about to get a lot worse. A whole week the risen Lord would make him wait, sharing that room with the ten other men to whom he had hurled his challenge: "Unless I see in His hands the print of the nails, and put my finger into the print of the nails, and put my hand into His side, I will not believe" (20:25). As each day passed, the case for skepticism was strengthened.

But then it happened. The room was suddenly filled with a great light. New evidence had arrived and stood now undeniable on the scene. Doubting Thomas sensed that his long-established thinking was about to be rather deeply shaken. However embarrassed, he rose and turned toward the entering light, bracing himself to learn a bit of good news.

VII.
CLEVER SAINTS AND WISE
乳

Developed in many contexts and over several centuries, the wisdom tradition contained in the Bible is varied and rich.

In what is probably its earliest stage, Israel's interest in the pursuit of wisdom is seen in those old accounts of the practical shrewdness of their ancestors. One recalls, for example, the cleverness of the Hebrew midwives at the beginning of Exodus, those ladies who outwitted the evil designs of Pharaoh. There was also young David, of course, who consistently tricked the king of Philistia in the closing chapters of 1 Samuel. Most of all, perhaps, one thinks of Jacob and how he outsmarted even the wily Laban. In these, as in many other instances over the centuries, it was sharp, artful thinking that guaranteed the family's survival, and it is clear that the storytellers of the Bible loved to describe how their forebears could out-think their opponents.

As Israel became a real political entity after the Exodus, there emerged the need to incorporate that ancient familial trait into public policies. Indeed, the need was pressing. Almost immediately after entering the Holy Land, Israel had been duped into an unwise treaty by a local group called the Gibeonites (Joshua 9), and the wiser Israelites began to ask themselves how a nation so easily deceived by the lackluster Gibeonites would fare against the likes of Egypt and Syria. It was necessary, then, to advance intelligent men to positions of national leadership, especially after Israel's adoption of a monarchy near the end of the eleventh century. As Israel endeavored to create a geopolitical place for itself near the western end of the Fertile Crescent, such men would be trained in the arts of diplomacy, finance, and international trade. Examples would include Elihoreph and Ahijah, who served in the court of Solomon (1 Kings 4:3).

Alongside this sophisticated cultivation of political prudence, Israel's search for wisdom was also preserved in the folk traditions of its non-governing citizens, especially the farmers, craftsmen, and local merchants.

This latter form of wisdom is contained mainly in short, pithy sayings, easily memorized from childhood, maxims of the sort collected and preserved in the Book of Proverbs. The wisdom in this book is traditional, in the sense that the emphasis falls on such themes as fidelity to inherited standards, respect for the teachings of parents and elders, adherence to Israel's historical legacy, and so forth. The tone is immensely conservative, recommending what may be called tried and true, safe and sane. The Book of Proverbs habitually asks "how?" not "why?" Wisdom there is mainly practical, not speculative. It has to do with sobriety of judgment, prudence in one's business affairs, personal discipline in the use of one's time, money, and other resources, strict marital fidelity, and the consequent joys of home, property, tradition, and family.

Quite different is the approach to wisdom taken in the Books of Job and Qoheleth, or Ecclesiastes. These two books are not traditional and conservative. They are better described as bold and probing. They do not ask "how?" but "why?" They undertake the investigation of those philosophical questions in which the Book of Proverbs showed no interest, such as man's sense of tragedy and futility in life. Indeed, individual pages of Ecclesiastes and Job are sometimes shocking in the boldness of the questions they put to God. Their voices push toward the outer limits of speculative reflection about the meaning of suffering and the temptation to despair. The author of Ecclesiastes, facing frustration throughout all of existence, seems perpetually on the brink of discouragement and despondency, sentiments so alien to the stern cheerfulness and cautious optimism of the Book of Proverbs.

Finally, the wisdom pursued in Holy Scripture is the Wisdom of God Himself, that Wisdom by which He created the world and continues to govern history. This Wisdom is described in Proverbs 8 and several parts of The Wisdom of Solomon and The Book of Ecclesiasticus, or Ben Sirach. It is the teaching of these texts that man's mind, purified by discipline and transformed by God's grace, can be illumined and elevated to the contemplation of this Divine Wisdom that gives structure and significance to all of reality.

৵৹

1. SHIPHRAH AND PUAH

Right from its beginning, the Book of Exodus is the account of a conflict between the liberating wisdom of God and the enslaving stratagems of Egypt. This confrontation between two kinds of knowledge is especially evident in the mounting tension between Moses and Pharaoh, as each man tries to outwit the other over the destiny of the Israelites.

For example, as Moses and Pharaoh challenge one another, plague by plague, each conceals from the other man his true plans for the story's final outcome. Moses pretends that he wants to take the Israelites into the desert for only a few days, whereas he has in mind, and intentionally hides from his opponent, a larger and bolder project. Pharaoh, for his part, proposes slight concessions to Moses from time to time, with no intention of ever giving in. He will go back on his every pledge.

Eventually, of course, Pharaoh will meet more than his match in this Moses, who not only was "learned in all the wisdom of the Egyptians" (Acts 7:22), but also was the spokesman for the all-wise God. It is an intended point of irony that Pharaoh will ultimately be defeated by his own shrewdness, a quality that the Bible calls "hardness of heart."

It is instructive to observe that the hostile cunning of Pharaoh against the Israelites is introduced in Exodus at the very commencement of the account. "Come, let us deal shrewdly with them," he says (1:10). The introduction of this important motif so early in Exodus stands in parallel with the story of deception near the beginning of Genesis and, in fact, serves to tie these two biblical books together. As the encounter between the Serpent and Eve is about to begin, the former is described as "more cunning than any beast of the field" (Genesis 3:1). Thus, both books, Genesis and Exodus, commence with a wily enemy endeavoring to deceive God's people and bring them to ruin.

This literary juxtaposition, nonetheless, mainly serves to introduce a contrast. On the one hand, the Serpent in Genesis is far too shrewd for Eve, and the woman is quickly outwitted and caused to fall. This is not what happens in Exodus, however, where Pharaoh utterly fails to outsmart the two Hebrew midwives, Shiphrah and Puah. These two wise women are thus contrasted with the gullible Eve.

The source of their wisdom, Exodus indicates, is that "the midwives feared God" (1:17). This assertion serves to introduce the biblical principle that "the fear of the LORD is the beginning of wisdom, and the knowledge of the Holy One is understanding" (Proverbs 1:7; Psalm 110[111]:10, LXX). Since they knew and feared God, there is no wonder that the midwives were able to outwit the hapless Pharaoh, who would boast that he knew not the Lord (Exodus 5:2).

Thus, for the first time in Exodus the Israelites "pull a fast one" on Pharaoh, demonstrating a superior wisdom that will eventually make them victorious over the Egyptians.

This theme of victorious wisdom introduced in the story of Shiphrah and Puah serves also, in turn, to tie Exodus back to the Joseph narrative at the end of Genesis. Joseph and Moses are portrayed as alike in their superiority over the wisdom of the Egyptian sages.

Moreover, just as Pharaoh was outwitted by two Hebrew women in the first chapter of Exodus, so his hostile policy is again thwarted by two more such women, the sister and mother of Moses, in the second chapter. When Pharaoh's daughter discovers the baby Moses in the basket floating on the Nile, she is tricked by Moses' sister into hiring the child's mother to nurse her own baby! Thus, the family of hostile Pharaoh is deceived into nurturing and raising the very instrument of his downfall. These early stories in Exodus serve, then, to show that Pharaoh, for all his vaunting and bluster, never stood a chance against Moses.

Shiphrah and Puah also take an honorable place among the wise women employed by the Lord to bring deliverance to His people on so many pages of Holy Scripture: Deborah and Jael, Abigail, Esther, Naomi and Ruth, Rahab of Jericho, Tamar in Genesis 38, Judith, Michal in 1 Samuel 19, Joab's "actress" in 2 Samuel 14, that millstone-tossing Shechemite lady who dispatched Abimelech in Judges 9, and the anonymous female citizen who supervised a much-needed beheading in 2 Samuel 20.

⸱ᴥ⸱

2. ABIGAIL, BEAUTIFUL AND WISE

In 1 Samuel 25, at a point roughly halfway through the description of David's exile, comes the endearing account of his meeting with Abigail and of their eventual marriage. Reckoned among the most winsome narratives in the Bible, it is a story interesting, and even intriguing, from several aspects. The principal interest of the biblical author himself is properly theological, especially the theme of wisdom.

Even though she will not become an active participant in the drama until verse 14, Abigail is immediately introduced with her husband,

Nabal, near the very beginning of the account. This stylistic arrangement allows the author to establish early what becomes a sustained contrast between the two characters throughout the story. Abigail is "a woman of good understanding and beautiful appearance," whereas her husband "was harsh and evil in his doings" (v. 3). The rest of the account, elaborating the differences between a wise, attractive woman and her sottish, offensive husband, thus becomes a narrative enactment of the tension between Wisdom and the Fool, a standard theme of the Bible's sapiential literature.

Nabal was rash, compulsively driven, hot-tempered, sharp-tongued, stubborn, stingy, impossible to reason with, and a very slow learner. A major feature of Nabal's moral imbecility was the failure to appreciate his wife's wisdom. Long habituated to ignoring her example and her counsel, he followed his own path to self-destruction. His household servants summed it up: "He is such a scoundrel that one cannot speak to him" (v. 17).

Notwithstanding the conditions of her marriage, however, Abigail is not a woman to sit around agonizing over her fate. On the contrary, she is the very embodiment of the resourceful, energetic, and "virtuous wife" described in Proverbs 31:10–31: loving and patient, disciplined, hard-working and efficiently organized, wise and discerning, endowed with a gentle disposition and pleasant speech. Abigail's household is so well ordered that, with no prior notice, she can promptly put together an enormous meal (including two hundred loaves of bread!) to feed David's entire army (1 Samuel 25:18). A woman of great practical insight, she acts with dispatch; three times in the one chapter we are told that she "made haste" (vv. 18, 23, 42). The attentive reader gains the impression of a woman who decided, years ago, that her very survival would require an energetic but disciplined approach to life.

To save her household, therefore, Abigail goes out to meet the outraged David. This latter, sadly, is not far behind Nabal in rashness of temper. Vowing an exorbitant retaliation for Nabal's arrogant affront, he too is on the point of playing the Fool (cf. Proverbs 14:17). But then Abigail, acting as David's own personal Lady Wisdom, comes to seek him out, giving the "soft answer [that] turns away wrath" (Proverbs 15:1), instructing him not to "answer a fool according to his folly, lest you also be like him" (26:4). As the personification of Wisdom on David's behalf, Abigail "has slaughtered her meat, / She has mixed her wine, /

She has also furnished her table. / She has sent out her maidens, / She cries out from the highest places of the city" (9:2–10).

In his hour of impending moral peril, then, David's deliverance comes from receiving the instruction of Wisdom (Proverbs 15:32–33). He is thus rescued from an evil course of action that his anger had caused to seem proper (16:25; Ecclesiastes 7:9). The wise Abigail exhorts him to patience and restraint. She persuades him to abandon his foolish vow of blood-vengeance and to leave retribution to a provident God.

Thus rescued from the edge of destruction, David recognizes and praises Abigail as a woman of sense and discretion. The ultimate, decisive difference between David and Nabal is that the one will listen to Abigail's exhortation and the other will not. The wise man gladly receives instruction and reproof, but the fool does not.

As the discerner of Wisdom, moreover, Abigail serves in a prophetic role. She perceives God's true purpose in history, foretelling David's ascent to the throne and the founding of his dynasty: "The LORD will certainly make for my lord an enduring house" (1 Samuel 25:28; see also v. 30). She asks for herself only to be "remembered" by David (25:31), a modest petition that is providentially granted in the marriage that ends this lovely story with both irony and extravagance.

※

3. HUSHAI THWARTS AHITHOPHEL

In calling Him "the Son of David," the early Christians expressed their conviction that Jesus was the fulfillment of everything Israel had been promised in that great historical figure, who was the father of Judah's messianic line. For this reason Christians studied carefully the life and career of Israel's second king, so as to miss no aspect of the prophecies associated with him. In fact, we find this detailed preoccupation with David already obvious in the Church's first sermon (Acts 2:29–36).

Moreover, in interpreting David through the lens of Christ, those Christians were not obliged to start from scratch, because Israel's prophets had bequeathed them a great deal of material interpretive of David's life and significance. One such prophet was Zechariah.

Zechariah had based one of his messianic prophecies on the figure of David as the latter fled from the rebellion of Absalom (2 Samuel

15—17). He remembered King David, crossing the Kidron Valley east-wards and ascending the Mount of Olives, rejected by his people. The king left in disgrace, riding on a donkey, the poor animal of the humble peasant. David was the very image of meekness. As he went, he suffered further humiliation from those who took advantage of his plight, but in his heart was no bitterness; he bore all with patience, planning no re-venge. Unlike the usurping Absalom who drove "chariots and horses, and fifty men to run before him" (2 Samuel 15:1), David rode on the back of a little donkey. The Prophet Zechariah, seeing all of this as a narrative prophetic of the greater David yet to come, exclaimed, "Re-joice greatly, O daughter of Zion! . . . Behold, your King is coming to you; . . . Lowly and riding on a donkey, / A colt, the foal of a donkey" (Zechariah 9:9). This oracle the early Christians saw strikingly fulfilled near the end of the earthly life of Jesus (Matthew 21:5).

Furthermore, amidst all King David suffered that day, there was even a foreshadowing of Judas the traitor. The man's name was Ahithophel, and he was one of David's trusted counselors. Truly, the resemblances between Judas and Ahithophel are remarkable. Ahithophel, joining the conspiracy against David (2 Samuel 15:12; 16:15, 23), sought to seize him by night (17:1), just east of Jerusalem (15:23), so that all his companions would flee (17:2). Judas, joining the plot against Jesus (Matthew 26:3–4, 14–16), led the conspirators to seize Him by night (26:47–48), just east of Jerusalem (26:36), causing His companions to flee (26:56). Whereas Ahithophel hanged himself when his treachery failed (2 Samuel 17:23), Judas hanged himself when his treachery suc-ceeded (Matthew 27:5). Just as Judas Iscariot, then, is the obvious trai-tor in the New Testament, Ahithophel is the obvious traitor in the Old. The one betrayed the "type," the other its fulfillment.

There was a good reason that Ahithophel's betrayal did not succeed like that of Judas, and the reason's name was Hushai the Archite. A sagacious man worthy of the office of "king's companion" (1 Chronicles 27:33), Hushai hoped to join the fleeing David's paltry force and par-take of his flight. From this plan he was dissuaded nonetheless. Meeting the king on the Mount of Olives, near the very site where Judas would later betray Jesus (2 Samuel 15:30–32; Luke 22:39), Hushai was per-suaded by David to return to Jerusalem in order to serve as the king's secret agent in the capital and thereby thwart the evil counsel of Ahithophel (2 Samuel 15:34–37). Going back to the city, Hushai succeeded completely, both frustrating Ahithophel's designs (17:5–14) and then disclosing Absalom's schemes to David (17:15–22). Joab and the army would do the rest.

This union of wisdom and personal loyalty, fused in the perilous setting of Absalom's rebellious court, renders Hushai one of the truly attractive figures in Holy Scripture. He also well exemplifies the biblical principle that true wisdom is tried by fire and strife. His obedience to David caused Hushai to do a dangerous thing, but he very bravely placed his wisdom at the service of his loyalty, rather than his own safety, and in doing so he became the instrument of God's intention to frustrate what even the biblical author thought the sounder counsel of David's betrayer: "For the Lord had purposed to defeat the good advice of Ahithophel, to the intent that the LORD might bring disaster on Absalom" (17:14).

&

4. ELIHOREPH AND AHIJAH

One sign of the greater complexity of Solomon's political administration (961–921 BC) is the fact that the king employed two scribes, or secretaries (1 Kings 4:3), whereas his father David had been content with just one (2 Samuel 8:17). Solomon's scribes were two brothers, Elihoreph and Ahijah, and it is doubtless significant that the name of their father, Shisha, was Egyptian. Solomon had recently married a daughter of Pharaoh Psousennes II (1 Kings 3:1), an event sealing his political and mercantile dealings with Egypt, and these two talented young men likely came to the new king's attention during the course of those negotiations. It is also not improbable that the two brothers saw in Solomon's enlightened reign in Israel a chance to make their escape from the meager prospects offered by Egypt's moribund Twenty-first Dynasty. Whatever the reason, Elihoreph and Ahijah came to Jerusalem to work for Solomon.

The dignity and prominence of the brothers' new office is implied by their being named immediately after Zadok the priest in the list of Solomon's court officers (4:1–6). Indeed, the royal scribes (*sopherim*, a word related to *sepher*, "book") of ancient kingdoms were extraordinarily important men, the administrators of what we today call the "state department," the overseers and instructors of diplomatic delegations, the authors of treaties, juridical decisions, contracts, royal decrees and other legislation, all kinds of state documents and other official papers that would eventually be handed over to the royal archivist (*mazkir*— 4:3) to be preserved for the instruction of future generations.

Thus, much of what we know of ancient history we ultimately owe to such men. Their hands held the stylus, brush, or pen that inscribed the Edict of Ammisaduqa, the laws of Eshnunna, Hammurabi's Code, the vassal treaties of Esarhaddon, the Amarna Letters, the Mari and Nuzi Tablets, the archives of Tut-ankh-Amon, the Aramaic papyri from Elephantine, and scores of other documents. The writings of such men also provided source material for historians like Herodotus, Thucydides, Polybius, Diadore of Sicily, Diogenes Laertius, Tacitus, Suetonius, and others. We would know precious little of ancient times except for the carefully preserved records of ancient scribes. Our debt to them is beyond calculation.

When they came to work for Solomon, then, Elihoreph and Ahijah stepped into a noble calling, exercising an office at Jerusalem later to be held by the likes of Shebna under King Hezekiah (2 Kings 18:18), Shaphan under King Josiah (22:3), and Jonathan under Judah's last king, Zedekiah (Jeremiah 37:15). Of the literary sources used by the later authors of Holy Scripture, the official transcripts of these men were surely among the most prominent, nor is it conceivable that we would even have the Books of Kings, Chronicles, and Ezra without them.

These considerations lead to another question: Did Solomon's two scribes write any parts of the biblical text itself? Truly, it is not hard to make a case that they did. Scholars commonly ascribe much of the two Books of Samuel (and even some individual narrative parts of the Pentateuch) to the work of historians in the court of Solomon, nor is it unreasonable to identify those historians as Elihoreph and Ahijah or the staff that worked under them. At the very least, the office held by these two men was such as to render it unthinkable that any writings from the Solomonic court would have been published without their supervision.

The scribal work of Elihoreph and Ahijah was part of a larger, official literary concern that characterized the reign of Solomon. It is to his era that textual historians trace much of the source material for certain parts of Holy Scripture. Moreover, that same fourth chapter (vv. 30–34) of 1 Kings goes on to speak of Solomon's own sapiential and literary culture, and the Book of Proverbs contains at least two bodies of writing under his name (10:1—22:16 and 25:1—29:27). Himself a man of letters (and the son of a poet), it is easy to picture Solomon staffing his court with men of literary talent, and we students of the Bible are the beneficiaries of that talent. To this day, when we read those marvelous accounts of David and his colorful contemporaries, it is intriguing to think of that rich material coming down to us through the hands of two young scribes from Egypt.

⤳

5. THE WORDS OF AGUR

Proverbs 30 contains the first of the book's three final collections of wisdom maxims, a collection called "the words of Agur, the son of Jakeh." The Hebrew text further identifies Agur and Jakeh as "of Massa," the same place in northern Arabia (Genesis 25:14; 1 Chronicles 1:30) from which came King Lemuel in the following chapter. Agur, the son of Jakeh, is not called a king, however, nor is he otherwise identified. It is reasonable to suppose, therefore, that he must have been a figure of some renown among the readers for whom the Book of Proverbs was intended, requiring no further introduction.

What we have in Proverbs 30 is a philosophical discourse delivered by Agur and recorded by his two disciples, otherwise unknown, named Ithiel and Ucal. Ancient history from places as diverse as China, India, Egypt, and Greece provides other examples of such discourses given by philosophers and transcribed by their disciples. One thinks, for instance, of the notes that Plato and Xenophon took at the feet of Socrates.

One also thinks, perhaps, of the "Deer Park Sermon" of Siddhartha Gautama, transcribed by Ananda or one of the Kasyapas. Unlike Siddhartha, however, whose recent enlightenment (*Bodhi*) prompted him to discern a relentless Chain of Causation in existence and to devise an ascetic system for dealing with it, Agur of Massa confessed himself completely bewildered by the whole thing: "Surely I am more stupid than any man, / And do not have the understanding of a man. / I neither learned wisdom / Nor have knowledge of the Holy One" (Proverbs 30:2, 3).

Such a sentiment makes Agur resemble Socrates more than Siddhartha. Socrates, we recall, once identified by the Delphic oracle as the world's wisest man, spent his life trying to prove the oracle wrong. Socrates finally concluded, however, that the oracle must be right because he discovered all reputedly wise men to be just as ignorant as himself, except that they were not aware of being ignorant. Socrates concluded that it was as though the oracle had declared, "Among yourselves, oh men, that man is the wisest who recognizes, like Socrates, that he is truly nobody of worth [*oudenos axsios*] with respect to wisdom." Socrates and Agur, then, both associate the quest of wisdom with a humble mind.

Whatever his resemblance to the wise Athenian, nonetheless, Agur more readily puts us in mind of the Psalmist, who confessed to God, "I was so foolish and ignorant; / I was like a beast before You" (Psalm 72[73]:22), and "Such knowledge is too wonderful for me; / It is high, I cannot attain it" (138[139]:6).

Whereas the philosophical humility of Socrates was spawned of epistemology—that is, the accepted limitations of the human being's ability to know—that of Agur was inspired rather by theology and cosmology, the sheer vastness of the myriad things God created to be known: "Who has ascended into heaven, or descended? / Who has gathered the wind in His fists? / Who has bound the waters in a garment? / Who has established all the ends of the earth?" (Proverbs 30:4). Agur's are the sorts of reflections we associate with God's final answer to Job (Job 38—39).

With scant confidence in his own intelligence, then, Agur began the quest of wisdom by trusting in "every word of God" (*kol 'imrath 'Eloah,* Proverbs 30:5), which word he described, exactly like the Psalmist, as "pure," *seruphah* (Psalm 118[119]:140). He then turned to prayer, the only explicit prayer in the whole Book of Proverbs, in which he begged the Almighty for a modest life, free of falsehood. The life that Agur craved from on high would be neither wealthy nor poor, in order to avoid both arrogance and desperation, either of which might lead him into sin.

Agur did not think very highly of his contemporaries, whom he described as disrespectful of authority and tradition, morally dissolute and socially irresponsible, insatiable in their appetites, and entertaining too high an opinion of themselves. If one looks closely at Agur's criticism, it is clear that his complaint against his contemporaries had a fourfold structure. In fact, Agur was especially fond of maxims based on the number four: the four things that are never satisfied, four things too hard to understand, four things the world cannot endure, four small but wise animals from whom men could learn useful traits, and the four things "which are stately in walk" (Proverbs 30:29).

Agur's was, in short, the simple, observant philosophy of a humble man, content to live in this world by the purity of God's word and a prayerful reliance on God's gifts, offending the Almighty neither by the food he put into his mouth nor by the words he caused to come forth from it.

୬୭

6. LEMUEL'S MOTHER

Destined someday to be the king of Massa, a small realm in northern Arabia (cf. Genesis 25:14; 1 Chronicles 1:30), Lemuel was grateful to a wise mother for several verses of practical instruction that would serve him well in the years ahead. That instruction, being brief, could be inscribed on a single small sheet of vellum or papyrus, and Lemuel probably had a number of copies made for his friends. As gifts, those copies he also shared with other kings in the region, so that his mother's instructions made the rounds of various royal courts, carried by emissaries otherwise dispatched to attend to the diplomatic and mercantile concerns of Massa.

In due course, one of those emissaries came to Jerusalem to arrange some commercial treaty or other with King Solomon. Lemuel, well acquainted with Solomon's universal reputation for wisdom (cf. 1 Kings 4:31), had sent along a copy of his mother's instructions as a personal gift.

Now it happened that Solomon was in the process, just then, of editing a collection of traditional wisdom proverbs. Gladly receiving Lemuel's little scroll, therefore, he read it promptly and was so impressed that he incorporated the maternal instructions verbatim into his collection. Thus now, three thousand years later, we read those brief instructions of Lemuel's mother in Proverbs 31:1–9.

Perhaps significant also is the context in which Solomon placed the instructions of Lemuel's mother in the Book of Proverbs. Namely, immediately in front of the famous description of the ideal wise woman (31:10–31). Was Solomon thereby paying the Queen Mother of Massa a compliment, suggesting that she herself exemplified that description?

I doubt that I am the only reader who has entertained this thought.

Although the Book of Proverbs several times recommends that a young man pay attention to the teaching of his mother (1:8; 6:20; 15:20), these verses from Lemuel's mother are the only example of maternal teaching explicitly contained in Proverbs. And, on reading this material, we gain the impression that it is not, on the whole, much different from the instruction that a young man received from his father. There are warnings against lust (31:3) and drinking alcohol (31:4), along with an exhortation to take care of the oppressed and the poor (31:5–9).

Some of the material here resembles that in other ancient collections of teaching intended for future rulers. For example, "The Instruction of King Meri-Kare," an Egyptian manuscript preserved (as Papyrus Leningrad 1116A) in St. Petersburg, contains a collection of such teaching from near the end of the third millennium before Christ.

Lemuel's royal mother obviously embodied a traditional form of wisdom, heavily accented with good sense and moral responsibility. In this respect her instruction is of whole cloth with the rest of the Book of Proverbs.

The most ancient form of the wisdom tradition, of which Lemuel's mother and the Book of Proverbs are good representatives, was not much concerned with the kinds of thorny speculative questions that preoccupied Ecclesiastes and the Book of Job. It did not normally raise theoretical reflections about the meaning and purpose of life. It contained nothing suggestive of the "cutting edge" of new ideas that might distract from the serious business of getting on with a good and useful life.

The inherited wisdom tended to ask "how" a person should live in a difficult world rather than "why" he should go on living in a difficult world. Instead of inquiring "Why do the innocent suffer?" it suggested ways of avoiding those sufferings that a man might bring upon himself by not living wisely.

The wisdom of Proverbs and Lemuel's mother may be called conservative and traditional, a wisdom proved repeatedly in the experience of previous generations. It would certainly discourage a young man from "marching to a different drummer" or "doing his own thing." It emphasized such themes as fidelity to inherited standards of responsibility, respect for the teachings of parents and elders, hard work, fiscal conservatism, sobriety, virtue, principled judgment, prudence in one's business affairs and matters of state, personal discipline in the use of time, money, and other resources, strict marital fidelity, and the consequent joys of home and family.

Although history has left us no other record of Lemuel, we are probably justified in thinking of him living to an old age on the throne of the kingdom of Massa, dying secure in the memory of grateful citizens who recalled his wise and benevolent reign. It should not surprise us, either, if some archeologist should someday uncover his tomb and find the inscription: "Here lies Lemuel, King of Massa, whose final words were, 'I owe it all to Mom.'"

༄

7. EZRA THE SCRIBE

Ezra, normally regarded as the major biblical figure in the fifth century before Christ, merits that high assessment as a priest, a scholar, an activist reformer, and a man of prayer.

On the traditional and reasonable presumption that the Artaxerxes spoken of in Ezra 7:7–11 is Artaxerxes I (465–425 BC), Ezra arrived at Jerusalem in 458, thirteen years before Nehemiah. His priestly lineage abundantly established (7:1–5), Ezra came from Babylon with a task clearly related to the official worship in the temple. Authorized by a letter from the emperor (7:11–28), he arrived with a retinue that included priests and other temple ministers (7:7; 8:2), as well as arrangements for finances and appointments for the temple (8:24–30). Subsequent events would demonstrate that the governance of the temple, especially the discipline of the clergy, was in need of a strong hand, and the hand was Ezra's.

Ezra was also a scholar, which the Bible indicates by calling him "a skilled scribe in the law of Moses" (7:6). The Hebrew word for scribe, *sopher*, is an active participle of the verb *saphar*, which originally meant "to count" but also, by extension, could mean "recount," or "narrate," and hence "write." When Ezra is identified as a *sopher*, then, that word is perhaps more accurately translated as "bookman," or even "man of letters." The rendering in the canonical Greek text, *grammateus*, suggesting "grammar" and other such English words, expresses the sense clearly. Indeed, there is a fairly strong tradition, which includes the erudite Saint Jerome, that Ezra was an editor of the Pentateuch (and author of the closing chapter of Deuteronomy, which records the death of Moses) while he was still living in Babylon.

Ezra was Jerusalem's major teacher of the Mosaic Law during the period after the Babylonian Exile. This is certainly how he is portrayed in one of the most memorable scenes associated with him, the public reading of the Torah in Nehemiah 8. Ezra had been engaged in editing the Torah, and the people wanted to hear it. They gathered to the east of the city, and as Ezra read the text in Hebrew, which by now was only a scholar's language, running translations were provided in the common spoken language, Aramaic. It was a scene of great emotion, with the experiences of conversion, remorse, and rejoicing mixed together.

Ezra was also an activist reformer. By temperament a resolute person, he was a confident and forceful leader who saw things in black and white, a man little given to nuanced views, someone who inspired trust by conveying a sense of certainty and command. He would have made neither a good discussion leader nor a reliable talk-show host.

Ezra was, however, a persuasive and decisive speaker, as we see in the great scene where he reprimanded those Jews, especially priests, who had married outside of their religion (Ezra 10). He gathered the offenders in the rain and simply overwhelmed them with the righteousness conveyed by his towering moral presence, persuading them to take steps deeply repugnant to very deep instincts and warmly cherished preferences. Under the barrage of steady rain and Ezra's firm invective, the crowd became completely cooperative. It was a turning point in Israel's history.

Before speaking to the people, however, Ezra fortified his soul with prayer (Ezra 9). He made this prayer with uplifted hands at the time of the vesperal sacrifice, during which it was usual to pray in this posture (cf. Psalms 134[133]:2–3; 141[140]:2). We especially note in his prayer that Ezra did not separate himself from this sin of the people, though he himself had not committed it; the sin involved "us" (vv. 6, 7, 10, 13, 15). Because of this solidarity he maintained with those for whom he prayed, Ezra was an effective intercessor. His cruciform posture during the evening sacrifice was theologically appropriate, because the Old Testament's evening sacrifice was a type of and preparation for that true oblation rendered at the evening of the world, when the Lamb of God, nailed to the Cross, lifted His hands to the Father in sacrificial prayer for the salvation of mankind. This was the true lifting up of the hands, the definitive evening sacrifice offered on Golgotha, by which God marked His seal on human destiny. Ezra was, in this respect, a type of Christ our Lord.

ॐ

8. THE SON OF SIRACH

Joshua ben Sirach, the author of the Book of Ecclesiasticus, lived and wrote in the early second century before Christ. Thus he was among the last authors of the Old Testament. Although he composed his work in Hebrew, most of the original text is now preserved only in fragments, the largest (containing 39:27—44:17) being found at Masada in 1964. For the past two thousand years, however, the Christian Church has preserved the entire Greek translation of Ecclesiasticus that was made by his grandson in Egypt sometime after 132 BC.

Ben Sirach represents Israel's older, more conservative pursuit of wisdom. That is to say, he especially cherishes the time-tested truths of experience, the practical lessons derived from antiquity through tradition. Thus, he is not given to theoretical speculations, the bold probing of problems of the sort we find in Qoheleth and Job. He is not much disposed to search out matters above his abilities (3:21) or engage in unwarranted curiosities (3:23). Often enough, he believes, such pursuits are largely pretentious (3:25).

For this reason, perhaps, Ben Sirach has sometimes been regarded as excessively pessimistic about human abilities. For example, Herman Melville, himself hardly an optimist, remarked, "And, now that I think of it, how well did those learned doctors who rejected for us this whole book of Sirach. I never read anything so calculated to destroy man's confidence in man" (*The Confidence Man*, Chapter 45). Well, speaking for myself, I could mention any number of books that accomplish this task far more effectively. *Moby Dick* comes to mind.

While Ben Sirach entertains no great hopes for men without God's grace, it is not the case that his attitude toward things human is cramped and narrow. Indeed, the very opposite is true. For starters, he clearly loves literature and is well versed in that of his nation, particularly the Torah and the Wisdom books. In addition, Ben Sirach has traveled widely and appreciates the personal enrichment available to the traveler (34:9–11). He especially values the scientific skills of medicine (38:1–8; contrast 2 Chronicles 16:12). His hymns (42:15—43:33), in addition, testify to both his regard for the wonders of nature and his personal abilities as a poet. Ben Sirach has lived a long time and reflected wisely on the varying fortunes of human life (51:13–22), but he is no pessimist.

While the perspective on wisdom in Ecclesiasticus closely follows Israel's older approach, which is characteristic of the Book of Proverbs, two differences are usefully noted.

First, Proverbs is essentially a compilation, in that it preserves its wisdom sayings in traditional forms derived from a variety of ancient sources. In Ecclesiasticus, by contrast, the wisdom sayings are distilled through the personal reflections and literary craft of a single teacher and writer. Thus, in Ben Sirach's portrayal of the ideal rabbinical sage (38:24—39:11), he may as well be giving us a description of himself. When he instructs the young man coming to the service of God to prepare his soul for temptation and adversity (2:1–5), he understands from experience whereof he speaks.

Second, Ben Sirach's perspective on wisdom, by reason of its extensive recourse to biography, is less abstract than that of Proverbs. That earlier book consisted mainly of apothegms that had already been employed for a long time in a thousand different contexts; well before they reached their literary form in the Book of Proverbs, those maxims had become general, universalized as it were, having lost the personal qualities they may have carried in their original contexts. Thus, there is nothing personal in Proverbs, in the sense of biographical. There is nothing comparable to Ben Sirach's "praise of famous men," which is one of the most remarkable and endearing parts of Ecclesiasticus (44:1—49:16).

In this lengthy section Ben Sirach, setting in review the revelation of God's wisdom in the lives of great men over an extended historical span, from Adam to Nehemiah, gives praise to God for that revelation. Even as he speaks of "praising famous men," it is really God who is given the glory: "The Lord has wrought great glory by them through His great power from the beginning" (44:2).

And this, surely, is the answer to be made to critics like Melville, who regard man as God's rival and imagine that God's glory must work to man's diminishment. Ben Sirach would have found that attitude rather strange, even a bit inhuman.

ॐ

9. APOLLOS OF ALEXANDRIA

Apollos was no ordinary man. Raised in the first century after the Incarnation in Alexandria, at that time the intellectual center of Greco-Roman civilization, this young Jew was educated in the rich mix of two great cultures, the Hebraic and the Hellenic. It was in the synagogue at Alexandria, around three centuries earlier, that the Hebrew Scriptures had first been translated into Greek, causing Moses to speak to the world in the tongue of Homer, and somber Job in the tones of Sophocles. Furthermore, it is entirely probable that Apollos was personally acquainted with the most famous member of the Alexandrian synagogue, the philosopher Philo (roughly 20 BC to AD 50), who employed the insights of Plato to interpret the Old Testament.

Apollos, sometime before Aquila and Priscilla met him at Ephesus, had become a disciple of John the Baptist, one of several indications that the religious movement associated with John's name had spread well beyond Palestine. It is perhaps in his connection with John the Baptist that Apollos appears the most extraordinary. Since "he knew only the baptism of John" (Acts 18:25), we would not have expected Apollos to be familiar with the Holy Spirit. Other individuals, after all, who had been baptized only into "John's baptism," had "not so much as heard whether there is a Holy Spirit" (19:2–3). The deficiency of John's baptism consisted in its inability to confer the Holy Spirit. In fact, John the Baptist had made this point himself: "I indeed baptized you with water, but He will baptize you with the Holy Spirit" (Mark 1:8). In the case of Apollos, nonetheless, we are told that he was, literally translated, "boiling with the Spirit" (*zeon to Pneumati*—Acts 18:25).

This description of Apollos suggests that he had already become something more than a disciple of John the Baptist. Even previously, we are told, he had been "instructed [*katechemenos,* "catechized"] in the *way* of the Lord" (18:25), the same "way" (*hodos*) in which Aquila and Priscilla will instruct him further (18:26). Inasmuch as The Acts of the Apostles several times employs the identical word "way" as a simple metaphor for the Christian life itself (16:17; 19:9, 23; 22:4; 24:14, 22), Luke's double application of this word to Apollos surely signifies that he was already pursuing the Christian faith, albeit with imperfect knowledge.

When they met Apollos in Ephesus early in the year 52, Aquila and Priscilla were doubtless concerned about the church at Corinth, which they, along with Paul, had left the previous year (18:18). As companions of the Apostle Paul during the eighteen months that he had evangelized that troublesome place (cf. 18:2–3, 9–11), it perhaps seemed to them that the wisdom of Apollos, "an eloquent man and mighty in the

Scriptures" (18:24), might be the very thing to renew the strength of the Corinthian congregation. In any case, Apollos wanted to go to Corinth, so Aquila and Priscilla, having further instructed him, wrote a letter of recommendation for him, "exhorting the disciples to receive him" (18:26–27).

Nor were they disappointed, inasmuch as Apollos "greatly helped those who had believed through grace; for he vigorously refuted the Jews publicly, showing from the Scriptures that Jesus is the Christ" (18:27–28). So successful was Apollos's ministry, moreover, that the Corinthian church experienced a whole new influx of converts.

Unfortunately, some of the new converts, perhaps attracted by the superior erudition of Apollos, assumed a supercilious attitude toward the original but less gifted members of the Corinthian congregation, among whom there were "not many wise according to the flesh, not many mighty, not many noble" (1 Corinthians 1:26). This latter group, thus spurned, began making indelicate comments about the "uppity newcomers in the parish," and before long the congregation was divided between those declaring "I am of Paul" and those proclaiming "I am of Apollos" (1:12). Utterly mortified by this development, Apollos returned to Ephesus.

He was present in Ephesus in the spring of 55, when an exasperated Paul wrote an epistle to address the sad situation at Corinth, which had meanwhile grown even worse. Paul had hoped that Apollos would carry that epistle to the Corinthian church for him, but Apollos evidently found the whole matter too uncomfortable (16:12). In the following year we find him working as a missionary in Crete with a lawyer named Zenas (Titus 3:13).

St. Jerome much later tells us that Apollos returned to Corinth as its bishop, but I am among those who doubt it. If Apollos had returned to Corinth, Eusebius of Caesarea could hardly have failed to speak of it in his history of the early Church. The congregation at Corinth, moreover, continued to manifest a serious divisiveness until the end of the century. About the year 96 they received a very firm letter of reprimand on that matter from St. Clement, the third bishop of Rome.

VIII.
GENTLE SAINTS
꿏

When someone opens the Four Gospels for the first time, even if he is yet an unbeliever, it seems hardly possible that he will fail to observe the compassion and gentleness of Jesus of Nazareth. Even though such a reader cannot yet correctly answer the question, "What do you think about the Christ? Whose Son is He?" (Matthew 22:42), he nonetheless finds vibrant in those pages a figure "who went about doing good" (Acts 10:38), a Person supremely attractive for His gentleness and mercy. Jesus Himself, moreover, drew attention to this trait, making it a motive for men to become His disciples. "Take My yoke upon you," He said, "and learn from Me, for I am gentle and lowly in heart" (Matthew 11:29).

Five aspects of this self-description of Jesus are especially striking and worthy of reflection.

First, the Greek word here translated as "gentle," *praüs*, conveys the sense of humility and heartfelt meekness. Indeed, the words "gentle" and "lowly in heart," placed together in this verse, form an adjectival hendiadys expressing a single idea. Significantly, *praüs* is also the adjective that Matthew uses to speak of those meek who will inherit the earth (5:5). With respect to the gentleness of Jesus Himself, this same evangelist cites a prophecy of Isaiah (42:2–3) that he sees fulfilled thereby: "He will not quarrel nor cry out, / Nor will anyone hear His voice in the streets. / A bruised reed He will not break, / And smoking flax He will not quench" (12:19–20).

Second, the immediate context of Jesus' invitation to "learn" from Him speaks of His communion with the Father: "All things have been delivered to Me by My Father, and no one knows the Son except the Father. Nor does anyone know the Father except the Son, and the one to whom the Son wills to reveal Him" (11:27). The gentleness of Jesus, then, is not simply a preferred psychological trait, as it were. Rather, it is revelatory of the gentleness of God. It shows forth the regard of the Father toward those who agree to "learn" from Jesus.

Third, there is nothing weak and feeble about the gentleness of Jesus. It is, rather, the gentleness of the divine strength. Those tempted to interpret the gentleness of Jesus as some sort of benign "nonjudgmentalism" and general tolerance are invited to examine more closely the very context in which Matthew speaks of it. Our understanding of Jesus' gentleness must be sufficiently energetic to include such sentiments as, "Woe to you, Chorazin! Woe to you, Bethsaida! . . . And you, Capernaum, who are exalted to heaven, will be brought down to Hades. . . . But I say to you that it shall be more tolerable for the land of Sodom in the day of judgment than for you" (11:21, 23, 24). Jesus discoursed of His communion with the Father and His gentleness toward men, Matthew informs us, at the very time (*en ekeino to kairo*— 11:25) that He spoke these very harsh words to the unrepentant cities of Galilee. Evidently the gentleness of Jesus is not incompatible with a generous measure of brimstone.

Fourth, Jesus' gentleness has special reference to His suffering and death. The other time when Matthew uses the adjective *praüs* to describe our Lord is found in the story of His dramatic entry into Jerusalem to inaugurate His Passion. Matthew quotes a prophecy of Zechariah (9:9), which Jesus thus fulfills: "Tell the daughter of Zion, 'Behold, your King is coming to you, / Lowly [*praüs*], and sitting on a donkey' " (21:5). The gentleness of Jesus is the humility of the Cross, that obedience by which He emptied Himself and took upon Himself the form of the Suffering Servant, whose redemptive suffering and death is so graphically described in the Book of Isaiah (cf. Philippians 2:7).

Finally, the gentleness of Jesus is not simply the context in which we learn from Him. It also pertains to the substance of what we learn. The Father does not reveal His Son to "the wise and prudent" of this world, but to the "babes" or "little ones" (*nepioi*, Matthew 11:25). These "little ones" are those who, because the Father reveals His Son to them, are able to recognize the King who comes to Jerusalem, gentle and sitting on a donkey. It is of them that this King, in that very context, declares, "Out of the mouths of babes [*nepioi*] and nursing infants You have perfected praise" (21:16). To learn from the gentle Christ, then, is to become like Him and thus find rest for our souls.

✣

1. THE RESPONSIBILITIES OF ADAM

When the Bible describes the creation of Eve, one gains the impression that our ancient mother was something, almost, of an afterthought. At least the sequence of events insinuates as much. Having formed Adam and put him in charge of the Garden, the Lord went on to shape "every beast of the field and every bird of the air," remarking as He did—by way of explanation—that "it is not good that man should be alone" (Genesis 2:18–19). It was only after failing to discover among those animals a completely suitable companion for Adam that the Lord cast him into a deep sleep, removed a rib, and so forth. That is to say, in the creation of both Eve and the animals, the guiding idea was to keep man from being alone.

Since God made man alone, it is very ironic that it was not good for man to be alone. Over and over in the Creation account the text says that "God saw everything that He had made, and indeed it was very good" (1:31). Yet, when He looks down on Adam, all alone, God says, "Hey, wait a minute, this is *not good*. I must do something so man will not be alone."

But why? To keep Adam from feeling lonesome? It is worth suggesting that Adam's being alone involved a bigger problem than mere loneliness. Indeed, still in the state of innocence, a measure of loneliness might have been very good for Adam, causing him to long more intensely for God. Not having a wife to think about or animals to care for, Adam might have given himself over to deeper pondering and more ardent prayer, a contemplative with fewer distractions. In fact, Adam's earliest life resembled rather closely that of a consecrated hermit, quietly tilling the soil, tending his vegetables, communing with his Maker in purity of heart.

I propose here that the real problem of Adam's being alone was that he had no other creature to whom he was "answerable." Very simply, nothing ever responded to him. Adam must have noticed that trees, left without wind or rain, give forth no voice. Surrounded by plants, Adam had neither living things to listen to nor, for all he could tell, living things that could listen to him. Nothing in his world "talked back." In his experience of these vegetative creatures, then, Adam had no real experience of "response." And hence no felt sense of being "responsible."

Until Eve and the animals entered his life, there were very severe limits to Adam's ability to be "answerable" and "responsible."

Surely God formed Eve and the animals in order to render Adam more "responsible," more "answerable," for this trait is nearly the essence of what it means to be a human being. In order to make Adam a completely responsible creature, then, God made Adam a social being. His conscience would henceforth be contoured, not only by his intellect's recognition of God's eternal law, but in part by a sense of being social, that imaginative perception that Henri Bergson called *le moi social*.

The beasts of the field and birds of the air were, of course, decidedly secondary in this procedure. Adam's true socialization came through his relationship to Eve, which is the biblical prototype of marriage. Eve, you see, *would* respond. She really would look Adam right in the eye and answer him back. She knew exactly what the words meant and she could use the words as well as Adam. The latter, now a husband, would find an entirely new dimension to the words "answerable" and "responsible."

And together Adam and Eve started the first family, the original nucleus of mutual responsibility. This responsibility constrained them, in turn, to fashion certain kinds of controls, stern restraints beyond those that Adam had known when he was still single. These restraints were also of a different quality. As a moral being, Adam had always been obliged to employ what Irving Babbitt called "the inner check" over his desires, but now his need for intentionally cultivated inhibition took on a social property. Adam had to learn the manly art of putting Eve before himself. In the earlier days he could, within limits, use the world rather much as he liked; now, however, there was someone else to be consulted. Back when he was yet all by himself, Adam had to speak the truth, whereas now he was obliged to speak the truth in charity. In the striking expression of Zbigniew Brzezinski, Adam and Eve together were now forced to contrive some "shared criteria of self-denial." In short, in order to be responsible, Adam and Eve became cultured and domesticated.

The latter participle, "domesticated," derived from the Latin word for "home" (*domus*), indicates the cultivation of discipline necessary to the proper humanizing of social life. The correct social inhibitions, learned in the family, are probably best regarded as exercises of artistic discipline, the proper influence of form on matter. Begotten and nurtured within the home, they are ever essential to social culture, the fundamental unit of which is the family. All of human society is but an extension of human families.

⁓

2. THE LAUGHTER OF ISAAC

Isaac is one of the most engaging figures in Holy Scripture, probably because he is the most associated with the exuberance of laughter.

Isaac was named for laughter, in fact, because that name, formed from the verbal root *shq*, literally means "he will laugh." It is ever a marvel and a grace, for sure, to hear a little infant laugh, and I confess, for my part, a preference for the view that babies, when they come to earth, bring along with them the laughter of the angels.

In the birth of Isaac, however, the circumstances attendant on his unexpected appearance in this world afforded an even ampler ground for mirth. No one felt this better than his mother, Sarah, who conceived him at the age of eighty-nine, and the happy laconism that she delivered, right after delivering her son, was smartly to the point: "God has made me laugh, and all who hear will laugh with me" (Genesis 21:6).

Truth to tell, the laughter had begun already, a year and more before. Abraham, when first he heard the tidings, bent himself upon the earth, prostrate in a solemn posture of devotion. The gravity of his reverence, however, and the deep mood indicated by his downward frame, were more than faintly muted by the smile that formed around his mouth. How should a ninety-nine-year-old man respond, after all, on being told, with respect to his eighty-nine-year-old wife, "I will bless her and also give you a son by her"? (17:16). Unfamiliar with a better rule for how to receive this sort of information, "Abraham fell on his face and laughed" (17:17).

Sarah herself first learned the news while eavesdropping, from within the tent, on a conversation between her husband and the Lord, whom he hosted outside. "Sarah your wife shall have a son," she heard the latter say. Her response? "Sarah laughed within herself," asserts the Sacred Text, a reaction that she was a tad too quick to disavow when questioned on the matter. "I did not laugh," she insisted. "No," the Lord pressed the point, "but you did laugh!" (18:9–15).

Her laughter was prompted, of course, by the sheer incongruity of the proposition, because "Abraham and Sarah were old, well advanced in age; and Sarah had passed the age of childbearing" (18:11). Did her laughter also betray a skepticism about the promise? A first reading of the text may suggest it did, because her laugh was accompanied by the remark, "After I have grown old, shall I have pleasure, my lord being old also?" (18:12). Nonetheless, our earliest Christian commentator on the passage evidently did not think this to be the case. He even counted Sarah among the heroes of faith: "By faith Sarah herself also received strength to conceive seed, and she bore a child when she was past the age, because she judged Him faithful who had promised" (Hebrews 11:11).

According to the full, Christian understanding of the Holy Scriptures, the joy of Abraham and Sarah at the promised birth of Isaac was burdened with the gold of prophecy, for his miraculous begetting foretold a later conception more miraculous still. Isaac was, in truth, a type and pledge of "Jesus Christ, the Son of David, the Son of Abraham" (Matthew 1:1). And Mary, mother of this Newer Isaac, having conceived Him in virginity just days before, made perfect her responding song of praise by remembering the mercy that God "spoke to our fathers, / To Abraham and to his seed forever" (Luke 1:55).

Did not Abraham himself anticipate with joy the later coming of that more distant Seed? Surely so, for even our Newer Isaac proclaimed, "Your father Abraham rejoiced to see My day, and he saw it and was glad" (John 8:56). Like Moses (5:46), Isaiah (12:41), and David (Matthew 22:43), Abraham was gifted to behold, in mystic vision, the final fulfillment of that primeval word, "But My covenant I will establish with Isaac" (Genesis 17:21).

In the second century, St. Irenaeus of Lyons expressed thus the mystery inherent in the figure of Isaac: "Abraham, knowing the Father through the Word, who made heaven and earth, confessed Him as God, and taught by a vision that the Son of God would become a Man among men, by whose arrival his seed would be as the stars of heaven, he longed to see that day, so that he too might embrace Christ, as it were; and beholding Him in the Spirit of prophecy, he rejoiced" (*Against the Heresies* 4.7.1).

෴

3. NEW TESTAMENT JOSEPH

There is something strongly impressive in the Bible's final remark on the life of St. Joseph: "Then [Jesus] went down with them and came to

Nazareth, and was subject to them . . . And Jesus increased in wisdom and stature, and in favor with God and men" (Luke 2:51–52). The Son of God was raised, that is to say, as any little boy should be raised, growing day by day in the practical and moral skills of life, the formation of character, even as He grew in height and build. While God's Son assumed humanity in His mother's womb, it was Joseph who taught Him what it means to be a man. Thus, Joseph was to leave the forming mark (*charakter* in Greek) of his own manhood on the God-Man. Jesus, in His hometown, was known as "the carpenter's son" (*ho tou tektonos huios*—Matthew 13:55).

Few if any writers have shown as much exegetical insight into St. Joseph, I think, as Bernard of Clairvaux, who preached a homily on this saint back in the twelfth century. Bernard spoke of Joseph as "the man of virtue," who "deserved to be so honored by God that he was called, and was believed to be, the father of God" (*meruit honorari a Deo ut pater Dei et dictus et creditus sit*).

Detecting the subtle suggestions dropped in the Gospel of St. Matthew, Bernard compared St. Joseph to his Old Testament counterpart, Joseph the Patriarch. Both men, Bernard noted, were men of chastity, unwilling to touch women who did not *belong* to them. Each man, likewise, was driven into Egypt by the ill-will (*invidia*) of others, in the first case by the older sons of Jacob, and by King Herod in the second. Both men were given divine messages in their dreams. The older Joseph "provided grain, not only for himself, but for all the people," while the later Joseph "received for safekeeping the Living Bread from heaven, both for himself and for the whole world."

In the biblical genealogies Jesus' lineage is traced back to David, not through His mother, but through Joseph, to whom Jesus had no biological relationship (Matthew 1:16; Luke 3:23–31). Thus, Jesus inherited the messianic title "Son of David," not through Mary, but through the man who served Him, literally, *in loco parentis*.

Bernard was impressed by the Davidic lineage of St. Joseph: "Truly of the house of David, this man [*vir iste*] Joseph truly descended from the royal stem, noble in lineage, more noble in mind. . . . Indeed was he a son of David, not only in flesh, but also in faith, in holiness, in devotion. The Lord found him as it were another David, a man after His own heart, to whom He could safely commit the most secret and most sacred purpose [*arcanum*] of His heart—to whom, as to another David,

He manifested the deep and concealed things of His wisdom, and whom He would not permit to be ignorant of the Mystery which none of the princes of this world have known. To him it was given to see what many kings and prophets had longed to see, but had not seen, and to hear, but had not heard. And he was given, not only to see and to hear, but also to carry, to lead, to embrace, to kiss, to nurture, and to guard" (*Super Missus Est Homiliae* 2.16).

Every vocation is unique, surely, in the sense that the Good Shepherd calls each of His sheep by its own proper name. Still, there was something more particularly unique about the vocation of St. Joseph. Just how does a man learn the proper form and method for being the foster-father of God's Son and the spouse of that divine Son's virgin mother? One suspects that there were no manuals on the subject. Joseph was obliged simply to follow God's call wherever it led. Like Abraham, "he went out, not knowing where he was going" (Hebrews 11:8). And if Abraham, in thus following God by faith, is called "our father" (Romans 4:12), there must be some sense in which St. Joseph serves as our foster-father.

With so distinctive and demanding a vocation, we might excuse Joseph if, on occasion, he sometimes felt anxious and insecure. The available evidence, however, indicates that this was not the case. Joseph appears four times in the Gospel of Matthew, and every single time he is sound asleep. Whatever troubles Joseph endured, they did not include insomnia. Joseph's vocation was not simply difficult; it was impossible. Consequently, he realized that all of it, in the end, depended on God, not himself.

※

4. PETER'S WIFE AND MOTHER-IN-LAW

An unbroken chorus of voices from the second century—including Tertullian, Papias of Hierapolis, Clement of Alexandria, Irenaeus of Lyons, and Dionysius of Corinth—testifies that the Apostle Peter was put to death during the Neronic persecution in Rome, which began in late AD 64, and that the Gospel according to Mark, composed in that context, substantially contains the preaching of St. Peter in that city. It is very instructive to follow that historical and literary link between Peter and Mark.

When Peter arrived in the city, perhaps only a year or so earlier, he may have found Mark there already, since St. Paul had asked Timothy to bring him to Rome (2 Timothy 4:11). In any case, near the end of the epistle that Peter himself sent from Rome about the year 63, he wrote: "She who is in Babylon, elect together with you, greets you; and so does Mark my son" (1 Peter 5:13).

It was natural that Peter, on arriving at Rome, took a particular interest in Mark, whom he had known as a very young man. Indeed, that earliest Jerusalem congregation, of which Peter was clearly the major leader, had regularly assembled in the very home where Mark grew up, and it was to that home that Peter himself returned after his miraculous deliverance from prison some two decades earlier (Acts 12:12).

When Mark left Rome sometime after Peter's death, he went to Alexandria in Egypt, carrying with him, not only a copy of the Gospel that he had recently composed (Eusebius, *Ecclesiastical History* 2.16.1), but also certain personal memories of the Galilean fisherman. This would explain why we find personal recollections about Peter preserved in the Alexandrian tradition. Peter is spoken of numerous times by Alexandria's two early catechists, Clement and Origen.

Most striking among those memories are the ones concerning Peter's family. Whereas St. Paul had already mentioned Peter's wife (1 Corinthians 9:5), it was Clement of Alexandria who referred to their children (*Stromateis* 3.6.52).

Clement is also our sole source for the information that Peter's wife died as a martyr, and his endearing reference is well worth quoting: "They say that blessed Peter, seeing his wife being led away to death, rejoiced because of her calling and her homeward liberation, and shouted out with glad encouragement and reassurance, addressing her by name, 'Remember the Lord' [*memneso, o haute, tou Kyriou*]. Such was the marriage of those blessed ones and their perfect attitude toward their dearest" (7.11.63).

Clement cites these memorable words from a popular source, "They say" (*phasi*), but a memory from so far away and of such antiquity (nearly a century and a half) needs an explanatory connection. That connection was surely Mark, St. Peter's younger assistant and a major historical link between the churches of Rome and Alexandria.

In exhorting his wife to "remember the Lord," Peter perhaps summoned to her mind a goodly number of precious recollections, one of them being the Lord's healing of her own mother very early in His ministry. In fact, Mark himself recorded that miracle as an almost eye-witness account, so original appears its setting and sequence: "But Simon's wife's mother lay sick with a fever, and they told Him about her at once. So He came and took her by the hand and lifted her up, and immediately the fever left her. And she served them" (Mark 1:30–31). Mark had doubtless heard Peter tell the story many times.

If the historians are right (and I think they are), Matthew and Luke depended on Mark as the source for their own versions of the story of Peter's mother-in-law. Moreover, one cannot fail to notice that these later accounts of the miracle are less vivid than Mark's. Luke, for instance, leaves out the detail about Jesus "taking her by the hand." An even greater simplification of the account is evident in Matthew, whose omission of all the other *dramatis personae* modifies the story into simply a person-to-person encounter between Jesus and the sick woman. Thus, Jesus Himself "sees" her lying feverish and acts on His own initiative. Then, at the end, Matthew says that the woman, when healed, "served Him" (8:15), rather than (as in Mark and Luke) "served them." Peter's mother-in-law is thus transformed into the model believer, raised up by the Lord to be His servant.

※

5. ANDREW, THE FIRST-CALLED

If a Bible-reader takes the care to notice him, the Apostle Andrew is among the most attractive individuals in all of Holy Scripture. A certain measure of careful attention is necessary to lay hold of this fact, nonetheless, for Andrew does not really "put himself forward." He does not come bounding forth impetuously from the biblical page, so to speak, like a David, a Moses, or a Paul. Indeed, this disinclination to draw explicit attention to himself is one of the very features that render Andrew so attractive.

To appreciate this quiet, self-effacing aspect of Andrew it may be useful to contrast him, in this respect, to his bolder, more emphatic brother, the Apostle Peter. Peter most certainly does draw attention to himself, which may be one of the reasons that he is invariably named first when the original Apostles are listed (cf. Mark 3:17–19; Acts 1:13; etc.). In the memory of the early Church, Peter would have been extremely difficult to overlook. He appears in Holy Scripture very much as an in-your-face apostle, if the term be allowed. It was he, after all, who flung himself into the lake and swam toward the risen Jesus, while the others came rowing to shore in their boats (John 21:7–8). On that occasion Peter was at least swimming toward the Lord and not attempting, as he had earlier done, to walk to Him on the surface of the water (Matthew 14:28–31).

Even though Peter often served as a spokesman for the others (cf. Matthew 19:27; Mark 1:36), one has the impression that he sometimes went out of his way to distinguish himself, to set himself apart, from the rest of the Apostles—"Even if all are made to stumble, yet I will not be" (Mark 14:29). A consummate alpha personality, Peter simply cannot be overlooked; like the very sun, a boisterous giant rejoicing to run his course, there is nothing hidden from his heat.

In his brother Andrew we find none of this. Andrew, on the contrary, appears not to draw attention to himself, but serves entirely as a conduit for others to come to the Lord. Even in that scene that prompts the Church to remember him as the first-called, he immediately went to share his blessing with his sibling. It is no wonder that he was known among the first Christians simply as "Andrew, Simon Peter's brother" (cf. John 1:38–42).

As the first-called of the Church, then, Andrew was apparently recognized to enjoy a kind of special access to the Lord. Thus, when the Greek-speaking visitors to Jerusalem approached Philip (besides Andrew, the only other apostle with a Greek name) saying, "Sir, we wish to see Jesus," Philip went first to Andrew so that the two of them might together facilitate that meeting (John 12:21–22). Evidently Philip felt the need to have the helpful, accessible Andrew by his side at that time.

In all of the Gospels, however, there is one scene that seems most clearly to reveal this trait of friendly, relaxed availability in Andrew, and that scene is in John's narrative of the multiplication of the loaves. Of the six New Testament stories on this theme, only John tells us of the special role of Andrew: "One of His disciples, Andrew, Simon Peter's brother, said to Him, 'There is a lad here who has five barley loaves and two small fish, but what are they among so many?'" (John 6:8–9).

Now, the attentive reader of Holy Scripture should be asking a question of the text at this point, namely, just how did Andrew know that there was a little boy present who was carrying those particular pieces of food? It is unlikely, after all, that a small boy would be holding all seven items in his hands at the same time. The five barley loaves and two little fish must have been carried in a sack of some sort. The lad was part of a large multitude that had been with Jesus for some days (Matthew 15:32), and his mother had packed him several meals in a lunch bag. By now, he has already eaten most of that food—the fresh fruit and sweets are gone, for instance. All the lad has left in that sack are five barley loaves, possibly a tad beyond their prime, and a couple of salted fish.

So how did Andrew know what was contained in that little boy's bag? Surely the answer is obvious. He noticed the child standing near him, maybe alone, perhaps a bit distracted, and he simply asked in a cordial, engaging way, "Say there, son, what all did your mama pack for you in that bag?" From such friendly inquiries are missions and ministries begun, and miracles born.

⚬

6. THE WIDOW IN THE TEMPLE

Though *naos* is the Greek noun properly used to refer to the temple at Jerusalem, in the New Testament we more often find the word *hieron* ("holy place") employed in this sense, particularly when the reference is to some specific part of the temple.

For example, *hieron* is the word of choice to designate the Court of Women, that precinct of the temple complex closed to Gentiles but open to Jewish women. Jewish men could congregate in that precinct as well, but the men were also free to move on to the Court of Israel, to which the women had no access. Thus, besides being the place in the temple where the women could pray (cf. Luke 2:37), the Court of Women was the one place in the temple where all Israelites could gather.

Thus, it naturally became the place where Jesus spoke when He taught in the temple (John 8:20; 18:20). It was there that His enemies found Him sitting and teaching one morning, when they came dragging a woman who had been taken in adultery during the preceding night (8:2–3).

Naturally, too, it was to the Court of Women that mothers brought their purification offerings after the birth of their children. Standing at that precinct's inner gate, they could look across and see the altar on which the designated lamb (or, in the case of the poor, the pair of turtle-doves—Luke 2:24) was offered on such occasions.

One of the notable features of the Court of Women was the *glazophylakion* or "treasury," thirteen trumpet-shaped receptacles placed there to receive the offerings of the faithful for the maintenance of the temple and its ministry. Because pagan coinage was often adorned with engravings of political leaders and images from mythology, such "idolatrous" money could not be placed in the temple treasury. For this reason there were moneychangers in the temple to provide the acceptable coinage for the offerings. Since they were not expected to work for free, the monetary exchange involved a measure of profit for the exchangers (much as we have today in international airports), and on at least one occasion our Lord seems to have manifested a rather dim view of such transactions.

One day the Lord called attention to a poor widow whom He saw casting her last two coins into the treasury. These coins (*lepta*) were so small that they had no strict equivalence in the imperial monetary system, and, because they would not be familiar to Mark's readers at Rome, he explained that two of them were needed to equal a single *quadrans* (12:42).

Jesus knew that these two small pieces of change were the sum of this poor widow's assets (*pace* Rudolph Bultmann who doubted how Jesus could possibly have known this!). Therefore it is significant that she gave both of them, holding back nothing for herself.

For Jesus this latter fact became a point of contrast between the widow and the wealthier benefactors of the temple (12:43f; Luke 21:4). Unlike the latter, this woman was giving "all her life" (*holon ton bion* in Mark 12:44). Jesus knew that, if a woman is reduced even to ten coins, the loss of a single one of them is a matter of considerable concern and industry (cf. Luke 15:8–10). Moreover, given the grandeur of the temple and the magnitude of its economic base, this lady might have been tempted to feel that her tiny gift was insignificant, even futile. Such is the context in which our Lord speaks of her bravery and generosity.

Our Lord's reaction was typical of Him, nor was this the only occasion on which He took compassion on a widow (cf. Luke 7:11–17). Indeed, He was obviously fond of an old story of a strikingly similar widow who likewise sacrificed her last resources to advance God's cause (1 Kings 17:8–16; Luke 4:25–26).

It is further significant that the Gospel accounts of this poor widow in the temple place her in the context of the Lord's Passion. In Mark she comes at the end of five stories of conflict between Jesus and His enemies (11:27—12:40) and immediately prior to His final great discourse (which commences with a remark about the grandeur of the temple!—13:1), while in Luke she appears in the chapter before the Sanhedrin's plot to kill Jesus (21:1–4; 22:1–6). Giving her *all* for God, this widow thus becomes a symbol or type of Christ Himself, who will lay down His life (*bios*) to advance God's cause.

✦

7. MOST EXCELLENT THEOPHILUS

Both Luke's Gospel (1:3) and the Book of Acts (1:1) are addressed to a man named Theophilus, whom Luke calls "most excellent [*kratistos*]." This honorific adjective, which in antiquity a person might use when approaching someone of a higher social class than himself, was deemed especially appropriate for addressing government officials. Indeed, Luke himself provides three examples of this usage: the letter of Lysias to the governor Felix (Acts 23:26), an address to the same man by Tertullus (24:3), and St. Paul's speech to the governor Festus (26:25). It is not surprising, then, that many interpreters of Holy Scripture think Theophilus was a Roman political figure. This is an attractive and likely suggestion.

Many of these same biblical interpreters go on to contend that Theophilus was perhaps a sympathetic Roman ruler, but still a pagan, whom Luke was endeavoring to convince of the truth of the Gospel. They argue, in other words, that Luke's intent in these two books was largely apologetic, rather like Paul arguing his case before Festus and Agrippa (26:2–23). These exegetes believe that Luke was thus recommending the merits of the Christian faith to the official Roman world as represented in Theophilus.

One may mention two reasons for believing that this line of interpretation is not very likely. First, though the Book of Acts does contain several apostolic speeches of an apologetic nature, Luke's two works on the whole are not marked by the directness and simplicity normally characteristic of an apologetic case. As many of those same biblical interpreters have shown, Luke's thought and style are theologically very complex and subtle. He was clearly directing his Gospel and the Acts of the Apostles to mature believers already inside the Church.

Second, Theophilus himself was certainly no pagan, because Luke

168

explicitly mentions his having been "catechized" (*katechethes*—Luke 1:4). This expression means that Theophilus had already received the normal basic instruction given within the Christian Church (1 Corinthians 14:19; Galatians 6:6). His experience in this respect was doubtless identical to that of Apollos, who also was "catechized" by Priscilla and Aquila (Acts 18:25).

The basic catechesis among Christians was essentially oral, rather than literary. Indeed, this is indicated even by the etymology of the word "catechesis": *kata-echo*, "by way of echo," an expression suggesting much recourse to repetition. The fundamental teaching in the Church was to have an echo quality, involving a generous amount of "repeat after me." Truly, this is how the Gospel itself is handed on to each new generation of believers: "I received from the Lord that which I also delivered to you" (1 Corinthians 11:23). Catechesis is thus no place for innovation and experiment.

Nonetheless, the New Testament also indicates that deeper explorations and more detailed explanations were provided for Christians who had already been catechized in the basics. The Epistle to the Hebrews, for example, clearly distinguishing between these two types of teaching (5:12—6:2), says "let us go on to perfection."

Similarly, it was Luke's intention to provide Theophilus with a deeper, more detailed, and "perfect understanding" of the doctrines of the faith, "just as those who from the beginning were eyewitnesses and ministers of the word delivered them to us" (Luke 1:2–3). It was to furnish this further instruction that Luke composed his Gospel and the Book of Acts.

Luke had in mind, of course, that these books would be read by other Christians besides Theophilus, and we would surely be mistaken if we imagined these books as intended for a private library. On the contrary, both works were composed for the very purpose which, in fact, they have always served in the Church—namely, the public proclamation of God's Word within the Church's worship. Indeed, both books make pointed references to God's people assembled for worship.

Why, then, is Theophilus himself the person addressed at the beginning of each work? Unless he is to be understood as a purely literary addressee, like the "Malcolm" of C. S. Lewis, the most reasonable explanation is that it was Theophilus who made the production of these books possible. At the very least this means that Theophilus supported

Luke while he wrote the Gospel and Acts. All of us, in this case, are very much in his debt.

⅌

8. MATTHIAS, CHOSEN BY LOT

Among the literary features that particularly adorn the Gospel of St. Luke are certain points of symmetry and polish that unite the beginning and ending of that work. Some of these are fairly direct and easy to perceive. For instance, there is the clear parallelism between the two congregations praying at the temple, one at the beginning of the Gospel (1:9, 10, 21) and the other at the end (24:53). Again, most readers will probably note the presence of the angels at both the beginning (1:11, 19, 26; 2:9, 13, 15) and the ending (22:43; 24:4) of Luke's narrative.

Fewer readers of Luke, perhaps, will observe that there is also a rolling of dice near both the beginning (1:9) and the ending (23:34) of that Gospel. However subtle, nonetheless, this symmetry was hardly lost on the refined *Schriftsgefühl* of St. Ambrose, who perceived therein a comparison and contrast between the levitical priesthood of Zacharias, chosen by lot to offer the incense, and that new priesthood by which Jesus offered His sacrifice on the Cross while the soldiers cast lots for His clothing. "So the priest was chosen by lot," he says with respect to Zacharias, and then he adds: "Perhaps on this account the soldiers cast lots for the Lord's garments. Since the Lord prepared to offer sacrifice for us in His temple, the shaking of the lots around Him would also fulfill the precept of the Law."

In addition to those tropes by which Luke unites the beginning and ending of his Gospel, there are also conspicuous lines of parallel between the early part of that Gospel and the early part of Luke's second work, the Acts of the Apostles. Both books commence, for example, with an address to "most excellent Theophilus," followed by the portrait of a congregation at prayer (Luke 1:10; Acts 1:14). And just as there were angels at the outset of Luke's Gospel, so we find them again at the beginning of Acts (1:10–11). Moreover, near the front of each book there is the descent of the Holy Spirit, who overshadows the Virgin Mary (Luke 1:35) and anoints the Church (Acts 1:4–8; 2:1–4), which is gathered with the Virgin Mary (1:14).

Once more, also, there is a replicated rolling of dice. Just as Zacharias is designated by lot to offer the incense at the beginning of Luke's Gospel, Matthias is chosen by lot to be numbered among the Apostles at the beginning of Acts (1:24–26). This latter juxtaposition, too, was detected by St. Ambrose, who thus commented on the choice of Zacharias by speaking of the choice of Matthias: "So the lot fell on the apostle Matthias, lest the choice of an apostle should seem to diverge from the command of the Old Law."

Before their casting of lots, the brethren narrowed their selection to a choice between two men with identical qualifications. Matthias and Joseph Barsabas both met the technical requirements for being numbered with the original Apostles (1:21–23). One remembered, however, that Judas Iscariot too had met those requirements. Clearly something more was needed, as their prayer acknowledged: "You, O Lord, know the hearts of all." God could read the hearts of both men, and, for reasons best known to Himself, He preferred Matthias.

God's preference of Matthias, nonetheless, implied no censure of the other man. Joseph Barsabas was not chosen for that particular apostolate, but there was no implied criticism of him. All through Holy Scripture, indeed, God continually chooses some individuals over others with a view to the divine purposes in history. While each of those choices necessarily implies a rejection of sorts, such rejections are not necessarily condemnations nor repudiations.

Thus, the Lord was not condemning the other sons of Abijah, years earlier, when he caused the lot to fall on Zacharias. It was simply the case that God chose Zacharias to offer incense that day, and not one of the other priests. Not because Zacharias was worthier than his brethren; it was simply that the all-knowing Lord had some rather specific intention in mind, an intention involving Zacharias's meeting, that day, with an archangel. God knew what He was about.

So with Matthias. The Lord had some specific plans for him. And while Matthias perhaps spent the rest of his life discovering what these plans were, he was keenly aware that God was reading his heart.

⸾⸾⸾

9. PRISCA AND HER HUSBAND

Aquila and his wife Prisca were tentmakers, originally from Pontus. When we first meet them, maybe in the winter of 49/50, they have recently arrived at Corinth from Rome. Luke tells us that they had departed from the capital because of a decree of the Emperor Claudius against the Jews (Acts 18:1–3), an edict also mentioned by other ancient sources. For example, some decades later the historian Suetonius wrote, "Because the Jews were continuously making disturbances, instigated by Chrestus, [Claudius] expelled them from Rome" (*Lives of the Caesars*, "Claudius" 25.4).

Although Luke says that Claudius "commanded all the Jews to depart from Rome" (Acts 18:2), and Suetonius uses the verb "expelled" (*expulit*), it appears that Rome had no shortage of Jews within the next few years. Perhaps these peremptory expressions of Luke and Suetonius should be understood in a broader and looser sense. It may be the case that Claudius simply forbade the Jews in Rome to assemble in public. This interpretation of the decree corresponds, in fact, to the testimony of Dio Cassius, who wrote somewhat later, "With respect to the Jews, who had again increased so greatly that because of their multitude it would have been difficult, without starting an uproar, to keep them out of the city, [Claudius] did not expel them, but he commanded them, while adhering to the form of life inherited from their fathers [*patrio bio*], not to hold meetings" (*History* 60.6). Such a prohibition, by putting an end to the regular synagogue services at Rome, would severely restrict observant Jewish life. Large numbers would have departed rather than be deprived of their regular synagogue worship. Perhaps this was the reason that the decree was popularly interpreted as a forced exile of the Jews from the capital city, an interpretation reflected in Luke and Suetonius.

Aquila and Prisca, then, were Jews exiled from Rome. When Paul met them at Corinth, were they also Christians? Perhaps. In either case, however, they had certainly heard of Christ, because there had been Roman Jewish Christians right from Pentecost (Acts 2:10). Indeed, the expression used by Suetonius in connection with the disturbances at Rome—"instigated by Chrestus [*impulsore Chresto*]"—seems to be a reference to Jesus the Christ, about whom the Jews at Rome were raising such a row.

If Aquila and Prisca were not already Christians when Paul first met them at Corinth, they became Christians very soon, joining him in the local ministry and tentmaking business in that city for the next eighteen months (Acts 18:11). Then, in the summer of 51, they journeyed with Paul to Ephesus (18:18–19), where they remained even after Paul left that city for a while. It was at Ephesus that they instructed the fervent convert Apollos (18:24–26). Paul came back to the city in 52, after Apollos had gone over to Corinth (Acts 18:27—19:1).

In the story of the instruction that Aquila and Prisca gave to Apollos, it is most noticeable that the lady is named before her husband, a fact which may suggest that she was a more prominent and memorable person than he (18:18, 26). This usage is not peculiar to Luke. Paul, too, when he refers to this couple, twice (of three times) names Prisca before her husband (Romans 16:3; 2 Timothy 4:19).

Aquila and Prisca were still with Paul in Ephesus in the spring of 55; indeed, one of the local parishes met in their home (1 Corinthians 16:19). Claudius having died in 54 (Dio Cassius, *History* 61.35), we find Aquila and Prisca back at Rome by the winter of 57/58; they also hosted one of the parish churches in that city (Romans 16:3–5). By the early 60s the couple once again moved to Ephesus, which is the last place we hear of them in Holy Scripture (2 Timothy 4:19).

Up to this point in their lives, it would seem, Aquila and Prisca had not yet met Luke, who later wrote about them. Luke, having remained at Philippi during the years 49 to 58 (Acts 16:16–17, 40; 17:1; 20:6, closely compared), was not with Paul during those first trips to Corinth and Ephesus, when he was with Aquila and Prisca. Later, when Luke himself was with Paul, the other two were not. As the third missionary journey drew to a close, Luke was at Paul's side continually, from the time he left Macedonia in the spring of 58 (Acts 20:6), during the two years of Caesarean imprisonment (Acts 24:27; Colossians 4:14; Philemon 24), throughout the subsequent voyage to Rome (Acts 27:1; 28:14), and, it would seem, during Paul's two years of house arrest there (Acts 28:30; 2 Timothy 4:11). By the time that Luke and Paul reached Rome, Aquila and Prisca were already back at Ephesus (4:19). During that prolonged period, then, Aquila and Prisca were always someplace else. However, when Luke finally did meet Prisca and her husband, sometime after Paul had been martyred, the couple became his source for much of the nearly five years of apostolic history covered in Acts 18—19.

Indeed, we suspect that Luke may have come to know them even better than did Paul. This suspicion would explain, at least, why the Acts of the Apostles habitually calls Prisca by the affectionate diminutive "Priscilla," or "little Prisca," a liberty that Paul never took when referring to the lady (though some later copyists of the Pauline manuscripts did). Along with the Mother of Jesus, Mary Magdalene, Joanna, and so many others, Aquila's wife became one of the many women that Luke interviewed in preparing to write his Gospel and the Acts of the Apostles.

⋙

10. LUKE THE PHYSICIAN

On the explicit testimony of Irenaeus of Lyons, St. Luke's authorship of one of the canonical Gospels and of that other work known as the Acts of the Apostles is rightly regarded as part of the unbroken, never seriously challenged tradition of the Church. But just who was Luke? Answering this question is more complicated.

Were Ephrem of Edessa and other Church Fathers correct in identifying Luke with Lucius of Cyrene in Acts 13:1? If so, then perhaps there is merit in thinking Luke to be the companion of Cleopas in the Emmaus story in Luke 24, as we find in Theophylact and some liturgical texts. Similarly, Epiphanius of Cyprus lists Luke among the "seventy" that Jesus sent out in Luke 10:1. This last theory, however, seems impossible, because Luke's own words (1:2) imply that he was *not* an immediate witness of Jesus' ministry.

In fact, all of the foregoing identifications are shaky at best, inasmuch as they contradict the more common patristic opinion that Luke was a Gentile, not a Jew. Indeed, this latter judgment seems better supported by Holy Scripture. For example, when Luke is mentioned in Colossians 4:14, he is clearly *not* included among those of Paul's companions who are "of the circumcision" in 4:10–11.

Apparently in accord with an opinion common in the fourth century, Eusebius and Jerome both say that Luke was a native of Antioch. This view would explain how the word "we" found its way into some manuscripts of Acts 11:28.

Indeed, from earliest times the Church Fathers, educated to a great sensitivity toward literary and historical details, presumed that whenever Luke used the word "we" in the Book of Acts, he was describing events of which he was an eyewitness. Following their insight on this point, I have long thought Luke to come from Troas, near the site of the ancient Troy, because the first "we" text (16:10–11) speaks of the voyage from Troas to Macedonia.

Thus, Luke was with Paul during the mission to Philippi (16:12–16). When the citizens of this city, opposed to anything that could be called "Jewish" (16:20–21), made life rough for Paul (16:22–24), he left the place (16:40), but he was careful to leave Luke, a Gentile, as the pastor of the new congregation there. Consequently, the "we" sections stop abruptly at Philippi, indicating that Luke was not a companion of Paul's travels in Acts 17—19. Indeed, when the word "we" next appears, it is nearly nine years later, again at Philippi (20:6).

Thus, it appears that Luke pastored the congregation at Philippi from the summer of AD 49 to the spring of 58. This reasonable hypothesis clarifies the identity of the "true companion" (literally "loyal yokefellow") whom Paul addresses in the Epistle to the Philippians (4:3). (For various reasons that I will not elaborate here, I believe Philippians was written from Ephesus sometime in the early 50s.) Luke was not named in that epistle, precisely because the Philippians understood the reference.

Beginning in the spring of 58, Luke once more became Paul's more-or-less-constant companion (Acts 20:13—21:17). He was sufficiently near him during the two years' imprisonment at Caesarea (24:27) to be mentioned in the epistles to Philemon (24) and the Colossians (4:14). He shared Paul's arduous voyage to Rome (Acts 27—28) and was at his side when Paul wrote his final epistle from that city (2 Timothy 4:11).

From these epistolary references we also know that Luke was a physician, and in this respect it is reasonable to venture another suggestion. Perhaps it was in prison at Caesarea, during long talks with Luke, that Paul became familiar with the recent medical theory about the head as the governing part of the body (a theory then so recent that it does not appear in our extant medical literature until Galen, more than a century later). Not until Luke was with him at Caesarea do we find Paul speaking of Christ as the "head" of the Church.

As early as the spring of 55, Paul had referred to the Church as "the body of Christ" (1 Corinthians 10:16–17; 12:12–27), a theme that he took up again in the Epistle to the Romans (12:1–5) early in the year 58. In those letters that he wrote from Caesarea, however, during a period when we know Luke was with him, Paul began to speak, not only of the Church as Christ's body (Colossians 3:15; Ephesians 2:16; 4:4, 12; 5:30), but of Christ as the Church's "head" (Colossians 1:18; Ephesians 1:22–23; 5:23), "from whom all the body, nourished and knit together by joints and ligaments, grows with the increase that is from God" (Colossians 2:19). Since this idea represents a clear development of Paul's earlier imagery, it is legitimate to inquire where Paul might have derived this idea. It seems reasonable to suppose that he learned it from the physician Luke.

Commentators have long remarked on Paul's influence on the theology of Luke, but perhaps that influence went both ways. Humanly speaking, we may wonder whether Paul, apart from what he discovered from conversations with his friend, physician, and fellow-missionary Luke, would ever have written, "Speaking the truth in love, [we] may grow up in all things into Him who is the head—Christ—from whom the whole body, joined and knit together by what every joint supplies, according to the effective working by which every part does its share, causes growth of the body for the edifying of itself in love" (Ephesians 4:15–16).

IX.

ALL THE KINGS' MEN

꙰

Many years ago a devout old woman of Irish extraction told me the story of her family's migration to the United States during the great potato famine, in the course of which crisis, she informed me, the Catholics in the old country could expect no help from that terrible Protestant monarch, Henry VIII. I did not remark on her inaccuracy, of course, not only because a young man does not correct a person more than twice his age, but also because Henry VIII was quite incidental to the story. The lady knew her family history well enough and could likely have named her ancestors for several generations back. Since the account she shared with me pertained to family—not political—history, the correct identification of the relevant British king was . . . well, irrelevant.

The early stories in the Bible fall very much into this category of "family history." In considerable detail they tell us what various members of the family were doing, such as who begot whom, but allusions to the larger social picture of the time, political references in particular, are scant at best. Such contextual information, if we are keen to have it, we must obtain elsewhere, especially from archeology.

Archeological texts indicate, for example, that there was a large westward migration of Semitic peoples, known as the *Habiru*, or Hebrews, across the Fertile Crescent early in the second millennium before Christ. The Bible says nothing about that extremely important social phenomenon. It only says that Abraham, who was called a Hebrew (Genesis 14:13), migrated west, along with his family, from Ur to Haran to Shechem to Egypt (11:31—12:10). That is to say, he went up and across the entire length of the Fertile Crescent. Both stories are historically based, but the biblical story pertains to family history.

Then, when Abraham does arrive in Egypt, he has an interesting run-in with the pharaoh who rules the country (12:11–20). That pharaoh, who was surely one of the most powerful political figures in the world at that time, the Bible does not identify. It could have been Amenemhet III, or Tutimaios I, or, for that matter, Henry VIII. It is a family story, after all; the Bible really doesn't care who the pharaoh was.

This insouciance to the larger social picture is clear right through the Joseph Narratives. These latter stories, although they remember the name of Potiphar, never identify the pharaoh pertinent to the events, and, when they do describe a major social innovation in Egyptian history (Genesis 47:13–26), that story is told solely within the perspective of the family's own history.

Indeed, even respecting the Exodus, the most important political event of that ancient family history, the Bible tells us nearly nothing of the larger social setting of the time. The varying fortunes of Egypt's Nineteenth Dynasty, its battles with the Nubians and Hittites, for instance, are never mentioned, nor do we catch the name of a single pharaoh. We do learn of Egypt's massive construction projects during that period, but only insofar as those projects touched the Bible's family history.

This perspective in the Bible does not seriously begin to change until the mid-tenth century BC. From then on, the biblical story starts to assume a larger social and political interest, undoubtedly related to the international concerns of the reign of Solomon (961–922 BC). Thus, it is not surprising that the first pharaoh identified by name in Holy Scripture is Sheshonq I (945–924 BC), founder of the Twenty-second Dynasty, who involved himself in the dynamics of Solomon's kingdom (1 Kings 11:40; 14:25).

From the mid-tenth century, biblical history, as narrated in Kings, Chronicles, and the prophetic books, was dated according to the reigns of the kings of Judah and Israel, a system that was transferred to the Persian emperors after the fall of those kingdoms (2 Chronicles 36:22; Nehemiah 2:1, etc.). This development, which effectively placed biblical history within the larger perspective of social and political history, attained a certain fullness when Luke dated the ministry of John the Baptist, the inauguration of the era of grace (Acts 1:22), "in the fifteenth year of the reign of Tiberius Caesar" (Luke 3:1).

This development of perspective also affirms a theological point: namely, that the "family God" of the Hebrews is likewise the Lord of universal history, including political history. He is to be adored and served even in the halls of government, where kings and their ministers are charged with the fortunes and destiny of nations.

༺༄

1. JOSEPH IN PHARAOH'S COURT

A stylistic point that distinguishes the Joseph story from the earlier Genesis narratives is its idealizing of the dominant personality. Genesis offers no parallel example of such a sustained interest in describing the shape of a specific character in terms of a moral ideal, a flawless or nearly flawless man, almost a type of perfection, a veritable saint right from the start of the story. In his patient suffering, moreover, his endurance of betrayal, his confidence in God's guidance, and his forgiveness of those who wronged him, Joseph embodies the highest norms of the Gospel.

The story of Joseph is told with images effecting a narrative coherence. For example, Joseph's different changes of fortune are symbolized in his clothing. His famous and elaborate tunic, which focuses the hatred of his brothers in 37:3–4, is dipped in blood in 37:23–32, thus symbolizing Joseph's alienation from his family. Then, in 39:12–18 his ill-fated encounter with Potiphar's wife is imaged in the loss of the cloak used as evidence to imprison him. His eventual release from prison again involves a change of clothing in 41:14, and finally a whole new wardrobe symbolizes his new state in 41:42.

Another component effecting narrative coherence is introduced by Joseph's two dreams in 37:5–10, in each of which his brothers bow down before him. This double prostration is prophetic, inasmuch as the brothers bow before him on each of their trips to Egypt (42:6; 43:26; 44:14; 50:18), and Joseph remembers the dreams on the first of these instances (42:9).

There is a very entertaining irony in Joseph's treatment of his brothers. He holds all the cards, as it were, and constantly deals from the bottom of the deck; he recognizes his siblings at once, whereas they do not know him (42:7–8). As he speaks through an interpreter, they never suspect that he understands every word they say among themselves (42:23). He plays little games at their expense, such as accusing them of being spies (42:9–16), returning their money (42:25), and setting them at table in the order of their ages (43:33). Moreover, Joseph knows exactly how long the famine will last; they don't. So when he sends them back for the upswing section of their yo-yo journey, he is quite confident that they will soon find themselves once again in Egypt.

As suspense mounts between the strategy of Joseph in Egypt and the reluctant maneuvering of Jacob back in Canaan, there is a corresponding emotional intensity in Joseph's own reaction to the ongoing drama. Outwardly, he is in full command of the situation. Inwardly, however, he can hardly contain the force of his feelings and is obliged to pull back for emotional relief (42:24; 43:30).

Both of these tensions are essential to the drama, and both are resolved simultaneously with Joseph's dramatic self-revelation in 45:1–4. When everyone arrives in Egypt, all suspense is over, and the story quietly ties up the loose ends of Genesis and prepares for Exodus.

While God's direction of events in the Joseph account consists in the providential oversight of human activity, we also note a special emphasis on the divine management, as it were, even of sinful activity. This story is a fine illustration of God's ability to bring good from evil. So the wise and forgiving Joseph can announce to his sinful brothers: "Do not therefore be grieved or angry with yourselves because you sold me here; for God sent me before you to preserve life" (45:5; also v. 7), and later: "But as for you, you meant evil against me; but God meant it for good" (50:20).

The story of Joseph, then, is an account of divine providence. Its clear thesis consists in the proposition that "all things work together for good to those who love God" (Romans 8:28). In everything that happens to Joseph, God is "with" him (Genesis 39:3, 5, 21–23). This affirmation of divine providence in the Joseph story is not simply implied in the text but also made explicit by its chief character. Moreover, Joseph's insights into God's working in history are explicitly regarded as coming from the Holy Spirit (in Genesis 41:38), reminding us that the general affirmation in Romans 8:28 is also contextualized by the theology of the Holy Spirit and especially by the principle that "as many as are led by the Spirit of God, these are the sons of God" (8:14).

%

2. THE TRAGIC FIGURE OF ABNER

Did we pay him more mind, the Bible's portrayal of Abner would surely appear as a case study in psychology and moral analysis. As Abner's *persona* is partly eclipsed, however, by his proximity to David, Saul, and other more obviously "complicated" figures, we may easily fail to notice the interesting moral complexity of his life and career.

A kinsman of Saul (1 Samuel 14:50), Abner was a military leader, part of the royal court, and a sharer at the king's private table. In one of the accounts, he is credited with originally bringing David to Saul's attention (17:55–57).

With David's rapid rise, however, the popular prestige of Abner was doubtless diminished as much as Saul's, nor is it unwarranted to guess at his reaction when David's superior military ability likewise earned him a place in the royal family and at the royal table. If the popular mind made David something of a rival to Saul, he was surely as much to Abner. Later, indeed, David's open jeering at Abner in the presence of the army strikes one as the taunt of a personal contender (26:5, 13–16).

But harder days for Abner lay ahead. As a royal relative and the recognized commander of Israel's army, his responsibilities were considerably increased after the death of Saul and Jonathan at the Battle of Mount Gilboa. Indeed, the political stability of the northern tribes greatly depended on his personal authority during those troubled years, nor could the house of Saul have stayed in power had it not been for the backing of Abner. Events would prove that Saul's lackluster heir, Ishbosheth, could occupy the throne only by Abner's assent.

Following the Battle of Mount Gilboa, the Israelites were divided between the northern tribes, nominally ruled by Ishbosheth, and the tribe of Judah under David, a division rendering it easy for the Philistines effectively to control most of the northern area west of the Jordan. This hapless situation, threatening to become permanent, posed for Abner a true moral dilemma.

He was an instinctively loyal man, principled, and innocent of personal ambition. The sundry loyalties of even such a man, nonetheless, may sometimes stand in conflict, and Abner was compelled in due course to choose between his expected adherence to the house of Saul and his more abiding concern for the nation's very survival. Long accustomed to viewing David through the eyes of Saul, Abner experienced much of the same conflict of loyalties that had plagued the conscience of Jonathan some years earlier, and his painful resolution to that conflict, like Jonathan's, would lead directly to the tragedy that ended his life.

When he did decide to join with David, Abner's moral authority in

Israel was such that he was able to bring with him, not only the army, but the various tribal elders of Israel (3:17–19).

Abner's decision, though it probably took shape over some period of time, was brought to abrupt closure when Ishbosheth accused him of disloyalty to the house of Saul (2 Samuel 3:7–11). Decisions about loyalty are particularly tough ones that often can go either way, so it is not surprising that not everyone would agree with Abner. The line of his critics and second-guessers extends from his murderer, Joab (3:24–30), all the way to certain modern commentators, one of whom writes of Abner's "treachery."

As we would expect, David himself took an opposite view of the matter (3:37), as did Solomon (1 Kings 2:32). Abner himself claimed that his decision was based on theological truth, not mere political expediency (2 Samuel 3:18). David, after all, had been anointed by Samuel and was recognized by the high priest Abiathar. Ishbosheth, in contrast, had nothing to recommend him beyond his descent from Saul, whose house the Lord had clearly repudiated.

Still, Holy Scripture does not disguise the fact that Abner's resolve, for all its high-minded adherence to principle, was not untainted by some element of the fleshly and the mundane. In the end it was a sense of disgust with Saul's son that drove Abner to David's side.

Nor does the biblical narrator himself say, in so many words, that Abner was an honorable man; he simply tells the story and lets the reader decide. (Indeed, he may not have known whether there was truth in Ishbosheth's accusation.) Only God, after all, can fully measure any man or his moral decisions.

⚜

3. BATHSHEBA, THE QUEEN MOTHER

The office of "Queen Mother" is one of the institutions by which the Bible distinguishes the kings of Judah from the kings of Israel. In fact, with the conspicuous exception of Jezebel, Holy Scripture hardly mentions the mothers of the kings of Israel, whereas the mothers of the kings of Judah are specifically named in nineteen of twenty-one cases. In the dynastic rule of the Davidic kings, their mothers were clearly persons of power and considerable influence. This institution reflected a complex political reality. While kings rather often had more than one wife, they each had only one mother, and often enough that mother's efforts played some significant role in her son's accession to the throne.

Indeed, the Hebrew word used to designate the Queen Mother, *gebirah*, is derived from the root *gabar*, signifying "strength." In Judah the mother of the king was "the power lady," possessed of a prestige and authority beyond her merely biological relationship to the king. Often spoken of as an essential person in the royal court (Jeremiah 22:26; 29:2), wearing her crown (13:18), and enthroned at the king's right hand (1 Kings 2:19), the *gebirah* was not a person to be taken lightly. Consequently it was a great advantage in the court to stand well in her favor. We cannot imagine anyone saying of the mother of a Davidic king, "Ah, but you see, she is, after all, *only* his mother."

The true grandeur of the Queen Mother's status is perhaps most obvious in the case of Maachah, the wife of Solomon's immediate successor, Rehoboam. When her son Abijah died after a reign of only three years (1 Kings 15:2), Maachah's personal authority within the realm was so formidable that there was evidently no one sufficiently powerful to remove her from office. Thus she continued in the position of *gebirah*, even though she was the grandmother, not the mother, of the king. Later, when her young grandson Asa grew sufficiently powerful to remove her as Queen Mother because of her idolatry (15:13), Maachah was so completely associated with that office that the name of Asa's own mother was lost from the biblical record. Indeed, even to speak of Maachah's "removal" from the office of Queen Mother indicates that the term signified much more than a merely biological relationship to the king.

In maintaining this institution of Queen Mother, the Kingdom of Judah resembled the political structures of Egypt, Mesopotamia, and, most significantly, the Hittites. After all, the first and most famous of Judah's *gebiroth* was Solomon's mother, Bathsheba, who was herself likely a Hittite. She had originally been married to a Hittite (2 Samuel 11:3), anyway, and it is reasonable to suppose her familiar with the office of Queen Mother in Hittite polity. What seems obvious from the biblical text is that Bathsheba's actions and example (1 Kings 1:15–34) established the power and importance of the Queen Mother in Judah.

The true place of the Queen Mother in Holy Scripture is amply illustrated by comparing two texts relative to Bathsheba. In each of them she is pictured as entering the throne room to speak to the king. In the first of these she is described as coming into the presence of her husband, King David: "And Bathsheba bowed and did homage to the king" (1 Kings 1:16). In the second instance, she comes into the presence of Solomon, her son: "And the king rose up to meet her and bowed down to her, and sat down on his throne and had a throne set for the king's mother; so she sat at his right hand" (2:19). A simple comparison of these texts indicates clearly the deference and honor with which a Davidic king expects his mother to be treated. If the king himself bows down before her, how much more his subjects?

It is hardly surprising, therefore, that Bible-believing Christians cultivate the deepest, most affectionate reverence for her of whose Son the angel said: "The Lord God will give Him the throne of His father David" (Luke 1:32). She has from the beginning been invoked as "the mother of my Lord" (1:43), and in their time of need believers have ever sought her intercession with her Son (John 2:1–11). As the Mother of Christ, she is mother to all who belong to Christ. They doubt not that forever in the kingdom of heaven she reigns as Queen and sovereign Lady, seated in glory at the right hand of great David's greater Son.

4. SOLOMON'S GOLD

A singular prosperity and peace characterized the long reign of Solomon, 961–922 BC. His father David, taking advantage of the decline of Babylon at the eastern end of the Fertile Crescent and the geopolitical vacuum created by the lackluster Twenty-first Dynasty of Egypt at its western end, had carved out a small empire for himself, subduing the Philistines, Edomites, Moabites, Ammonites, and Syrians, and making mercantile arrangements with the seagoing Phoenicians to the north. To all of this fortune Solomon fell heir when David died in 961.

It is possible that in all of history Solomon had no equal in his ability to read both maps and ledgers. His father having incorporated the Edomites to the south, Solomon controlled the port and Gulf of Aqaba (Elath) and the Red Sea. This extensive waterway afforded access to ports along the west coast of the Arabian peninsula, the east of Africa, and, through the Indian Ocean, a thousand other places. To the north Israel was bordered by the Phoenicians, whose shipping merchants were delivering and picking up cargo at ports all around the Mediterranean basin. Looking at this picture, Solomon decided to go into business, serving as the middleman between the Phoenician markets in the

Mediterranean and the sundry mercantile opportunities around the Red Sea. It would prove to be a time of booming material affluence.

Besides the favorable geopolitical situation, several other recent developments aided the prosperity attendant on Solomon's reign. First, it was the beginning of the Iron Age in that part of the world, with its greatly improved axes, hoes, scythes, plowshares, and other tools and farming implements, leading to less labor and increased productivity. Second, the greater use of calcium oxide to seal cisterns and wells allowed for improved water conservation and, in turn, greatly increased agricultural yields. Third, the adoption of a common alphabet in the eastern Mediterranean world permitted more efficient bookkeeping, uniform bills of lading, invoices, and other forms of written communication essential to commerce. Fourth, use of the camel greatly increased. This animal, already important in the economy of the Fertile Crescent, served as Solomon's chief vehicle of commerce along the overland trade routes extending north-south between the Gulf of Aqaba and the Phoenician ports of Tyre and Sidon. Solomon's reign was, therefore, a period of enormous prosperity, in describing which the Bible speaks repeatedly of gold.

Besides economic prosperity, however, Solomon's reign was also a period of several attendant social changes that would prove significant, though not invariably beneficent, as time went on. First, the prosperity itself, especially the agricultural productivity, enhanced the people's diet, lengthening the average life expectancy, lowering the age of puberty and menarche, and thus increasing the population. Second, the need for labor in the commercial sector drew many farmers from the land to enjoy the less onerous life of merchants, caravan drivers, and so forth. This meant fewer and larger farms, now rendered more productive by better tools and a greater water supply. At the same time, with fewer farms, fewer people were now able to control the food market—and prices. These higher prices, along with the lower wages inevitably prompted by the swelling of the urban labor force, became subjects on which the prophets of the coming centuries ventured a remark or two, consistently negative. Fourth, the centralization of commerce under Solomon's political control led to higher taxes and a breakdown of local tribal loyalties that had served, up to that point, to provide traditional stability to the people. Fifth, and related to the higher taxes, among the northern tribes there was a growing discontent with the south, especially the royal and priestly establishment at Jerusalem. The better farmland and the bulk of the nation's wealth were found in the north; yet the king and his capital were in the south, at Jerusalem. Finally, Solomon's economic and political ties with Phoenicia eventually led to the deep religious and moral infidelities symbolically associated with the most famous of these Phoenicians, a lady named Jezebel.

Indeed, the Bible indicates that a political and social crisis was already on the horizon near the end of Solomon's reign. In Egypt Pharaoh Sheshonq I inaugurated the Twenty-second Dynasty. It was he who gave asylum to Solomon's enemy Jeroboam, the very man who would come back and instigate the civil war and the secession of the northern tribes after Solomon's death in 922. Shortly afterwards Sheshonq himself would invade the Holy Land and bring it under his overall political influence.

For all his gold and glory, then, Solomon set the stage for many of the chosen people's future troubles. Indeed, Israel never fully recovered from all that prosperity.

๛

5. ASA AND HIS GRANDMOTHER

Asa (913–873 BC) was Judah's initial "reform" king, in this respect a forerunner to Hezekiah and Josiah. He was the first of those very few kings of whom it was said that he "did what was right in the eyes of the LORD, as did his father David" (1 Kings 15:11).

When Asa came to the throne as David's fourth successor, the realm was not doing very well. During the reign of Asa's grandfather, Rehoboam, Judah's financial state had been greatly weakened by incessant war with the Northern Kingdom (15:6) and by an invasion from Egypt (14:25–26). Hardly better was the nation's spiritual state, for idolatry and gross immorality were rife (14:22–23). Rehoboam was followed on the throne by Asa's father, Abijah, but the latter too "walked in all the sins of his father, which he had done before him" (15:3).

These problems seem not to have daunted the young Asa, who cleaned up Judah's idolatry and immorality with such dispatch and efficiency that 1 Kings could account for the work in a single verse (15:12).

Although the longer description of Asa's reign in 1 Chronicles 14—16 describes in greater detail some of the more serious problems he encountered, there is reason to believe that Asa's greatest single headache came from his . . . grandmother!

Had Asa's accession to the throne followed traditional policy on the point, this grandmother, known to history as Maachah the Younger, would have retired to spend her remaining days rocking and knitting in some quiet corner of the palace, occasionally stopping to dandle a grandchild or take some cookies from the oven. Her role as queen mother, or *gebirah*, would have been assumed by Asa's own mother.

As it happened, however, the old lady did not step down, and evidently, on the day that Asa took the throne, no one in the realm was sufficiently powerful to make her step down, not even the new king.

Maachah doubtless enjoyed occupying what was a very powerful position in ancient courts. Since royal sons were hardly disposed to decline reasonable requests from their mothers (cf. 1 Kings 2:17), it was no small advantage for other members of the court to cultivate the favor of the *gebirah*. Her special place in the realm is further indicated by the fact that the Books of Kings normally list the names of the mothers of the kings of Judah.

The case of Maachah demonstrates that an especially shrewd *gebirah*, were she also unscrupulous, might manage to maintain her position at court even after the death of her son. A woman so powerful, after all, was able to put quite a number of people in her debt over the years, influential and well-placed individuals on whom she might rely later on to keep her in power. The Bible's truly singular example of this was Athaliah, the mother of Ahaziah, who actually usurped the realm itself during the years 842–837 BC (2 Kings 11).

Maachah herself never went so far, but she did manage to hold on to her privileged position at court after the accession of Asa (1 Kings 15:10). She had been around for quite a while and was well acquainted with the ways of power. Named for her grandmother, Maacah the Elder, a Geshurite princess married to David (2 Samuel 3:3), this younger Maachah was a daughter of Absalom. She was still a child during the three years that she spent with her father in his exile in Geshur (2 Samuel 13:38). Doubtless it was there that she first learned the ways of idolatry.

For Maachah was most certainly an idolatress. Raised in the easygoing atmosphere of her Uncle Solomon's court after the death of her own father, she further learned the lessons of idolatry along with the habits of political power. Given in marriage to her cousin Rehoboam, who would eventually succeed Solomon on the throne, Maachah knew that someday, when her son Abijah became king, she would become the *gebirah*. She longed for the day.

That day, when it came, did not last very long, for Abijah reigned only three years. No matter, for the determined Maachah somehow found the means to stay in power for a while longer. Except for her idolatry, Asa might have left her in place for good. But the king, as his position grew stronger, was in a reforming mood, and Maachah stood in the way of his reforms. "You know, Granny," he finally said to her one day, "it's about time for you to take up knitting" (1 Kings 15:13; 2 Chronicles 15:16).

꒰ꙮ꒱

6. THE DECISIONS OF JEHOSHAPHAT

Although the Prophet Eliezer leveled a half-verse of criticism against King Jehoshaphat near the end of his life (2 Chronicles 20:37), the Bible is, on the whole, rather positive in its assessment of that king of Judah. An earlier historian of the period summed it up: "And he walked in all the ways of his father Asa. He did not turn aside from them, doing what was right in the eyes of the LORD" (1 Kings 22:43).

Still, it is instructive to examine some unforeseen results of certain practical choices made by Jehoshaphat during the course of his admittedly virtuous life, because those unintended consequences bear witness to the human condition of sinful helplessness, our native inability to accomplish the good we will (cf. Romans 7:15–19). However pure his intentions, it is a fact that some terrible things came to pass by reason of Jehoshaphat's political decisions. Indeed, they nearly led to the downfall of the house of David.

When he took his place on the throne of Judah in 873, Jehoshaphat resolved that there would be no more fighting with the kingdom of Israel. As much as anyone, he was sick of the strife that had ravaged the Promised Land for half a century, ever since the division of the region into two kingdoms at the death of Solomon in 922. The reign of Jehoshaphat's own father, Asa, had been particularly bellicose. "Now there was war between Asa and Baasha king of Israel all their days," wrote that same historian of the period (1 Kings 15:16, 32).

Naturally, so much warfare exacted a heavy toll from Judah, in loss of life, disruption of families, devastated crops, impaired commerce, and swollen taxation, leading to a general weakening of the economy and the social order. None of this fighting, furthermore, had accomplished much. Since the only sane reason for a nation to wage a war is to *decide* something, hardly any national experience is so disheartening as an indecisive war, and Judah, by this time, was very disheartened.

The ensuing damage to the social edifice was even more severe in the kingdom of Israel, or at least we may infer so from its greater political disquiet. Israel, in addition to fighting with Judah, had been afflicted with civil unrest and dynastic strife. Whereas Jehoshaphat was Judah's fourth king after Solomon, Israel had had as many dynasties during that same period (15:25—16:23). Surely, then, Israel too might appreciate some relief from conflict.

Two other recent political changes likewise hinted that the time for peacemaking had arrived. First, barely four years before Jehoshaphat became king of Judah, Israel had crowned a new king whose name was Ahab. This new man, Jehoshaphat could see, was chiefly interested in making money by commercial ties with Phoenicia. Indeed, Ahab had married a Phoenician princess named Jezebel and served as a mercantile partner of his father-in-law, Ethbaal of Sidon. Ahab would have no interest in continuing the old fight with Judah.

Second, a much larger menace now loomed darkly in the east, where the shadowy Assyrian began to feel the movement of his might. Before long the warring Shalmaneser III (859–824 BC) would start his march to the Great Sea, and if the little nations lying along the path of that trampling march, like Israel and Judah, were to meet his threat, they had better resolve their smaller problems.

Sizing up the entire geopolitical situation, therefore, "Jehoshaphat made peace with the king of Israel" (22:44). In fact, Jehoshaphat went a very significant step further to seal that peace by arranging the marriage of his own son Jehoram, the crown prince, to Princess Athaliah, the daughter of Ahab and Jezebel. The two crown houses thus became, as it were, a single family, so that Jehoshaphat could say to Ahab, some years later, "I am as you are, my people as your people, my horses as your horses" (22:4).

Hardly could Jehoshaphat have known to what bad consequences his best intentions would lead. Within three years both his son and his son's son would be dead, and Athaliah, now queen in her own right, would nearly destroy the house of David (2 Kings 11:1). In fact, until the fall of Jerusalem nearly three centuries later, Judah never saw a darker hour. And all this from one good man's untimely decisions. Such is the power of evil in man's fallen history.

⋙

7. JOSIAH AND DEUTERONOMY

When Josiah was born in 648 BC, the geopolitical prospects of the Kingdom of Judah did not appear too bad, for the Assyrian Empire, which had long oppressed the area, was on the verge of the decline that would bring it down before the century's end.

From a religious perspective, nonetheless, the situation in Judah was bad indeed. Manasseh (687–642 BC), the very wicked king who was Josiah's grandfather, had established Canaanite and Assyrian worship in Jerusalem itself, resorting even to the sacrifice of one of his sons, an act for which he was roundly denounced (2 Kings 21:1–15). From an apocryphal work called *The Ascension of Isaiah* (5:1–14), we know that the atrocities of this depraved king included his causing the Prophet Isaiah to be sawn in half (cf. Hebrews 11:37). Besides the melancholy biblical account of his reign, Manasseh is mentioned several times in Assyrian records, always as a subject king of the Assyrian Empire.

Josiah was six years old when his grandfather died in 642, to be succeeded by the boy's unpopular father, Amon (2 Kings 21:19–26; 2 Chronicles 33:21–25). When the latter was assassinated two years later, little Josiah acceded to the throne at age eight.

We know almost nothing of his early regency period, but Josiah soon became his own man. In 632, near his sixteenth birthday, he experienced a religious conversion, pointing him in a new direction. Four years later, on assuming the full powers of the throne, Josiah began a large-scale reform of the religious life of Judah, an ambitious project now rendered possible by the growing disarray of the Assyrian Empire (2 Chronicles 34:1–17). It was also in that very year that the Lord sent Jerusalem one of the greatest prophets, a young man named Jeremiah. From a religious point of view, then, things were starting to look better.

Nonetheless, the best was yet to come. Among the features of Josiah's reform was a thorough purging of the Jerusalem temple to rid it of all vestiges of idolatry. In 622, during the course of this work, the renovators discovered a very ancient manuscript, which historians identify as either the whole or central section of the Book of Deuteronomy. It had been lost for many years. After 622, therefore, Josiah had in hand a very specific text on which to base his continuing reform of Judah's religious life. Point by point, he and his reformers began to implement the prescriptions of Deuteronomy (2 Chronicles 34:8–33), including the restoration of the Passover (35:1–19). For this reason, historians customarily refer to Josiah's efforts as the Deuteronomic Reform.

Because several generations of "Deuteronomists" would continue to make that book the basis of Judah's religious life, the ferment and effects of Josiah's reform were to outlive the king himself. In the following century, those Deuteronomic scholars would serve as the backbone of Judah's survival, and even flourishing, during the Babylonian Captivity. During that time of exile, it was under the impulse of Deuteronomic theology that they would edit and unify much of the historical material contained in the Bible.

The royal sponsorship of the Deuteronomic Reform came to an end, however, in the year 609. It happened in this way: As the Prophet Nahum had foretold, the Assyrian capital of Nineveh fell to the Babylonians in 612, but a good part of the defeated army survived. Moving north to Haran, at the top of the Fertile Crescent, this remnant continued to hold out for three years, waiting desperately for help expected from Egypt. In 609 Egypt's new Pharaoh, Neco II, to whom it was obvious that his country's advantage lay in stopping the rise of the Neo-Babylonian Empire, determined to go to the aid of those Assyrians. With some Greek mercenaries, Neco moved up into Palestine, planning to join the Assyrians at Carchemish on the Euphrates. King Josiah of Judah, however, had ideas of his own. Knowing firsthand the evils of Assyria, he decided to throw in his lot with the Babylonians, so he led the army of Judah to meet Neco's forces at the Megiddo pass. In the ensuing battle, the great Josiah was killed at age thirty-nine (2 Kings 23; 2 Chronicles 35).

For Judah his passing was an unmitigated tragedy. The strong, devout Josiah was followed on the throne by a series of quislings, who governed an ever-diminishing nation until Jerusalem's destruction in 587 BC.

☙

8. THE ANOINTED CYRUS

It is truly remarkable that God spoke of a pagan ruler, a Persian emperor, as "His anointed . . . Cyrus" (Isaiah 45:1) and called him "My shepherd" (44:28). Perhaps the extraordinary distinction accorded to Cyrus by these references is set in greater relief if we recall that the Hebrew word for "anointed" is *messiah* (in Greek *christos*), and that when God otherwise speaks of "My Anointed" in the Old Testament, the reference is to David or to Christ (Psalm 132[131]:17). The designation of Cyrus as "My shepherd," likewise, puts the attentive reader in mind of David (cf. 2 Samuel 5:2; Psalm 78[77]:71). Who, then, was this Cyrus, of whom the Lord God speaks in these messianic and covenantal terms?

He was Cyrus II of Anshan, an ancient country within the territory of modern Iran. It lay to the northeast of the Fertile Crescent, just under the Caspian Sea. After the fall of Nineveh in 612 BC, Anshan, traditionally subject to the Assyrians, became a vassal state of the Medes. In 550 its king, Cyrus II, defeated the Medes, thus becoming ruler of the entire empire of the Medes and Persians. In order to gain this ascendancy, Cyrus had accepted the help of the Babylonians, who apparently did not reflect that a victorious Cyrus would soon prove to be a greater threat to them than the Medes had ever been.

When their new danger did finally dawn on the Babylonians, they promptly formed a defensive pact with several countries, including Lydia, a kingdom situated in the west of the large peninsula that we now call Turkey. Before challenging Babylon, therefore, Cyrus determined it would be better to conquer Babylon's ally, Lydia. Accordingly, the king of Lydia, Croesus, having received assurances of military help from Egypt and Sparta, prepared to move east against Cyrus.

Prior to making that move, however, King Croesus of Lydia resolved to seek an oracular word from the god Apollo, whose shrine was at Delphi, as well as from other sources of divination (Herodotus 1.46–47). It was apparently in reference to all this feverish oracular activity that the Book of Isaiah commented that God "frustrates the signs of the babblers, / And drives diviners mad" (44:25). At the time, in fact, many predictions were being made about the struggle soon to ensue (Herodotus, 1.53–54; Isaiah 40:8; 47:12–13; 55:10–11).

On the strength of what Croesus learned, or, alas, *thought* he learned, from Apollo at Delphi, he prepared to attack Cyrus. Cyrus himself did not wait for his opponent to arrive. In the winter of 547/6 BC he launched his own attack, catching Croesus by surprise, taking his capital city of Sardis, and incorporating Lydia into his own growing empire.

The fall of Lydia struck panic among the Greeks (cf. Isaiah 41:5–6), who realized that rather soon they too would have to face the growing Persian Empire. (They would do so early in the following century, in the unforgettable battles of Marathon, Thermopylae, Salamis, and Plataea.) The panic of the Greeks, however, was nothing to that of the Babylonians. They knew that they were next on Cyrus's list.

To the Jews, however, and other peoples oppressed by the Babylonians, the recent victory of Cyrus over Lydia augured their own deliverance, so they watched his military progress with no little excitement (cf. Isaiah 41:1–4). Over and over, Israel was told not to fear, because God was about to deliver them from the Babylonians (41:8–15; 43:1, 5; 44:8; 51:7, 12; 54:4, 14). They did not have to wait very long. On October 13, 539, Cyrus captured Babylon by a shrewd tactical maneuver that immortalized his fame in military history (Herodotus 1.190–191).

As we know from a record Cyrus left to posterity, an inscription on a clay barrel called the "Cyrus Cylinder," this Persian ruler of Babylon promptly proclaimed himself a servant of the Babylonian sun god, Marduk. In the Bible, nonetheless, Cyrus is ever regarded as the historical instrument of the true God, Israel's God. It was Cyrus who brought the Babylonian Captivity to an end in 538, authorizing the return of the chosen people to their homeland, along with the restoration of the sacred vessels of Jerusalem's temple, which he ordered to be rebuilt (2 Chronicles 36:22–23; Ezra 1:1–8; 4:3; 5:13–17; 6:3). Even as Holy Scripture describes the Emperor Cyrus in terms otherwise associated with King David, this Gentile messiah—as it were—is rightly regarded as another type and foreshadowing of the true Messiah and Shepherd, Jesus the Lord, who delivers His people from a captivity more bitter than that of Babylon, restores them to the Promised Land, and builds for them a better temple.

☙

9. NEHEMIAH OF THE PERSIAN COURT

Nehemiah is arguably the Bible's best example of a man of the world who was also a godly man, deeply reflective and much given to prayer.

A Jew trained in the diplomatic and executive skills of the Persian court, Nehemiah was possessed of a firm grasp on how to get things done. The Bible calls him a royal cupbearer, but this term should not make us think of a simple domestic servant. That bearing of the cup at the king's table was but the symbolic function of an individual of great importance in the realm. The term "royal chamberlain" comes closer to the modern idiom, for this was no menial position. The Persian art of the period shows that the cupbearer ranked second, right after the crown prince, in the gradations of the royal court. Archeology indicates that sometimes cupbearers were buried in the same crypts as the emperor's own family. Nehemiah, then, was a high official of the realm, the ancient equivalent to our "prime minister." All important business with the crown passed through his hands.

In December of the year 445 (Nehemiah 1:1), certain fellow Jews came from Jerusalem to see Nehemiah at the court of Artaxerxes I, bearing the sad news that some local opposition back in the Holy Land, evidently implementing an official decree, had put a stop to the construction of the walls around the city of Jerusalem (1:2–3). It is impossible that Nehemiah did not know this already, but the firsthand report gave him a strong new impression of the full tragedy of the situation. It threw him into a depression for days, a depression accompanied by fasting and prayer (1:4). This is our first of many examples of Nehemiah in prayer.

Fortified by prayer and fasting, Nehemiah prepared to argue his case before Artaxerxes. He bided his time until the following spring; it was Nisan, the month of the Passover. Doubtless Nehemiah was waiting for the most opportune and advantageous moment, watching the movement of government, carefully observing the emperor's moods and attitudes. He resolved finally to display his feelings; it was not an inadvertent dropping of his guard, but a calculated move (2:1), and the emperor, as expected, noticed (2:2). There was a sudden tense moment, because ancient potentates liked to be surrounded by happy, healthy faces (cf. Daniel 1:10–13!). Nehemiah stated the matter quickly and succinctly, for Persian emperors were busy, efficient men, not famous for their patience. In addition, they could be terribly fickle and capricious (cf. Esther 4:11!). Nehemiah knew all this, and even while he spoke to Artaxerxes, he continued to speak to God in his heart (2:4). His brief prayer was clearly efficacious, because he managed to make his complaint without criticizing either the emperor or anyone in the Persian government.

Nehemiah was the consummate diplomat, schooled in the arts of an international court. In that scene with Artaxerxes, for example, he only answered the emperor's question. He made no request until the king explicitly asked for one, and we observe that the request, made at precisely the moment when it should have been made, was immediately granted.

Likewise, throughout the book named after him, we ever find Nehemiah playing a cool, deft hand, maintaining strict control over the cards held close to his chest. His several opponents, always obliged to guess what hand he was holding, ever acting in the dark, were no match for him. In every instance we watch Nehemiah disclosing only as much information as was needed to accomplish what he had in mind. If anyone wants to examine what it means to be as cunning as a serpent (which Jesus our Lord commands us to be), he will discover no better example than Nehemiah.

For a man accustomed to dealing with the administration of an empire that stretched from the Khyber Pass to the Danube River, the modest organization required for building the walls of Jerusalem was scarcely a challenge. Sections of the work were apportioned to various families, villages, and professions, and the construction of the walls was completed in record time. Overseeing this construction all the while, the self-possessed, reflective Nehemiah talked with God in short, frequent, and fervent prayers that are interspersed throughout the narrative (2:8, 10, 20; 3:36–37; 4:9; 5:13, 19; 6:14, 16; 13:14, 22, 31, 39).

ॐ

10. MORDECAI VERSUS HAMAN

However bitter the feelings between them, the conflict of Haman and Mordecai was more than a personal fight. It rather closely resembled, in fact, the resumption of a family feud.

It is important to see that the strife between Mordecai and Haman was older than either of them. If Haman hated the Jews, as surely he did (Esther 3:10; 8:5; 9:24), it was hardly surprising. He was, after all, an Amalekite, descended from King Agag (3:1), whose realm had been conquered by Israel's first monarch, Saul the son of Kish, of the tribe of Benjamin (1 Samuel 15:1–8). As for Mordecai, he also was of the tribe of Benjamin and the grandson of another man named Kish (Esther

2:5–6). The encounter of these two men involved an ancient grudge.

Thus, the earliest commentator on this story, Flavius Josephus, called attention to the immemorial resentment contained in Haman's hatred of Mordecai: "Now there was a certain Haman, the son of Amedatha, an Amalekite by birth, who was accustomed to approach the king. . . . And when he wished to punish Mordecai, he thought it too insignificant a thing to request of the king that he alone should be punished; he resolved, rather, to annihilate the whole nation, for he was naturally an enemy of the Jews, because the Amalekites, to which he belonged, had earlier been destroyed by them" (*Antiquities of the Jews* 11.6.5).

These circumstances form no little part of the irony of the Book of Esther, in which two ancient adversaries encounter each other anew, as it were, in the far-off country of Persia. This time their battle is fought, not with military weapons, but with the might of wisdom. The combat of Haman and Mordecai moves its battle lines to the field of practical wit. The triumph that the Jew wins over the Amalekite in this instance is a victory of the mind.

Haman, the highest official of the Persian court (Esther 3:1), represents a perverse and malicious philosophy. He belongs to that class of men whom Jeremiah described as "wise to do evil" (Jeremiah 4:22) and of whom Isaiah said they are "wise in their own eyes, / And prudent in their own sight" (Isaiah 5:21). Haman violates all the rules of true wisdom. First, he permits himself to be filled with rage (Esther 3:5; 5:9; cf. Proverbs 21:24; 29:22). Second, moved by passion, he reacts precipitously and without caution (Esther 3:6; cf. Proverbs 14:17, 29). Third, he becomes imprudent in his speech (Esther 5:10–13; cf. Proverbs 12:23).

Mordecai too is an official of the realm, described as sitting "within the king's gate" (Esther 2:21), an expression meaning that he is a judge or magistrate who adjudicates legal cases. (Indeed, we also know Mordecai from a contemporary Persian document that refers to him as "Marduka.") Though hardly the wisest man in Holy Scripture, he has more than enough wisdom to outwit Haman.

Josephus speaks of Mordecai's wisdom (*sophia*), born of his reverence for the Torah (*nomos*). Mordecai is not moved by passion, is not precipitous to act, nor does he rashly speak his plans to others. In all these things he shows himself a true sage and man of self-control (cf. Proverbs 12:23; 13:3; 16:32), worthy to replace the arrogant Haman (Esther 6:1–14).

Consequently, what finally ensues in the encounter of these two men is exactly what the Bible's wisdom literature would lead us to expect (Proverbs 11:8; 26:27; Psalm 7:14–16; Ecclesiastes 10:8). Haman is put to death (Esther 7:10), whereas Mordecai is given the signet ring of the king (8:2, 8) and honored in the sight of the nation (8:15).

When old King Saul, the earlier son of Kish, defeated Agag centuries before, his failure to kill that Amalekite had earned him the censure of Samuel (1 Kings 15:9, 20–23). Indeed, that was the occasion, we recall, when the Lord regretted having made Saul the king (15:11). In the Book of Esther, however, the situation is set aright. The moral failure of the earlier Benjaminite is not duplicated in the case of Mordecai. Haman is not spared, but dies the death he deserves.

With respect to that ancient feud, there is a further irony in the story of Mordecai and Haman. Whereas Saul, the first descendant of Kish, had despoiled Agag without killing him, this second descendant of Kish, Mordecai, kills the Agagites without despoiling them (Esther 9:10).

⚬҄

11. CORNELIUS THE CENTURION

Among the polarities employed in the Bible's treatment of salvation, that of universality and holiness is perhaps the easiest to describe. Universality is wide, and holiness narrow. We are bidden by the former, "Come to Me, all you who labor and are heavy laden, and I will give you rest" (Matthew 11:28), while the latter declares, "Unless you repent you will all likewise perish" (Luke 13:3, 5). The first is inclusive and brims with encouragement, whereas the second is restrictive and hurls out a challenge. Thus, when the principle of universality proclaims that God "desires all men to be saved" (1 Timothy 2:4), the principle of holiness answers that "narrow is the gate and difficult is the way which leads to life, and there are few who find it" (Matthew 7:14).

The tension inherent in this polarity is first theological, to be sure, hinting at the mysterious confrontation of God's freedom with man's. But because salvation is worked out in history, we are not surprised to find the tension between universality and holiness taking shape in discrete contingent forms. For example, against the backdrop of the Roman Empire's political universality, the Acts of the Apostles portrays the strain that the early Church felt between her universal call to mission within that world and the stern demand laid upon her to be a people set apart from it. That is to say, the theological tension assumes flesh as a tension of history, and then again, issuing from the pen of St. Luke, a tension of narrative.

Within Luke's lengthy account of how that theological tension was maintained by the counterweights of history, the conversion of Cornelius and his friends is of central importance. So the story is worth revisiting under the aspect of that consideration.

Cornelius's entrance into the Christian Church is especially significant, not only because he is a Gentile, but also because, in his military office, he represents the Roman Empire. In this representation Cornelius is prefigured by Luke's earlier centurion at the foot of the Cross, who pronounced Rome's final verdict, as it were, on Jesus of Nazareth: "Certainly this was a righteous man!" (Contrast Luke 23:47 with Matthew 27:54 and Mark 15:39.) In this adjudication the representative of a political universality receives the grace to discern, by the light of universal norms of righteousness, that Jesus at least meets the common standards of a moral claim. In this respect he takes Rome's first step in favor of Jesus and is, thereby, the forerunner of Cornelius. It is for this reason that the Acts of the Apostles will end in Rome (28:13–16).

The story of Cornelius is told with great care. Indeed, it is told twice, once by Luke as narrator and once by Cornelius himself. (Peter's part is also told twice, by the way, once by Luke and once by Peter.) As angelic announcements solemnly indicated the beginning of the Gospel (Luke 1:11, 26; 2:9), so this coming mission to the Roman Empire is announced by an angel (Acts 10:3). The calling of Cornelius is, for Luke, a decisive step in the universalizing of the Gospel, foreseen by the prophetic Simeon's "light to bring revelation to the Gentiles" (Luke 2:32). It is Peter's reception of this centurion into the Church that prepares the universal mission (and trip to Rome) of Paul, himself converted in the previous chapter.

In the tale of Cornelius, even the time frame is easy to find. Since we know that the angel instructed him on one of the weekly Jewish fast days (Monday or Thursday), and since we should presume that Peter would not have traveled from Joppa to Caesarea on a Sabbath, we may be quite sure that the "four days" of the story began on a Monday (Acts 10:9, 24, 30).

These references to fast days (and the maintenance of the "canonical hours" —10:3, 30) are also relevant to our theme, for they indicate the "holiness" pole in the tension of salvation. Cornelius represents, not only the universality of grace, but the restricting efforts of spiritual discipline. Luke describes him as "a devout man and one who feared God with all his household, who gave alms generously to the people, and prayed to God always" (10:2). Praying, fasting, and giving alms are not incidental to the story. Cornelius is told, on the contrary, "your prayer has been heard, and your alms are remembered in the sight of God" (10:31). Both universality and holiness pertain to the picture.

X.
SAINTS UNDER PRESSURE
乷

One does not have to live very long, I think, to perceive a certain per-
verseness about this world, life's strange but innate contrariness that
cripples man's stride and corrodes his hope. Indeed, in terms of plain
empirical verification, few lines of Holy Scripture seem supported by
more and better evidence than St. Paul's testimony that "creation was
subjected to futility" (Romans 8:20).

This dark sense of things is what the ancient Greeks called "tragedy," a subject they appear to have pondered more than most. The root
word for this expression means "goat" (*tragos*), an animal commonly
associated with stubbornness, mischief, aberrance, and even damnation
(Matthew 25:32–33).

The Greeks observed that however slight the flaw in the fabric of a
human life, implacable *tragodia* seemed ever able to spy it out and rip
that life to shreds. They transmitted endless stories illustrating this theme.

In one such account, the hero Theseus, returning to Athens after
slaying the Minotaur on Crete, neglected to alter his ship's sail from
black to white, the color that his father Aegeus had instructed him to
hoist, on his return, to signify his victory. When Aegeus, waiting on the
shore, beheld instead the black sail atop his son's returning ship, he
rashly presumed that Theseus had perished, and not waiting for confir-
mation of the matter, he flung himself in despair from a high precipice
and was dashed to death on the rocks below. Thus, poor Theseus, though
triumphant over the menacing Minotaur, returned only to find that a
more formidable and relentless foe, impossible either to envision or resist, had turned his brief joy into lasting sadness (Plutarch, *Lives*,
"Theseus" 22). The impetuosity of his father had conspired with his
own slight and momentary inattention to devour the substance of his
hope. Once again, the smallest flaw in his life's fabric became the entrance point of tragedy.

But even without the dramatic pangs of tragedy, the Greeks realized, life in this world was usually hard, very often a struggle, even a kind of combat. Young people needed to learn this lesson early, a need that explains why Homer's *Iliad*, which portrays life as a battlefield, served as an essential text of classical Greek education. The truer and deeper warfare portrayed in the Iliad, after all, is the struggle to excel, to be virtuous, *aristevein* (*Iliad* 6.208; 11.784). (Classical Greek education's other essential text was Homer's *Odyssey*, which sketches life as a journey.)

Classical paganism's greatest moral effort to deal with the toughness of life, including its tragic sense, was the philosophy known as Stoicism. The Stoic, realizing that most events in life—virtually all things outside himself—lay beyond his ability to control, resolved to bring discipline and serenity into his soul by putting aside his passions, bridling the reckless ambitions of his mind and will, and striving for inner freedom. One of the more notable Stoics, Epictetus, remarked that it was solely by abandoning the desire to master things outside himself that a man could gain mastery within himself. Only this inner mastery could mitigate the trials and misfortunes of life.

Holy Scripture, tracing all evil in the world, including especially death, to man's infidelity to God, normally uses the experience of evil as the occasion for calling man to repentance. This theme appears repeatedly in the Bible's historical and prophetic books. Job and Qoheleth, along with some of the psalms, do include speculation about the structure of tragedy, but this line of thought remains exceptional in Holy Scripture.

More prominent is the theme of the Cross, which provides the key, not to unlock the correct explanation of evil, but to open a door to ultimate deliverance. It is the promise of the Cross that "God will wipe away every tear from their eyes; there shall be no more death, nor sorrow, nor crying. There shall be no more pain, for the former things have passed away" (Revelation 21:4).

Short of that eschatological exchange of sorrow for joy, however, the Bible never essays to diminish the stark seriousness of human suffering. Certain pages of Holy Scripture, were they understood apart from themes like divine providence and the abiding primacy of grace, would be unbearably dark. The saints, in short, seem to live ever under pressure.

X. SAINTS UNDER PRESSURE

⅗

1. THE EYES OF LEAH

The Lord looked out for Leah. He had to. Nobody else would.

Well, all right, I exaggerate. Leah's father Laban also looked out for her, at least in the sense of making sure she was married before her younger sister. Nor, let it be said, was this an easy thing to do. When Jacob arrived at Padan-Aram, he immediately fell in love with that younger sister, Rachel, whom the Bible describes as "beautiful of form and appearance." It was Rachel that Jacob had in mind to marry (Genesis 29:17–18).

With respect to Leah's physical appearance, Holy Scripture comments only on her eyes, which are said to be *rakkoth*. Although the root of this adjective means "weak" (hence "sickly" in the Septuagint, "bleary" in the Vulgate, and "delicate" in the New King James), the word more likely indicates that her eyes were tender or gentle. (The medieval Jewish commentator Rashi speculated that Leah's eyes were wasting away with continual weeping, at the thought that she might have to marry Jacob's older brother Esau!) Perhaps the Sacred Text mentions only Leah's eyes because these were her sole attractive aspect. Anyway, Jacob was not in love with her.

For Leah the impending marriage of her younger sister was something of a disadvantage, because, as Laban explained, "It must not be done so in our country, to give the younger before the firstborn" (29:26). On the other hand, this explanation may have been merely an excuse, and Laban definitely needed an excuse for what he did. Determined that his older daughter should not go unwed, he furtively substituted Leah into Jacob's bed on the wedding night. Jacob, discovering the substitution the next morning, remarked to his father-in-law at breakfast that the move had been a bit sneaky, a kind of thing not entirely acceptable among gentlemen (29:24–25). But the matter was settled, and not much could be done about it. Laban gave Rachel to Jacob as a second wife, and the young man would just have to make the best of it.

Leah, for her part, certainly felt the indignity of the situation, always conscious of not being her husband's first choice. Jacob "loved Rachel more than Leah," the Bible tells us (29:30); indeed, it literally says that Jacob *hated* Leah (29:31). He must not have hated her too much, though, because she was often pregnant. Moreover, that same verse goes on to say that Leah's frequent pregnancies demonstrated that the Lord Himself was looking out for her.

He was also looking out for Leah's husband. The Lord had promised Jacob a large progeny (28:14), but Jacob had gone and fallen in love with Rachel, a woman who would die in giving birth to her second son. Had the young man been permitted to follow his own plans, God's promise would not, humanly speaking, have been fulfilled.

Leah, on the other hand, gave Jacob six sons and a daughter. Although she had not been part of Jacob's plans, Leah was a most important component in God's plan, for from her body leapt the royal and priestly bloodlines of the realm. Leah's third son, Levi, became the primogenitor of Israel's priesthood, including Moses, Aaron, Zachary, and John the Baptist. Her fourth son, Judah, was the ancestor of the house of David, the kingly family, including "Joseph the husband of Mary, of whom was born Jesus who is called Christ" (Matthew 1:16). Indeed, the Lord was looking out for Leah.

We have here a biblical example of God's use of someone's deception as an instrument of His providence. Indeed, there is a special irony to Leah's story in this respect. If Jacob thought Laban's substitution of Leah for Rachel in the marriage bed had been a bit too undercover (so to speak), he should know. Jacob, intimately acquainted with all manner of underhanded activity, had barely removed the disguise by which he deceived his father Isaac and stole the blessing intended for Esau. Since he had pulled that little trick to the disadvantage of an older brother, there was some justice in Jacob's being tricked, in turn, to the advantage of an older sister. And the Lord was at work in it all. Just as God had used Jacob's deception of Isaac as a means to accomplish His salvific will, He used Laban's deception of Jacob for the same purpose.

Finally, it was Leah, not Rachel, who would lie buried beside Jacob her husband in the cave of the field of Machpelah, before Mamre, in the inheritance of Judah, her fourth-born.

ॐ

2. THE TRAGEDY OF JEPHTHAH

By way of preparing us for the establishment of Israel's monarchy near the end of the eleventh century BC, the Book of Judges ends with a discouraging analysis of the moral climate of the period prior to that of the kings: "In those days there was no king in Israel; everyone did what was right in his own eyes" (21:25). Since the identical words appear earlier, at the beginning of the account of Micah and the Danites (17:6), we are likely correct in thinking that this melancholy assessment pertains especially to the wild and, frankly, disedifying stories that lie between those two verses: the migration of the Danites and their kidnapping of Micah, the gory account of Gibeah and the Levite's concubine, Israel's war with Benjamin, and the abduction of the virgins of Jabesh Gilead. Indeed, the startling similarity between this last narrative and the Roman legend of the rape of the Sabines tends to strengthen one's impression of raw paganism in these stories. Truly, they are among the harshest and most disheartening pages in Holy Scripture.

Earlier accounts in the Book of Judges, however, also indicate a considerable lack of moral direction throughout Israel during that early period. The stories of Jephthah, for example. Did the Bible not explicitly tell us that "the Spirit of the LORD came upon Jephthah" (Judges 11:29), some of us might really wonder. Even so, quite a number of students of Holy Scripture, over the years, must have shaken their heads in bewilderment at the behavior of Jephthah.

Most conspicuous in this respect, surely, is the story of Jephthah's sacrifice of his own daughter (11:29–40). Although various commentators have endeavored to "explain away" the obvious meaning of this story, such explanations will not stand up to literary and historical scrutiny. However uncomfortable it makes us, Jephthah really did offer his daughter in sacrifice.

Other writers, perhaps taking their cue from the story of Herod Antipas and John the Baptist (cf. Mark 6:22–29), have spoken of a "rash oath" on the part of Jephthah. Dante, for example, read the text this way (cf. *Paradiso* 5:64–68). However, there is nothing in the account of Jephthah to suggest that the vow was incautious on his part, except in its unexpected result. It is portrayed, rather, as his deliberate pledge to sacrifice a human life, an oath that Jephthah apparently believed he would fulfill by sacrificing a slave or some other person less significant than his own daughter. The literal meaning of the narrative is very plain.

It is also conspicuous for its lack of moral comment, the author using a restraint markedly in contrast to other places where the Holy Scripture speaks of human sacrifice (cf. 2 Kings 16:3; 17:17; 21:6;

Jeremiah 7:31; Micah 6:7). Likewise, the tragedy of Jephthah and his daughter is told in the starkest terms, with emphasis on his own grief and on the daughter's bravery in accepting her allotted fate and her compassion for the dereliction of her father. There is no doubt or hesitation in the mind of either of them. Unlike the case of Abraham, God does not intervene to save the situation. Nor would Jephthah be long in following his daughter in death (Judges 12:7). A great sense of irony and doom hangs over this whole story, told as an unmitigated tragedy.

The oath of Jephthah, once he makes it, seems to carry an ironlike inevitability which, from a purely literary perspective, may put one in mind of the Greek tragedies. Indeed, readers have often remarked on the thematic similarity between the stories of Jephthah and Agamemnon, who also sacrificed a daughter in connection with a military operation. Dante (*Paradiso* 5:64–72), for instance, believed that the stories would always be remembered together. Arguably more prominent, however, are the ways in which these two accounts stand in contrast. First, unlike Jephthah, Agamemnon is not struck by a misfortune unforeseen; his sacrifice of Iphigeneia is planned and very deliberate. Second, unlike the bloody details in Aeschylus's portrayal of the sacrifice of Iphigeneia, the Bible's narrative is very sober and subdued; there is no direct mention of the sacrifice itself. Indeed, from a strictly dramatic (as distinct from theological) point of view, it may be argued that the sense of inevitable doom in the biblical story of Jephthah is even more "Greek" than the Greek tragedy.

⨯

3. SAMSON THE NAZIRITE

As a lifelong Nazirite, Samson was supposed to live a completely consecrated existence, an undistracted life, singular of intent, pure in purpose. That was, at least, the plan.

The biblical noun "Nazirite," derived from the Semitic root *nzr*, meaning "to set apart," referred to those who vowed to perform some special work in God's service. During the time of that service, the Nazirite's dedication to his vow was indicated by certain ritual and ascetic practices. Indeed, the Nazirite lived very much as the priest did during his own days of liturgical ministry. For example, both men maintained a strict ritual purity and abstained from wine and alcohol. In

206

addition, the hair of the Nazirite was not cut until the completion of the vow (Numbers 6:1–21).

Directed to a specific task, the Nazirite's commitment normally lasted for only a determined period. Nonetheless, Holy Scripture indicates three instances in which the Nazirite's special consecration was to last for his entire lifetime. In two of these instances, Samuel and John the Baptist, the purity of their dedication appears to have been perfect and above reproach all the days of their lives (1 Samuel 1:11, especially in the LXX; Luke 1:15; 7:33).

Prior to Samuel and John the Baptist, however, there was Samson (Judges 13:7), and, in the case of Samson, the maintenance of his life-long Nazirite consecration became a bit . . . well, complicated.

Arguably the most memorable characteristic of Samson was his immense, Spirit-endowed strength (Judges 13:25), which he displayed in such vigorous, wholesome pursuits as ripping lions apart with his bare hands (14:6), snapping strong ropes as though they were thin threads (15:14; 16:12), toting heavy city gates up to inconvenient places (16:3), all the while burning the harvests and bashing the heads of deserving Philistines (14:19; 15:5, 8, 15). Such rollicking exhibitions of brawn, tending as they did to keep God's enemies in check and off-balance, were entirely commendable, and Samson spent a good twenty years doing what he did best (15:20).

Nonetheless, Samson was not in every respect a man of strength. No, and his distinct weakness was women. Though he eschewed strong drink, Samson did not avoid women. Far from it. On two occasions he fell in love, each time, alas, rather unwisely. Each of the women that Samson loved betrayed him. The first was the unnamed Philistine wife of his youth, and the other a mysterious lady named Delilah, who sealed the tragedy of his last years.

There is a serial correspondence between these two stories of Samson in his youth and in his later days. First, each woman is used by the Philistines to "entice" the strong man (14:15; 16:5). Second, in each story Samson is bound with "new ropes" (15:12–13; 16:8, 12). Third, in both cases the breaking of these ropes is compared to a destruction by fire (15:14; 16:9). Fourth, both women want to know a secret, which Samson, finally unable to endure their insistent pouting, rashly discloses to them (14:16–17; 16:16–17).

The close correspondence in detail between these two narratives, however, serves chiefly to heighten the contrast between them. We perceive that Samson in the second story has become, as it were, a different man. In the first account, Samson is "in command," both of himself and of the situation. In the second, Samson is in command of neither. Twenty years separate the two accounts, and Samson is no longer young. Nor, for that matter, is he any longer virtuous. Just prior to falling in love with Delilah, in fact, he had already become involved with a prostitute (16:1).

In short, the aging Nazirite falls. Seduced unto the loss of his hair, the outward sign of his inner consecration, Samson is suddenly bereft of his great strength (16:17–20). And then, as though to guarantee that His Nazirite will never look at another woman, God permits Samson to be blinded. Unseeing, but faintly sensing the pagan world about him, Samson spends the ensuing years, day by day, grinding the Philistine grain (16:21).

But all these things, even Samson's fall, are parts of God's providential plan (14:4). As tragic as any figure that ever graced the theatres of ancient Greece, blind Samson bides his time, and at last, though he cannot see the light of it, there dawns the day of his deliverance. As the multitude of Samson's taunters assemble in their temple, he knows what he will do. Sensing the strength that returned slowly to his frame as the hair returned slowly to his head, Samson resolves to redeem his tarnished life by the sacrifice of a selfless death. Praying for the grace to do so (16:28–30), he wreaks his final destruction on the Philistines by forcing one last display of his mighty strength.

❧

4. DAVID'S WOMEN

King David made Abigail a happy woman, but she was the exception. Over the other women along his path, as far as we can tell, David invariably cast a shadow dark and tragic.

There was Bathsheba, for example, whom the king lured into sin, which sin further prompted him, in due course, to murder her husband. Indeed, King David caused conflict even in the household of Bathsheba's birth. Her grandfather, Ahithophel, conspired against him (15:12), whereas her father, Eliam, was one of his military leaders (2 Samuel 11:4; 23:34). The little else we know of Bathsheba's life includes the death of the first child she bore to the king (2 Samuel 12:15–18) and that distinct whiff of awkwardness attendant on their final meeting (1 Kings 1:15–16).

Then there was Michal, Saul's younger daughter and David's first wife. Her fascination with the new hero (18:20), himself already popular among the local women (18:6–7), probably shielded Michal's girlish heart from knowing, at first, that she was only a pawn in the deeper plans of Saul (18:21). Soon, nonetheless, her devotion to her husband obliged the young lady to take sides against her father and then lie about it (19:11–17).

Saul, for his part, had other plans for Michal. At David's exile, she was taken away from him and given as wife to Palti, of whom we know only that he loved her—perhaps the sole man that ever did—and was the father of her five children (Josephus, *Antiquities* 7.4.3). David himself also married again, first to Abigail, then to Ahinoam. All three of these marriages are mentioned together, as though to indicate that "things were over" between Michal and David (25:43–44).

After the death of Saul, however, in the peace negotiations that David conducted with the party of the late king, he demanded that Michal be returned to him. Accordingly, she was abducted from Palti, who reacted in one of the Bible's most poignant lines: "Then her husband went along with her to Bahurim, weeping behind her" (2 Samuel 3:16). Thus, Saul was not the last man to deal with Michal as a political pawn.

Michal became but a trophy in David's court, and perhaps it was the bitterness of her life, in part, that prompted Michal to sarcasm about the king's dancing before the Ark (6:16, 20). No king is safely mocked to his face, however, and apparently Michal was never again invited to the royal bed (6:21–23). Forcibly exiled from her one devoted husband and five children, did Michal ever know another day of happiness?

Merab, Michal's older sister (1 Samuel 14:49), was a third woman to whom the thought of David meant nothing but misery. As the daughter that Saul promised in marriage to whatever warrior defeated Goliath (17:25; 18:17), Merab seemed destined to become the wife of David, but the wedding was called off, perhaps because Saul learned of the younger sister's preference. Merab was given, instead, to Dariel the Meholathite (18:19–20; 2 Samuel 21:8), to whom she bore five sons. We would like to add that they all lived happily ever after.

We would like to say that, but in fact they did not live happily ever after. Years later the delayed shadow of David fell at last across the path of Merab. The king, constrained to hand over seven descendants of Saul to satisfy an ancient grudge of the Gibeonites (21:1–6), chose the five sons of Merab to be of their number (21:8). Then, in one of the truly tenebrous lines of Scripture, the Gibeonites "hanged them on the hill before the LORD" (21:9). With that last notice of her tragedy, the loss of all five children on a single day, forlorn Merab disappeared from history, mentioned by neither Chronicles nor Josephus.

And last there was sad Rizpah, Saul's concubine who bore him two sons. When these two were joined with the five sons of Merab to make up the seven slain by the avenging Gibeonites (21:8), Rizpah stood lonely, wretched guard over those suspended corpses decomposing in the sun; "she did not allow the birds of the air to rest on them by day nor the beasts of the field by night" (21:10). This desperate labor of devotion earned Rizpah the respect of King David himself, who had caused to overflow her cup of sorrow, even unto flood (21:11–14).

⽞

5. NABOTH AND HIS INHERITANCE

Naboth was a conservative. He could even be called a hopeless conservative, because he was also an anachronism. The moving times had passed him by, and his desperate cause was doomed from the start.

But even to speak of Naboth's "cause" is probably misleading, for he was certainly no activist nor agitator, no reactionary nor leader of a movement. On the contrary, Naboth was a quiet, private man who wanted only to be left alone, free to grow his grapes on the little plot his fathers had planted for roughly three centuries.

There had been a time, and not so very long before, when Naboth's modest aspirations represented an ideal. Even a century earlier, during the reign of Solomon (961–922 BC), it was said that "Judah and Israel dwelt safely, each man under his vine and his fig tree" (1 Kings 4:25). Truth to tell, the Mosaic ordinance, taken literally, prescribed that no man's farm, the land bequeathed by his father, should ever pass definitively out of the family. In due course, rather, those same inherited fields would be handed on to the next generation, so that household and real estate would remain forever inseparable (Leviticus 25:23; Numbers 36:7).

But by Naboth's day the times had changed, and fewer folks felt tied so to their land. Indeed, in large measure Solomon himself, by introducing new mercantile enterprises and fiscal policies, had been responsible for the change. Thanks to the peace that David's sword had brought to the region, international trade started to boom in the second half of the tenth century before Christ. By shrewd geopolitical maneuvers, Solomon joined the vast shipping interests of the Mediterranean to the extensive mercantile empire of Sheba, spread through the Red Sea, the Gulf of Aden, the Arabian Sea, the Indian Ocean, the Bay of Bengal, and waters more exotic still.

As a consequence of these adventures, new and lucrative employment was to be had in Israel's expanding cities, jobs much easier than the long hours and back-bending labor of the small family farm. Little wonder, then, that many Israelites began to adopt a less-than-literal understanding of the ancient rules about not letting their land be lost from the family. Attracted by the prospect of a brighter future in the city, working at any of the scores of new professions spawned by Solomon's economic success, many citizens simply forfeited the inheritance of their fathers.

This rich economic development meant, of course, fewer farmers and larger farms. This adjustment created no immediate problems of labor, nonetheless, because the larger farms were more efficiently cultivated with tools made from a recently smelted metal called iron. Plowshare blades, axes, hoes, and scythes were sturdier than ever. Furthermore, farmers learned to seal the walls of their wells and cisterns with calcium oxide, thus preserving the precious water needed for irrigation. Food production increased enormously.

The enhanced nutrition not only lowered the infant mortality rate, it also led to earlier puberty and menarche, thus increasing the birth rate. The larger and healthier population provided the expanding work force needed for the economic boom. In short, as far as the bankers and financiers were concerned, the times were bright, and the future looked brighter. Seldom any more did one hear his elders talk of "the good old days" prior to this new, advanced era.

Not every man, however, fell into step with the march of progress, and a hundred years later there were still some stubborn, godly souls who, reading the Mosaic mandates rather close to the letter, maintained the homesteads very much as their forebears had done. Naboth, whose story is told in 1 Kings 21, was one of these dogged holdouts. When

King Ahab, coveting Naboth's vineyard in Jezreel, sought to buy or swap for it, he was met by the owner's emphatic "No!"

Because Ahab's queen was a ruthless woman, not scrupulous about such matters as suborned perjury and the shedding of blood, Naboth paid for his conservatism with the price of his life. Like his contemporary Elijah, this brave vine-grower stood defenseless but defiant before raw power and cruel injustice. This baffling Naboth's hearty answer to Ahab (21:3) may serve as a battle cry for every true conservative: "The LORD forbid that I should give the inheritance of my fathers to you!"

⊰৹

6. MICAIAH'S FORCED PROPHECY

Besides surprised, Micaiah ben Imlah was feeling more than faintly puzzled. A messenger had just arrived from the palace in Samaria, summoning him to a large consultation of prophets that King Ahab had assembled to consider some new military option. Ahab, for reasons that Micaiah could only guess, wanted him to be a part of that consultation. Why? After all, the king had never been especially happy about Micaiah's earlier prophecies.

The time was 850 BC, roughly three years since King Ahab had joined forces with Ben-Hadad of Damascus, along with other allies in the region, to withstand the forces of the Assyrian emperor, Shalmaneser III, at the battle of Qarqar. So far, their *ad hoc* military league had been successful in discouraging further invasions from Assyria, and as long as there was a possible threat from that quarter, it seemed, peace would continue between Israel and Damascus (1 Kings 22:1).

But Ahab learned that peace with Damascus came at a price, and, notwithstanding the advantage that he enjoyed by maintaining this good relationship with Ben-Hadad, it truly rankled him that the latter still occupied an ancient Israelite city, Ramoth Gilead. The secure return of all Israelite cities had been one of the pledges exacted from Ben-Hadad several years earlier, when Ahab had defeated him at the battle of Aphek (20:1–34). The pledge was not being honored. Besides, Ahab recalled, even at the battle of Qarqar, when he had joined forces with Ben-Hadad to meet the Assyrians, he himself had put no fewer than two thousand chariots on the field, eight hundred more than came from Damascus. Ahab was confident, then, that he could settle accounts properly with this Ben-Hadad with sufficient show of force.

Micaiah ben Imlah knew most of this already. What puzzled him was the fact that King Ahab was seeking his own prophetic word about attacking Damascus. After all, there were four hundred "yes prophets" at court already, who would tell his majesty exactly what he wanted to hear. Chief among them was Zedekiah ben Chenaanah, a thoroughly uncivil and surly fellow much given to theatrical flourish on matters of prophecy (22:11).

The royal messenger indicated to Micaiah that Ahab had little choice. King Jehoshaphat of Judah, he explained, on whom Ahab was relying for military assistance, was apparently having second thoughts on the business. Recently arrived at court in Samaria, the king of Judah was not entirely convinced by the enthusiasm of these four hundred "yes prophets" encouraging Ahab to go to war. Suspecting them to be nothing more than groveling sycophants, Jehoshaphat wanted to make certain that the planned attack on Damascus was really God's will. So he requested that a new voice be added to the discussion. Ahab agreed to summon Micaiah, but reluctantly, for he added "I hate him, because he does not prophesy good concerning me, but evil" (22:2–8).

The king's messenger to Micaiah pleaded with the prophet, then, not to upset the royal plans. Four hundred prophets, surely, could not be wrong. "Please," he said, "let your word be like the word of one of them, and speak encouragement" (22:13). But Micaiah made him no such promise.

Arriving at the gate of Samaria, where the two kings were enthroned in regal splendor, Micaiah resolved to be sarcastic with Ahab. This fool of a king was determined to wage war? Well, then, let him. "Go and prosper," Micaiah announced in a singsong voice, "for the LORD will deliver it into the hand of the king!" Ahab, however, would not let the matter rest. When he insisted on knowing "the truth in the name of the LORD," Micaiah gave him an undiluted dose, prophesying not only Israel's defeat at the hands of Ben-Hadad, but also Ahab's own death in the battle. Turning to Jehoshaphat when he heard these words, Ahab exclaimed: "Did I not tell you he would not prophesy good concerning me, but evil?" (22:15–18).

Micaiah was promptly dispatched to prison until Ahab should return from battle, but he knew that the king would never come home. His own prophetic efforts that day had gone for naught, faced as he was with a moral buffoon forcing him, by a "no-win" question, to make a "no-win" prophecy. The Lord had determined Ahab's destruction (22:19–23). Realizing this, Micaiah headed off to prison. At least he would never again be called to court!

⚜

7. THE HOME LIFE OF HOSEA

Hosea's vocation was most unusual (if that is the word we want). It all had to do with his truly miserable home life. Hosea was not directed, like Jeremiah (Jeremiah 16:1), to remain celibate, nor was he admonished, like Ezekiel (Ezekiel 24:15–18), not to weep at the death of his wife. Oh no, Jeremiah and Ezekiel were shirkers beside Hosea. God told him, rather, to go marry a whore and beget children of her (Hosea 1:2). More than that, he was commanded to love the woman (3:1).

The setting of Hosea's life was the Northern Kingdom in the mid-eighth century before Christ, during the long reign of Jeroboam II (1:1), of whom the Bible says (surprise!) that "he did evil in the sight of the LORD" (2 Kings 14:24). Just a few decades before Israel fell to Assyria in 722, it was a time of national apostasy, when "the LORD saw that the affliction of Israel was very bitter; and whether bond or free, there was no helper for Israel" (14:26).

Like his slightly earlier contemporary Amos, Hosea sensed the impending doom and felt the same frustration at the people's refusal to repent in the face of that coming disaster. Unlike Amos, however, Hosea had relatively little to say about social sins, such as war crimes and the oppression of the poor; he was more directly concerned with that form of idolatry known as syncretism—that is, the combining of the true religion with elements, both doctrinal and ritual, from pagan religion.

In particular Hosea was concerned with the worship of Baal, the Canaanite god of rain and fertility (Hosea 2:17). It was not accidental, Hosea believed, that the prohibition against idolatry was the very first of the commandments, because ultimately all sin is rooted in the violation of that commandment. Israel had thus sown the wind and would reap the whirlwind (8:7).

So why marry a prostitute? The message of that action was really quite simple. God had betrothed Israel to Himself in the Covenant of Mount Sinai, which several of the prophets described in the metaphors of marriage. Thus, Israel's adherence to the religion of the Canaanites, to their god Baal, was on the order of marital infidelity. Idolatry was a form of adultery. Israel was continually unfaithful in her marriage commitment to the Lord, and the Lord, as the faithful Husband of the Covenant, suffered the pains of her repeated infidelities. God suffered these pains precisely because of His own continuing fidelity to Israel.

God commanded Hosea, then, to go out and marry this whore named Gomer (1:3), a woman who would be unfaithful to him repeatedly. Hosea did so, and the rest of his life was filled with sadness and disappointment, as over and over again he forgave and took back his faithless wife. This, he said, was God's own experience with His chosen people, constantly forgiving their repeated infidelities. He felt in his own pulse, as it were, the longing of God to bring Israel once again to the early desert days of the divine espousals, "As in the days of her youth, / As in the day when she came up from the land of Egypt" (2:15).

Hosea, in the very circumstances of his marriage, was to embody God's experience of the Covenant and to know through the pains of his own soul the deep grief of the divine heart. This feature of Hosea's vocation marks him as one of the Bible's most special messengers, participating, even by the details of his prophetic life, in the very suffering of God, the mystery of our Blood-redemption on the Cross. "Who is wise?" asks Hosea; "Let him understand these things" (14:9).

Perhaps the most poignant scene in this very poignant book is found in chapter 3, where Hosea must go down to the slave market and, with great embarrassment amid a jeering crowd ("Chastity begins at home!"), buy back the mother of his children, who has fallen so low as to lose her freedom. The price of a slave is thirty shekels of silver (cf. Exodus 21:32; Leviticus 27:4; Matthew 26:15), but Hosea does not even have enough money to close the deal. He is obliged to "scrape together" the resources to make the purchase, throwing in some measures of barley from the family kitchen. Nonetheless, he does so, because he still loves this unworthy wife, and, like God, he is resolved to take her back once again. These few verses form one of the most moving scenes in the whole Bible.

This wife of Hosea bore him children, to whom he was directed to give very improbable names, names symbolic of Israel's sins (1:4–8). These children, born in such a miserable home, also experienced the dereliction that was being visited on Israel in that deranged and chaotic time of apostasy.

༂

8. THE TRIAL OF SUSANNAH

When Martin Luther determined to limit the books of the Old Testament to those in the classical rabbinical canon, one of the casualties of his decision was the fast-moving story that opens the canonical Greek text of the Book of Daniel and forms chapter 13 of its traditional Latin version. Namely, the account of chaste Susannah and her lecherous detractors. Because of Luther's decision, a good number of ardent Bible-readers nowadays are unfamiliar with this marvelous story.

A pity, surely, for it is no exaggeration to say that all generations of Christians before Luther, and most Christians even after him, were very familiar with the biblical account of the beautiful and wise Susannah—the tale of the two lustful elders who attempted to seduce this virtuous lady by threats, their perjured testimony against her when she refused them, the death sentence imposed for her alleged adultery, and the dramatic emergence of young Daniel to vindicate her innocence and confound her accusers.

In general, the early Christians did not doubt that the story of Susannah is integral to the Book of Daniel. In all of Christian history there is not a single Greek or Latin manuscript of the Book of Daniel without the story of Susannah. In the third century, Origen testified that the story was "found in every church of Christ in that Greek copy that the Greeks use." This impression is also supported in the history of Christian art. Already in the second century we find the first of six mural icons drawn from the Susannah story on the walls of the Roman catacombs. Spread throughout Italy and Gaul, there are seven extant examples of scenes from the Susannah chapter in bas relief on Christian sarcophagi from the first few centuries.

Susannah has ever been held in the highest regard by Christians, especially for her faith, chastity, holiness of life, and patience in affliction. "In the sense of the Gospel," wrote Hippolytus of Rome, "Susannah despised those who can kill the body, in order that she might save her soul from death." Christians have been particularly impressed that Susannah, when falsely accused, spoke not a word to defend herself but sought in prayer the justice of God.

Nor is it without interest that Susannah's temptation and subsequent trial took place in a garden (*paradeiso*). This new "paradise" is contrasted with the garden of Genesis 3, where Eve was tempted, justly accused, and finally banished. "As formerly the devil was disguised in the serpent in the garden," wrote Hippolytus, "so now is he concealed in the two elders, whom he arouses with his own lust, that he might once again seduce Eve."

It was inevitable that Susannah be compared to Joseph, in the case of Potiphar's wife. Indeed, the resemblance between the two stories is remarkable: Joseph and Susannah both resistant to assaults against their chastity, both falsely accused by those who lusted after them, maintaining silence when accused, condemned in a foreign country, and finally vindicated by a providential intervention. No wonder that Christian readers have repeatedly elaborated comparisons between the two, whether in respect to their chastity under severe trial, to their being falsely indicted and condemned by their tempters, or to their patient silence when accused.

But if Susannah is to be likened to the unjustly accused Joseph, how much more to Jesus in the context of His Passion? Both Jesus and Susannah were betrayed in a garden, after all, a circumstance that would prompt Maximus of Turin to compare the two lustful elders with Judas Iscariot. For St. Jerome, the sorely tried and unjustly accused Susannah was a "type" of the Lord in His saving Passion, both of them maliciously accused by false witnesses. Both, likewise, remained silent when indicted. Jerome, when he read of the resounding clamor raised for the execution of Susannah, thought immediately of the loud "Crucify him" against the Lord on Good Friday.

This comparison of the contrived criminal trials of Jesus and Susannah inevitably led Maximus of Turin to contrast the judgments of Daniel and Pontius Pilate. Both men claimed to be "innocent of the blood" about to be shed. How different, nonetheless, the two cases! Whereas Jesus was handed over to the crowd by the cowardice of Pilate, Susannah was saved from the crowd by the bravery of Daniel.

⁊꙼

9. JOHN THE BAPTIST AND THE PROPHETS

The Lord's assessment of John the Baptist as "more than a prophet" was no denial that John the Baptist was a prophet (Luke 7:26). Indeed, He said, "there is not a greater prophet than John the Baptist" (7:28). A common persuasion on this point commenced early. John's own father "was filled with the Holy Spirit, and prophesied" (1:67), with respect to his newborn son: "And you, child, will be called the prophet of the Highest" (1:76). John's contemporaries, moreover, certainly regarded him as a prophet (20:6), as even Herod knew (Matthew 14:5).

Although our Lord said that "among those born of women there has not risen one greater than John the Baptist" (Matthew 11:11), only Luke thought to provide us with the name of the woman who gave John birth. In fact, Luke went into some detail to tell of that lady named Elizabeth and the circumstances surrounding her unexpected conception of a son in her advanced years. The Angel Gabriel, who had been somewhat quiet in Israel after the days of Daniel, appeared to Elizabeth's husband and predicted the pregnancy (Luke 1:13).

Moreover, God clearly intended to leave a special mark on John even before his birth. Six months into the gestation, Elizabeth received another visitor, this one human, her young kinswoman from Galilee named Mary. At Mary's greeting, John's mother sensed another Presence, as "the babe leaped in her womb" (1:41). Mary, in fact, like a new Ark of the Covenant, bore within her body God's newly incarnate Son, whose Father chose her greeting and that moment to sanctify the unborn John the Baptist. This event fulfilled an earlier prediction of Gabriel with respect to John: "He will also be filled with the Holy Spirit, even from his mother's womb" (1:15). In drawing our attention to John's prophetic consecration before his birth, Luke portrays him in the likeness of the Prophet Jeremiah, to whom God said, "Before I formed you in the womb I knew you; / Before you were born I sanctified you; / I ordained you a prophet to the nations" (Jeremiah 1:5).

If John resembled Jeremiah, however, his resemblance to the Prophet Elijah was even more pronounced. Once again, it was the Angel Gabriel, who used of John the very words with which the Prophet Malachi foretold the return of Elijah: "And he will turn many of the children of Israel to the Lord their God. He will also go before Him in the spirit and power of Elijah, 'to turn the hearts of the fathers to the children,' and the disobedient to the wisdom of the just, to make ready a people prepared for the Lord" (Luke 1:16–17; Malachi 4:5–6).

Since Elijah's return had been predicted in the last of the Old Testament's prophetic books, there was considerable expectation on the matter, even among the Lord's Apostles (Matthew 17:10). Although

John himself denied that he really was Elijah in a literal sense (John 1:21), he surely felt some affinity to that earlier prophet; he even dressed like him (Matthew 3:4 [and 11:8]; 2 Kings 1:8).

Whatever John felt about the matter, nonetheless, Jesus Himself asserted that "Elijah has come already," and, when He asserted this, "the disciples understood that He spoke to them of John the Baptist" (Matthew 17:12–13). John's affinity to Elijah was more than haberdashery, however, for his appearance in this world introduced the days in which "the kingdom of heaven suffers violence, and the violent take it by force. For all the prophets and the law prophesied until John. And if you are willing to receive it, he is Elijah who is to come" (11:12–14).

The "violence" associated with John was readily discerned in his asceticism, which prompted his enemies to say, "He has a demon" (11:18). Violence was also evident in his apocalyptic preaching, all about "the wrath to come," with axes laid to the roots of trees and the burning of chaff with unquenchable fire (3:7–12). John's hearers could never tell God that they had not been warned!

One of these was Herod Antipas, whom Herodias manipulated into beheading the violent John (Mark 6:14–29). Resenting the Baptist's condemnation of her "meaningful and fulfilling," albeit adulterous, relationship with Antipas, Herodias had longed for that day of vengeance. Indeed, in the New Testament triangle of the anemic Antipas, the hateful Herodias, and the relentless John, we have a striking parallel to the Old Testament triangle of the anemic Ahab, the hateful Jezebel, and, of course, the unrelenting Elijah.

⁂

10. THE WIDOW OF NAIN

For its blending of compassion, brevity, and dramatic resolution, few episodes in the Gospels, I think, surpass the story of the widow of Nain.

The scene (Luke 7:11–17) is unforgettable. Two large and very different crowds of people, neither at first aware of the other, are about to meet in the narrow confines of a village street. The first, a wailing funeral cortege, winds its mournful way toward the cemetery (discovered by modern archeology) that lies east of the city. The dead man is borne on an open bier, the only son of his widowed mother. Before this procession ever leaves the village, however, it encounters the second crowd, which comes marching in from the opposite direction. These two large masses of people, slowing down as they draw nigh, now meet in the tight confines of the narrow street.

On an ordinary day, ordinary decency and universal custom would dictate, of course, that the advantage of passage should be conceded to the funeral procession. This is not, however, an ordinary day, nor is this second group of people an ordinary assembly. It is the Church of Jesus Christ, who walks out in front of her as the Author and Perfecter of her faith.

Jesus, looking with compassion on the bereaved woman (7:13; compare John 11:33), steps forward and tells her to stop weeping. Then, very deliberately, He extends His hand and touches the bier, bringing the procession to an abrupt stop. Completely in charge of this utterly dramatic situation, He addresses the corpse, "Young man, I say to you, arise." The latter does so, and Jesus restores him to his mother. It is a scene of tender mercy and enormous majesty.

As this story of the widow of Nain is found only in Luke among the evangelists, it seems best to study it first within the literary framework of that Gospel, where it is situated in both a general and an immediate context.

In its immediate context, this narrative directly follows the account of Jesus' healing of the centurion's servant (7:1–10). In each instance the miracle is the Lord's response to the interests and affections of a third party, namely, the centurion and the widow. There is also a contrast between the two accounts that was noticed by St. Cyril of Alexandria many centuries ago: "But observe how He joins miracle to miracle; in the prior instance, the healing of the centurion's servant, He was offered an invitation. Here, however, He draws near without being invited. . . . To me it seems that He purposely made this next miracle to follow the first" (*Homily 36 on Luke*).

Likewise in its immediate context, Luke's story of what happened at Nain is directly followed by his account of the delegation that John the Baptist sends to Jesus from prison (7:18–23). Jesus, in His response to that delegation, refers explicitly to the raising of the dead. The event at Nain, then, is preparatory to the very next narrative in Luke's sequence.

Certain aspects of this story are significant within the yet more general context of Lukan themes. For instance, Luke's very wording of the miracle, in which Jesus "presented him to his mother," is found verbatim in the Greek text of 1 Kings 17:23, where Elijah restored her dead son to the woman of Zarephath. Luke had spoken of this woman earlier (4:26).

Likewise, Jesus' compassion for the bereaved widow is of whole cloth with Luke's attention to this sustained trait of the Lord's ministry. One thinks of the crippled woman that Jesus heals in the synagogue (13:10–17), the sinful woman whose ministry He accepts in the house of the Pharisee (7:36–50), and the two sisters at Bethany (10:38–42).

Within the larger reference of Luke's theology, however, the most important detail in this story would seem to be his reference to Jesus as "Lord" in 7:13—"When the *Lord* saw her . . ." This is the first time that Luke refers to Jesus by that title which is His by virtue of His Resurrection (Acts 2:34–36) and by which He is invoked in the act of saving faith (1 Corinthians 8:6; 12:3; Philippians 2:11). From this point on in Luke's Gospel, Jesus will often be called "Lord" (e.g., 10:1, 41; 11:39; 12:42; 13:15); indeed, Luke calls Him by this title in the very next story, the account of the delegation of John the Baptist (7:19 in the manuscripts preferred here). It is most significant, however, that Luke first calls Jesus "Lord" in the context of His manifest authority over death.

ॐ

11. THE STONING OF STEPHEN

Generations of preachers have employed no little ingenuity, and sometimes a fair measure of eloquence, to expound the theological reasons for celebrating St. Stephen's Day so close to Christmas. It is not to slight those rhetorical efforts that one reflects that "the feast of Stephen" was celebrated long before anyone thought of celebrating the birthday of the Savior. Stephen, that is to say, got into the liturgical calendar first. Indeed, there is good reason to think that St. Stephen's is among the oldest feast days in the Christian Church. Moreover, except for the days of Holy Week and the paschal cycle itself, it is possible that the annual commemoration of the martyrdom of St. Stephen is the oldest feast day in the Christian liturgical calendar.

We know, first of all, that very early the dates of the martyrs' deaths were commemorated annually in their local churches. *The Martyrdom of Polycarp*, from Smyrna in AD 156, is our earliest explicit witness to this custom, but it seems already to have been traditional. Stephen, the first martyr after the death of Jesus, was venerated in the earliest church, Jerusalem, from which all other Christian churches derived their liturgical precedents. Furthermore, primitive chronological collections affirm that the martyrdom of St. Stephen occurred on December 26 in the very year of our Redemption, and this was arguably the view of Eusebius of Caesarea. In short, then, when good King Wenceslaus, centuries later, "looked out on the feast of Stephen," he was observing a commemoration that Christians have observed, literally, from the very beginning.

In Luke's description of Stephen's martyrdom, several features are worthy of remark.

First, like the Savior (John 20:19; Hebrews 13:12), Stephen is executed outside the city wall (Acts 7:58), because even in this massive miscarriage of basic justice, Stephen's murderers adhere to the Mosaic prescription (Leviticus 24:14; Numbers 15:35–36). This is ironic, because in Lukan theology this exit from Jerusalem, for the murder of Stephen, symbolizes that outward movement of the witness from Jerusalem that is so strong a theme in the Book of Acts (1:8).

Second, and also as a feature of considerable irony, it is in this scene that St. Paul is first introduced in the Acts of the Apostles (7:58). This introduction of the Apostle to the Gentiles, at exactly this point in the narrative of Acts, is of a piece with the theological significance of Stephen's dying outside of the walls. Later on, praying in a state of trance, Paul will say to Jesus, "And when the blood of Your martyr Stephen was shed, I also was standing by consenting to his death, and guarding the clothes of those who were killing him" (22:20).

Third, there is a powerful emphasis on the Holy Spirit. It was early said that Stephen was "full of the Holy Spirit" (6:3, 5), but the statement is repeated once again in the context of his death (7:55). This emphasis, which relates Stephen's death to the pentecostal outpouring, reflects the conviction of the early Church that martyrdom is the supreme charism of the Christian life, the final and crowning gift of the Holy Spirit that definitively seals and consecrates the testimony, the *martyria*, of the Church and the believer. We meet this conviction somewhat later in *The Martyrdom of Polycarp* and in the earliest treatises on martyrdom by the Christian apologists.

Lastly, there is a dramatic change in Stephen's tone. Having bitterly denounced the Jews in his testimony before the Sanhedrin (7:51–53), Stephen finishes his life by committing his soul to the Lord and devoutly praying for his persecutors (7:59–60). Luke thus takes great care to observe the similarities between the deaths of Jesus and Stephen (Luke 23:34, 46), as Irenaeus of Lyons early noted (*Against the Heresies* 3.12.13).

Dante's portrayal of the scene is especially memorable:

> Then I saw people incited in a fire of wrath
> to kill a young man [*giovinetto*] by stoning, loudly
> calling out to one another, 'Kill him, kill him!' [*Martira, martira!*]
> And him I saw, bowed down by the death
> that already laid him prone upon the earth,
> but he ever made with his eyes a door into heaven,
> praying to the high Lord [*all'alto Sire*], in so great a struggle,
> that He would pardon his persecutors,
> with a gaze deserving of mercy (*Purgatorio* 15:106–114).

XI.

INTERCEDING SAINTS

When the saints on earth beseech the Lord, new things begin to happen. First, they happen in heaven, and then they happen on earth, so that God's will is done on earth as it is in heaven. This is the meaning of intercession.

To appreciate the correct context and dimensions of the intercession of the saints, it is useful to consult the picture of it that the Bible provides. In that picture, intercession truly commences, not on earth, but in heaven, and it begins, not with speech, but with silence. "When He opened the seventh seal," says the definitive source on this subject, "there was silence in heaven for about half an hour" (Revelation 8:1). Why silence in heaven? Perhaps that silence at the seventh seal corresponds to the divine rest of the seventh day (Genesis 2:2; Hebrews 4:1–11).

One recalls also the ominous silence that preceded the unleashing of God's judgment on Egypt at the time of the Exodus. When did God's almighty Word leap down from heaven "as a fierce man of war into the land of destruction," visiting Egypt with ten plagues? It happened, we are told, "while all things were in quiet silence" (Wisdom of Solomon 18:14–16). Here in Revelation as well, there is deep silence just prior to the falling of the final plagues, when God's trumpets of judgment are sounded (Revelation 8:6–12).

Likewise, the intercession begins, not with men, but with angels. Seven of them, actually. St. John portrays the scene: "And I saw the seven angels who stand before God, and to them were given seven trumpets" (Revelation 8:2). Seven angels? Yes. In fact, one of those seven had introduced himself earlier in the Bible: "I am Raphael, one of the seven holy angels, which present the prayers of the saints, and which go in and out before the glory of the Holy One" (Tobit 12:15; cf. 1 Enoch 20:1–7). These are the seven angels of the intercession, permanent ministers before the Throne of God.

These holy seven are going to blow their seven trumpets. Why? Because incense is about to be burned, and the burning of incense is to be accompanied by the sounding of trumpets (2 Chronicles 29:27–28). Indeed, there is quite a bit of this incense to be burned:

"Then another angel, having a golden censer, came and stood at the altar. He was given much incense, that he should offer *it* with the prayers of all the saints upon the golden altar which was before the throne. And the smoke of the incense, with the prayers of the saints, ascended before God from the angel's hand" (Revelation 8:3–4).

The prayers of the saints, offered on earth, are ennobled and enriched by their incorporation into the heavenly worship. These earthly prayers ascend to God in communion with the prayers offered in heaven by "the spirits of just men made perfect" (Hebrews 12:23), symbolized in the twenty-four elders in whose hands are "golden bowls full of incense, which are the prayers of the saints" (Revelation 5:8).

It is from the incorporation of these earthly prayers into the heavenly worship that things will now begin to happen on earth: "Then the angel took the censer, filled it with fire from the altar, and threw *it* to the earth. And there were noises, thunderings, lightnings, and an earthquake. So the seven angels who had the seven trumpets prepared to sound" (8:5–6).

Things will now change on earth in response to what happens in heaven. It is from God's very altar that the divine judgment is poured upon human history. Corresponding to the seven trumpets that brought down the walls of Jericho, that ancient city which threatened Israel's full entrance into the Promised Land, the seven angels will now sound seven trumpets introducing the divine intervention in the affairs of men (8:7–21; 11:15–19). The course of history is changed. This is what happens when the saints pray.

Thus, the biblical teaching on the intercession of the saints is inseparable from the Church's faith in the communion of the saints. This creedal confession testifies that all worship is one, whether in heaven or on earth. To speak to God, to praise and bless Him, is to join our voices to a much larger liturgy that includes the heavenly Jerusalem, an innumerable company of angels, the general assembly and church of the firstborn who are registered in heaven, and Jesus the Mediator of the new covenant (Hebrews 12:22–24). This communion of the saints is what causes the earth to change, and the things that happen thereon.

⤳

1. THE INTERCESSIONS OF ABRAHAM

Abraham was a man of powerful prayer. This is hardly surprising, because the Scriptures call him "the friend of God" (2 Chronicles 20:7; Isaiah 41:8; Daniel 3:35 [LXX]; Judith 8:22 [Vulgate]; James 2:23), and God, like the rest of us in this respect, delights in doing favors for His friends. Thus, even after God declared to Abimelech, "Indeed you *are* a dead man," He went on to promise that Abraham "will pray for you and you shall live" (Genesis 20:3, 7). And, indeed, "Abraham prayed to God; and God healed Abimelech" (20:17).

As God's friend, Abraham was blessed with what the Bible calls *parresia*, confidence or even boldness (Ephesians 3:12; Hebrews 4:16), in his approach to the Lord on matters of concern. Like the stalwart widow in the Gospel parable on this subject (Luke 18:1–8), Abraham could be rather persistent, perhaps a tad nagging, when he brought some point of concern to the attention of the Almighty. Accustomed to that mercantile dickering ever common in the Middle East, Abraham knew how to chaffer his way to a bargain, and he incorporated this skill too into his prayer, as it were.

An important feature of such "haggling" is that it must appear reasonable. Since the Lord Himself created the structures of reason, that is to say, Abraham thought an appeal to reasonableness a legitimate aspect of his discussions with God. He got rather good at making this appeal.

The evidence for it stands in Genesis 18:16–33, where "God's friend," fearing that the divine plan to destroy Sodom meant that his nephew Lot might perish, summoned all his mental resources to talk the Almighty out of it. He commenced by asking a perfectly reasonable question having to do with the nature of the divine justice: "Would You also destroy the righteous with the wicked?" God wouldn't, of course; the question itself was rhetorical. Thus, Abraham the haggler had already intruded his foot into God's doorway.

The point about the divine justice implicitly conceded, then, Abraham went on to advance another question having to do with the idea of due proportion inherent in the very concept of justice. He submitted a reasonable hypothesis on the point, followed by an inquiry: "Suppose there were fifty righteous within the city; would You also destroy the place and not spare *it* for the fifty righteous that were in it?"

However sober this conjecture may have seemed as a speculative proposition, Abraham's argument, nonetheless, abruptly swung into a more persuasive mode, as though the Lord, inwardly weighing His options, needed an extra nudge in the right direction: "Far be it from You to do such a thing as this," Abraham entreated, "to slay the righteous with the wicked, so that the righteous should be as the wicked; far be it from You! Shall not the Judge of all the earth do right?"

Thus pushed on the point, God answered Abraham's hypothesis with an "if" of His own: "*If* I find in Sodom fifty righteous within the city," He responded, "then I will spare all the place for their sakes" (18:26). "Aha," Abraham thought to himself, "the principle of the thing, at least, has been established; now let's get working on that price." After all, God had earlier expressed some faint touch of misgiving about the recent reports from Sodom (18:21), nor was Abraham, for his part, very confident that he could actually find the required fifty. That many righteous men in Sodom was awfully iffy indeed. God's friend determined, then, to chip away at that figure and see how much he could scale it down.

Any master haggler was familiar with the method. One began with a touch of personal deference and a very modest reduction in the sticker price: "Indeed now, I who *am but* dust and ashes have taken it upon myself to speak to the Lord: Suppose there were five less than the fifty righteous; would You destroy all the city for *lack of* five?" This new proposition, carefully worded, subtly ignores that the "five less" is subtracted, not from the total number of citizens in Sodom, but from the already low number of fifty. Nonetheless, the Lord accedes: "If I find there forty-five, I will not destroy *it*." Continuing thus, Abraham resolutely worked the figure down to only ten righteous. The Lord, patient through the process but still resolved about Sodom, finally just had to walk away. Abraham was, after all, His friend.

※

2. ABRAHAM'S SERVANT

The doctrine of divine providence is asserted in the biblical thesis that "all things work together for good to those who love God" (Romans 8:28). This "working together" of historical events under divine governance for particular and interrelated purposes is a mystery, of course, but a mystery in two senses.

First, divine providence is a mystery in the sense that it is humanly inscrutable, exceeding even the furthest reaches of our thought, and is known only by faith. That is to say, it pertains to divine revelation. It is not the general, natural *pronoia* of the Stoics and Middle Platonists, but a special providence revealed by God's particular interventions in the structure of history. For this reason Holy Scripture never attempts to explain it. Although the Bible affirms divine providence, it teaches no theory of the matter.

Second, divine providence is also a mystery in the sense that we are initiated into it. It is rendered accessible, that is, to our revelatory experience of it, the discernment of which is a gift of the Holy Spirit. It is particular and personal, sensed through the coherent structure of events. For this reason Holy Scripture not only affirms divine providence, but also portrays the mystery of it through narratives about events.

The Old Testament's story of Joseph is perhaps the most elaborate example of such a narrative. We do not discern how, in the Joseph story, "all things *work together* for good to those who love God," but the narrative enables us to perceive it intuitively, buried deep in the events of Joseph's life and conferring coherence on that life. At the end of the story we are able to say, with Joseph, "So *it was* not you *who* sent me here, but God" (Genesis 45:8).

In some cases, we are able to sense God's providential purpose in a biblical story by the insinuated dynamics of the story itself, without our attention being drawn to it by any explicit statement. Examples of this are found in the Book of Ruth and, with far greater subtlety, the Book of Esther. In the latter story, in fact, God's intrusive activity in the events is so subtle that He is not even mentioned!

In other instances the Bible conveys the providential nature of a story by the direct insertion of it through the voice of the narrator. Through such an insertion, the story takes on an entirely different flavor, being transfigured, so to speak, from secular to sacred. For instance, the tale of David's escape from Saul at Hachilah (1 Samuel 26) is transformed into an account of divine providence by the plain statement that "they *were* all asleep, because a deep sleep from the LORD had fallen on them" (26:12). Similarly the biblical narrator says, in the context of Absalom's revolt, that "the LORD had purposed to defeat the good advice of Ahithophel, to the intent that the LORD might bring disaster on Absalom" (2 Samuel 17:14).

Another literary method of conveying the providential purpose in a biblical story is to place the affirmation of it in the mouth of one of the characters. As we have seen, this is the method followed in the Joseph story, in the scene where he reveals himself to his brothers (Genesis 45:5–7; 50:15–20).

Another and very fetching example of this literary device is found in Genesis 24, which describes the journey of Abraham's servant to Mesopotamia in order to find a suitable bride for Isaac (namely, Rebekah). In this exquisitely crafted account of God's historical intervention in response to prayer, two features should especially be noted.

First, the story is told twice, initially by the narrator (24:1–26) and then a second time by a character within the narrative itself, namely the servant (24:34–48). This deliberate doubling of the story, which obliges the reader to think about its implications a second time, also serves the purpose of placing the theme of divine providence more completely within the fabric of the tale. In the first telling, the reader is struck by how quickly the servant's prayer is heard—"And it happened, before he had finished speaking" (24:15). This promptness of God's response is emphasized in the second telling—"before I had finished speaking in my heart" (24:45). God is encountered in the servant's experience of the event that comes crashing in, as it were, on his prayer.

Second, the doubling of the narrative is not artificial. It is essential, rather, to the motive of Rebekah and her family in their decision that she should accompany the servant back to Abraham's home and become the wife of Isaac. That is to say, the characters themselves are made aware that God has *spoken* through the narrated events. *They* perceive God's providence: "The thing [*dabar*] comes from the LORD; we cannot speak [*dabber*] to you either bad or good. Here *is* Rebekah before you; take *her* and go, and let her be your master's son's wife, as the LORD has spoken [*dibber*]" (24:50–51). The event itself, the "thing," was a "word" from God, a *dabar*. That is to say, given the servant's testimony, it was clear that all things had worked together "for good to those who love God."

⁊⁌

3. MOSES ON THE MOUNTAIN

Not least among the features endearing the Prophet Moses to the mind of a believer is the memory of his efficacious and powerful intercession for God's people in the hour of their apostasy. Thus, when St. Symeon the New Theologian sought to praise someone for this same quality, he could do no better than to compare him to Moses. "I know a man," he wrote, "who desired the salvation of his brethren so fervently that he often sought God with burning tears and with his whole heart, in an excess of zeal worthy of Moses, that either his brethren might be saved with him, or that he might be condemned with them. For he was bound to them in the Holy Spirit by such a bond of love that he did not even wish to enter the kingdom of heaven if to do so meant being separated from them" (*Book of Divine Love*, Homily 54.1).

The biblical text that St. Symeon has in mind here is Exodus 32:32, where Moses prayed for sinful Israel in these words: "Yet now, if You will forgive their sin—but if not, I pray, blot me out of Your book which You have written." That fervent prayer was more than a bare intercession; it was Moses' generous self-offering by an association of himself with the people's guilt.

The context of that prayer is worth a detailed examination. There is, to begin with, a two-leveled scene: Moses is on top of Mount Sinai with God, while Aaron is down in the valley with the Israelites. Just prior to the prayer, two things have been transpiring simultaneously, both of them having to do with Aaron. On the mountain Moses has been receiving from the Lord a series of ordinances and statutes governing the consecration, vestments, liturgical instruments, and other matters concerning the Aaronic priesthood (Exodus 25—31).

Meanwhile, however, Aaron was down in the valley proving himself unworthy of that priesthood, for the Bible describes his complicity in the construction and cult of the golden calf. At the people's first idolatrous impulse, Aaron acceded to their wishes. "Break off the golden earrings," he instructed them, "which *are* in the ears of your wives, you sons, and your daughters, and bring *them* to me." And when they did so, "he received *the gold* from their hand, and he fashioned it with an engraving tool, and made a molded calf" (32:2–4).

In this whole episode Aaron is portrayed as craven and double-minded, a hireling and no shepherd. Though very much involved in the people's sin, he would never admit this association in their guilt. He becomes, rather, a classical example of rationalizing an infidelity, not regarding his action as the apostasy it was, but rather (as the saying goes) as "accepting people where they are." "You know the people," he would tell Moses, "they *are set* on evil" (32:22). Refusing thus to assume responsibility, he attempts to disentangle himself from the people's sin.

In a line that the biblical author must have regarded as a kind of mockery, the irresponsible and cowardly Aaron endeavors, moreover, to minimize his own considerable role in the matter, claiming that when the Israelites gave him the gold, "I cast it into the fire, and this calf came out" (32:24).

Actively taking part in their apostasy, Aaron did not love the people enough to resist them. His attitude is described as the very opposite of that of Moses, whose prayer united him to the guilt of the people, even though he himself had not shared in their sin.

The self-sacrificing prayer of Moses, in which he deliberately associates himself with the guilt of the people, demonstrates an important quality of intercessory prayer in Holy Scripture. The biblical intercessor never stands apart from the state of those for whom he prays. Moses' wish to be blotted from God's book rather than see the Israelites perish is clearly repeated in the soul of St. Paul, who wrote of those same Israelites: "I could wish that I myself were accursed from Christ for my brethren, my countrymen according to the flesh" (Romans 9:3).

The Bible's supreme and defining example of this sacrificial intercession is that of the Suffering Servant who "*was* wounded for our transgressions" (Isaiah 53:5), and "was numbered with the transgressors" (53:12), and who, though He knew not sin, became sin for us, "that we might become the righteousness of God in Him" (2 Corinthians 5:21).

᪐

4. JOB AND HIS COMFORTERS

Job is a discomforting book, for it deals with a very thorny question: the suffering of those who do not deserve to suffer. Job is portrayed as an eminently just man. He has fulfilled all of his responsibilities and more. He has offended in nothing. Indeed, Job has lived as the very embodiment of the ideals set forth in Israel's "traditional wisdom," as contained in the Book of Proverbs. Well could Job expect, then, the happiness that the Book of Proverbs confidently held out to those who adhered to the dictates of Israel's traditional wisdom. Instead, however, he is visited with all manner of evil, disgrace, humiliation, and suffering.

Various possible answers to Job's questions are tried, weighed, and mostly found wanting. For this reason the book may be described, like the Book of Ecclesiastes, as speculative. Its answers are tentative rather than definitive. Its mental map is not entirely filled in. Its themes are more probed than proved. It ends on the note of faith in God but, like Ecclesiastes, it permits speculative thought to explore the darker, more mysterious dimensions of that faith.

Job himself is given two lifetimes, a before and an after, with the period of his trial being the central dividing point of his allotted days. Thus, he lives 140 years, exactly twice the normal span of a man's life (see Psalm 89[90]:10). Each of his first seven sons and three daughters is *replaced* at the end of the story, and all of his original livestock is exactly doubled (Job 1:3; 42:12).

A very important word in the Book of Job, of course, is the verb "to comfort" (*niham*). Near the story's beginning, this is what Job's friends come to do (2:11), and the expression appears several more times, whether in the verbal form (7:13; 16:2; 21:34; 29:25) or as the cognate noun (6:10). Whereas Job's friends fail utterly in their efforts to comfort him throughout almost the entire book, they succeed at the end (42:11), after the resolution of Job's conflict by God's intervention.

One may argue that the proper key to understanding the Book of Job does not appear until the last chapter thereof. This key commences with the Lord's word to Eliphaz the Temanite, who represents all of Job's comforters: "'Now therefore, take for yourselves seven bulls and seven rams, go to My servant Job, and offer up for yourselves a burnt offering; and My servant Job shall pray for you. For I will accept him, lest I deal with you *according to your* folly; because you have not spoken of Me *what is* right, as My servant Job *has*.' So Eliphaz the Temanite and Bildad the Shuhite *and* Zophar the Naamathite went and did as the LORD commanded them; for the LORD had accepted Job. And the LORD restored Job's losses when he prayed for his friends. Indeed, the LORD gave Job twice as much as he had before" (Job 42:8–10).

In this passage near the very end of the book, Job appears preeminently as an effective petitioner on behalf of his friends. These men are restored to God's favor by Job's praying for them, and Job himself is restored *by* his praying for them. The story of Job is thus interpreted through the singular mystery of intercessory prayer. Moreover, this explanation of Job was not lost on earlier readers of the book. For example, the Prophet Ezekiel, remembering Job's prayer more than his patience, listed him with Noah and Daniel, all three of whom he took to be men endowed with singular powers of intercession before the Most High (Ezekiel 14:14–20).

Indeed, this theme of Job's intercessory prayer appears early in the book. We learn of Job's intercession before we discover anything else about him. Concerned for the welfare of his ten children, we are told, Job "would rise early in the morning and offer burnt offerings *according to* the number of them all" (Job 1:5). Indeed, between Job's intercessions at the beginning and the end of the book, we may regard chapters 2 through 37 as a kind of Satanic distraction to Job's life of prayer. About halfway through the book, Job's final prayer is prophesied by Eliphaz in a verse of great irony: "You will make your prayer to Him, / He will hear you, / And you will pay your vows" (22:27). To show that this prophecy has been fulfilled, it is to Eliphaz that God directs His rebuke and command at the end of the story (42:7–8). Job's wisdom, then, has to do with his prayer for those he loves.

⳺

5. JEREMIAH AND JERUSALEM'S TRAGEDY

God spoke to and through the prophets, and some of those prophets, on occasion, spoke back to God. None of them did so, however, as often and fervently as Jeremiah. Jeremiah was a man of prayer.

This trait, discernible throughout the man's life and ministry, is introduced right from the opening scene in the book that bears his name. That scene, the account of his call when he was still very young, consists entirely of a conversation between himself and God (1:4–14). Such conversations between the Lord and this prophet, moreover, are a unique and distinguishing characteristic of Jeremiah among the prophetic books (cf. 4:5–21; 9:1–6; 11:1–5, 18–23; 12:1–6; 14:1–22; 15:10–21; 17:12–19; 18:19–23; 20:7–18; 23:9–12; 24:1–5; 32:16–26). The prayers of Jeremiah, intense in their tone and unique in their frequency, are essential to the understanding of his message and his historical significance.

If, especially after the tragic death of King Josiah at the Battle of Megiddo in 609 BC, Jeremiah's prayers became progressively darker, this trait reflected but the deepening shadows of his life, and these shadows, in turn, were cast by the inevitable, trampling fate that trod its way toward Jerusalem. Nearly all of the Book of Jeremiah was composed under the grim, gathering cloud that stormed forth at last in 587, when the Babylonian invader came to destroy Jerusalem and its temple. The inevitability of that coming destruction had been foretold by Huldah the prophetess in 622 (cf. 2 Kings 22:16–17), and the keenly perceptive Jeremiah discerned its taking shape in the politics and cultural life of his day.

Interpreting that approaching doom was the very substance of Jeremiah's ministry, and his prayer was integral to that interpretation. The Lord was on the point of destroying the very institutions that He had for centuries cultivated and sustained, and in the heart of Jeremiah the city's looming destruction assumed metaphysical dimensions. It suggested to his mind both the overthrow of nature and the dissolution of history. Thus, it was Jeremiah's destiny to assume the impending tragedy of Israel into the fabric of his own heart, an experience that filled him with a deep feeling of radical alienation from God. He struggled in the darkness: "O the Hope of Israel, his Savior in time of trouble, / Why should You be like a stranger in the land, / And like a traveler *who* turns aside to tarry for a night?" (14:8) . . . "Will you surely be to me like an unreliable stream, / *As* waters *that* fail?" (15:18) . . . "Do not be a terror to me; / You *are* my hope in the day of doom" (17:17).

Jeremiah's prayer was shaped, therefore, by the contours of Israel's tragedy: "Oh, that my head were waters, / And my eyes a fountain of tears, / That I might weep day and night / For the slain of the daughter of my people!" (9:1) . . . "Woe is me, my mother, / That you have borne me, / A man of strife and a man of contention to the whole earth!" (15:10) . . . "But *His word* was in my heart like a burning fire / Shut up in my bones; / I was weary of holding it back" (20:9).

His was an extremely lonely life. Most of Jerusalem's citizens, suffering from chronic shallowness and terminal optimism, thought him something of an oddity and a nuisance, maybe even a public menace. They accused him (37:14), conspired against him (18:18), seized him (26:8), sought his life (11:21), struck him and put him in stocks (20:2), imprisoned him (32:3), kidnapped him (chs. 42—43), threw him in a deep pit where he nearly died from hunger (38:6–9). In short, Jeremiah was obliged to "go it alone." His was a more than ordinary personal desolation, inasmuch as he embraced a life of consecrated celibacy and asceticism as a prophetic sign of Jerusalem's approaching devastation (16:1–5).

Because the shape of his own soul was formed by his internal identification with the tragic history of his people, there was a special effi-
cacy in Jeremiah's prayer for them. So much was this the case that on
three occasions the Lord felt obliged, as it were, to order Jeremiah to
stop praying! (7:16; 11:14; 14:11). It was as though the prophet's intercession was so persuasive and effective that God Himself would be unable to resist. It was largely as an intercessor that Israel later thought of
Jeremiah, described in the dream of Judas Maccabaeus as "a lover of
the brethren, who prays much for the people, and for the holy city"
(2 Maccabees 15:14).

𝕴

6. THE SYRO-PHOENICIAN WOMAN

Of all the sundry intercessions of the saints, there are none so dear to
the Almighty as the prayers of parents for their children. There seem to
be several reasons for this.

First, when we pray for our offspring, we appeal, in a sense, to those
sentiments that lie deepest in the Deity. Begotten of faith, conceived in
the profound instincts of the heart, the petitions of fathers and mothers
for their sons and daughters appear in a special way to gladden that
parental impulse radical to God's own being. And should it happen, as
often it does, that our parental prayers are of the anxious sort, weighed
down by fret and freighted with worry, our heavenly Father recognizes
in them a reflection of the solicitude He feels for all His children, who
frequently wander and are always at risk. When, then, with worried Job
we rise early in the morning and offer the daily oblation according to
the number of our progeny, in order to "sanctify them," concerned as
we are lest any of them sin in their heart (Job 1:5), this offering is surely
received on high by God's most gracious and paternal favor.

A second reason why these pleadings for our offspring are so pleasing to God is that they tend to be particularly humble and self-effacing.
When we implore the divine mercy for our children, the mind offers no
asylum to haughty thoughts or an arrogant temper. If a child suffers, if
a child is in danger, if a child is threatened or lost in any of the myriad
ways that children can be threatened or lost, we rather promptly learn
humility. Indeed, we become utterly shameless in our begging. Like the
Shunammite, we fling ourselves to the earth and cling to the feet of the
prophet (2 Kings 4:27). With the nobleman of Capernaum we cry to

236

the Lord, "Sir, come down before my child dies!" (John 4:49). Maybe more than any other form of petition, then, the intercessions we offer for our offspring take on the quality of abject pleading, accompanied by profound sentiments of self-abasement.

A third reason for the special quality of prayer for our children comes from the demand that such prayer makes on the resources of our belief. A man who beholds his son convulsing, helpless on the ground, is brought up short by the weakness of his own faith. "O faithless generation," he is told, "how long shall I bear with you?" Even then, nonetheless, he finds somewhere down in his soul the wherewithal to cry back, "Lord, I believe; help my unbelief!" (Mark 9:14–24). And how does a believing father act when his daughter lies at death's door? How is faith expressed? We may take our example from Jairus, who brought that very problem to Jesus: "And when he saw Him, he fell at His feet and begged Him earnestly, saying, 'My little daughter lies at the point of death. Come and lay Your hands on her, that she may be healed, and she will live'" (5:22–23).

A fourth reason why such prayer is so dear to God is that, like the love that inspires it, this prayer takes on the quality of self-sacrifice. Even when we do not explicitly say so, the Lord senses that we would willingly suffer in place of our young ones—would hand ourselves over, as it were, on their behalf. Our sentiments in such times are those of David, who would have died in place of Absalom (2 Samuel 18:33). The impulse of such prayer touches the mystery of the Cross, where the Good Shepherd laid down His life for the sheep.

All the qualities of this prayer may be discerned in the intercession that the Syro-Phoenician or Canaanite woman made for her afflicted daughter. It was, first of all, a prayer of faith. Jesus remarked, indeed, on the greatness of her faith (Matthew 15:28). It was also a prayer of the most profound humility, in which she came to Jesus "and fell at His feet" (Mark 7:25). And the sacrificial nature of her prayer is readily perceived in the response this Gentile woman gave to Jesus' assertion that "it is not good to take the children's bread and throw *it* to the little dogs" (7:27). Far from taking personal offense at this deliberate rebuff, the woman gracefully turned the last shred of her pride into a burnt offering for her suffering daughter: "Yes, Lord, yet even the little dogs under the table eat from the children's crumbs" (7:28). Hers was the prayer of faith and humility, because it was the prayer of parental love.

It was also the prayer of self-sacrifice for the sake of love, to the Father who knows and honors such love.

৵৹

7. THE CENTURION AND HIS SERVANT

Among those sections that the Gospels of Matthew and Luke, independent of Mark, have in common, almost all are directly didactic. That is to say, those sections almost invariably consist of the explicit teachings of Jesus, with no attention to events in Jesus' life. Those shared sections convey, for instance, the sort of material we find in Matthew's Sermon on the Mount (chapters 5—7) and Luke's Sermon on the Plain (6:20–49). When, on the other hand, Matthew and Luke do tell a common story about Jesus' life, Mark has that story too.

The clear exception to this pattern is Matthew's and Luke's narrative of the centurion who sought healing for his cherished servant (Matthew 8:5–13; Luke 7:1–10). As an account of a person beseeching the Lord on behalf of someone else, this shared narrative resembles other stories in the Gospels, such as Jairus and the Syro-Phoenician woman praying for their daughters (Mark 5:23; 7:24–30), another man and a centurion pleading for their sons (9:17; John 4:46–53), Martha and Mary of Bethany interceding for their brother (11:3). These are all accounts of petitionary prayer on behalf of loved ones.

Such stories surely had a great influence on the patterns of Christian intercessory prayer. We note, for instance, that the petitions in these accounts are addressed to Jesus. Although in Jesus' specific teaching about prayer, the normal emphasis was on prayer addressed to the heavenly Father (Luke 11:2) in Jesus' name (John 15:16), the emphasis is different in these particular Gospel stories. One of their singular values is that they unambiguously answer a practical question that might arise among Christians, namely, "If one of your loved ones gets sick, is there some special Trinitarian protocol to follow, or is it all right just to take the problem right to Jesus?"

However, the idea of taking one's problems "right to Jesus" is surely not to be understood in the sense of forgoing the mediating prayer of others. It is not as though the unique mediation of Jesus our Lord (1 Timothy 2:5) excludes certain saints from mediating on behalf of other saints, and these various Gospel stories are the proof of it. In fact, it is the entire point and the whole business of the foregoing stories to validate such mediation. This is called intercessory prayer.

To see how this works out, let us return to the story of the centurion pleading on behalf of his servant. If we compare the differing accounts of this event in Matthew and Luke, we first observe that Matthew's is the shorter and simpler version. In this account the centurion simply goes to Jesus, requesting that the Lord speak the commanding word so that the servant will be healed. It takes only six verses.

In Luke, however, the story requires ten verses and is considerably more complicated. First, the centurion himself does not approach Jesus directly. He sends some friends who will speak for him. Now this is interesting, because it introduces another level of mediation. The friends are interceding for the centurion, who is in turn interceding for his servant. We have here the beginnings of a prayer chain, as it were.

Then, when Jesus starts moving towards the centurion's home, the latter dispatches another group of friends, who will speak the famous words that characterize this story: "I am not worthy that You should enter under my roof" (7:6). It is surely significant that the centurion does not speak these words, deeply personal as they are, to Jesus directly. Others say them to Jesus on the centurion's behalf. In Luke's version of the story, in fact, there is no face-to-face encounter of the centurion with Jesus at all. The centurion's faith is conveyed by those he chooses to intercede for him.

Finally, in Luke's version of the story, there is a striking parallel, surely deliberate, between this centurion and Cornelius in chapter 10 of the Acts of the Apostles. Both of these centurions send others to speak on their behalf, and in each case the one solicited—Jesus in the first and Simon Peter in the second—goes immediately to respond to the need. At this point the two stories form a contrast. In the first instance the centurion, wanting to spare Jesus the uncleanness of entering a Gentile house, solicits His aid from a distance. In the case of Peter and Cornelius, however, the barrier between Jew and Gentile has now been removed forever, and Peter comes to his home.

꙾

8. TWO DECEASED SAINTS

In the normal course of the life in Christ, not all our communication with God is direct and immediate. The saints not only pray directly to God in Christ; they also seek the intercession of the other saints.

Thus the communion of the saints includes also a communication among the saints.

Consequently, when the saints gather for worship, the Apostle Paul insists that their prayers include intercession, *enteuchsis* (1 Timothy 2:1), a discipline for which he himself sets the example, both by praying for other Christians (1 Thessalonians 1:2; Philemon 4) and by depending on their prayers for him (2 Corinthians 1:11; Philippians 1:19; Philemon 22). Another good example was provided by the church at Jerusalem during Peter's imprisonment, when "constant prayer was offered to God for him by the church" (Acts 12:5).

Indeed, the saints normally seek that intercession. Several years before he was able to visit the Christians at Rome, for instance, Paul was already beseeching the Lord on their behalf (Romans 1:9), and he went on to "beg" (*parakalo*) them to "strive together with [him] in prayers" that he might come to visit them (15:30–32). This expression, "strive together [*synagonisasthai*] in prayers," contains a compound of the verb (*agonizomenos*) that Paul used to describe the intercessions of Epaphras on behalf of the church at Colossae (Colossians 4:12).

Holy Scripture abounds with examples of such intercession. For instance, those Greeks who "wish to see Jesus" initiate their approach through a saint named Philip. And how does Philip answer them? He brings the matter to the attention of yet another saint named Andrew, and then the two of them intercede with Jesus (John 12:20–22). Two saints, in other words, agree together to petition the Lord on behalf of those who made the original request (Matthew 18:19). Such is the communication among the saints.

A further example of this intercession of the saints is found in the story of Tabitha, the seamstress of Joppa. Tabitha died what the Acts of the Apostles indicates was a premature death, for we are told that she perished of a sickness. Tabitha's bereaved companions, learning that the Apostle Peter was currently visiting in the nearby town of Lydda, "sent two men to him, imploring [*parakalountes*] him not to delay in coming to them" (9:38). We observe here the dynamics of Christian intercession. At Tabitha's death the congregation at Joppa was not content to "go to God directly." They sought, rather, the intercession of Peter, and to obtain that intercession they sent, not one, but two men to "implore" Peter on their behalf. It is clear that "imploring the saints," communication among the saints, took place all through this episode.

Later generations of the saints would call this process a "prayer chain."

One is impressed by the several similarities between this story of Tabitha and another biblical account of intercession, the Gospel narrative of the raising of Jairus's daughter. First, each case involves a premature death, the daughter of Jairus being only twelve years old (Mark 5:42; Luke 8:42). Second, in both episodes attention is drawn to the people weeping near the corpse (Matthew 9:23; Mark 5:38; Luke 8:52; Acts 9:39). Third, in each instance the curious bystanders are dismissed from the room prior to the raising from the dead (Matthew 9:25; Mark 5:37; Luke 8:51; Acts 9:40). Fourth, both Jesus and Peter take the hand of the one deceased (Matthew 9:25; Mark 5:41; Luke 8:54; Acts 9:41). Fifth, there is a resemblance between these two accounts even in the wording of the formulas used to raise the dead persons. This similarity is clearest in Mark, who alone transcribes the original Aramaic of Jesus' command, "Little girl, arise": *Talitha, koum* (5:41). We note that a difference of only one letter separates this word *talitha* from the Aramaic name "Tabitha," for which Luke provides the Greek translation *Dorkas*, meaning "antelope" or "gazelle" (Acts 9:40). Thus, Peter's Aramaic command to the deceased seamstress of Joppa was, *Tabitha, koum.*

Finally, and perhaps most significantly, in each case there is an intercession, literally an "imploring," and it is instructive to observe that the same word, *parakalo*, is used with respect both to imploring Jesus (Mark 5:23; Luke 8:41) and to imploring Peter (Acts 8:38). In the context of prayer, that is to say, the saints speak to the saints in a way resembling the way they speak to Jesus. Thus, this identical verb, *parakalo*, is employed by Paul both to "implore" the Lord in his affliction (2 Corinthians 12:8) and to "implore" the saints at Rome to pray for him (Romans 15:30).

XII.
THE FORTITUDE OF THE SAINTS
⚬

Judges 8:4–9 records the incident in which Gideon, leading his three hundred exhausted and hungry warriors in pursuit of fifteen thousand escaping Midianites, requested loaves of bread from the cities of Succoth and Penuel. This request was entirely reasonable. Gideon's small force, by routing the Midianite army at the hill of Moreh (7:19–22), had effectively delivered all Israel, including Succoth and Penuel, from seven years of oppression (6:1). Now there remained only a modest mopping-up operation to subdue the last vestiges of the fleeing Midianite force, led by Zebah and Zalmunna. Providing Gideon's little army with a bit of bread was the very least to be expected from those cities that benefited from that army's victory.

Yet, the leaders of Succoth and Penuel refused Gideon's petition. The Sacred Text tells us why: *"Are* the hands of Zebah and Zalmunna now in your hand, that we should give bread to your army?"* (8:6). That is to say, the men of those two cities, Succoth and Penuel, were afraid to take the chance. If they were to give bread to Gideon's forces and then Gideon should lose the battle to Zebah and Zalmunna, the Midianites would retaliate against the cities that had provided the requested assistance. (One recalls the vengeance of Saul against the priests of Nob, who honored an identical request from David; see 1 Samuel 21:1–7; 22:6–19.) In short, until the battle was actually over, the men of Succoth and Penuel decided to play it safe. No bread, then, for Gideon's men.

This story illustrates the difference between those who play it safe and those who play for keeps. By boldly marching his three hundred men into the massive Midianite camp ("as numerous as locusts; and their camels *were* without number, as the sand by the seashore in multitude"—7:12), Gideon had played for keeps. This story emphasizes the fortitude of his army by its contrast to the cowardice of Succoth and Penuel. Gideon won that battle, because the Lord took his side. In some of the battles that men fight on this earth, you see, God does take sides. Never, however, does He take the side of the coward.

This story also illustrates why the virtue of fortitude is necessary for all the other virtues, as a condition and catalyst. The history of moral philosophy insists that no other virtue is possible without the virtue of fortitude, certainly not justice nor charity. The man deficient in fortitude will not measure up in anything else. In the words of Ambrose of Milan, "In the mediocre soul there is no fortitude, which alone defends the adornment of all the virtues" (*De Officiis* 1.39). For this reason, the man least deserving of our trust, on any matter whatever, is the coward. Fortitude, wrote Thomas Aquinas, is "the general virtue, or rather, the condition of any virtue" (*generalis virtus, vel potius, conditio cuiuslibet virtutis—Summa Theologica* Ia IIae, Q. 123, Art. 2). Thus, the leaders of Succoth and Penuel, falling short in fortitude, failed in an elementary duty of justice and charity.

In Holy Scripture this fortitude especially characterizes the prophets, even more than the warriors. Indeed, the biblical warriors, like Jonathan, Jehoshaphat, and Judas Maccabeus, literally had a fighting chance of coming out of the battle alive. The prophets, no. Of the prophets it was said that the Israelites "beat one, killed one, and stoned another" (Matthew 21:35). So many of them sacrificed their lives in God's service that it became common to speak of "the blood of the prophets" (Revelation 16:6; 18:24; cf. Matthew 23:37; Romans 11:3; 1 Thessalonians 2:15).

Except for the power of God's Word, the prophets sallied forth unarmed. They had nothing else in their favor when they confronted their contemporaries, and most especially the men of power whom God called them to challenge. The prophets, then, possessed the supreme fortitude (*andreia*) of which Aristotle wrote that "he is properly called a 'man of fortitude' [*andreios*] who is fearless in the face of a noble death [*ton kalon thanaton*] and those things that lead to death" (*Nicomachean Ethics* 3.6.10). This is the example we behold in Samuel confronting Saul, Nathan accusing David, Elijah encountering Ahab, Amos reprimanding Jeroboam, Isaiah challenging Ahaz, Jeremiah standing up to Zedekiah, Daniel opposing Nebuchadnezzar, and John the Baptist facing Herod. These and the other prophets were men of fortitude, aware that they were not the masters of their lives. Having received their lives from God by way of stewardship, they committed entirely to Him the day and circumstances of their deaths. This was the font and source of their fearlessness.

કૂ

1. NOAH THE PREACHER

Noah's construction of the ark represented his faith, the foundation of his righteousness. According to the Epistle to the Hebrews, "By faith Noah, being divinely warned of things not yet seen, moved with godly fear, prepared an ark for the saving of his household, by which he condemned the world and became heir of the righteousness which is according to faith" (11:7).

But Noah not only lived in righteousness; he also proclaimed righteousness. The Apostle Peter referred to him as "a preacher of righteousness" (2 Peter 2:5), and late in the first century Clement of Rome wrote that "Noah preached repentance, and those who heeded him were saved" (*First Epistle* 7.6).

This picture of Noah as a righteous preacher of repentance came to the early Christians from Jewish lore about that famous builder of the ark. Flavius Josephus wrote of Noah's relationship to his contemporaries in this way: "Noah was most uncomfortable with their actions, and, not at all happy with their conduct, he persuaded them to improve their dispositions and their actions. Seeing, nonetheless, that they did not obey him but remained slaves to their own wicked desires, he feared that they would slay him, together with his wife and children, as well as the spouses of the latter, so he departed out of that land" (*Antiquities* 13.1). Unable to convert his contemporaries, Noah then followed the divine leading to build an ark for the delivery of his family. He knew that God intended to flood the earth and destroy its wicked.

In the New Testament both the ark and the flood are understood as having to do with the mystery of baptism. Thus, St. Peter, writing of Christ's descent into hell after His death, proceeded immediately to treat of Noah, the flood, our own baptisms, and the Lord's Resurrection. For the early Christians, these were all components of the same mystery of regeneration: "For Christ also suffered once for sins, the just for the unjust, that He might bring us to God, being put to death in the flesh but made alive by the Spirit, by whom also He went and preached to the spirits in prison, who formerly were disobedient, when once the Divine longsuffering waited in the days of Noah, while *the* ark was being prepared, in which a few, that is, eight souls, were saved through water. There is also an antitype which now saves us—baptism (not the removal of the filth of the flesh, but the answer of a good conscience toward God), through the resurrection of Jesus Christ" (1 Peter 3:18–21). If we are to understand the story of Noah as the early Christians understood it, then, we must examine its relationship to repentance and baptism.

We may start by considering the symbolism of water itself, especially water as threatening and destructive. The water in the Noah story is not the great life-sustaining fluid; it is utterly menacing, rather, and it is specifically menacing to sin. Like the flood of Noah, baptism is destructive. Baptism has been given to the world because the world is full of sin, and through this water of baptism we are delivered from the sinful world. To be baptized means that we deliberately drown our sins in repentance. Whether we speak of the baptismal type in the Deluge, therefore, or of the fulfillment of that type in baptism itself, we must start with sin.

Thus, the Bible's flood account begins with a description of a world full of sin (Genesis 6:1–5, 11–13), ending with God's sorrow at having made man and His resolve to destroy man from the earth (6:6–7). God does not destroy the world in wrath, but in sorrow, and only our repentance at Noah's preaching can spare us this great sorrow of God.

We are baptized, therefore, because we are sinners, and our sins are destroyed in the mystery of baptism: "Arise and be baptized, and wash away your sins, calling on the name of the Lord" (Acts 22:16). Or earlier, "Repent, and let every one of you be baptized in the name of Jesus Christ for the remission of sins" (2:38). Unlike Noah's contemporaries, we ourselves hearken to his preaching. That is to say, we submit to this new baptismal flood because we repent at the witness of Noah. Baptism presupposes and requires this repentance of our sins, this conversion of our hearts to the apostolic word of Noah. In repentance we plunge ourselves into the deeper mystery of Noah's flood, which is the death and Resurrection of Christ our Lord (Romans 6:3; Colossians 2:12).

⚓

2. SAMUEL, BEARER OF BAD NEWS

Samuel's lifetime, mostly the second half of the eleventh century before Christ, was an age of transitions, in two of which Samuel himself was directly involved. These were the destruction of the shrine at Shiloh in his youth, and Israel's establishment of the monarchy during his declining years. In both cases Samuel, the last of Israel's Judges, was obliged to be the bearer of bad news.

He was a mere boy when, shortly before 1050 BC, Samuel was taken to Shiloh, consecrated to God, and placed under the guidance of that shrine's last priest, Eli (1 Samuel 1:24–28; 2:11, 18–20). Shiloh had been a central shrine of Israel for about a century and a half, ever since Joshua fixed it as the meeting place of the twelve tribes (Joshua 18:1). It was from there that the tribal representatives went forth to survey the Promised Land, and back to Shiloh they returned to cast lots for the division of the land (18:8–10; 19:51). During the ensuing period of Israel's judges, 1200 to 1050, Shiloh remained a regular place of pilgrimage (Judges 21:19; 1 Samuel 1:3, 7). At some point during that period, the Ark of the Covenant, previously placed at Bethel (Judges 20:26–27), was moved to Shiloh. It was near the Ark, within the shrine, that the boy Samuel slept, at least sometimes (1 Samuel 3:3).

One such night, indeed, provided what is perhaps the best-known scene in Samuel's life. Three times the sleeping lad, hearing his name called out in the night, rose and went to learn what Eli wanted of him. Eli, however, had not called him. Finally, this aged priest, suspecting the truth, instructed Samuel, should he hear his name invoked again, to answer, "Speak, LORD, for Your servant hears" (3:3–9). Samuel, yet abiding near the Ark, did so, and the Lord did speak to him, giving the boy his first experience of prophecy. It concerned the coming destruction of Shiloh and the end of Eli's priesthood (3:11–14). Samuel was obliged to bear the bad news (3:17–18).

Shiloh's destruction followed shortly after, when the Ark of the Covenant, carried into battle with the Philistines, was captured by them, and Eli himself fell dead at the news (4:1–22). Thus, "all Israel from Dan to Beersheba knew that Samuel *had been* established as a prophet of the LORD" (3:20). Although some prophets continued to dwell at Shiloh (cf. 1 Kings 14:2, 4), its priests settled at Nob (1 Samuel 14:3; 22:11). Samuel moved back to Ramah (7:17), his birthplace, and the Ark, though returned to Israel, was never again installed at Shiloh. The Lord had abandoned the site (Psalm 77[78]:60), making it a symbol of the fate awaiting any city that forsakes His covenant (Jeremiah 7:12, 14).

Israel's movement to monarchy occurred some thirty years later, around 1020, and here again Samuel served as the bearer of bad news. Though his own instincts opposed the idea of kingship, regarding it at first as a rebellion against God's covenant, it is possible that Samuel bore some of the blame. His failure to discipline his sons, after all, was the immediate reason given for the need of a king (1 Samuel 8:1–5). There is an irony here. Samuel himself had witnessed how Eli's failure to discipline his sons had earlier led to the destruction of Shiloh (1 Samuel 2:12–17, 22–25). It is no little paradox that Samuel, ever the visionary of the future, should be suddenly confronted with déjà vu.

As in that earlier case, however, Samuel prayed (8:6), and once again God spoke to him, instructing him to accede to the people's clamor for a king (8:7–8). Indeed, Samuel was the man God wanted to anoint that king (10:1). Nonetheless, as Israel's "seer" (9:9), he was also directed to foretell to the people the dire consequences of their choice, and the sad list of evils that the seer predicted as attendant on the institution of kingship (8:11–18) was a prophecy amply fulfilled in the following centuries. It was truly bad news.

Even though Samuel's hopes for the kingship had never been high, Israel's first king, Saul, was especially disappointing. Samuel endured him for twenty years. In the Lord's final word to His prophet, near the end of the century, He commanded Samuel to stop moping about the problem and to anoint David as the new king (16:1). He obediently did so (16:2–13), though he died before David could assume the throne (25:1). In Holy Scripture Samuel thus appears as the prophetic link joining Israel's kings to its earlier history.

⁊

3. NATHAN'S GODLY NARRATIVE

Probably the most important person in the life of King David was the Prophet Nathan. His very name means "gift," and Nathan was certainly God's generous gift to the king. Were it not for Nathan, in truth, we have no reason to believe that the Bible's final word on David would be any more favorable than the Bible's final word on King Saul.

David, himself a prophet (Acts 2:29, 30), had lost his way, not only succumbing to an adulterous passion, but even initiating a cunning plot of murder, so it was Nathan's divinely appointed task to call him back from sin to the path of repentance (2 Samuel 12). As was noted by

Saint John Chrysostom, "one prophet was sent to another" (*Peri Metanoias* 2.2.8). Nathan was assigned to do for David what the Apostles were appointed to do for all mankind—to preach repentance and the remission of sins (Luke 24:47).

Among the various ways by which to preach repentance to sinners, Nathan's inspired choice is that of the parable, a preference evidently favored also by a certain Prophet from Galilee at a later period. Nathan tells David the story of the ewe lamb, a narrative surely to be numbered among the Bible's finest examples of what T. S. Eliot called "the moral imagination." By means of storytelling Nathan successfully engages the king's own sense of decency and justice. He skillfully stimulates David's return to "the permanent things."

Nathan's method, of course, is to cloak the king's sinful actions within the folds of his own homespun. As Nathan's account progresses, David becomes morally aroused, with no suspicion that he is himself the villain of the narrative. Finally he pronounces the anticipated moral judgment, or, as the Scripture says, "David's anger was greatly aroused against the man, and he said to Nathan, '*As* the LORD lives, the man who has done this shall surely die!'" It is at this point, finally, that the prophet's impeaching finger is thrust at the royal face: "You *are* the man!" (12:5, 7).

It is important to observe that, in preaching repentance from sin, Nathan does not "preach down" to the sinner. He does not assume the "higher moral ground." On the contrary, the prophet's story compels David himself to seize that ground. Nathan does not directly accuse the king until after he causes the king to accuse himself. Nathan's method is to transform the sinner's imagination within a drama, until at last David is disclosed in the character of the villain. Again in the words of Chrysostom, "Nathan wove a dramatic scene, secretly concealing his weapon" (*op. cit.*, 2.2.9).

Moreover, even as David is explicitly condemned, he is implicitly affirmed. That is to say, in order to impugn the very worst in David, Nathan addresses himself to the very best in David—his innate, more deeply abiding sense of right and wrong. As a result of this preaching, the king's condemnation of his sins springs forth from his own conscience. David becomes his own accuser: "I have sinned against the LORD" (12:13). Thus, Nathan's preaching functions very much like the crowing of the nocturnal rooster that dramatically awakened the sleeping conscience of Simon Peter (Matthew 26:75).

One may further argue that this narrative of Nathan also provides the key for understanding biblical parables in general. Simply put, the parables of Holy Scripture are not to be interpreted "from outside," but to be engaged from within. These are imaginative stories of the human heart. We do not so much interpret the parables as we permit the parables to interpret us. They are narrative invitations. They summon us hearers of the Word to become parabolic, so to speak. They are mirrors of the soul, stories about our inner selves; we enter them by searching the inner caverns of the heart and mind. Otherwise we remain "outsiders."

While this is a universally valid principle for all interpretation of Holy Scripture, it is perhaps most obviously at work in our Lord's story of the sower and his seed. Examined closely, this narrative is actually a parable about the function of parables (Mark 4:1–20). In describing the differing destinies of the various hearers of God's word, the Lord is actually addressing the question of our spiritual state as we attend to the story. The parable of the sower serves to turn us to the examination of our hearts, whether they be invaded by bird or infested by thorns, and so on. The terrible question posed here is whether or not we ourselves are simply "outsiders" to the parable (4:11).

~~

4. THE HARSH WORD OF AHIJAH

The similarities between Samuel and Ahijah are truly striking. Both of them prophets from Shiloh, both were likewise appointed to designate new kings for Israel: Saul in the case of Samuel, Jeroboam in the case of Ahijah. Both of those kings, each of whom reigned roughly twenty years, proved to be failures. Finally, toward the end of their reigns, the same two prophets, both of them now quite old, were once again commissioned to announce the downfalls of the aforesaid kings and the impending changes of dynasty. Thus, Samuel prophesied the rise of David (1 Samuel 13:14), and Ahijah foretold the coming of Baasha (1 Kings 14:14).

Although the story of Samuel, because of its greater length and the richer detail in its telling, is doubtless the better known of the two, the account of Ahijah is no less dramatic and every bit as memorable.

Ahijah first appears on the biblical scene late in the reign of Solomon. By way of preparing for his appearance, Holy Scripture tells of the evils attendant on Solomon's rule (11:1–9) and the external political enemies who rise to challenge his kingdom (11:14–25). It is at this point that the Bible introduces young Jeroboam, whom Solomon has appointed an overseer for the northern tribes. As Jeroboam leaves Jerusalem to undertake his new responsibilities, he is met by the Prophet Ahijah, who abruptly proceeds to tear his clothing into twelve parts. Having thereby gained his total attention, Ahijah explains to the young man that these twelve parts represent Israel's twelve tribes, and he goes on to prophesy that Jeroboam will govern ten of those tribes, leaving only two tribes for the dynasty of David (11:26–39). All of this prophecy is fulfilled in the events that immediately follow the death of Solomon (11:30—12:16).

We do not again hear of Ahijah for a long time, nor does the Bible give us reason to suppose that Jeroboam further consults the prophet for advice in the governance of the realm. Unlike David, whose reign benefited from the prophetic counsel of Nathan, Jeroboam puts all thought of God behind him (14:9). On one occasion when he is accosted by an anonymous prophet from Judah, Jeroboam asks for the man's prayers but pays no heed to his prophetic warning (13:1–9). Furthermore, if Jeroboam had conferred with the Prophet Ahijah, whom God sent to him in the first place, he likely would not have erected those two golden calves at Bethel and Dan, thereby *doubling* the ancient infidelity of Aaron. (Compare 12:28 with Exodus 32:4, 8).

No, Jeroboam does not place himself under the judgment and discipline of the prophetic word. He is one of those men who want God on their side, without being on God's side. Craving the divine aid without the divine ordinance, Jeroboam will not consult Ahijah again for many years.

When he does so, it is because his son is sick, and he sends his wife to the prophet in hopes of obtaining a favorable word. Jeroboam sends her, moreover, in disguise, evidently too embarrassed to let Ahijah know who it is that seeks that word. The prophet himself, by this time, has grown very old, and his sight is failing.

Foolish Jeroboam, thinking to deceive the prophetic vision. Ahijah had been able to read the signs of the times during the reign of Solomon, but Jeroboam now fancies he can deceive the old seer with such a clumsy ruse. Inwardly guided by the Almighty, Ahijah reads the situation perfectly, and the Lord himself dictates "thus and thus" what he is to say.

The awful asperity of Ahijah's word to Jeroboam is enhanced by the ironies of the scene. At the doorway, deeply anxious for her sick child, arrives this woman clothed in a hopeless disguise. At her footfall, before one syllable escapes her lips, she is already detected by an old blind man, greeting her with a harshness hardly surpassed on any page of Holy Scripture (14:6–16), informing her, not only that the child will die, but that he will be the last in the family even to find his way to a grave. All the others will be devoured by dogs and birds. Mercy now is found no more, nor tenderness, but terrifying, unspeakable finality. God's last word to Jeroboam, the man who "made Israel to sin," is a kind of paradigm of damnation itself: "Depart from Me, you cursed, into the everlasting fire." Ahijah speaks for the God who reads hearts and is not mocked.

⚜

5. ELIJAH THE TISHBITE

Elijah was a robust sort of fellow, but this had been a very strenuous day. It began early that morning, when he met on Mount Carmel with King Ahab, two groups of the prophets of Baal totaling eight hundred and fifty, and an apparently large number of other Israelites (1 Kings 18). This ecumenical convention, which Elijah himself had suggested to the king, had a very practical purpose. After forty-two months without rain (James 5:17), a terrible drought lay on the land, and something simply had to be done about it. Elijah suggested a plan for putting an end to the problem, and Ahab was sufficiently desperate to try just about anything.

Elijah proposed that they choose two bulls to be offered in sacrifice, one by the prophets of Baal and one by himself. This recommendation met everyone's approval. The prophets of Baal (with whom, it may be said, Elijah already had a somewhat strained relationship) should have suspected something sly was afoot, when they themselves were obliged to supply Elijah with a bull. He had not brought one.

However, for two reasons, these gentlemen were a bit overconfident. First, Baal was a storm god, who knew a thing or two about rain. Elijah's Lord, on the other hand, had revealed Himself in the desert, where water was scarce. He would not know much about storms, atmospheric conditions, and that kind of thing. Second, the prophets of Baal enjoyed both royal patronage and the advantage of numbers. This would not be much of a contest, they were sure. Moreover, Elijah even agreed to let them go first.

It did not take the eight hundred and fifty very long to cut up their bull for sacrifice, and, while they were doing it, Elijah announced "no fire." They would have to persuade Baal, who was a storm god, after all, to send down lightning to get the flames going. Strangely, no one objected.

They worked hard all morning, trying to draw Baal's attention to the matter at hand, yelling out their prayers, jumping up and down on the altar (Baalism, you understand, was a seeker-friendly religion), and making a general commotion. Finally, they took knives and began to gash themselves (well, so much for seeker-friendly). Somebody declared this had worked in the past. It was no go today, however.

Elijah appeared to enjoy the show, cheering the Baalists on to greater exertions, suggesting that Baal was perchance asleep, or having a conversation with some other god perhaps, or maybe was on a trip. Elijah encouraged them to yell louder.

Finally, when they were rather worn out by mid-afternoon, Elijah suddenly announced, "My turn!" He jumped up, constructed a rather impressive altar, and cut up the second bull on it. Then, he had twelve barrels of sea water dragged up the side of Mount Carmel and poured all over the sacrifice. The prophets of Baal thought this last maneuver was a bit show-offy.

From this point on, everything started to happen all at once. Elijah said a quick two-verse prayer, and abruptly, from a cloudless sky, there fell a bolt of fire that "consumed the burnt sacrifice, and the wood and the stones and the dust, and it licked up the water" (1 Kings 18:38).

The theological question of the day being thus settled, Elijah had the crowd round up the Baalist prophets, who were promptly marched down the northeast corner of Mount Carmel to the dry bed of the Kishon River, where they were all put to death. Elijah was not a man of half-measures. He well knew that this was the very place where Barak's army had defeated the forces of Sisera centuries before.

Elijah himself stayed on the mountain and gave himself to prayer. Notwithstanding that impressive bolt of lightning, after all, there was still no rain! He prayed seven times (three times had been enough to raise a dead person in the previous chapter), and then they saw the first cloud, "small as a man's hand," coming from over the sea. "Better head for home," Elijah said to Ahab, while the sky grew black with clouds and wind. At this point, indeed, Elijah himself jumped up and ran out ahead of Ahab's chariot. The mind's eye may see him even now, this wild prophet with streaming hair, rushing through the thunder and the lightning bolts, running well ahead of the panicking, wide-eyed, panting, galloping horses, racing through the darkness and the rain, all those seventeen miles from Mount Carmel to Jezreel.

Recalling the scene a millennium later, St. James calmly remarked that Elijah "was a man with a nature like ours" (James 5:17). I am grateful that James made that point, because, to tell the truth, I think I might have missed it. James himself, I am prepared to believe, may have been of like nature with Elijah. As for anybody else I know, well, I am not so dead sure about it.

⁂

6. AMOS: PROPHECY WRITTEN DOWN

After the death of Solomon in 922 BC, the ten northern tribes rebelled against the Davidic royal house at Jerusalem and, under the leadership of King Jeroboam I, established themselves as an independent realm. Most often called simply Israel, that kingdom is also known in the Bible as Samaria (its later capital), Ephraim (its principal tribe), and "the House of Joseph" (father of Ephraim and Manasseh). This Kingdom of Israel lasted exactly two centuries, coming to an end in 722, when the Assyrian Emperor Sargon II conquered it, deporting the masses of its population to the eastern end of the Fertile Crescent, the area known as Mesopotamia. To this very day we refer to those deportees as the "Ten Lost Tribes."

The biblical sources ascribe the eventual downfall of that rebellious kingdom to its sustained infidelity to God's Law, a spiritually dangerous political and mercantile alliance with the Phoenicians, its materialistic idolatry, and the high level of oppression effected by its venal and unjust economics. In all these various evils Israel's kings had led the way.

Nonetheless, throughout its history, God repeatedly sent prophets to the Northern Kingdom to warn them of the dangerous path they were pursuing. In the ninth century the most famous of these prophets were Elijah, Micaiah, and Elisha. In the following century, only a generation before Israel's downfall and deportation, God sent them Amos, who foresaw and foretold the nation's coming tragedy, regarding it as God's just punishment of their national apostasy.

There are several features to be noted about the prophetic ministry of Amos. First, he was a "social prophet," concerned mainly with military atrocities, political oppression, and economic injustice. In this respect his ministry continued a prophetic theme earlier witnessed in Elijah's denunciation of the injustice of Ahab and Jezebel (cf. 1 Kings 21).

Second, Amos was the Bible's original "literary prophet," meaning that he was the first biblical prophet whose extended oracles were consigned to writing in a single book. In this respect he may be regarded as a point of transition between earlier prophets like Elijah and such later prophets as Jeremiah. This was new. The very act of writing down the oracles of God's prophets manifested a fresh insight, a heightened awareness that the divinely prophetic message was possessed of a permanent relevance beyond the circumstances of its original time and place. Someone, perhaps Amos himself, believed that his message had about it a timeless value and that his words were worth recording for the generations yet to come. The origin of the Book of Amos lay in that conviction.

Third, Amos, though he preached in the Northern Kingdom, was himself a southerner, coming from among the shepherds of the village of Tekoah in Judah. One day, sometime around the year 750, he suddenly showed up at the northern shrine of Bethel, near the border of Judah, and began his ministry of preaching the Word of the Lord. He mainly denounced vice and corruption, announcing that the patience of God was nearly exhausted. The prophet's dramatic appearance at Bethel met the resistance of Amaziah, the priest of that idolatrous shrine, who wrote to King Jeroboam II, complaining of Amos's interference where it was not wanted: "The land is not able to bear all his words." By way of response, Amos insisted that his unappreciated appearance to the northern shrine was not his own idea. He had been perfectly content, he said, to remain "a sheepbreeder / And a tender of sycamore fruit," but God had called him to "prophesy to My people Israel." It was in this context that Amos foretold Israel's impending disaster: "Jeroboam shall die by the sword, / And Israel shall surely be led away captive" (Amos 7:10–15).

Fourth, Amos's prophetic denunciations were not limited to one nation. On the contrary, he extended his message to Israel's closest neighbors, Syria, Philistia, Phoenicia, Edom, Ammon, Moab, and his own native Judah. These all he denounced for an assortment of social atrocities, including international slave trade, the murder of pregnant women, and other crimes associated with unbridled warfare. This larger, more general dimension of his message is surely one of the reasons that the prophecies of Amos were written down for future generations.

ॐ

7. MICAH OF MORESHETH

Not least among the many results of Solomon's political reforms and progressive fiscal policies was the emergence of an economic elite. Benefiting from Israel's more emphatic mercantile economy, which freed them from working fairly long hours on fairly small farms, this economic elite naturally became, as well, a cultural elite, enjoying the twin advantages of greater leisure and more interesting ways to fill it. They were transformed, in other words, into the trendsetters of their day, the sort that Adam Smith would later call the "people of fashion."

Remembering that our word "school" derives from the Greek word for "leisure," we are not surprised that some of Israel's emerging elite, by way of filling their enhanced leisure hours, acquired an education. And a good deal of that education was certainly literary, for the evidence suggests that at least two significant blocks of Israel's literature were put to pen during the reign of Solomon: the foundational document embodied in the Book of Proverbs, and the historical material incorporated into the Books of Joshua, Judges, and Samuel.

Access to literacy in Israel was also progressive, gradually extending to individuals from other classes. Such progressive extension would explain why, for instance, Elijah, Micaiah, Elisha, and the other prophets of the ninth century did not write books, while those of the eighth century did. It is also instructive, as well as pertinent to our theme, that these later prophets (Amos, Hosea, Isaiah, and Micah), when they did assume the pen, held it rather like a dart directed at the elite class— aimed, that is, against those very trendsetters who chiefly benefited from the new economy.

In doing this, the eighth-century prophets were among the first social critics to direct attention to what Adam Smith would later call the "two different schemes or systems of morality." On the meaning of this distinction Smith is worth quoting at length: "In every civilized society, in every society where the distinction of ranks has once been completely established, there have always been two different schemes or systems of morality current at the same time, of which the one may be called strict or austere, the other one liberal, or, if you will, the loose system. The former is generally admired and revered by the common people; the latter is commonly more esteemed and adopted by what are called the people of fashion."

In Israel the "strict or austere system" was the inherited ethics of the Mosaic Law and the prescriptive wisdom of Proverbs. Strong on restraint and swift to warn against the dangers of self-indulgence, this traditional morality was extremely useful for those whose station in life left them no wiggle space for moral mistakes. A conservative morality based in part on a conservative economy, it was, as Smith said, "generally admired and revered by the common people." Amos, for instance, and Micah. And, in his saner moments, even Solomon!

The new commercial prosperity, however, had now spawned a new, "progressive" style of conduct, the morality that Smith identified as "commonly more esteemed and adopted by what are called people of fashion." Removed to greater length from likely ruin, these latter could abide a riskier style of life. Their larger bank accounts enabled them— to stay here with Smith's own words—to afford a measure of "luxury," "the pursuit of pleasure," "some degree of intemperance," and an occasional "breach of chastity." Folk of this sort, moreover, were commonly found in the cities, where the banks were and the counting houses, while the adherents of the older, more austere morality lived out on the farmland and in the smaller villages.

It is hardly a wonder, then, that one of the first prophetic pens directed against the elite morality should come from a small village. Moresheth, to be precise, and the prophet's name was Micah. Also first to foretell the downfall of that big city Jerusalem because of her big-city sins, Micah filled seven chapters with invective against the social evils inevitable in a morality determined solely by unrestrained consumerism and the raw concerns of market. In his counsel that man should do justly, love mercy, and walk humbly with his God, Micah represents the literary and theological link that joins the prophets to the older, common morality of Moses and the Book of Proverbs.

ॐ

8. ZEPHANIAH AND THE DAY OF THE LORD

The Scythians were Eurasian nomads who for centuries roamed the vast grasslands along the Dniepr, the Don, and the Volga. In Assyrian records they are known as the Ashguzai, and in the Bible, which calls them the Ashkenaz, they are descendants of Gomer, in the second generation after Noah (Genesis 10:3; 1 Chronicles 1:6). In ancient Persian their name, as preserved in an inscription of Darius, was corrupted to Skusha, from which was derived the Greek name by which we still call them, Scythians. In Greek mythology, the patriarch of the race was said to be Scythes, the son of Heracles (Herodotus 4.10). Antiquity remembered them as fearsome mounted archers.

In the seventh century before Christ, the Scythians wandered into the notice of history when they passed down through the Caucasian Gates and encroached on the Assyrian Empire. Although this contact was originally hostile, Esarhaddon (681–668) made allies of them, giving his daughter in marriage to the Scythian king, Bartatua. The Assyrians hoped to keep the newcomers around for a while, to help against the rising Babylonians and Medes.

The Scythians, however, could do pretty much what they wanted, because the Assyrian Empire was in full decline after Esarhaddon (and would collapse completely in 612). Moreover, these nomads rarely remained long in one place, and sometime between 630 and 625 they determined to go on a raiding expedition down the western half of the Fertile Crescent. They actually had designs on Egypt, according to Herodotus, who left us a record of what ensued: "When they arrived in that part of Syria called Palestine, Psammetichus, the King of Egypt [Psamtek I, 664–610], met them with gifts and supplications to advance no further" (1.105). Although thus bought off from invading Egypt, the Scythian hordes menaced much of the Holy Land, destroying the Philistine cities of Ashkelon and Ashdod.

Although the Medes, in due course, drove these invaders to the northern frontiers of the Mediterranean and up toward the Black Sea, they remained a threat to the Fertile Crescent for a long time. In the early years of the sixth century, Jeremiah still thought of them as a force to be reckoned with (51:27), and centuries later the Apostle Paul used their name as a synonym for barbarians (Colossians 3:11).

Herodotus says that the Scythian ascendancy in Asia lasted twenty-eight years, but their invasion of the Holy Land probably lasted for a only a few months. Even this brief time, nonetheless, was sufficient to inspire panic among the populace; they had already heard of those terrifying mounted archers whom even the Assyrians preferred not to fight.

One of Israel's prophets took this Scythian invasion as a sign of God's impending wrath. His name was Zephaniah. The Scythian attack came early in the reign of Josiah of Judah (640–609), before the Deuteronomic Reform that began in 622. Thus, Zephaniah was a contemporary of Jeremiah (Zephaniah 1:1). This dating would also explain Zephaniah's preoccupation with popular religious syncretism, involving the worship of the Phoenician Baal, the Ammonite Milcom, and the Philistine Dagon (1:4–5, 9). It was chiefly against this syncretism that Josiah's reform of 622 would be directed (2 Chronicles 34:8–33).

The imagery of warfare, of which the Scythians were currently providing a vivid example, prompted Zephaniah to view the judgment of God in terms of a cosmic overthrow, an undoing, as it were, of the work of Creation, especially of days five and six: "'I will utterly consume everything / From the face of the land ['*adamah*],' / Says the LORD; / 'I will consume man ['*adam*] and beast; / I will consume the birds of the heavens, / The fish of the sea . . . / I will cut off man ['*adam*] from the face of the land ['*adamah*],' / Says the LORD" (Zephaniah 1:2–3). Because man ('*adam*) is taken from the very earth ('*adamah*), this cutting out of the very ground from under human existence is the worst punishment Zephaniah could imagine; man's life is left "up in the air."

Zephaniah arguably gives us the Bible's most detailed picture of the *Dies Irae*, "the day of the LORD" (1:14–16). It will visit all nations, not just local folks like the Philistines (2:4–7) and the small nations east of the Jordan (2:8–11), but also the Ethiopians at the southwestern edge of the Fertile Crescent (2:12) and the Assyrians at its other end (2:13–15). Most of all, warns Zephaniah, it will visit God's holy city, Jerusalem (3:1–4). God will cut off all nations (3:6).

For all these dire warnings, Zephaniah must finally be regarded as a prophet of hope, because God is faithful to His promises. After the divine visitation of wrath has passed, God's people are once again summoned to sing the renewal of grace (3:14–20). Even as man waited for the divine judgment, he was told, "Be silent in the presence of the Lord

GOD" (1:7). And when His wrath is spent, this Lord God promises, "I will gather those who sorrow" (3:18).

౩౯

9. NAHUM AND NINEVEH

In at least one respect, Nahum is unique in all of the Bible—what he announced was exactly what his contemporaries most wanted to hear!

In general it may be said that the biblical prophets are "countervailing." That is to say, most of the time we find them resisting, even denouncing, the popular mind of their day. They usually speak in a direction about 180 degrees at variance with the temper of their times. Thus, if God's people are content and self-satisfied, the biblical prophets step in and give them something to worry about. If, on the other hand, God's people are depressed and weary, the prophets' word to them is normally encouraging and full of promise. In short, the word of the prophet is most often just the opposite of what the people are disposed to hear, a feature that tends to render the prophet a tad unpopular in his own time. It is easy to show that this countervailing disposition rules in most of the Bible's prophetic books.

Not in the Book of Nahum, however. His was a word that all expected and no one was sad to hear! Shortly before the fall of the Assyrian capital, Nineveh, in 612, Nahum announced its coming destruction in the most vivid terms. to the universal jubilation of his listeners. Assyria, after all, was the scourge of its time. Ever since its rise a few centuries earlier, the empire ruled from Nineveh had inflicted countless sufferings across the Fertile Crescent. As prophesied by Amos, the Assyrians under Emperor Sargon II had conquered the Kingdom of Israel in 722, carrying away the ten northern tribes to a bitter captivity, and other nations of the Middle East suffered an identical fate. The Assyrians, moreover, destroyed the Phoenician capital of Tyre and conquered the Nile Delta. Meanwhile, the nations of Judah, Syria, Ammon, Moab, and Edom were held under Assyrian subjection and tribute. In 701, only a miraculous intervention had preserved Jerusalem itself from destruction by the Emperor Sennacherib.

Given that they were roughly the ancient world's equivalent to the Third Reich, it is not surprising that the Assyrians were thoroughly and roundly hated throughout the lands of the Bible. We recall with what reluctance the Prophet Jonah had preached repentance to the

Ninevites back in the eighth century, for he did not *want* them to repent!

By the beginning of the seventh century, nonetheless, a new empire was rising to challenge Assyria—namely, a rejuvenated Babylon. Perhaps the latter power seemed harmless at first. We recall that King Hezekiah of Judah, late in his reign, received a Babylonian delegation, foolishly showing them the treasures of his kingdom, never suspecting that these Babylonians would soon return to claim that treasure. Isaiah, however, a keen interpreter of his times, foresaw it all.

Neither in the Bible nor in other ancient records is it clear exactly how the Assyrian Empire arrived at the decline that marked its existence by the mid-seventh century, though one suspects that it had simply grown too large to be manageable. More than one empire in history has been taught the danger of having too many borders to defend. In 614, when combined forces of Babylonians and Medes destroyed Assyria's older capital, the city of Ashur, the Prophet Nahum sensed that the end of its newer capital, Nineveh, was not far off. The three chapters of his prophecies should be dated between 614 and 612.

Nineveh, the Assyrian capital, was a most impressive city for that time. Its containing wall was 8 miles long and embraced about 1,850 acres, or 2.89 square miles. It was full of palaces built by Sennacherib, Esarhaddon, and Ashurbanipal. Its temples to Ishtar and Nabu were world famous. It was full of wealth drawn from the whole region between Egypt and the Persian Gulf. Most Assyrians may have thought that the empire and its capital would last forever. Not so, said Nahum, going on to described Nineveh's impending destruction in very colorful scenes that depict the scarlet tunics of the invading armies, the rumbling of horses' hooves and chariot wheels, the brandishing of spears, the flaming torches put to the buildings. In short, "Woe to the bloody city!" (Nahum 3:1).

Such a fate, says Nahum, must hang over every nation that rebels against the rule of God, for "who can stand before His indignation? And who can endure the fierceness of His anger?" (1:6).

☙

10. OBADIAH AND THE EDOMITES

Convinced that God speaks at specific points in history, the canonical editors of the Holy Scriptures often ascribe particular time frames to the messages of the prophets. Frequently they specify these occasions by reference to the reigns of certain kings. Thus we are informed that Isaiah was called "in the year that King Uzziah died" (Isaiah 6:1), that Zechariah heard God's voice "in the eighth month of the second year of Darius" (Zechariah 1:1), and that John the Baptist began his ministry "in the fifteenth year of the reign of Tiberias Caesar" (Luke 3:1). Such time references may be determined in other ways; thus we learn that Jeremiah received a prophetic word immediately after the fall of Jerusalem (Jeremiah 40:1) and that Amos began to preach "two years before the earthquake" (Amos 1:1). This kind of information is so standard in Holy Scripture that, in those cases where it is missing, we should presume that it simply was not available to the biblical editors.

One such case is the prophecy of Obadiah. Though a dozen or so men in the Bible bore that name, the absence of a genealogical reference at the beginning of the Book of Obadiah makes it difficult to identify our prophet with any of them. Was he the Obadiah known to Elijah in 1 Kings 18? This identification, favored in some Jewish sources and in standard works of Christian hagiography, is obviously attractive, but it collapses under the book's internal evidence. The author of the Book of Obadiah was clearly from Judah, not the Northern Kingdom, and the past events to which he refers occurred much later than the ninth century before Christ.

The one thing we do know for certain about the author of the Book of Obadiah is that he took a decidedly dim view of the Edomites. Nor was Obadiah alone in that respect, for there is reason to believe that more than one Israelite was somewhat tried by Deuteronomy's injunction not to despise the Edomite (23:7). Those descendants of Esau, after all, had obstructed the chosen people's way to the Promised Land in the days of Moses (Numbers 20:21), and according to the Prophet Amos in the eighth century the Edomites, having "cast off all pity" (Amos 1:11), were involved in international slave trade (1:6, 9).

Edom's most memorable offenses, however, occurred when the Babylonians destroyed Jerusalem in 587. At that time they rejoiced at the city's downfall (Lamentations 4:21), exploiting its misfortune in a vengeful way (Ezekiel 25:12). Most serious of all was the vile complicity of the Edomites in the demolition of Solomon's temple, an outrage for which they are explicitly blamed in 1 Esdras 4:45.

This final offense likewise inspired a line of Psalm 136(137), a lament composed in captivity "by the rivers of Babylon" (v. 1) where the exiles sat and wept, remembering Zion. Reflecting on the holy city's recent, ruthless destruction, the psalmist bitterly recalled Edom's share in the matter: "Remember, O LORD, against the sons of Edom / The day of Jerusalem, / Who said, 'Raze *it*, raze *it*, / To its very foundation!'" (v. 7).

Obadiah's prophecy testifies that his own rancor toward the Edomites was prompted by the identical recollection. He particularly blames them for rejoicing at Jerusalem's downfall, despoiling the city, blocking the path of escape against those who fled, and handing the refugees over to their captors (vv. 12–14). He can scarcely forget that the descendants of Esau were, in fact, blood relatives of the Israelites. Like Amos, who had earlier accused Edom of pursuing "his brother with the sword" (Amos 1:11), Obadiah speaks of "violence against your brother Jacob" (v. 10). His words stand forever in Holy Scripture as a warning to those who rejoice at or take advantage of the tribulations of others, or who neglect the ancestral ties that should prompt a readier compassion.

The prophetic doom pronounced by the Bible against the Edomites was vindicated in their displacement by the Nabateans in the fourth century BC. Forced to migrate to southern Palestine, they were eventually subjugated by John Hyrcanus (134–104). From that point on, they were simply assimilated into Judaism. One of them, named Herod, even became a king of the Jews, but he always sensed that someday a real descendant of David might appear on the scene and challenge his claim to the throne. It made him very nervous and unreasonable.

ॐ

11. HAGGAI AND THE PRINCIPLES OF STEWARDSHIP

When the Persian emperor Cyrus permitted Jews to return home from the Babylonian Captivity in 538 BC, relatively few of them did. Most of the Jews in exile, having established homes and businesses in the eastern half of the Fertile Crescent, were little disposed to return to a land that had suffered the ravages of war, and most of those who did come home were younger and relatively poor. Also, they were nearly all unmarried men.

Moreover, the new life awaiting these men was frugal. The available area of the Promised Land was only about twenty square miles around the city of Jerusalem, which was in ruins. It was not politically independent but belonged to the administrative district of Samaria, part of the fifth Persian satrapy.

This southern part of the Holy Land, which was never especially fertile, had not been farmed in half a century, and trees and wild brush can grow very thick and tall on farmland left fallow for so long. Moreover, the newcomers immediately faced a series of crop failures and meager harvests, sending up prices in a population already impoverished.

Still, farming was about the only way a young man could make a living in this region, for there were no other industries. Those who had not managed to obtain land often found themselves unemployed.

The rest of the Holy Land was largely populated by half-Jews and non-Jews who were opposed to the return of these newcomers. Not only were jobs scarce, but those who went out looking for work might be mugged or shot at: "*There were* no wages for man nor any hire for beast; / There was no peace from the enemy for whoever went out or came in" (Zechariah 8:10).

It is scarcely surprising, then, that many of the returned exiles, struggling to make a meager living, soon forgot that one of the purposes of their return was to restore Israel's authentic worship in a new temple. Year after year, this project was neglected, as folks became ever more preoccupied with their own concerns. Eighteen years went by, to the second year of King Darius (Haggai 1:1—late August of the year 520), and still they were saying, "The time has not come, the time that the LORD's house should be built" (Haggai 1:2).

The Prophet Haggai was among those who lamented this state of affairs (Ezra 5:1) and saw that it was proving ruinous to the spiritual life of the people. Their growing selfishness and materialism would finally corrupt, he feared, the important spiritual lessons that they had learned during the Babylonian Captivity. It was time to speak up.

The problem, Haggai saw, was that the people were not putting God first. According to their way of thinking, they would finally get around to building God's house when they had finished building their own. If the Lord would simply let them "get a little more out of the hole," they would eventually do something for God. That is to say, let us seek the Kingdom of God in second or third place, but certainly not first.

Haggai knew how fallacious this reasoning was. Nearly two decades had passed, and Solomon's temple was still in ruins. The basic law for godly living, Haggai saw, was to seek *first* the Kingdom of Heaven. If a man wants "to get a little ahead" before he starts giving something to God, it will probably never happen.

Indeed, Haggai perceived, things tended to get worse: "You have sown much, and bring in little; / You eat, but do not have enough; / You drink, but you are not filled with drink; / You clothe yourself, but no one is warm; / And he who earns wages, / Earns wages *to put* into a bag with holes" (Haggai 1:6). This text is the Bible's first reference to minted coins and purses, and already the purses have holes in the bottom!

Those who put God anywhere but first will never have *enough*, Haggai taught. There has never been a self-centered man who thought he had enough. God's blessing, moreover, does not fall on such folk: "'*You* looked for much, but indeed *it came to* little; and when you brought it home, I blew it away. Why?' says the LORD of hosts. Because of My house that *is in* ruins, while every one of you runs to his own house" (1:9).

His contemporaries, fortunately, paid attention to Haggai. They built that new temple in the next four years (Ezra 6:15).

⳥

12. THE MAN BORN BLIND

Whenever the Gospel of St. John says that Jesus "sees" someone, the verb denotes more than the bare act of vision. If John takes the care to remark that Jesus "sees," this is invariably a prelude to some transformation; some work of grace is at hand. Thus does Jesus "see" Nathaniel (John 1:47, 50), the paralytic at the pool (5:6), the weeping Mary of Bethany (11:33), and His two dear ones at the foot of the Cross (19:26).

Thus, too, does St. John introduce the story of the man born blind, for he says that Jesus, "passing by, *saw* a man blind from birth" (9:1). This is a most important detail. The blind man himself, after all, cannot see Jesus, so Jesus must first see him. This is a story about the primacy of grace, illustrating the truth that it is "not that we loved God, but that He loved us" (1 John 4:10). This story begins, then, with a man that Jesus saw, and it ends with that same man seeing Jesus: "You have both *seen* Him and it is He who is talking with you" (John 9:37, emphasis added).

As they behold the blind man, the Lord's disciples are plagued by a theological problem—namely, whose fault is it that the man was born blind? They phrase this question in a curious and most interesting way:

"Rabbi, who sinned, this man or his parents, that he was born blind?" (9:2). Jesus answers immediately, of course, that neither sinned, but that is not the last time this question will appear in the story. After his healing, both the man and his parents will be subpoenaed for interrogation by the Lord's enemies, who have their own ideas about "who sinned." The latter will say of Jesus, "We know that this Man is a sinner" (9:24). Then, when he refuses to agree with them, the man himself is pronounced guilty: "You were completely born in sins" (9:34). They thus provide their own answer to the question first posed by the disciples.

There is a deeper blindness in the story, nonetheless, an unrepentance that is the real sin. Thus, at the very end of the account, Jesus gives a further response to the original query, "Who sinned?" To those hard of heart who condemned the man born blind, the Lord asserts, "If you were blind, you would have no sin; but now you say, 'We see.' Therefore, your sin remains" (9:41). This is the story's final answer to its first question. Thus, the problem of "who sinned" is an interpretive key to the whole narrative.

There is another opposition in this story, a contrast between the purely speculative question of the disciples and the practical action of Jesus. Faced with this phenomenon of blindness, the disciples want to assign the proper blame for the situation, whereas Jesus wants to change it. They look to a human cause, He to a divine purpose ("that the works of God should be revealed in him"—9:3).

The enemies of Jesus in this story are also theorists. They *know* that Jesus "is not from God" (9:16), because His interpretation of the Law differs from theirs. By way of contrast, the man born blind begins with no theory. Indeed, he is a practical empiricist, who knows what he sees: "One thing I know: that though I was blind, now I see" (9:25). For him, any theories about "who sinned" must commence with certain established facts, facts as plain as the mud that he washed from his eyes.

Commencing with these facts, the man will reason his way to others, and one may observe a transformation in his regard for Jesus. It is ironic, moreover, that the interrogation of the Lord's enemies becomes the impetus driving him to an ever more comprehensive recognition. Immediately after the healing, he speaks simply of "a Man called Jesus" (9:11). When pushed on the point, however, he finds himself forced to a new conclusion about Jesus: "He is a prophet" (9:17). As he argues with Jesus' enemies, logic compels him to admit that Jesus comes from

God (9:32). Finally, he recognizes that Jesus is the Son of God, and at his last appearance in this story the man born blind is prostrate before Him in adoration (9:35–38).

This intricate narrative is an illustration of a theme introduced early in the Gospel of John. As He begins to heal the blind man, Jesus announces, "I am the light of the world" (9:5), a self-identification paraphrasing a line near the beginning of the Gospel: "That was the true Light which gives light to every man coming into the world" (1:9). This man born blind, then, is the image of all to whom the true Light appears.

XIII.
QUESTERS AND QUESTIONERS
 ॐ

Two of the shortest parables in the Gospels are those of the treasure in the field and the pearl of great price. Probably because they are similar in structure and theme, the New Testament preserves them in sequence: "Again, the kingdom of heaven is like a treasure hidden in a field, which a man found and hid; and for joy over it he goes and sells all that he has and buys that field. Again, the kingdom of heaven is like a merchant seeking beautiful pearls, who, when he had found one pearl of great price, went and sold all that he had and bought it" (Matthew 13:44–46). Common to both parables are the elements of discovery, value, sale, and purchase.

The latter three themes—value, sale, and purchase—are particularly strong in uniting these parables. The kingdom of heaven is portrayed as a reality of incomparable value, the attaining of which is worth more than everything else put together. Indeed, the sale of all that we have, in order to purchase this incomparable treasure, is a dominant Gospel motif quite apart from the parables. For example, Matthew somewhat later records our Lord's words to the rich young man: "If you want to be perfect, go, sell what you have and give to the poor, and you will have treasure in heaven; and come, follow Me" (19:21).

Moreover, a comparison of this latter passage with the parable of the hidden treasure is very instructive. Indeed, I suggest that, in order to understand either account—the treasure in the field and the rich young man—it is useful to juxtapose them, because they manifestly deal with the identical moral situation. The dilemma of the rich young man, who wants to "have eternal life" (19:16), is indistinguishable from the opportunity of the man who finds the treasure buried in the field. The responses of the two men, however, are exactly opposite. In the case of the man in the parable, there is joy in his very despoiling: "for *joy* over it he goes and sells all that he has." However, in the case of the young man whom Jesus invites to make the identical decision, there is nothing but sadness: "But when the young man heard that saying, he went away *sorrowful*, for he had great possessions" (19:22). What for the one individual is a reason for joy is for the other man an occasion of sorrow. The difference is entirely in their responses.

Comparing the two parables themselves—the treasure in the field and the pearl of great price—we discern that one of their common components, namely the element of "discovery," also provides a point of contrast between them. In the parable of the treasure in the field, it is essential to the story that the treasure is *hidden*, concealed, not out in the open. Only one man discovers the whereabouts of the treasure, and he proceeds to act on the information in the greatest secrecy. This is, after all, *buried* treasure, bearing an air of escapade, evoking a sense of adventure. This parable prompts us to crouch quietly under the full moon and listen. We hearken to the hooting of the owl. Frogs croak in the distant marsh, and crickets sing in the hedge. We hold our breath to hear the steady delving of the spade into the sod some three steps northeast of the shadow cast by the bottom branch of the sycamore tree. Buried treasure, you see, is the very stuff of romance, and the Lord's parable about it suggests that the Gospel embodies some secret allure for the searcher, some whispered mystery that beckons to the soul of the adventurer.

Just one verse later, however, when we come to the parable of the pearl, all this hushed atmosphere of mystery is changed. The kingdom no longer signifies the discovery of something secret but of something quite public. The pearl is not buried anywhere. On the contrary, it is exposed in the marketplace. It is out there where everyone can see it. This pearl of the kingdom becomes the subject of human assessment and calculation. People look at it, appraise it, compare it to other pearls. The kingdom thus becomes an historical component of human interest, activity, study, decision, and enterprise.

This pearl of great price may thus be likened to the star that beguiled the Magi; it was up there with all the other stars. In a sense, it even had to compete with those other stars in order to gain the interest and seal the allegiance of the wise. It was the attraction of this one star, this single pearl in the heavens, that fascinated their minds and drove them to the far reaches of their search. This was the star that whispered to their hearts: "If you want to be perfect, go, sell all that you have, and come, follow Me."

꒛

1. THE QUEEN OF SHEBA

The realm of Sheba, or Saba as the place is called in ancient Assyrian documents, was situated at the extreme southern tip of the Arabian peninsula, the area now known as Yemen. From those same Assyrian texts, as well as from inscriptions found at Sheba's capital city, Mâreb, we know a thing or two about the history of the place during the first millennium before Christ.

First, we know that Sheba flourished most of that time as a major mercantile link between the Far East and the southern Mediterranean, and a glance at a map of the area quickly explains why this should be the case. Sitting on both sides of the corner formed by the Red Sea and Gulf of Aden, Sheba dominated the narrow Straits of Bab el Mandeb by which these two waters are joined. This meant that Sheba could effectively control the traffic coming down from those twin horns formed at the north of the Red Sea by the Gulf of Suez and the Gulf of Aqaba. Likewise, through the Gulf of Aden, Sheba was open to shipping on the Arabian Sea, the Indian Ocean, the Bay of Bengal, and places beyond. Thus, with respect to sea travel Sheba was the tangent point of two great mercantile spheres.

Some of the business, in fact, stood nearby. Immediately to the north of Sheba was Ophir, probably to be identified with Havila, a region celebrated for its gold (e.g., see Genesis 2:11; Job 22:24; 28:16). Over to the west lay Ethiopia, or Cush, a kingdom sufficiently imposing to control Egypt for some periods, and, from the south, there extended the horn of Somalia. As Asia's vital southern link with Africa, then, Sheba was in a position to gain, hold, and control great wealth.

Second, we also know the names of five of the queens of Sheba. As all of these lived in the eighth and seventh centuries, however, none of them can be identified with that Queen of Sheba who came to visit Solomon in the mid-tenth century before Christ. A pity, in truth, for some of us would dearly like to know the lady's name.

Doubtless her appearance in Solomon's court was related to the latter's recent entrance into the powerful circles of international commerce. Through his extensive dealings with the Phoenicians, whose ships docked in harbors on all three continents bordering the Mediterranean basin, Solomon's port at Elath on the Gulf of Aqaba became an important link in a new mercantile chain that now stretched from Ceylon in the southeast to Gibraltar in the northwest. The queen's arrival at his court, then, was clear evidence that Solomon had become a "player" on the big scene.

The event surely signified more, however. After all, Solomon was still far from being the queen's equal in the world of international commerce. Indeed, his recently gained status in this respect depended entirely on his hegemony over the land of Edom, which contained the port of Elath, for this was Solomon's sole connection with the Gulf of Aqaba. If royal visitations, therefore, depended on "rank" among the international powers, we would expect Solomon to be visiting the Queen of Sheba rather than vice versa.

Holy Scripture is clear that this was not the case. We are told that the Queen of Sheba, who could have handled her commercial relationship with Solomon through the usual business channels, was prompted solely by a desire to see for herself whether this new king was as wise and discerning as his reputation proclaimed. Nor was the lady disappointed at what she saw: "I did not believe the words until I came and saw with my own eyes; and indeed the half was not told me. Your wisdom and prosperity exceed the fame of which I heard" (1 Kings 10:7).

In the Gospels of Matthew (12:42) and Luke (11:31) this royal Gentile, "the Queen of the South," becomes a type of the true seeker and believer. In both places she is contrasted with the Lord's enemies, the unbelievers who refuse to recognize that "a greater than Solomon is here." Accordingly, Sheba's magnificent lady is made a figure of Mother Church, standing rapturously in the presence of the wiser Solomon. We make our own her praise and proclamation before the throne of Christ: "Happy *are* your men and happy *are* these your servants, who stand continually before you *and* hear your wisdom! Blessed be the LORD your God, who delighted in you, setting you on the throne of Israel!" (1 Kings 10:8–9).

◈

2. BILDAD THE SHUHITE

Bildad, Job's second "comforter," is described as coming from the ancient and well-known city of Shuah, situated on the right bank of the Euphrates, between the mouths of the Balikh and Khabur rivers, south of Carchemish. This is well to the east of the Promised Land. If it is the case that the name of this city is related to one of Abraham's sons by Keturah (cf. Genesis 25:2; 1 Chronicles 1:32), the Israelites would certainly have regarded the city as very eastern, indeed, "eastward . . . to the country of the east" (Genesis 25:6).

Bildad (whose arguments are found in Job 8, 18, and 25) thus represents the wisdom of ancient Mesopotamia, the very culture that gave the human race the art of writing. Indeed, starting with the Sumerians, near the end of the fourth millennium before Christ, Mesopotamia is the absolute font of all literary culture.

The literary culture of ancient Mesopotamia itself was engaged in many philosophical and moral concerns, such as the origins of the world and the Great Flood. Thus, it is from this region that we have inherited the famous Sumerian and Akkadian mythologies recorded on cuneiform tablets that narrate the stories of Gilgamesh, Adapa, Nergal, and Ereshkigal. As one can see from Bildad's own words transcribed in the biblical account, this was also a culture that meditated deeply on the shortness and vanity of human life. It does not surprise us, then, that the people of Mesopotamia reflected likewise on the afterlife and the netherworld. Indeed, several accounts of this concern have also been preserved on ancient clay tablets from this region.

Along with his persuasion that life is short and the future uncertain, Bildad was also fairly sure that people finally get what they deserve.

Job's children, for example. One recalls that Job himself had been rather preoccupied with concern about his children, especially their moral state. His sons and daughters, born into a wealthy household, are portrayed in the Bible as uncommonly frivolous, definitely of the "partying" type. In fact, they threw a whoop-de-do every day, moving the reveling site from house to house. Job was so anxious about this incessant fun and frivolity that he commenced rising up early each morning to offer an individual sacrifice for each of his children (Job 1:5). And what happened to them? Well, sure enough, all of the revelers were wiped out simultaneously, perishing in the midst of one of their daily entertainments (2:18–19).

But this is exactly what we should have expected, Bildad reflected. People do die young, very much like papyrus reeds. "While it *is* yet green *and* not cut down, / It withers before any *other* plant" (8:11–12). Moreover, even as Job had suspected might be the case, Bildad speculated that those young people perhaps brought God's wrath down on their own heads: "If your sons have sinned against Him, He has cast them away for their transgression" (8:4). This is a pretty rough thing to say to a grieving father.

On the other hand, Bildad contended, the same divine justice that punished Job's children can also serve to sustain Job himself in the years to come: "If you would earnestly seek God / And make your supplication to the Almighty, / If you *were* pure and upright, / Surely now He would awake for you, / And prosper your rightful dwelling place. / Though your beginning was small, / Yet your latter end would increase abundantly. . . . He will yet fill your mouth with laughing, / And your lips with rejoicing" (8:5–7, 21). It is a point of no little irony that, whatever the shortcomings of Bildad's moral reasoning, the end of the book does portray Job as larger and more joyous, in fact, than he was at the beginning.

Bildad's moral reasoning, which is certainly on trial in the Book of Job, was the derived traditional experience, possessed of simple, straightforward answers learned from those who went before (8:8). His moral reasoning was very traditional, quite identical to that of the Book of Proverbs. According to this moral reasoning, at least one thing was certain—things go very badly for bad people (cf. Job 18:5–21). When pushed further, nonetheless, Bildad was obliged to concede that there is no such thing as a completely just man. This was the burden of his final and shortest speech (25:1–6), best summarized, perhaps, by the thesis that "all have sinned and fall short of the glory of God" (Romans 3:23).

Like Job himself, Bildad struggles with a true moral problem. Accustomed to viewing all evil as associated with moral failing, his mind is deeply perplexed by the sight of a good man in suffering.

⳾

3. THE BAPTISM OF NAAMAN

Naaman's is the most interesting story of a Gentile who came to the faith and worship of Israel's God. A general in the service of King Ben-Hadad II of Syria during the ninth century before Christ, he was persuaded by a little Israelite girl, a captive of the Syrians, to make a pilgrimage to Israel in hopes of being cleansed of his leprosy. Fortunately for Naaman, the Prophet Elisha was in residence at the time, for whom the curing of leprosy was a small part of a day's work.

We know on the authority of Jesus Himself that Naaman's story signified God's plans for the salvation of the Gentiles (Luke 4:27; 2 Kings 5:15–17). That is to say, what happened to Naaman prefigured the Christian mission to the nations. An especially ironic feature of this story is that this Gentile confessed the true God during a time when many in Israel were engaged in the worship of false gods. He obeyed the Lord's prophet when not a few of that prophet's coreligionists were refusing to do so.

And just what did Elisha oblige Naaman to do? "Go," he told him, "wash in the Jordan seven times" (2 Kings 5:10). This order seems simple enough, but Naaman evidently expected something a bit more sudden and dramatic: "I said to myself, 'He will surely come out *to me*, and stand and call on the name of the LORD his God, and wave his hand over the place, and heal the leprosy'" (5:11).

Naaman, you see, though a religious man, did not yet know about sacraments, and the action required of him by Elisha—dipping into the Jordan seven times—had a distinctly sacramental quality. It was not "only a symbol," but a symbolic action specifically designated by God for the granting of grace. It actually accomplished something.

By bathing in the Jordan, Naaman would be doing a thing of great moment. He would be identifying with the Israelites who went through that river as their passage into the Promised Land. A whole generation of them had been baptized, as it were, in the Jordan, as the previous generation had been baptized in the Red Sea (1 Corinthians 10:2). Just as those ancient events had foreshadowed the Christian sacrament of baptism (10:11), Naaman's mystic sevenfold immersion in that same mystic river was to serve as a prophecy of the future baptizing of the nations.

What was required of Naaman was the "obedience of faith" (*hypakoe pisteos*—Romans 1:5; 16:26, author's translation). Unless he did what he was told, he would remain a leper. John Chrysostom thus compared Naaman to the blind man whom Jesus commanded to wash his eyes in the pool of Siloam; both were required to make the same act of obedience in faith (*Homilies on John* 56). Naaman received from Elisha essentially the same command that the newly converted Paul would someday receive from Ananias: "Arise and be baptized, and wash away your sins, calling on the name of the Lord" (Acts 22:16).

Naaman did not understand any of this. What, after all, was so special about the Jordan River? "*Are* not the Abanah and the Pharpar, the rivers of Damascus, better than all the waters of Israel?" Naaman was not yet converted. He still resisted doing something he did not understand. "So he turned and went away in a rage" (2 Kings 5:12).

Naaman's loyal friends, however, eventually persuaded him to obey the prophet, "so he went down and dipped seven times in the Jordan, according to the saying of the man of God; and his flesh was restored like the flesh of a little child, and he was clean" (5:14). By way of prophetic prefiguration, Naaman submitted to the stern exhortation of the Apostle Peter, "Repent, and let every one of you be baptized in the name of Jesus Christ for the remission of sins" (Acts 2:38). He went, he washed, he was cleansed.

It is in such terms that the Church of Jesus Christ has ever read the story of Naaman. That little girl who sent Naaman to be baptized, said Ambrose of Milan, "bore the mien of the Church and represented her image"—*speciem habebat Ecclesiae et figuram representabat* (*De Sacramentis* 2.8). "It was not for nothing," wrote Irenaeus of Lyons, "but for our instruction, that Naaman of old, suffering from leprosy, was cleansed by being baptized [*on baptistheis ekathaireto*]. For as we are lepers by sin, we are made clean from our old transgressions through [*dia*] the sacred water and the invoking of the Lord, being spiritually regenerated as newborn children, even as the Lord declared, 'Unless a man be born again through water and the Spirit, he shall not enter into the Kingdom of God'" (Fragment 34).

༝༖

4. TOBIAS AND THE ANGEL

The Church's belief in the ministry of the guardian angels is amply supported by our Lord's warning, "Take heed that you do not despise one of these little ones, for I say to you that in heaven their angels always see the face of My Father who is in heaven" (Matthew 18:10). Luke, likewise, in referring to Peter's angel, testifies to that belief among the early Christians (Acts 12:15). Both references indicate that the guardian angels were already well known to the readers of the Gospels of Matthew and Luke.

As in other instances of Christian belief, it was originally from the Jews that the Church inherited this belief in the ministry of the guardian angels. The Psalmist had declared, "The angel of the LORD encamps all around those who fear Him, / And delivers them" (Psalm 33[34]:7). And again, "He shall give His angels charge over you, / To keep you in all your ways" (90[91]:11).

The clearest illustration of Jewish belief in the guardian angels is found in the Book of Tobit, preserved in the Septuagint. It is the story of an exiled Israelite family living in Mesopotamia during the late eighth century before Christ, and the central core of the account concerns the long journey that the young man, Tobias, makes on behalf of his recently blinded father, Tobit. In this narrative the original purpose of Tobias's trip—to collect a debt in order to preserve the family from destitution—is transcended and enriched in a variety of ways, not the least of which is the young man's discovery of a godly wife.

Prior to setting out on this journey, however, the young man and his parents are visited by a stranger who offers to guide Tobias along the way, and at the story's end the stranger is identified as Raphael, "one of the seven holy angels, which present the prayers of the saints, and which go in and out before the glory of the Holy One" (Tobit 12:15; cf. Revelation 1:4).

This revelation does not take place until the end of the book, however, when the journey is over. Thus, Tobit and his family, like Abraham in Genesis 18, Gideon in Judges 6, and the parents of Samson in Judges 13, receive an angel "unwittingly" (Hebrews 13:2). Even unaware of Raphael's true identity, nonetheless, Tobit twice unwittingly makes reference to a "good angel" who will accompany his son on the journey (Tobit 5:16, 21). Likewise, when the trip is over, but before he learns Raphael's identity, Tobit blesses God's "holy angels" (11:14). Tobias had traveled with the angel even without knowing it.

The journey on which Raphael proposed to lead Tobias, from Nineveh to Rages, was a fairly long one, about 200 miles, and rather much uphill. Yet, in the oldest extant manuscript containing the Book of Tobit (*Codex Sinaiticus*), a copyist's hand inserted the remark that their trip required only two days! Recalling that the swift army of Alexander needed ten days to march the same distance (cf. Plutarch, *Lives*, "Alexander" 42), one is prompted to reflect on the unsuspected advantages of traveling with an angelic companion.

They also brought along the family dog, so we see Tobias traveling with both an angelic and an animal companion, representing the twin worlds of spirit and biology, those two realms of experience in which man travels through this world.

St. Jerome, who tells us that he translated the Book of Tobit from Greek into Latin in the course of a single night, was intrigued by that dog. Although he must have been pretty tired as he came to the end of his candlelight labor during the morning hours, Jerome was still sufficiently alert to do something rather imaginative with that dog. He actually altered the text of the Book of Tobit, a thing he felt free to do, since he did not believe the book to be canonical (a distinctly eccentric view among the Latin Fathers, be it noted). Jerome inserted a detail—or, more accurately, a *tail*—in the Vulgate's description of Tobias's return: "Then the dog, which had been with them in the way, ran before, and coming as if it had brought the news, showed his joy by fawning and wagging his tail." Neither that tail nor its wagging is found in the Septuagint version of Tobit. Jerome made it all up.

It is not difficult to discern why the prankish Jerome engaged in this little witticism. Struck by the story's resemblance to Homer's *Odyssey*, which also tells of a man's journey back to the home of his father, Jerome remembered Argus, the dog of Odysseus, the first friend to recognize that ancient traveler on his return to Ithaca. The old and weakened Argus, Homer wrote, when he recognized his master's voice, "endeavored to wag his tail" (*Odyssey* 17.302).

There was more than a joke involved here, however. Jerome correctly regarded the trip of Tobias, like the travels of Odysseus, as a symbol of man's journey through this world, returning to the paternal home. Tobias thus takes his place with Gilgamesh, Theseus, Jason and the Argonauts, Aeneas, and the other great travelers of literature. It is the Bible's teaching that we do not make this trip alone. We are accompanied by "an angel of peace, a faithful guide, a guardian of our souls and bodies."

❧

5. THE QUESTIONS OF HABAKKUK

Although its opening verse provides no evidence by which to date the Book of Habakkuk, its canonical position between Nahum and Zephaniah apparently represents an ancient persuasion that Habakkuk prophesied during the same period. Moreover, Habakkuk's reference to the Neo-Babylonians (1:6) confirms that persuasion. We do well to date him, then, in the late seventh century before Christ, a period of great trial and turmoil in Judah. Indeed, any reader of Habakkuk can see that he was dealing with considerable trial and turmoil. Within that period, furthermore, the death of King Josiah in 609 was easily the most devastating event in the life of Judah, the crisis evoking Jeremiah's great temple sermon (chapters 7 and 26). The salutary words of Habakkuk may fit that context better than any other.

After Josiah's passing, and until Jerusalem's fall in 587, the throne at Jerusalem was occupied by a series of men whose political incompetence was surpassed only by their shocking moral shortcomings. Scandal was everywhere, and to many it seemed that the entire moral order was falling to pieces. The minds of thoughtful men were asking: Is the Lord a just God? Does the world that He made truly stand on a vindicating principle of righteousness? Such, too, were the queries addressed by Habakkuk.

The ministry of Habakkuk followed shortly after those two other prophets who had dealt with themes germane to the question of ultimate justice: Zephaniah with his apocalyptic imagery of "the Day of the Lord" as the day of judgment, and Nahum with his assessment of the downfall of Nineveh as a manifestation of the righteous judgment of God. Each in his own way, both men proclaimed: "He will come again in glory to judge."

Yet, in a certain respect Habakkuk's vocation was not like theirs. After Zephaniah and Nahum had spoken to their countrymen in the name of God, Habakkuk was charged to speak to God in the name of his countrymen. Whereas most of the biblical prophets proclaimed to men the messages and mandates of the Almighty, Habakkuk addressed to the Almighty those problems most plaguing the minds of men. Thus St. Jerome called Habakkuk a "wrestler with God," because he touches themes that appear in Ecclesiastes and some of the Psalms. He also resembles, in this respect, the Book of Job.

It is very significant that the early compilers of Holy Scripture placed Habakkuk among the prophets, because they thereby acknowledged that the Holy Spirit may speak to man, not only through the external word that he cannot help but hear, but also through the internal word that he cannot help but speak. In that magnificent dialogue that is the first chapter of Habakkuk, it is not only the answers of God that are divinely inspired, but also the questions of Habakkuk himself. It is God who places those very questions in his questing mind. They too are revelatory.

We would utterly fail to understand Habakkuk, however, if we saw in him only a philosophical questioner. He is essentially a man of faith, rather, whose questions invariably take the form of prayer. It is God that he queries, not simply his own thoughts: "O LORD, how long shall I cry, / And You will not hear? . . . Are You not from everlasting, / O LORD my God, my Holy One? . . . *Why* do You make men like fish of the sea, / Like creeping things *that have* no ruler over them?" (Habakkuk 1:2, 12, 14). All of Habakkuk's message is structured in the form of conversation with God in prayer.

God's answer is, of course, the line so beloved in the New Testament: "The just shall live by faith" (2:4; Romans 1:17; Galatians 3:11). This is the principle that Habakkuk is told to write out in large letters on a billboard, as it were, in script so tall and plain that the runner (or jogger) passing by is not obliged to slow down in order to read it: "Though it tarries, wait for it; / Because it will surely come, / It will not tarry" (Habakkuk 2:3; Hebrews 10:37–38). This is the faith exemplified in Habakkuk himself, when the fig tree no longer blossoms, nor is fruit found on the vine, and the labor of the olive fails, and the fields yield no food, when the flock is cut off from the fold, and there is no herd in the stalls. What does God's wrestler say then? "Yet I will rejoice in the LORD, / I will joy in the God of my salvation" (3:17–18). The full dimension of Habakkuk's faith was best appreciated by St. Jerome, who translated that last clause into Latin as: "*Exultabo in Deo* Jesu *meo.*"

⚶

6. THE SOMBER QOHELETH

In the final analysis, the choice of a philosophy is . . . well, a choice. A person really does decide to look at existence from a particular point of view, to interpret the world in a certain way. The reason that this determination must involve a choice is the undeniable fact that the world itself can be regarded from more than one perspective. By presenting us with a variety of conflicting impressions, existence invites us, as it were, to consider it from different, even contradictory angles. A truly sensitive thinker is aware that he is making a philosophical choice. All real thinking is free thinking.

Take the Stoic, for instance. The Stoic deliberately *chooses* to defy all the evidence suggesting that existence is chaotic. Because he is convinced by a contrary impression about the world, the Stoic holds at bay all the reasons for supposing that existence is only a meaningless jumble. He looks out on the world and says, "I discern around me so much evidence of design and meaningful structure (*logos*) that I am determined to base my life and thought on the presumption of cosmic order. Consequently, when I experience what seems to be chaos in existence, and especially when I am besieged by misfortunes, I shall yet hold fast my conviction that this world is founded on a mysterious depth of meaning that binds it all together. Therefore, I will deliberately regard all misfortunes and disasters as integral components of a larger picture that my limited understanding simply cannot contain. Accordingly, my moral efforts will be directed to maintaining patience and serenity in the face of adversity." This is the attitude we see in Epictetus, Seneca, Jane Austen, and the world's other great Stoics.

The nihilist, on the other hand, makes the opposite philosophical choice. "The world provides so much evidence of radical disarray," he says, "so many indications that nothing really makes sense, that personal integrity obliges me to regard existence as meaningless and chaotic. No matter how sensible some things appear, it is an observable fact that everything eventually comes to nothing (*nihil*). Even in those cases, then, when existence does appear to make sense, I will regard that impression as subjective and illusory. Accordingly, my moral efforts will be directed to maintaining patience and serenity, as I liberate myself from such illusions." Sartre's existentialism may be taken as a recent example of this philosophical option, but there are other forms of it.

For example, Siddhartha Gautama, known to history as the Enlightened One, or Buddha, should be included among the nihilists, notwithstanding the great differences that separate him from the more modern varieties. According to his own account, Gautama's *Enlightenment* consisted in a discovery of the moral path required to escape the radical vexation that plagues existence. This vexation, Gautama believed, consists of three components: the impermanence (*anicca*) of existence, the radical unreality (*anatta*) of the self, and the sorrow (*dukkha*) that results from these perceptions. Any other view of existence, he believed, is an exercise in illusion, and his true task is to escape such illusions. If we were to express Gautama's interpretation of the world in a single sentence, then, it might be: "Vanity of vanities, and all is vanity."

Ironically, however, it was not Gautama who immortalized that formula, but a divinely inspired author of Holy Scripture. We know his thought from the book that bears his name, Qoheleth, or, in Greek, Ecclesiastes.

Qoheleth is not only the most somber of the biblical authors; he is one of the darkest writers in the entire history of philosophy. For him, all of existence is vexation of heart and spirit (Ecclesiastes 1:14; 2:11, 17, 22, 26; 4:4, 6, 16; 6:9). Empirical evidence, he believes, does not support the thesis of a moral universe (3:16; 4:1; 5:8; 7:15; 8:12, 14). Happiness is supremely elusive (5:10–12; 6:1–9), and nothing is ever as it appears (9:11; 10:6). The very sequences of times and seasons, which elsewhere in the Bible represent God's covenanted care for man (Genesis 8:22; Psalm 103[104]:19–24), provoke in the mind of Qoheleth only the deepest sense of ennui (Ecclesiastes 1:3–8; 3:2–8). Even if wisdom can be attained—which prospect he deems unlikely (7:23–24)—wisdom and grief are inseparable (1:18).

For all that, Qoheleth is no Buddhist. If "Vanity of vanities, and all is vanity" best summarizes a final philosophical choice for Gautama, for Qoheleth it represents only a vexing impression with which his believing mind struggles. In spite of this impression, Qoheleth remains a man of faith, and ultimately his philosophical choice is inseparable from that faith. Believing in a supreme God—and very unlike Gautama in this respect—Qoheleth never embraces the thesis of radical chaos. The root problem in the world is not the world. It is the human heart's rebellion against God: "Truly, this only I have found: / That God made man upright, / But they have sought out many schemes" (7:29). In spite of all appearances, then, Qoheleth never loses his conviction that God is the final judge of all human decisions (3:17; 5:6). God's sovereignty over man's destiny must never be forgotten (11:9—12:1). However dark the path that man treads, he must in faith continue to "fear God and keep His commandments, / For this is man's all. / For God will bring every work into judgment, / Including every secret thing, / Whether good or evil" (12:13–14).

ॐ

7. THE QUESTIONS OF MALACHI

The Book of Malachi, the last of the books to be included in the prophetic section of the Hebrew Bible, seems to come from the mid-fifth century BC. Thus, the prophetic ministry of its author at Jerusalem was roughly contemporary to the mission of Ezra and the government of Nehemiah. It was also the period of Artaxerxes I in Persia and of Pericles in Athens.

The preoccupations of Malachi, in fact, are very much those of Ezra and Nehemiah. Jerusalem's temple had been rebuilt at the end of the previous century, and the sacrifices and ritual were once again routine parts of the worship of the people. Indeed, everything had become a little too routine, it seemed to Malachi, and void of deep commitment. Above all, Malachi detected a disturbing skepticism manifested in the religious questions that people were asking. The very foundation of faith was being called into doubt. "It is useless to serve God," the Israelites were saying, "What profit *is it* that we have kept His ordinance, / And that we have walked as mourners / Before the LORD of hosts?" (Malachi 3:14).

This widespread skepticism had led to spiritual indifference, stinginess, and apathy, it seemed to Malachi, not only among the people themselves, but also in their priestly leadership. Instead of offering God their best, the people were insulting Him by the poor quality of their offerings (1:6–9), bringing Him what was blemished and imperfect (1:14) and thus defiling His table (1:12).

In addition, the people were failing to place their own domestic economies on the firm foundation of the tithe, a sin that Malachi describes as "robbing" God (3:7–10). No wonder that their service to God was experienced as a "weariness" (1:13). Moreover, because of widespread intermarriage with unbelievers, an offense equally deplored at that time by Ezra and Nehemiah, family life itself was no longer based on devotion to the true God (2:11).

Malachi believed that the lack of respect and reverence towards the practices and integrity of worship were but symptoms of the deep skepticism that was deadly to the spirit. But skepticism is also deadly to the intellect, the prophet knew, because undisciplined questioning tends to eviscerate the processes of thought. Ironically, however, skepticism is a malady best answered by being questioned within a disciplined discourse. One thinks of those other skeptics of that same fifth century, the Sophists, and how their antagonist, Socrates, kept pressing them with the proper questions calculated to put structure into their thought.

Malachi, too, was a great asker of questions, much given to argument and challenging discourse. A contemporary of that great Athenian philosopher, Malachi has even been called "the Hebrew Socrates," by reason of a certain similarity of tone and style. Like Socrates, Malachi is fond of dialectics, the question and counterquestion method of getting at the meat of things.

Thus, Malachi's is a book of questions and counterquestions. Ten times in these four chapters he begins with "you say," followed with some question put by a supposed interlocutor. Questions addressed back to these questioners by Malachi himself are found fifteen times, so that a considerable portion of the book is composed of this extended questioning process. This method of arguing by counterquestion eventually became a standard rabbinical device much evidenced in both the New Testament and the Talmud. One can hardly fail to notice, for instance, how very often in the Gospels Jesus answers a question with another question.

Malachi, however, for all his interest in provoking people to disciplined thought, was more a prophet than a philosopher. Abstract speculation was the furthest thing from his mind, and his opposition to skepticism was inspired by his moral intensity and earnestness. These are among Malachi's major characteristics.

Whatever his likeness to Socrates, then, Malachi really stands closer to Elijah. Indeed, it was Malachi himself who clearly foretold a kind of reappearance of Elijah, that "Messenger of the covenant" (3:1) who would come to prepare "the great and dreadful day of the LORD" (4:5). Malachi's prophecy of Elijah's return was taken up with enthusiasm by Sirach three centuries later (48:10–11) and was interpreted in the New Testament as a reference to John the Baptist (Matthew 17:1–13; Luke 1:13–17).

As Malachi was the last of the books added to the prophetic section of the Hebrew Bible, he had an influence on Jewish expectations far beyond what one might expect from the brevity of his work. Indeed, the early Christians seem to have been very much preoccupied with the message of Malachi (e.g., Romans 9:13), especially with his prophecy of the "pure offering" that the Gentiles would offer to God "from the rising of the sun, even to its going down" (Malachi 1:11; *Didache* 14:3; Justin Martyr, *Dialogue* 28, 41, 116, 117; Irenaeus of Lyons, *Adversus Haereses* 4.17.5; Clement of Alexandria, *Stromateis* 5.14; Tertullian, *Adversus Marcionem* 3.22; 4.1).

୫୨

8. THE JOURNEY OF THE MAGI

Among the notable features proper to the Gospel according to St. Matthew is the way it includes the verb "to adore" (*proskyneo*) in passages where that verb does not appear in parallel accounts in the other Gospels. Thus, Matthew describes various people falling in adoration before Christ in scenes where they are not said to be doing so in the other Gospel versions of the same stories. These instances include the accounts of the cleansing of the leper (8:2), the petition of Jairus (9:18), the walking on the water (14:33), the prayer of the Canaanite woman (15:25), and the request of Zebedee's wife for her two sons (20:20). A pronounced emphasis on Christward adoration, then, is a distinguishing characteristic of Matthew's narrative.

There is, furthermore, a special parallelism between the first and last instances of this verb in Matthew's composition. These are the two scenes of the coming of the Magi, near the beginning of the Gospel, and the Great Commission to the Church at the very end. In the former of these, the verb *proskyneo*, "to adore," is found three times (2:2, 8, 11), which is Matthew's highest concentration of that word in a single scene. A literal reading of the Great Commission passage makes it appear that the Eleven Apostles are actually bowed over in adoration before the risen Jesus at the very time when the Great Commission is given to them (28:9). Thus, not only does Matthew portray various individuals adoring the Lord, but his entire Gospel can be said to begin and to end with that picture in mind.

There is a further important parallelism between the Christmas story of the Magi and the account of the Great Commission; namely, the theme of the Church's universal calling. Whereas Matthew ends his story with the Apostles' being sent forth with the command, "Go therefore and make disciples of all the nations" (28:19), he begins his whole account with a kind of foreshadowing of that final mission by the arrival of the Magi, those wise searchers from the East who come to adore the newborn King of Israel. These two passages, then, thus embrace Matthew's entire story of Jesus.

There is more suggested by the juxtaposition of these parallel texts, however, for the very purpose of the Great Commission is to transform the whole of humanity as the rightful heirs of the Magi. Like the stars themselves, the Apostles are sent forth to lead all nations into that path first followed by the wise men from the East.

Indeed, St. Paul compared the Apostles to those very heavens that "declare the glory of God," quoting in their regard the Psalmist's affirmation that "Their line has gone out through all the earth, / And their words to the ends of the world" (Psalm 18[19]:4; Romans 10:18). The stars and the Apostles proclaim the same universal message, and that message is the Gospel.

These Magi have come to the Messiah, moreover, precisely because they are star-watchers. "For we have seen His star in the East," they affirm, "and have come to worship [or adore] Him" (Matthew 2:2). Likewise, the mission of the Apostles is to bring all nations even unto Bethlehem, that "house of the Bread" (for such is the meaning of "Bethlehem"), where all who eat the one loaf are one body in Christ, to join with the Magi in their eternal adoration.

This adoration takes place within the "house," which is the Church formed by those who break and share the one Bread: "And when they had come into the *house*, they saw the young Child with Mary His mother, and fell down and worshiped [or adored] Him" (Matthew 2:11). That is to say, when the Magi entered the *house*, they found what we all find portrayed on a central icon up near the altar, the mother holding and presenting the Child for the adoration of those who have followed the star into the house of the Bread.

For this reason, it was entirely proper that the Apostles, as they were being commissioned for the great work of universal evangelism, should manifest in their very posture the Christward adoration which is the final goal of that evangelism (Matthew 28:9).

Finally, while the Magi were instructed by what they read in those heavens that declare the glory of God, they did not pursue their quest among the stars but upon the earth. They found the answer to their quest, that is to say, in a particular place and at a particular time. They accepted the spatial/temporal, fleshly limitations that God Himself assumed.

৯৯

9. THE MISSIONS OF PHILIP

Stephen and Philip were the first two of seven Greek-speaking men ordained by the Apostles by way of dealing with the "complaint against the Hebrews by the Hellenists" at Jerusalem (Acts 6:1–6). Let us here speak of Philip.

When Stephen was martyred, a great persecution of Christians broke out, many of whom, consequently, fled from Jerusalem (8:1, 4; 11:19). Philip was one of these (8:5). He eventually settled in Caesarea, a coastal city to the north (8:40), where he raised a family of four daughters, all of whom were graced with the gift of prophecy (21:9; Eusebius, *Ecclesiastical History* 3.31.5).

Nearly two decades later, in the spring of 58, the Apostle Paul, on his final trip to Jerusalem, was a guest at Philip's home in Caesarea. Luke accompanied him, and they remained in Philip's house "many days" (21:8, 10). As far as we may discern from the Sacred Text, this was Luke's first meeting with Philip, nor is there solid evidence that they ever met again. It is reasonable, then, to suppose that this visit was the occasion on which Philip shared with Luke the details of his two earlier missions, the first in Samaria and the other along the Palestinian coast from Gaza to Caesarea. These missions Luke recorded in Acts 8.

Although Jesus had already gained some converts among the Samaritans (John 4:40–41), His post-Resurrection directive to bear witness in Samaria (Acts 1:8) seems first to have been followed by Philip. It was a massive success (8:5–13). The mother church back in Jerusalem, learning of the fruitfulness of Philip's ministry among the Samaritans, "sent Peter and John to them, who, when they had come down, prayed for them that they might receive the Holy Spirit" (8:14–15).

Luke's account here is marked by a gentle irony. Luke had earlier recorded the Apostle John's reprehensible impulse to call fire from heaven on the heads of those Samaritans (Luke 9:52–54). Now, however, as a result of Philip's ministry, John is commissioned to call down on the Samaritans the true fire from heaven, the holy flames of transformation. He and Peter "laid hands on them," Luke tells us, "and they received the Holy Spirit" (8:17). This was the beginning of a still larger Samaritan mission (8:25).

Philip's conversion of the Samaritans was a pivotal development in the mission of the early Church, because if these Jewish Christians could share the Gospel with the Samaritans, they could share it with anyone. They would indeed be "witnesses to Me in Jerusalem, and in all Judea and Samaria, and to the end of the earth" (1:8). Thus, the Pentecost of the Jews in Acts 2 is followed by the Pentecost of the Samaritans in Acts 8, which in turn is followed by a Pentecost of the Gentiles in Acts 10.

Philip, meanwhile, was instructed by an angel to proceed south toward the coastal road near Gaza (8:26), a route much used by pilgrims who came to Jerusalem from Egypt and other parts of Africa. Here Philip is directed by the Holy Spirit to encounter one such pilgrim, an "Ethiopian," a word at that time normally referent to Nubians who lived between Aswan and Khartoum in Upper Egypt and the Sudan. This man, a treasury official in the service of the queen mother, was returning from Jerusalem, where he had been to worship (8:27–29).

As Philip approached the man's carriage, which was either parked or making its way very slowly along the crowded road, he heard the pilgrim reading the Book of Isaiah. There was nothing particularly remarkable about this, for in antiquity it was normal to read in an audible voice, especially a work of literary merit. (So much was reading considered an auditory exercise in olden times that Augustine remarked at some length on Ambrose's strange custom of reading silently—*Confessions* 6.3.3).

Philip overhears the prophetic reading, interprets the Isaian text in the light of the Christian Gospel, and, in one of the swiftest conversions ever recorded, brings the man to baptismal faith (Acts 8:30–39).

It is also significant that this conversion takes place near Gaza, an ancient capital of the Philistines, as though to symbolize the Christian reconciliation of the Israelites with those European invaders whom they had bitterly battled for possession of the Holy Land more than a thousand years before.

His new convert properly baptized and sent along his way, Philip, walking north along the coast, "preached in all the cities till he came to Caesarea" (8:40), where Luke would interview him nearly two decades later.

※

10. THE JOURNEYS OF TITUS

Luke was the Church's first historian, but it is uncanny the things he left out of the Acts of the Apostles. Perhaps most notable among the omissions is any reference to Titus. Luke certainly knew Titus, who visited Macedonia sometime in AD 56/57 (2 Corinthians 7:6), a period when Luke lived there (comparing Acts 16:10 and 20:6).

Perhaps Luke's silence about Titus is not overly surprising, on the other hand, because there were several of Paul's other companions that he did not mention; Epaphras and Demas come to mind, both of whom were certainly known to Luke (cf. Colossians 4:12–14). Nor, for that matter, does Luke mention the brothers Tertius and Quartus (Romans 16:22–23), though he does refer to their older sibling, Secundus (Acts 20:4). (So, then, what became of Primus?)

Titus first appears in the New Testament as an associate of Paul during the latter's second post-conversion journey to Jerusalem in 51. The relevant timetable seems to stand as follows: If we date Paul's conversion about 34, his first post-conversion visit to Jerusalem was in 37, three years later (Galatians 1:18; Acts 9:26–30). His second such visit, then, which we know occurred fourteen years after that (Galatians 2:1), was in 51.

This timetable fits perfectly with what we may discern in Acts. From an inscription discovered at Delphi, it is clear that Gallio became proconsul of Greece in June of 51, which gives us our earliest possible date for Paul's appearance before Gallio (Acts 18:12–17). It was after that event that Paul crossed over to Ephesus (18:18–20). He did not stay long in Ephesus. Some manuscripts of Acts 18:21 indicate that he was in a hurry to arrive at Jerusalem for a coming feast, which would have to have been an autumnal feast, perhaps Sukkoth. This was Paul's second such visit, the one documented in Galatians 2:1, which also indicates that Titus was with him. He had evidently joined Paul's company during the previous two years.

The sudden appearance of this Gentile Christian in the Jerusalem church was a bit awkward, "because of false brethren secretly brought in" (Galatians 2:4). These demanded that Titus be circumcised. In spite of some Western manuscripts to the contrary, along with Augustine, Luther, and others, it seems certain that Paul did *not* give in on this point, putting Titus as a "test case" on the matter of Gentile circumcision. James, Peter, and John took his side on the question (2:3–9).

Titus next appears sometime in 56. From Ephesus Paul had previously dispatched him, as his own "partner and fellow worker" (2 Corinthians 8:23), to visit the chronically troubled church at Corinth. Paul himself later headed westward to Troas, having arranged to meet Titus there, in order to receive a report about the Corinthians. When he arrived at Troas, however, Titus was not there (2:12–13). Perhaps he had been unable to obtain passage. Sometimes cruises from Neapolis to Troas were delayed. After all, because the current through the Dardanelles flowed southwestward (the Black Sea being considerably cooler than the more rapidly evaporating and saltier waters of the Aegean), ships going east from Neapolis to Troas sometimes took much longer than ships sailing in the opposite direction. As we may see by comparing Acts 16:11 and 20:6, they could take more than three times as long. In any event, the anxious Paul decided to cross over to Macedonia (Acts 20:1), where he happily found Titus (2 Corinthians 7:6). Titus himself was overjoyed by the changes he could report about the Corinthian church, where he had been so well received (7:13—8:6, 16).

It seems to have been in late 56 that Paul took Titus to Crete, where he left him to oversee the new missions there (Titus 1:5–9). He himself went back to Macedonia and Illyricum (Romans 15:19). From somewhere in that region, Paul wrote an epistle to Titus, instructing him with respect to the ministries on Crete. He asked Titus to return to him, however, whenever Artemas or Tychicus should arrive in Crete to take his place in the mission. Paul mentioned that he planned to spend that winter of 56–57 at Nicopolis, a city of Epirus, south of Dalmatia (3:12). One suspects that Titus did return, because it would appear that Titus joined Paul and was still with him even during some of his time in Rome (61–62). When we last hear of Titus, Paul had sent him from Rome back to Dalmatia (2 Timothy 4:10). Titus was clearly a loyal man on whom the Apostle could rely, a minister who would not abuse his position (2 Corinthians 13:17–18).

৵

11. THE FLIGHT OF ONESIMUS

Philemon lived in Colossae, a city in southwest Phrygia, near Laodicea and Hierapolis (Colossians 4:13) in the Lycus Valley. His wife's name was Apphia (Philemon 2). Onesimus was his slave.

Although the Acts of the Apostles does not mention a visit to Colossae by the Apostle Paul, he certainly evangelized Philemon, at either Colossae or perhaps Ephesus, sometime during those three years (AD 52–55) that Paul spent as a missionary in the latter city (Acts 20:31). Anyway, Philemon became a Christian.

We would not know any of these things except for a letter that Paul wrote to Philemon from prison at Caesarea, sometime between 58 and 60 (Acts 24:27). While there, Paul had received a surprise visit from Onesimus, Philemon's slave, who had fled from his master and had come all the way to Caesarea to seek out the apostle.

It is not entirely clear what Onesimus expected of Paul, whom he had likely met some five or so years earlier, in the company of Philemon. His approach to Paul, right there in a jail guarded by Roman soldiers, was rather bold. In the Roman Empire, runaway slaves were branded on the forehead by a hot iron with the letter "F" for *fugitivus*.

Nor had Paul given any explicit indication that he opposed the institution of slavery; on the contrary, he had urged each man, including slaves, to maintain the social position he held at the time of his conversion (1 Corinthians 7:21–24). Paul's attitude toward slaves was perfectly clear: "*Exhort* bondservants to be obedient to their own masters, to be well pleasing in all *things*, not answering back" (Titus 2:9). So what did Onesimus expect?

Whatever he expected, Paul did what Paul did best. He evangelized and baptized the runaway slave right there in the prison (Philemon 10), surrounded by an impressive company of the Church's finest: Mark, Luke, and several others (Philemon 23–24; Colossians 4:7–14).

But now Paul had a problem: What was he to do with Onesimus? What approach should he take with his friend Philemon, who might be rather upset about the flight of a slave? After all, Onesimus was a law-breaker, to whom Roman law extended no mercy. Would Philemon show mercy?

In fact, Paul was not the only person in antiquity to face a problem of this sort. A few years later, Pliny the Younger (62–113) received the runaway servant of a friend, to whom he wrote a letter explaining the matter (*Epistolae* 9.21). Pliny exercised the greatest diplomacy in the affair, stressing the repentance of the fugitive, urging clemency for his offense, gently interceding by diplomacy instead of applying pressure based on mutual friendship.

Paul's approach to Philemon is similar in each of these respects, but he also appeals to more explicit Christian motives. After all, Philemon and Onesimus are now brothers by baptism. He subtly addresses Philemon's sense of compassion. In an epistle of only twenty-five verses, Paul mentions five times that he is writing from prison! He calls Onesimus "my son" (v. 10), perhaps suggesting that he might take personally any harm that came to the runaway. Paul stresses his solidarity with the slave (vv. 12, 17). He reminds Philemon what a generous person Philemon is (vv. 5–7), a reputation that he must now live up to. He almost makes it sound as though Philemon had sent the slave to take care of the apostle (v. 13). Still, Paul leaves the matter to Philemon's conscience (v. 21).

When Onesimus returned to Philemon, he was accompanied by Tychicus, "a beloved brother, faithful minister, and fellow servant in the Lord" (Colossians 4:7–9). The two travelers were carrying three letters: a personal letter to Philemon, in which all these matters were expressed; a communal letter to the Colossian church; another letter to the church at Laodicea (probably to be identified with the work known in most manuscripts as "The Epistle to the Ephesians"). These letters were to be shared as appropriate (Colossians 4:16). From the Muratorian Fragment we know that the Epistle to Philemon was contained in the earliest collections of Paul's epistles.

As for Onesimus himself, he was probably a very young fellow at the time of his flight, and Philemon certainly set him free on his return. He remained an active missionary in the region, and decades later Ignatius of Antioch knew him as the bishop of Ephesus (*Ignatius to the Ephesians* 1.3; 2.1; 6.2).

XIV.
VISIONARIES AND CONTEMPLATIVES
꙳

On "day one" (*yom 'ehad*) of Creation, God's word is described as creating only one thing, light. This light is the beginning of His works, the first reality "outside God" to exist. And just as "day one" is the root of all the succeeding days of Creation, this light, the first of His works, is the font and foundation of everything else that God makes. It is the substratum of all created existence.

The world is not chaotic. Its formation is not the result of the random activity of physical and chemical forces. To say that the world is created is to assert that it is intelligently designed and replete with intelligible meaning, and this meaning is what the Bible calls "light."

In this respect the Bible confirms what our reason already tells us. No truly rational person, examining the structure of the world, will reach a different conclusion. Those who do so are "without excuse"; indeed, they are said to "suppress the truth" (Romans 1:18, 20). For this reason, the denial of the light is the supreme offense, because "this is the condemnation, that the light has come into the world, and men loved darkness rather than light" (John 3:19).

By this light God has revealed Himself in His Creation, so that "His invisible *attributes* are clearly seen, being understood by the things that are made" (Romans 1:20). Seeing requires light. These attributes of God are clearly seen because God's first act of Creation is the shedding of light. The baseline of all things, then, is light. Everything else that exists is the extension of an inner luminosity.

This light at the heart of created being is effected by God's first word spoken outside of Himself, "Let there be light." And just as "day one" is the root of all the succeeding days of Creation, so this first word of God, "Let there be light," is the font and foundation of everything else that God will ever say. Light is both the principle and summation of His word.

Moreover, God created the light first, because He Himself is light: "This is the message which we have heard from Him and declare to you, that God is light and in Him is no darkness at all" (1 John 1:5). Truly, He is "the Father of lights" (James 1:17).

That first light created by the word of God in Genesis was not the light of the sun, of course, because the sun was not fashioned until the fourth day. Indeed, the first and underlying light of Creation is not a physical thing at all. It is a spiritual, metaphysical light, rather, the inner luminosity of truth, the radiance embodied in everything else that God makes. This is the light "which only the light-giving Light, who is God Himself, could have made. . . . He is His own eternal Light and is also the giver of light" (Augustine of Hippo, *Reply to Faustus* 22.8–9).

It is this first light that separates Creation from chaos, the topsy-turviness of nonbeing described in the Hebrew text as *tohu wabohu*, formlessness and void (Genesis 1:2). Outside of this light, there is only the darkness that the Bible calls night. (Night, then, is not the mere absence of the sun. As the simplest reader of the Bible can see, there were three evenings and mornings before there was ever a sunrise or sunset.) Nighttime abides in Creation as the vestigial symbol of the nonexistence that preceded God's initial word of Creation. Darkness describes that which is outside of God's word.

It is the teaching of the New Testament that that primordial light of Creation is identical with the life that is in God's eternal Word: "In Him was life, and the life was the light of men" (John 1:4). Thus, when this consubstantial Word of God became flesh and dwelt among us, the inner light of the world became manifest in history.

The divine glory shining on the human face of God's eternal Word fulfills the prophecy implied in the initial words of Creation, "Let there be light!" In the historical revelation of God's eternal Word, we are given to behold what God first spoke: "For it is the God who commanded light to shine out of darkness, who has shone in our hearts to *give* the light of the knowledge of the glory of God in the face of Jesus Christ" (2 Corinthians 4:6).

For this reason Christians look upon all created things through the light that shines on the face of Christ. In the beginning God said, "Let there be light." "Now, however, He has said nothing at all, but Himself has become the light for us" (John Chrysostom, *Homilies on Second Corinthians* 8.3).

The task of turning our faces toward that light is supremely the mission of the Bible's visionaries and contemplatives.

⊰๑

1. ENOCH WALKED WITH GOD

After the Epistle to the Hebrews gives its initial definition of faith as "the substance of things hoped for, the evidence of things not seen" (11:1), there follows the famous list of the "great cloud of witnesses" (12:1), those "elders" who "obtained a good testimony" by exemplifying such faith (11:2).

One can hardly fail to observe, in this list, the strong emphasis on death with respect to this saving faith. Throughout Hebrews 11, death is *the* test of faith. While this test is clearest in the instances of Abel (v. 4), Abraham (vv. 17–18), Jacob (v. 21), Joseph (v. 22), Moses' parents (v. 23), and the later witnesses (vv. 32–39), it is also implied in the cases of Noah (v. 7), Sarah (v. 12), Isaac (v. 20), and Moses (vv. 25–26). In short, in the Epistle to the Hebrews, faith has to do with how one dies, and "these all died in faith" (v. 13).

This emphasis on death in the context of faith renders very interesting the inclusion of Enoch among the list of faith's exemplars, for Holy Scripture indicates that Enoch departed this world in some way other than death. Indeed, in Genesis 5, the genealogy that includes Enoch's name employs the verb "died" eight times with respect to the patriarchs from Adam to Lamech, but in the case of Enoch, "the seventh from Adam" (Jude 14), Genesis says simply he "walked with God; and he was not found [*ouk eurisketo*], for God removed [*metetheken*] him" (Genesis 5:24, author's translation).

By way of commentary on this passage, the Epistle to the Hebrews says, "By faith Enoch was removed [*metethe*] so that he should not see death, 'and was not found [*ouk eurisketo*], because God removed [*metetheken*] him'; for before his removal [*metatheseos*] he was witnessed to have pleased [*euariestekenai*] God" (11:5, author's translation).

That ancient "witness," cited here in the Epistle to the Hebrews, is found in the Book of Wisdom, where Enoch is thus described: "He was pleasing [*euarestos*] to God and was beloved of Him, so that, living among sinners, he was removed [*metetethe*]. He was snatched away so that evil would not alter his understanding, nor deceit beguile his soul. For the malice of what is worthless takes away things of worth, and the roving of passion subverts a guileless mind. Made perfect [*teleotheis*] in a short time, he filled out massive times, for his soul pleased [*areste*] God. So He rushed him from the midst of evil" (4:10–14).

Such is the biblical witness about the "short time" that Enoch spent on this earth (a mere 365 years, according to Genesis 5:23). Unlike the other heroes listed in Hebrews 11, Enoch did not die in faith, for the unusual reason that he did not die at all. He nonetheless deserved a place in that heroic list, we are told, because "he pleased God" by his faith. Thus, when we believers "come boldly to the throne of grace" (Hebrews 4:16), when we approach "the general assembly and church of the firstborn *who are* registered in heaven" (12:23), there stands Enoch among "the spirits of just men made perfect [*teteleiomenon*]."

Living before both Noah and Moses, Enoch was participant in neither of the covenants associated with these men. Not a single line of Holy Scripture was yet written for him to read. Much less did Enoch ever hear the message of salvation preached by the Apostles. Yet, he was so pleasing to God by his faith as to be snatched away before his time, not suffering that common lot of death from which the Almighty spared not even His own Son.

What, exactly, did Enoch *believe*, then, that he should be such a champion of faith for the Church until the end of time? The Epistle to the Hebrews explains: "But without faith *it is* impossible to please *Him*, for he who comes to God must believe that He is, and *that* He is a rewarder of those who diligently seek Him" (11:6). This was the sum total of all that Enoch's faith told Him—God's existence and his own duty to seek God to obtain the singular blessing that Holy Scripture ascribes to him.

It is the Bible's portrayal of Enoch, then, that affords us some hope for the salvation of those millions of human beings who must pass their lives on that bare minimum of theological information, for which Enoch rendered such a marvelous account. We may dare to hope that some of them, too, have found their way into the cloud of witnesses.

⅗

2. ELIPHAZ THE TEMANITE

Job is addressed eight times by his three comforters, an arrangement that permits the first of those speakers, Eliphaz the Temanite, to address him three times. It is probably because he is the eldest of the three men (cf. Job 15:10) that Eliphaz speaks first, and this is surely also the reason why, near the end of the book, God addresses Eliphaz directly as the spokesman of the group (42:7).

A native of Teman, Eliphaz exemplifies the ancient wisdom of Edom (cf. Genesis 36:11), concerning which Jeremiah inquired, "*Is* wisdom no more in Teman? Has counsel perished from the prudent? Has their wisdom vanished?" (Jeremiah 49:7). Eliphaz represents, then, the "wisdom of the south," the great desert region of the Negev and even Arabia, where only the wise can survive.

In his initial response to Job (chapters 4—5), Eliphaz appeals to his own personal religious experience. Eliphaz, unlike the other two comforters, is a visionary. He has seen (4:8; 5:3) and heard (4:16) the presence of the divine claims in an experience of such subtlety that he calls it a "whisper" (*shemets*—4:12). This deep sense of the divine absolute, born of Eliphaz's religious experience, forced upon his mind a strongly binding conviction of the divine purity and justice. This profound certainty in his soul became the lens through which Eliphaz interprets the sundry enigmas of life, notably the problem of human suffering.

If we compare Eliphaz to Job's other two comforters, moreover, we observe a gradated but distinct decline in the matter of wisdom. Eliphaz begins the discussion by invoking his own direct spiritual experience, his *veda*. The second comforter, however, Bildad the Shuhite, can appeal to no personal experience of his own, but only to the experience of his elders, so what was a true insight in the case of Eliphaz declines to only an inherited theory in the case of Bildad. Living mystical insight becomes merely an inherited moral belief.

The decline progresses further in the case of Job's third comforter, because Zophar the Naamathite, unlike Bildad, is unable to invoke even the tradition of his elders. He is familiar with neither the living experience of Eliphaz nor the inherited learning of Bildad; his is simply the voice of established prejudice.

In these three men, then, we watch insight decline into theory, and then theory harden into a settled, unexamined opinion. As they individually address Job, moreover, each man seems progressively less assured of his position. And being less assured of his position, each man waxes increasingly more strident against Job.

Consequently, along with the decline of moral authority among these three men, there is a corresponding decline in politeness, as though each man is obliged to raise the volume of his voice in inverse proportion to his sense of assurance. Thus, we find that Eliphaz, at least when he begins, is also the most compassionate and polite of the three comforters.

Still, Eliphaz is shocked by Job's tone. Instead of asking God to renew His mercies, Job has been cursing his own life. And since God the Creator is the source of that life, Job's lament hardly reflects well on God. This perverse attitude of Job, Eliphaz reasons, must be the source of the problem. Job's affliction, consequently, is not an inexplicable mystery, as Job has argued, but the result of Job's own attitude toward God. Job's lament, Eliphaz believes, is essentially selfish, expressing only Job's subjective pain. Therefore, Eliphaz becomes more severe in his criticism of Job, referring to him as "foolish" (5:2, 3).

This severity becomes the dominant temper of Eliphaz's second and third speeches (chapters 15 and 22), where he no longer demonstrates deference and compassion. His former sympathy and concern for Job are no longer possible now, because Eliphaz has repeatedly listened to Job professing his innocence. Job, Eliphaz believes, by emphatically denying a moral causality with respect to his afflictions, menaces the moral structure of the world.

Therefore, Eliphaz responds with aggression and even a tone of threat. Is Job older than Adam, he asks, or as old as wisdom itself (15:7; cf. Proverbs 8:25), that he should engage in such dangerous speculations about the hidden purposes of God?

The irony here, of course, is that Job is the only one whose discourse manifests even a shred of intellectual humility. Job has never, like Eliphaz (4:12–21), claimed to discern the divine mind.

What should finally be said, then, of this Edomite's argument against the suffering Job? Though it is too severe and personally insensitive, Eliphaz does make a basically reliable case. Indeed, in God's final revelation to Job near the end of the book, we meet some of the very themes that initially appeared in the first discourse of Eliphaz. Moreover, in the final verses of his first speech (5:25–26), Eliphaz ironically foretells the blessings that Job will receive at the end of the story (42:12–17). However much, then, Eliphaz managed to misinterpret the implications of his religious experience, that experience itself was valid and sound.

ॐ

3. THE MANIFOLD MESSAGE OF JOEL

Arguably the greatest merit of the Book of Joel is that it provided the text for the Church's very first sermon at nine o'clock on the morning of Pentecost (Acts 2:14–21).

We know rather little about the man himself. Except for the opening verse of his book, the prophet is never otherwise mentioned in the rest of the Old Testament, even though twelve other biblical characters bear the same name. Unlike almost all of the other biblical prophets, no editorial care was taken to give an appropriate context and indication of dates to his prophetic words. Thus, the proper placing of Joel in his own historical setting is unusually difficult. His words tend, therefore, to take on a certain indefinite and even timeless character uncommon in biblical literature.

That said, Joel's reference to the international slave trade (3:4–8), a preoccupation also of Amos (1:6–9), may suggest that he prophesied in the eighth century. Such a dating would also explain why this book traditionally appears in the Bible between Hosea and Amos, two other prophets preoccupied with the social evils of that century. A dating in the eighth century would likewise make Joel a contemporary of Hesiod, the notable social critic of the Greeks. Curiously, it is in respect to the slave trade that Joel does, in fact, refer to the Greeks, or more properly "the Ionians" (*haiyowanim*—Joel 3:6).

The context of Joel's prophecy was some extraordinary visitation of locusts, in which the harvest of an entire season was destroyed, endangering the people's survival during the following winter. (This agrarian concern also puts us in mind of Hesiod.) The whole population was facing famine. Joel's response to the situation may be summarized like this: "You think you are having a rough time now? Just wait. The present disaster is only a warm-up exercise for the Lord's Day, the time of His visitation in judgment. For those who refuse to repent, far worse things lie in store."

Joel's prophecies present the reader, therefore, with a sustained call to repentance, fasting, and prayer, which is why Joel 2:12–19, the prophet's summons to "sanctify a fast," has for centuries been read in the West on Ash Wednesday, the beginning of the Lenten observance.

Lenten appeals to Joel are hardly limited to the West, however. In the Paschal Letter that Athanasius of Alexandria wrote at the beginning of Lent in 329, he cited that same text of Joel (*Epistolae* 1.4). Indeed, it has always been proper, in both East and West, to invoke Joel with respect to repentance at any time. Leo I of Rome cited that identical passage in a sermon delivered during the September Ember Days (*Sermones* 88.1), and Gregory the Theologian elaborated it in a lengthy series of comments on the prophets (*Orationes* 2.59).

Joel, however, knew about other things besides repentance and fasting. He especially foresaw and foretold the great outpouring of the Holy Spirit as a defining sign of the final times. Thus, on the morning of Pentecost, it was to Joel that the Church first turned to describe and interpret her own new existence in the world and the beginnings of her ministry to the nations.

For this reason, the Fathers of the Church found a goodly measure of the Gospel right there in the Book of Joel. Do we search for the Incarnation? Irenaeus of Lyons believed that when Joel proclaimed, "The LORD also will roar from Zion, / And utter His voice from Jerusalem" (3:16), Christ "specified the place of His coming" (*Adversus Haereses* 3.20.4). Or do we search for the Church? Cyprian of Carthage sees her in Joel's reference (2:16) to the Bride coming forth from her chamber (*Testimonia* 19). Salvation by faith? Because the Apostle Peter (Acts 2:21) quoted Joel's very words—"Whoever calls on the name of the LORD shall be saved" (2:32)—to this effect, wrote John Chrysostom, "We know that he foretold salvation through faith, for he did not remain silent on this point" (*Homiliae in Actus* 5). Baptism? Theophanes the Hymnographer wrote, "As Joel prophesied, rivers of miracles, which are the all-glorious apostles of the Lord, pour forth remission upon Judah, watering those who cry, 'Bless the Lord, all you works of the Lord'" (Eighth Ode in second tone for October 19). But Joel more especially spoke of the gifts of the Holy Spirit. It was to Joel, consequently, that Justin Martyr turned to speak of those "gifts which, from the grace of that Spirit's power, He gives to those who believe in Him, as He thinks each one worthy" (*Dialogue* 87.3).

It is significant that the message of Joel, proclaimed at both the beginning of Lent and the end of the paschal season, sets the tone for the most important period of the Church's liturgical year.

⚕

4. THE VISION OF ISAIAH

Augustine of Hippo, after his spiritual conversion in 386, and in preparation for his planned baptism in Milan during the Easter vigil in the
following spring, was wondering which part of Holy Scripture he should
read by way of making his heart ready for that great event. So, from his
retreat at Cassiacum, he wrote to Ambrose, the bishop of Milan, seeking his counsel on the matter. Augustine's recollection of that occasion
is worth citing at length: "By letter I informed Your bishop Ambrose,
that holy man, both of my former errors and present intention, so that
he could advise me as to which of Your books it would be best for me to
read, so that I could become more prepared and better fitted to receive
so great a grace. He recommended the prophet Isaiah. I believe that he
did so because this is a more manifest prophet of the Gospel and of the
calling of the Gentiles than are the other writers" (*Confessions* 9.5.13).
Alas, Augustine goes on to note, he was unable to understand Isaiah at
that time and was obliged to put it aside until he became more mature
in the Christian faith.

This is sometimes the case with Isaiah. He is not easy. Some measure of spiritual maturity is required, if one is to read him with profit.
The biblical scholar Sheldon Blank wrote of Isaiah: "If you hear him
you grow confused because he upsets your notions, if you go with him
you run into trouble because you are pushing against the crowd, if you
deny him you feel guilty because you know he is right." However difficult Isaiah can be to understand, it would be even harder to overesti-
mate the importance of that prophet in Christian theology. After the
Psalter, in fact, the New Testament cites the Book of Isaiah more often
than any other work of the Old Testament, and so vivid and detailed
were his prophecies of Christ our Lord that he has been called "the fifth
evangelist."

God's call to Isaiah came in an overwhelming experience of the
divine holiness. He himself recorded the year; it was 742 BC, "the year
that King Uzziah died" (Isaiah 6:1). While in prayer in the temple,
Isaiah beheld the Lord, high and lifted up, and His train filled the entire
structure. He heard the alternate chanting of those mysterious beings of
fire, the majestic seraphim, six-winged, many-eyed, soaring aloft, borne

on their pinions, singing the triumphal hymn, shouting, proclaiming, and saying: "Holy, holy, holy *is* the LORD of hosts; / The whole earth *is* full of His glory!" (6:3).

Suddenly Isaiah felt himself filthy and soiled: "Woe *is* me, for I am undone! / Because I *am* a man of unclean lips, / And I dwell in the midst of a people of unclean lips; / For my eyes have seen the King, / The LORD of hosts" (6:5). At this point one of the seraphim approached the altar in the temple with a pair of tongs and removed a burning coal. This fiery ember, so hot that even the angel of fire dared not touch it except with tongs, he rammed into the mouth of Isaiah, purging his lips so that he might proclaim God's holy prophetic Word.

After his overwhelming experience of the divine holiness, Isaiah was never again the same. Throughout the rest of the book that bears Isaiah's name, God is called *"the Holy One* of Israel." This expression is distinctly Isaian. It is found twenty-six times throughout the various parts of the Book of Isaiah, whereas it appears only six other times in the remainder of the Hebrew Bible.

But can God be seen? Does not Holy Scripture insist that "no one has seen God at any time" (John 1:18)? When Isaiah, then, "saw the Lord sitting on a throne, high and lifted up" (Isaiah 6:1), just whom did he see? Just whose glory, filling heaven and earth, did he contemplate?

The Gospel of St. John explicitly answers this question. To interpret the hardness of heart that Jesus met from His enemies in the officialdom of Judah, John quotes two verses from that very chapter in which Isaiah described his vision in the temple (Isaiah 6:9–10; John 12:40). Isaiah, John insists, had already prophesied these things at the time of his inaugural vision. Then, John goes on to identify Jesus as the very figure that Isaiah saw high and lifted up in the temple: "These things Isaiah said when he saw His glory and spoke of Him" (12:41).

It was this vision of Isaiah in the temple, then, that has prompted Christians to refer to that ancient prophet as "the fifth evangelist." It was given to Isaiah, seven and a half centuries before the Incarnation, to behold in mystic, prophetic illumination "the light of the knowledge of the glory of God in the face of Jesus Christ" (2 Corinthians 4:6). Isaiah, who knew very well that "no one has seen God at any time," nonetheless perceived in his prophetic summons that "the only begotten Son, who is in the bosom of the Father, He has declared *Him*" (John 1:18).

๛

5. DANIEL, MAN OF PRAYER

The Book of Daniel is a difficult work. Not only is it full of mysteries hard to unravel, but we encounter enigmatic features about the text even before we begin to read it.

First, by calling Daniel a prophet I am contradicting much of contemporary biblical scholarship, which prefers to describe the book named after him as "apocalyptic" rather than prophetic. This distinction, however, introduced as an instrument of literary history, is a bit artificial and, I think, not especially helpful even to that end. In addition, Jesus did call him "Daniel the prophet" (Matthew 24:15), and I am disposed to trust Jesus on the point.

Second, it is a fact that the Book of Daniel is not contained in the prophetic books (*nebi'im*) of the Hebrew Scriptures; it is found, rather, in that canon's final section, the "Writings" (*ketubhim*). Apparently not everyone in antiquity was agreed on the book's authority. Although Josephus says that a copy of Daniel was shown to Alexander the Great (*Antiquities* 11.8.5), Ben Sirach, writing early in the second century before Christ, did not include Daniel with Isaiah, Jeremiah, Ezekiel, and the twelve minor prophets (Ecclesiasticus 44:50). The decision to include Daniel in the Holy Scriptures, therefore, was made some time after the canon of the prophetic writings was closed. Thus, to be included in the Bible at all, it had to be placed in the final section, the "Writings."

Third, even to speak of Daniel as part of the Hebrew Scriptures is to stretch the matter a tad, because most of Daniel was written in Aramaic, the ancient language of Syria.

Fourth, the Book of Daniel, as preserved in the traditional Masoretic text of the Old Testament (and Protestant Bibles generally), is defective by two chapters. These chapters, the story of Susanna at the beginning of the book and the account of Bel and the Snake at its end, are preserved in the Greek text of Daniel handed down in the Christian Church. In spite of the rejection of these two chapters by the Jews (and later by the Protestants), they were surely contained in the Hebrew/Aramaic text of Daniel at the time of the New Testament. The strongest evidence for this view is the fact that both chapters were included in the Greek translation of Daniel rendered by Theodotion in the second century AD. The exclusion of these two sections from the Christian Bible, therefore, is unwarranted.

If the Book of Daniel is fraught with difficulties, however, the prophet himself is not. Indeed, the Bible's portrayal of him is fairly plain and straightforward. For starters, we know that he lived a good long life. Already active in the year 603 (Daniel 2:1), he was still going strong in 536 (10:1). A fearless man, not intimidated by lions' dens and other petty threats, he served the Babylonian and Persian emperors during that whole period, all the while remaining a devout and loyal Jew.

In this respect Daniel resembled the ancient Joseph, who had served in the royal court of Egypt. The kings in both cases gave their two servants special clothing to signify their status (Genesis 41:42; Daniel 5:29).

Daniel also matched Joseph in the interpretation of dreams, a gift in which both men were contrasted to the pagan soothsayers (compare Genesis 41 and Daniel 4). Both Joseph and Daniel, moreover, had revelatory dreams of their own (Genesis 37:5–10; Daniel 7—8).

Although several of the prophets recorded their visions (Ezekiel preeminently), proportionately more of the text of Daniel is taken up with visionary material than is the case with any other biblical writer except the author of the Book of Revelation.

In particular, Daniel was a man of disciplined devotion, who regularly went before the Lord three times each day in prayer and thanksgiving (6:10). Since one of those times was the hour of the evening sacrifice (9:21), we may presume that the other two were at the hour of the morning sacrifice and at noon (cf. Psalms 56[55]:17). Daniel is thus among our earliest witnesses to the keeping of the "canonical" hours of prayer, a discipline taken over by the early Christians without separation from their Jewish roots (cf. Acts 1:14 with 2:1, 15; 3:1; 10:3, 9, 30).

The contemplative and visionary aspects of Daniel's devotion, though certainly divine gifts, were also the fruit of his sustained application to the discipline of prayer. He set his heart to understand and to humble himself before God (10:12). A man "in whom *is* the Spirit of the Holy God," a man of "knowledge and understanding" (5:11–12), Daniel did not falter. He was no more likely to omit his daily prayer from fear of the lions than for any other trifling reason (6:11–17). This fidelity was the secret to his life and vocation.

6. THE COMPLEX EZEKIEL

Historians of the subject seem agreed that Judaism as a "world religion"—a religion sufficiently *portable* to be carried anywhere in the world—was largely the product of the Babylonian Captivity. It was during those four decades (587–538 BC) in exile from the Holy Land that Israel perfected, and learned mainly to rely on, the *moveable* institutions that were to give it defining shape and vitality for the next two and a half millennia: canonical Scriptures, synagogue, rabbinical authority and scholarship, the rituals of domestic piety and personal discipline. During most of the time since 586 BC, in fact, Judaism has not even possessed some of its earlier formative institutions, such as the temple and its priesthood.

Now among the individual figures who contributed to that important development during the Babylonian Captivity, surely none was more significant than the priest and prophet Ezekiel, who had already gone to Babylon eleven years earlier as a political hostage. So essential was Ezekiel during that formative time that he has sometimes been called "the father of Judaism." Surely J. T. Bunn was correct in describing his work as "a watershed in biblical literature."

On the other hand, hardly any other person in Holy Scripture has been interpreted from such a wide range of improbable and contradictory perspectives. Whereas he has been called a "prophet and theologian" (G. von Rad), even "the Calvin of the Old Testament" (R. Kittel), other judgments have been less kind. Thus, R. H. Pfeiffer referred to Ezekiel as "the first fanatic in the Bible" (an estimate to which, one imagines, Elijah might take exception), while one reviewer spoke of "a crazy loner with bad news." Harsher yet was E. C. Broome, who, bidding farewell to good sense, described Ezekiel's "unconscious sexual regression, schizophrenic withdrawal, delusions of persecution and grandeur." Heavens! Let a young fellow have a vision or two of fiery wheels and eyes and such, and some folks will think the very worst of him.

Perhaps more generous was the archeologist W. F. Albright, who described Ezekiel as "one of the greatest spiritual figures of all time," but only, he added, "in spite of his tendency to abnormality." Hmm, this was evidently only a tendency, we are given to understand, not a genuine, full-blooded abnormality. I suppose Dr. Albright expected us to find solace in this thought.

By way of response, A. J. Tkacik remarked that we should perhaps regard Ezekiel "as unusual rather than abnormal." This too may be small comfort, because Tkacik does Ezekiel the injustice of rendering him more normal ("normal, but not mediocre"!) by interpreting the visionary parts of his prophecies as literary devices rather than real ecstatic experiences. Such an approach makes the prophet more normal only by making him less interesting. I suspect many of us, anyway, would prefer an eccentric prophet to a boring one.

The great variety of these judgments, it would seem, testifies to the complexity of the subject, for Ezekiel was surely a complex man. Mystical, even clairvoyant, he was also very logically methodical, never incoherent, nor aimless, nor rambling. However ecstatic his visions, he had clearly reflected on them with calm and thoughtful deliberation before writing them down. Seldom, if ever, has the entranced appeared so rational.

Ezekiel must likewise be counted among the most educated and cultured men of Holy Scripture. Thoroughly familiar with all the biblical literature that preceded him, even Job, he also shows himself conversant with a vast breadth of other information about an unusual number of subjects: ancient mythologies, various wisdom traditions, geopolitical complexities, international trade, military matters, history and geography.

Most curious is Ezekiel's sense of geographical and chronological precision. His narrative sometimes supplies the place and usually the exact date of his visions, thus introducing into the Bible a larger dose of "autobiography" than is found in any other prophet. Indeed, we may think of Ezekiel as the first "diarist" in Western religious history, for his book reads as a sort of spiritual journal.

Most of all, however, there is Ezekiel's preoccupation with God's Holy Spirit, of whom he speaks more than any other of Israel's prophets and who is the source of his visionary wisdom.

※

7. JOHN AND THE DIVINE LIGHT

It is often remarked that the omission of the Transfiguration account from the Fourth Gospel is properly explained by the fact that Jesus *always* appears transfigured in that Gospel. In its every scene, including the Passion narrative, Jesus is suffused with the radiance of the divine light. "We beheld His glory," says St. John in the prologue, "the glory as of the only begotten of the Father" (1:14).

That prologue, which sets the theme for the entire story, is peculiar to John, whose Gospel otherwise adheres to the exact time span covered by the earliest apostolic preaching, namely, "all the time that the Lord Jesus went in and out among us, beginning from the baptism of John to that day when He was taken up from us" (Acts 1:21–22). Adherence to this same primitive time frame is also characteristic of the message of Peter and Paul (10:36–42; 13:23–31), as well as the earliest of the Gospels, Mark. So too John, except for his prologue.

Matthew and Luke had expanded that original time frame by adding the stories of Jesus' conception, birth, and infancy. John's prologue, however, escapes the confines of time altogether, rising to God's eternity, where "in the beginning was the Word, and the Word was with God, and the Word was God" (John 1:1). Only then does this Gospel begin to speak of the ministry of John the Baptist (1:6, 15).

The Jesus presented in John's Gospel, then, is the eternal Word, in whom "was life, and the life was the light of men" (1:4). Becoming flesh and dwelling among us (1:14), He is the living revelation of God on this earth. Even though "no one has seen God at any time," John says, "the only begotten Son, who is in the bosom of the Father, He has declared *Him*" (1:18).

These themes will appear again in the Lord's Last Supper discourse and the long intercession that He prays at the end of it. There will He speak of His being "the way, the truth, and the life" (14:6) and refer to the glory that He had with the Father before the world began (17:5, 24).

John's contemplative gaze at the glory of God on the face of Jesus also determines other features of his Gospel. We observe, for instance, his treatment of Jesus' miracles. Although his narrative very intentionally includes fewer of these than do the other Gospels (20:30; 21:25), John provides them greater theological elaboration.

John limits the number of recorded miracles, which he calls "signs," to the sacred figure seven. Leading to the commitment of faith, these seven signs commence with the fine wine of the wedding feast: "This beginning [*arche*, the same word as in 1:1] of signs Jesus did in Cana of Galilee, and manifested His glory; and His disciples *believed* in Him"

(2:11, emphasis added). The second sign John identifies as the curing of the nobleman's son (4:46–54); as in the first case, the man himself "*believed,* and his whole household" (4:53, emphasis added). Next comes the curing of the paralytic at the pool (5:1–15), followed by the miracle of the bread (6:1–14), the walking on the water (6:15–21), and the healing of the man born blind (9:1–41). The final and culminating sign is the raising of Lazarus from the dead (11:1–44).

John's recording of these revelatory signs is accompanied by theological comments on their significance, either in the detailed conversations of the narrative itself (as in the raising of Lazarus and the healing of the blind man) or by the Lord's own further elaboration (as in the Bread of Life discourse). Thus, each of these events in the Lord's life and ministry becomes a window through which we perceive the divine glory, and Jesus is transfigured with light through the whole narrative. In addition, two lengthy conversations, one with Nicodemus (3:1–21) and the other with the Samaritan woman (4:5–42), sound the depths of the revelation that takes place in the narrative.

At the end of the seven signs, John summarizes the tragedy of the unbelief with which the enemies of Jesus responded to His revelation (12:37–41). This unbelief leads immediately to the Lord's Passion, which is introduced by the great Last Supper discourse.

In every scene, then, from the Lord's appearance at John's baptismal site all the way through the Lord's death and Resurrection, the divine light appears among men. John records all these things that we readers too may "believe that Jesus is the Christ, the Son of God" (20:31).

⁓

8. MARY OF BETHANY

Mary of Bethany is identified by name in only two of the Gospels, Luke (10:38–42) and John (11:1–32; 12:1–8). In both places she is described through a studied contrast with some other character.

In Luke's story, Mary is contrasted with her (probably older) sister Martha, the latter being described as "distracted with much serving" and "worried and troubled about many things." One of the reasons Martha was so busy—or at least Martha thought so—was that Mary was not helping her in the kitchen and at table. So she approached Jesus with the request, "Lord, do You not care that my sister has left me to serve alone? Therefore tell her to help me." And just what was Mary doing that Martha found so inadequate? Well, she "sat at Jesus' feet and heard His word." It seems evident that Martha took her sister's more quiet activity to be either a sign of, or an excuse for, laziness.

By way of response, Jesus corrected not Mary, but Martha. He even pointed to the superiority of Mary's peaceful occupation, claiming that she "has chosen that good [lit., *better*] part, which will not be taken away from her."

Without getting too technical on the point here, it is important that the adjective (*agathe*) in this story be translated, not simply as "good" (as in the KJV and other English translations), but as "better" (following the Vulgate). As manifest in many examples in both the Septuagint and the New Testament, the use of a simple adjective to convey a comparative sense, or even as a superlative, is often found in Koine Greek, when two or more things are, in context, being compared. (Thus, for instance, it would have been "better," not simply "good," if Judas had not been born, in Matthew 26:24.)

According to Jesus, then, what Mary was doing was not only good; it was *better* than what Martha was doing. Consequently, it is no wonder that this verse from Luke has ever been used in the Church to contend for the superiority of contemplation over other kinds of activity. Moreover, along with Paul's thesis on the preference of consecrated celibacy over marriage (1 Corinthians 7:25–40), this text has always served to argue for the objective excellence of monasticism over other settings of the Christian life. Both of these exegetical inferences are sound and reasonable.

In order better to understand, however, how Mary represents a Christian contemplative life, it would be useful to consider her activity—sitting and listening to Jesus' word—within the context of Luke's larger story. First, this description of Mary of Bethany supports a comparison with the activity of Jesus' own mother, who "kept all these things and pondered *them* in her heart" (2:19, 51).

Second, both women are portrayed as the true contemplatives described in the parable of the sower. Recall that in Luke's version of that parable, the seeds "*that* fell on the good ground are those who, having heard the word with a noble and good [*agathe*] heart, keep *it* and bear fruit with patience" (8:15). That is to say, Christian contemplation involves the hearing of God's word in purity of heart.

Third, this theme is indicated in Luke's distinctive version of another word of Jesus: "My mother and My brothers are those who hear the word of God and do it" (8:21). Fourth, even when a woman in the crowd cried out to bless the mother of Jesus, the Lord responded by pointing to His mother's true blessedness: "More than that, blessed *are* those who hear the word of God and keep it" (11:27–28). Mary of Bethany, then, sitting at Jesus' feet to hear His word, exemplifies a theme deep in Luke's interest.

In the Gospel according to John, Mary of Bethany is contrasted with Judas Iscariot. It was Mary who, just six days before the Passover, "took a pound of very costly oil of spikenard, anointed the feet of Jesus, and wiped His feet with her hair" (John 12:3). That ointment was valued at three hundred pieces of silver by Judas, the thieving apostolic bookkeeper, who would soon betray Jesus for one-tenth of that amount. We who know, trust, and love Jesus as God's Son and our Savior are shocked by the crass response of Judas, which proved that he was already on the side of Jesus' enemies. How could anything done for the love of Jesus be thought extravagant or overly generous? This is obvious to us. It was obvious to Mary of Bethany, as well. She knew it by sitting quietly at Jesus' feet and listening.

ॐ

9. MARY MAGDALENE AT THE TOMB

The post-Resurrection stories of the New Testament, analyzed from a literary perspective, fall into two categories, each with its own set of interests.

The first of these we may think of as apologetic and kerygmatic. That is to say, certain stories are part of the Church's witness to the world; they stress the reality of the Lord's Resurrection. Thus, one notices considerable emphasis on the eyewitness testimony, just as there might be in a courtroom. Indeed, in 1 Corinthians 15:3–8 there is an early list of qualified witnesses well known among the early Christians. One notes the heavy accent on apostolic authority; in the main, the people listed here were official spokesmen for the Church, her authorized witnesses to the world (cf. also Acts 1:21–22). Official testimony had to be clear and unmistakable, emphasizing the identity of the risen Christ beyond doubt. We find exactly this kind of emphasis in a few of the Gospel accounts (Luke 24:36–43; John 21:24–29).

But there is a second kind of post-Resurrection story with an

310

emphasis very different from the first kind. To appreciate this difference, one may begin by noting who is absent in the first type of story—the women! How could these women be witnesses to the world? After all, even the Church had not believed them!

Thus, in Paul's list of official witnesses, there is not a single word about the Lord's appearances to the women. On the contrary, he says that the risen Jesus "was seen by Cephas" (1 Corinthians 15:5). Now when we turn to the Gospels themselves, quite a different emphasis shows itself. Indeed, here we read: "Now when *He* rose early on the first *day* of the week, He appeared first to Mary Magdalene" (Mark 16:9). In the official list in 1 Corinthians 15, she is not even mentioned. The contrast is striking.

In the second sort of story we are no longer concerned so much with the Church's witness to the world; we are, rather, dealing with the Church's inner memory, her devout and tender meditation on that first Easter morning and the ensuing days. In these accounts, the first apparitions are made to the women (Matthew 28:9; Luke 20:11–18). Indeed, the women are not even believed by the Apostles when they announce the empty tomb and the vision of angels (Mark 16:11; Luke 24:1–11).

In this second type of story, then, we are dealing less with official testimony than with a kind of prayerful meditation. Thus, the Lord is not necessarily recognized right away. The two disciples on the way to Emmaus and the seven disciples out at the Sea of Galilee do not know Him until some crucial point in the account. And the context of the recognition has something very spiritual about it: the disciples on the road recognize Him in the act of the breaking of the bread, and the seven on the lake once again share a meal of bread and fish. In these stories we are not dealing with the Church's testimony to the world, but with the Church's inner life of communion with the risen Lord.

Such a story is that of Mary Magdalene in John 20:11–18. Like the bride in the Song of Solomon (3:1–4), she rises early while it is still dark and goes out seeking Him whom her soul loves, the one whom she calls "my Lord." In an image reminiscent of both Genesis and the Song of Solomon, she comes to the garden of His burial (19:41). Indeed, she first takes Him to be the gardener, which, as the new Adam, He most certainly is. Her eyes blinded by tears, she does not at once know Him. He speaks to her, but even then she does not recognize His voice. The dramatic moment of recognition arrives when the risen Jesus pronounces her own name: "Mary." Only then does she know Him as "Rabbouni," "my Teacher."

In this story, then, Christians perceive in Mary Magdalene an image of themselves meeting their risen Lord and Good Shepherd: "the sheep hear his voice; and he calls his own sheep by name . . . , for they know his voice" (John 10:3–4). This narrative of Mary Magdalene is an affirmation that Christian identity comes of recognizing the voice of Christ, who speaks our own name in the mystery of salvation: "the Son of God, who loved *me* and gave Himself for *me*" (Galatians 2:20, emphasis added). This is truly an "in-house" memory of the Church; it can only be understood within the community of salvation, for it describes a wisdom not otherwise available to this world.

⋙

10. THE MOTHER OF JESUS

Since she appears only in the New Testament, it seems strange to think of the Virgin Mary as pertaining to the Old Testament. Yet, such a perspective is consonant with the thought of St. Paul, who described the Lord Jesus as "born of a woman, born under the law" (Galatians 4:4). This is why Amadeus of Lausanne, in the twelfth century, spoke of Mary as containing the mysteries of all the Old Testament saints.

There is a sense in which all of Old Testament history finds its fulfillment in the "Be it done unto me" of the young maiden of Nazareth. When Dante called the Virgin Mary the *termine fisso d'etterno consiglio*— "the fixed goal of the eternal plan" (Paradiso 33.3), he meant that her "yes" to God's summons was the Old Testament's final and culminating act of faith, through which God Himself assumed a human role in history. She thus represents the culmination of God's long providential and prophetic cultivation of a people proper unto Himself, intent solely on the doing of His will.

Since all of God's historical preparation found its fulfillment in the assent of that soul who gave herself over completely to the outpouring of the Holy Spirit, it is through the Virgin Mother of Christ that the whole of the Old Testament is filtered into the Incarnation.

It is Luke who describes Gabriel's visit to Mary and their important conversation, seeking Mary's assent to God's mystery. And just as Luke's Gospel begins with the Holy Spirit's descent to the Virgin Mary, so

Luke's second volume, the Book of Acts, commences with the Holy Spirit's descent to the Church. At this latter event, too, the mother of Jesus stands at the very center (cf. Acts 1:14), the very first among the disciples of her Son.

All of this sense of Mary's particular role in the drama of salvation is conveyed when her cousin Elizabeth addresses her as "the mother of my Lord" (Luke 1:43). When Elizabeth calls her "blessed," Luke tells us, it is because "Elizabeth was filled with the Holy Spirit" (1:41). Likewise filled with the Holy Spirit, surely, are all those subsequent generations that have called her "blessed" (Luke 1:48).

In the Gospel of John, the treatment of the Virgin Mary is extremely subtle and delicate. First, John never calls her by her own name; each time she appears, she is simply referenced as "the mother of Jesus." And she appears in that Gospel only twice, once near the beginning (2:1–11) and once near the end (19:25–27). It is also noteworthy that in both of these she is addressed by Jesus as "Woman," a title of respect not adequately represented in our English idiom.

In the earlier of these two cases, the story of the marriage at Cana, Mary's intervention on behalf of the embarrassed wedding party leads to the initial manifestation of His glory, the "sign" of the transformation of the water into wine. Not put off by an initial refusal that the Lord used to test her faith, she told the wedding servants: "Do whatever He tells you." Her faith in the power of Jesus' word thus led to the faith of the other disciples as Jesus "manifested His glory."

Even though Jesus' hour had not yet arrived (2:4), His mother's perfect faith brought about a foreshadowing of the abundant grace effected in His atoning redemption. At that event, which formed a new family, she thus became the first and a model among those who "believed" (see also Luke 1:45).

When the mother of Jesus appears in the Gospel of John for the second time, the Lord's "hour" has certainly arrived (12:23; 13:1; 17:1), and Mary now stands beneath the Cross of redemption with "the beloved disciple" (who remains similarly anonymous in John's Gospel). Indeed, in this place the mother of Jesus is the first mentioned among those four disciples who form the nucleus of the new community of faith (in contrast to the four soldiers also present at the Cross and representative of the forces of this world). Once again, a new family is formed: "Woman, behold your son! . . . . Behold your mother!" And "from that hour that disciple took her to his own" (19:26–27). The mother of Jesus now becomes the mother of all Christian believers, of whom the anonymous "beloved disciple" is the representative, who now takes her to his own home.

ABOUT THE AUTHOR:

Patrick Henry Reardon is pastor of All Saints Antiochian Orthodox Church in Chicago, Illinois, and Senior Editor of *Touchstone: A Journal of Mere Christianity.*

ALSO BY PATRICK HENRY REARDON:

Christ in the Psalms

A highly inspirational book of meditations on the Psalms by one of the most insightful and challenging Orthodox writers of our day. Avoiding both syrupy sentimentality and arid scholasticism, *Christ in the Psalms* takes the reader on a thought-provoking and enlightening pilgrimage through this beloved "Prayer Book" of the Church.

Which psalms were quoted most frequently in the New Testament, and how were they interpreted? How has the Church historically understood and utilized the various psalms in her liturgical life? How can we perceive the image of Christ shining through the psalms? Lively and highly devotional, thought-provoking yet warm and practical, *Christ in the Psalms* sheds a world of insight upon each psalm, and offers practical advice for how to make the Psalter a part of our daily lives.

Paperback, 328 pages (ISBN 1-888212-20-9) Order No. 004927—$17.95*

*plus applicable tax and postage & handling charges.
Please call Conciliar Press at 800-967-7377 for complete ordering information.

OTHER BOOKS OF INTEREST:

Romans: A Gospel for All
by Fr. Lawrence Farley

The Apostle Paul lived within a swirl of controversy. False Christians—Judaizers—dogged his every step, slandering his motives, denying his apostolic authority, and seeking to overthrow his Gospel teaching. They argued their case loudly, and Paul knew that he must give the literary performance of his life. The result was the Epistle to the Romans, in which he demonstrates the truth of his Gospel—a Gospel for all men—and thereby vindicates his apostolic authority.

Paperback, 208 pages (ISBN 1-888212-51-9) Order No. 005675—$14.95*

The Prison Epistles:
Philippians – Ephesians – Colossians – Philemon
by Fr. Lawrence Farley

From the depths of a Roman prison, words of encouragement and instruction flowed from the tongue of the great Apostle Paul. Written down by scribes, his words went forth as a series of letters to Christian communities throughout the Roman Empire. The Apostle Paul may have been fettered and shackled to a series of Roman guards, but the Word he preached remained unfettered and free.

Contains commentaries on the epistles to the Philippians, Ephesians, Colossians, and Philemon—which were written while the Apostle Paul was in prison.

Paperback, 224 pages (ISBN 1-888212-52-7) Order No. 006034—$15.95*

THE ORTHODOX STUDY BIBLE:
New Testament and Psalms

An edition of the New Testament and Psalms that offers Bible study aids written from an Orthodox perspective. Prepared under the direction of canonical Orthodox theologians and hierarchs, *The Orthodox Study Bible* presents a remarkable combination of historic theological insights and practical instruction in Christian living. *The Orthodox Study Bible* also provides a personal guide to help you apply biblical truths to your daily life with such excellent aids as: carefully prepared study notes on the text; a chart of Scripture readings to offer guidance for daily devotions; a guide for morning and evening prayers; readings for feast days; quotations from early Church Fathers such as St. John Chrysostom,

St. Ignatius of Antioch, St. Gregory of Nyssa, and St. Athanasius; a glossary of Orthodox Christian terminology; and the New King James Version translation with center-column cross references and translation notes.

Genuine Leather Edition—$49.95*; Hardcover Edition—$29.95*; Paperback Edition—$23.95*

Journey to the Kingdom: Reflections on the Sunday Gospels
by Fr. John Mack

Reflections on selected Sunday Gospel readings. Father John's insights into familiar Bible passages that we have often heard, but may not truly have understood, are excellent. He takes us through the highlights of the church year and lovingly opens up the Gospel stories to us with patristic and biblical wisdom. Many of the reflections are filled with stories of the saints, as well as observations about living in the twenty-first century that lead us to ask deeper questions about our own lives. *Journey to the Kingdom* deals with sin and grace, repentance and confession, living by faith, and many other needful topics.

Paperback, 208 pages (ISBN 1-888212-27-6) Order No. 005132—$13.95*

*plus applicable tax and postage & handling charges.
Please call Conciliar Press at 800-967-7377 for complete ordering information.